Capitalist Diversity on Europe's Periphery

A volume in the series

Cornell Studies in Political Economy
edited by Peter J. Katzenstein

A list of titles in this series is available at www.cornellpress.cornell.edu.

Capitalist Diversity on Europe's Periphery

Dorothee Bohle
and Béla Greskovits

Cornell University Press
Ithaca and London

First published 2012 by Cornell University Press
First printing, Cornell Paperbacks, 2012
Printed in the United States of America

Library of Congress Cataloging-in-Publication Data

Bohle, Dorothee, 1964–
    Capitalist diversity on Europe's periphery / Dorothee Bohle and Béla Greskovits.
        p. cm. — (Cornell studies in political economy)
    Includes bibliographical references and index.
    ISBN 978-0-8014-5110-2 (cloth : alk. paper)
    ISBN 978-0-8014-7815-4 (pbk. : alk. paper)
    1. Capitalism—Europe, Eastern.   2. Capitalism—Europe, Central.
3. Post-communism—Economic aspects—Europe, Eastern.   4. Post-communism—Economic aspects—Europe, Central.   5. Europe, Eastern—Economic conditions—21st century.   6. Europe, Central—Economic conditions—21st century.   I. Greskovits, Béla, 1953–   II. Title.
III. Series: Cornell studies in political economy.
    HC244.B674   2012
    330.12'20947—dc23   2012007508

Cornell University Press strives to use environmentally responsible suppliers and materials to the fullest extent possible in the publishing of its books. Such materials include vegetable-based, low-VOC inks and acid-free papers that are recycled, totally chlorine-free, or partly composed of nonwood fibers. For further information, visit our website at www.cornellpress.cornell.edu.

Cloth printing   10 9 8 7 6 5 4 3 2 1
Paperback printing   10 9 8 7 6 5 4 3 2 1

To the Memory of Peter Mair

Contents

List of Figures and Tables   ix
Acknowledgments   xi
Abbreviations   xiii

Introduction: The Success, Fragility, and Diversity
   of Postsocialist Capitalism   1

1. **Capitalist Diversity after Socialism**   7
   Comparing East European Capitalisms   9
   Polanyian Varieties   13
   Postsocialist Regime Concepts   17
   Matrixes of Institutions and Performances   25
   Puzzles of the Small State Pattern   53

2. **Paths to Postsocialist Capitalism**   55
   Leaving the East   58
   Mobilizing Consent   62
   Returning to the West: Transnationalization and
     European Integration   82

3. **Nation Builders and Neoliberals: The Baltic States**   96
   Origins of the National and Nationalizing Projects 98
   Exclusionary and Inclusionary Democracies   99
   The Politics of Early Economic Reforms   104
   Nationalist Social Contracts   113

Constructing the Estonian Success Story   124
Internationalization, European Integration, and
  the Baltic Economic Miracle   131

4. Manufacturing Miracles and Welfare State Problems:
   The Visegrád Group   138
   Unsuccessful Experiments and Double-Edged Inheritances   139
   Welfarist Social Contracts   152
   Rival Manufacturing Miracles   161
   Contesting the Euro   172

5. Neocorporatism and Weak States:
   The Southeastern European Countries   182
   Labor's Won Battles and Lost Wars   184
   Postsocialist Capitalism in Strong and Weak States   197
   Neocorporatist Balancing versus Crisis-Driven Path Corrections   211

6. The Return of Hard Times   223
   Recession, Austerity, and No Alternatives: The Baltic States   227
   Semicore Specialization, Polarized Democracy, and
     Austerity: The Visegrád Model in Peril   237
   The Crisis, Neocorporatism, and Weak States:
     Southeastern Europe   248
   Responsible Government or the Specter of Ungovernability   255

Conclusion: Postsocialist Capitalism Twenty Years On   259
   Legacies, Initial Choices, and Repressed Alternatives   260
   Market, Welfare, Democracy, and Identity:
     Compatibilities and Trade-offs   263
   Virtues and Vices of Deep International Integration   265
   Global Convergence versus Capitalist Diversity   267
   New Global Transformations   269

Index   275

Figures and Tables

Figures

1.1. Institutional foundations of capitalist democracy's goods,
      bads, and tensions   21
1.2. Neoliberal regime   23
1.3. Nonregime   23
1.4. Embedded neoliberal regime   23
1.5. Neocorporatist regime   23
2.1. Postsocialist regime formation: The first phase   82
2.2. Postsocialist regime formation: International factors   94
3.1. At-risk-of-poverty rate after social transfers   117
5.1. Origins of inward FDI stock in Southeastern Europe and
      East Central European subregions   210

Tables

1.1. Performance in opening and regulating markets,
      1989–98 and 1999–2007   26
1.2. Compensation for economic transformation costs,
      1989–98 and 1999–2007   32
1.3. Compensation for social transformation costs,
      1989–95 and 1999–2006   35
1.4. Indicators of democratic government, 1989–98 and 1999–2007   39
1.5. Trends in social partnership institutions, 1989–98 and 1999–2007   41
1.6. State capacity, 1996–98 and 2000–2008   ·   43
1.7. Semicore and semiperipheral profiles of international
      economic integration, 1989–98 and 1999–2007   45

1.8. Social cohesion, material loss, and existential stress,
  1990s and early 2000s   49
1.9. Macroeconomic (in)stability, 1989–98 and 1999–2007   52
3.1. Hopes and fears about the euro, mid-2000s   111
3.2. Ethnic aspects of social dislocation, 1993   120
4.1. FDI in the Visegrád countries and the NICs, late 2000s 171
5.1. Slovenia's strategy of economic restructuring, mid-2000s 204
6.1. Exposure to the global crisis, mid-2000s   225
6.2. Sources of political stability and capacity for
  crisis management, mid- and late 2000s   232

Acknowledgments

It is with great pleasure that we lay down our text and think about all those persons whose support, encouragement, and friendship have been crucial throughout the years of this intellectual journey, especially those at Central European University in Budapest and the European University Institute in Florence.

At Central European University we profited tremendously from the vibrant academic environment of the Political Economy Research Group. Many presentations and discussions with our colleagues and doctoral students helped us to develop our arguments. We are especially grateful to the early cohort of PERG members. Magdalena Bernaciak, Anil Duman, Zdeněk Kudrna, Lucia Kureková, Kristin Nickel Makszin, Gergő Medve-Bálint, Tibor Meszman, Andrej Nosko, Vera Šćepanović, and Kateřina Svíčková: thank you for investing so much into making PERG the stimulating place it has become.

Central European University generously granted us a long leave of absence, which we spent at the Department of Political and Social Sciences of the European University Institute. This was a most rewarding experience. The department was unique in its hospitality and as an intellectual community, and thanks to the open-minded colleagues, staff and students as well as the visiting fellows, we always found people eager to exchange thoughts with us. Among them, our special thanks go to our colleague and friend László Bruszt, as well as to Emese Bálint and Jázmin, for sharing with us so many happy moments of our academic and everyday life in Florence.

We benefited from the conversations we had with Marta Arretche, Rainer Bauböck, Mabel Berezin, Pepper Culpepper, Donatella Della Porta, Grzegorz Ekiert, Mark Franklin, Adrienne Héritier, Wade Jacoby, Erin Jenne, Terry Karl, Michael Keating, Martin Kohli, Hanspeter Kriesi, Philippe Schmitter, Roger Schoenman, Graham Smith, Sven Steinmo, Richard Swedberg, and

Alexander Trechsel, and the comments we received at workshops and conferences at EUI. Special thanks are due to Thomas Bourke and Peter Kennealy, who were most helpful whenever we needed any support from the library. Outside of CEU and EUI, Katharina Bluhm, David Brown, Valerie Bunce, Jan Drahokoupil, Aida Hozic, Herbert Kitschelt, David Ost, and Dieter Plehwe supported us at various moments of our endeavor.

Many colleagues read parts of our manuscript, some read the whole, and some even several versions. All of them gave us immensely helpful comments. We are deeply grateful to László Bruszt, Danica Fink-Hafner, Éva Fodor, György Greskovits, Vello Pettai, Jan-Hinrik Meyer-Sahling, Jörg Rössel, Vera Šćepanović, Sidney Tarrow, and Višnja Vukov. Sid Tarrow encouraged us to focus more explicitly on Karl Polanyi.

This book would not have seen the light of day without the continuous and enthusiastic support of our Cornell University Press editors, Roger Haydon and Peter Katzenstein. Peter's work on small states has been most inspiring for our study, and he has had the wonderful gift of instilling confidence in us in those very moments when we felt daunted by the tasks ahead. We are also very grateful for his and an anonymous reviewer's detailed comments on the manuscript, which greatly helped us to clarify our thoughts. We are especially fortunate to have worked with two wonderful manuscript and copy editors, Susan Specter and Gavin Lewis, whose contribution improved our text's quality significantly.

It is customary to thank partners for their emotional and intellectual support during the writing of a book. This being a book actually co-authored by partners, matters are slightly more complicated for us. While each of us took responsibility for drafting first versions of single chapters, rarely was it the case that a draft survived the critical intervention of the other. At times, this was an emotionally and intellectually challenging cooperation, and we have certainly cursed each other for destroying precious arguments, and for forcing each other to revisit sections or chapters that we thought already closed. But we always knew that we needed and inspired each other deeply.

As we put the finishing touches to the manuscript, we learned of the tragic death of Peter Mair. Of all colleagues and new friends at EUI, he was the most amazing. He was a wonderful person, a great scholar, and a brilliant mind, and his support for us was never ending. When our time at EUI came to an end, our friendship with Peter did not. Like so many people around us, we feel privileged to have known him, and we are deeply saddened by his untimely death. It is to his memory that we dedicate the book.

Abbreviations

AmCham	American Chamber of Commerce
BRIC	Brazil, Russia, India, China
BS	Bank of Slovenia
CDR	Democratic Convention of Romania
CEFTA	Central European Free Trade Area
CIS	Commonwealth of Independent States
CME	Coordinated market economy
CMEA	Council for Mutual Economic Assistance
CNB	Croatian National Bank
ČSSD	Czech Social Democratic Party
DME	Dependent market economy
EBRD	European Bank for Reconstruction and Development
EC	European Commission
EMU	Economic and Monetary Union
ERM	Exchange rate mechanism
ÉT	Interest Reconciliation Council (Hungary)
EU	European Union
EUR	Euros
FDI	Foreign direct investment
FIDESZ-MPSZ	Alliance of Young Democrats–Hungarian Civic Alliance
HDZ	Croatian Democratic Union
HZDS	Peoples' Party–Movement for a Democratic Slovakia
IFIs	International financial institutions
IMF	International Monetary Fund
Jobbik	Movement for a Better Hungary
KNSB	Confederation of Independent Trade Unions in Bulgaria
KOZ	Confederation of Trade Unions (Slovakia)

LFS	Labor force survey
LDDP	Lithuanian Democratic Labor Party
LME	Liberal market economy
LPR	League of Polish Families
MDF	Hungarian Democratic Forum
MEBO	Management employee buyout
MNB	National Bank of Hungary
MPS	Mont Pelerin Society
MSZOSZ	National Federation of Hungarian Trade Unions
MSZP	Hungarian Socialist Party
NBČ	National Bank of the Czech Republic
NBP	National Bank of Poland
NBS	National Bank of Slovakia
NDC	Notional defined contribution
NICs	Newly industrializing countries
ODS	Civic Democratic Party (Czech Republic)
PAYG	Pay as you go
PDSR	Romanian Social Democratic Party
PiS	Law and Justice Party (Poland)
PO	Civic Platform (Polish party)
PPS	Purchasing power standard
PSL	Polish Peasant Party
R&D	Research and development
RSHD	Czechoslovak (later Czech and Slovak) Councils of Economic and Social Agreement
SDK	Slovak Democratic Coalition
SDL	Party of the Democratic Left (Slovakia)
SDS	Slovenian Democratic Party
SLD	Alliance of the Democratic Left (Poland)
Smer	Direction–Social Democracy (Slovak party)
SMK	Party of the Hungarian Coalition (Slovakia)
SNS	Slovak National Party
SOE	State-owned enterprise
SRP	Self-Defense (Polish party)
SZDSZ	Alliance of Free Democrats (Hungary)
TNCs	Transnational corporations
TOP 09	Tradition Responsibility Prosperity 09 (Czech party)
USD	U.S. dollars
VoC	Varieties of capitalism
VV	Public Affairs (Czech party)
ZUS	Social Insurance Institution (Poland)

Capitalist Diversity on
Europe's Periphery

Introduction

The Success, Fragility, and Diversity of Postsocialist Capitalism

This book has grown out of our long-standing interest in the success, fragility, and diversity of East Central Europe's new capitalist order. All three aspects have occupied center stage in the debates on postsocialist transformation and European integration. The view that the region's states exhibit the maximum of success that any postsocialist country can achieve is still widely shared by comparativists, even if the recent global crisis casts a shadow over these states' earlier accomplishments. This positive assessment is based on the fact that after the fall of socialism East Central Europe—which for the purpose of this book includes the Baltic states of Estonia, Latvia, and Lithuania; the Visegrád group of the Czech and Slovak republics, Hungary, and Poland; as well as Slovenia, Bulgaria, Romania, and Croatia—managed to adopt the key institutions of market economy and democracy, and joined the European Union (EU).

These successes were neither predicted nor easily achieved. Rather, throughout the 1990s many scholars doubted that the seeds of capitalist democracy would ever take root in postsocialist soil. Some questioned its feasibility on grounds of missing cultural, political, or economic preconditions, or of past legacies inimical to a new order. Others were skeptical because they thought that building markets and democracy simultaneously from scratch imposed mutually incompatible tasks. The international context in which the Cold War ended also contributed to pessimism. It was argued that the neoliberal global economy left the postsocialist newcomers little room for emulating the Western democracies' postwar pattern of fast growth with equity and political stability.

These multiple handicaps can explain the ironic fact that scenarios of the new market societies' destabilization or breakdown were elaborated in greater detail by early transitologists than that of the collapse of socialism had ever been by Sovietologists. Indeed, the gloomy prophecies have not been entirely wrong. Despite advances toward more consolidated situations, the new order remained fragile. East Central European capitalism was born amidst the crisis of the early 1990s, stayed vulnerable in its aftermath, and proved crisis-prone in the late 2000s. Yet against all odds, these societies have remained both capitalist and democratic—at least so far. With our study of their efforts to survive in hard times, we aim to contribute to the field of political economy of contemporary capitalism in three ways.

First, while advanced market societies' solutions to the problem that Karl Polanyi considered endemic to capitalism, namely the fundamental conflicts between market efficiency, social cohesion, and political legitimacy, have been subject to thorough study, this book elaborates on the unique efforts to resolve these conflicts on Europe's less advanced periphery. It answers the question: What has made capitalist democracy possible under adverse conditions? Second, while earlier research specified the impact of interwar Western experiences on postwar progress, this book stresses the unintended contribution of the socialist system to capitalist development in its aftermath. We trace the ways in which the assets and liabilities left behind by socialism have influenced the shape of new market societies.

Third, while comparative political economists have identified a variety of institutional ensembles in which advanced capitalism exists and competes in world markets, we argue that the breakdown of socialism has led to the emergence of no less diverse institutional configurations with asymmetric strengths and weaknesses. In order to understand the peculiar factors and consequences of institutional diversity, we develop a Polanyi-inspired typology of capitalist varieties and use it for static and dynamic comparisons of the East Central European cases.

Scholars have proposed competing paradigms, such as neoliberalism, welfare capitalism, and corporatism, to describe the new capitalism's defining features. This book enters the debate with the suggestion that none of these perspectives alone can lead to a satisfactory characterization. Once the socialist system fell apart, its pieces began to move on different but patterned rather than random trajectories, which produced a diversity of market societies instead of a single variant. Nevertheless, borrowing from Albert Hirschman, we propose that "however incompatible the various theories might be, each might still have its 'hour of truth' and/or its 'country of truth' as it applies in a given country or group of countries during a stretch of time."[1]

Our typology classifies the new regimes according to the vigor with which, and the forms in which transformative actors have used state power to build market economies pursuing the goals of neoliberalism, and to simultaneously preserve social cohesion and political legitimacy in line with the agendas of

1. Albert O. Hirschman, "Rival Views of Market Society," in *Rival Views of Market Society and Other Recent Essays* (Cambridge: Harvard University Press, 1992), 137.

welfare capitalism and democratic or neocorporatist government. On these dimensions postsocialist capitalism is differently configured across cases and over time. Concretely, the book traces the emergence from the transformation of East Central European societies of three capitalisms: a *neoliberal* type in the Baltic states, an *embedded neoliberal* type in the Visegrád countries, and a *neocorporatist* type in Slovenia.

In summary, the distinctive features of the Baltic neoliberal regime consist of a combination of market radicalism with meager compensation for transformation costs, together with severe limitation of citizens' and organized social groups' influence in democratic politics and policymaking. In turn, the Visegrád states' embedded neoliberalism is characterized by a permanent search for compromises between market transformation and social cohesion in more inclusive but not always efficient systems of democratic government.

Slovenia has combined the least radical strategy of marketization with the region's most generous efforts to compensate transformation's losers. Moreover, uniquely in the postsocialist world, this country exhibits many features of a democratic corporatist polity, where negotiated multilevel relationships among business, labor, and the state orient political rivals toward compromise solutions. Finally, we propose that via different paths and with delays Bulgaria and Romania have adopted many features of the neoliberal model, and Croatia those of the embedded neoliberal regime. Chapter 1 reviews the broader academic debates in which our typology originates, and operationalizes and empirically establishes the East Central European capitalist varieties.

Tracing the origins and logics of emergence of the three regimes raises complex questions about the role of domestic agency and external influence, past legacies and current political decisions, and institutional imitation and innovation. The key question is how far the East Central European countries have themselves influenced the direction of their postsocialist history. Is it not the case that their paths, rather than being actually chosen by these small states, have been externally imposed or determined by their past, or are purely accidental? Without doubt, manifold external influences and the region's legacies have impacted these countries' own transformative agency since the breakdown of socialism. Yet external pressures and inherited constraints have to be reconciled with the fact that the region's new social order exhibits nontrivial variation in patterns of capitalism with profound implications for economic and political freedom, stability, and welfare. This diversity and frequent conflicts over various features of capitalist models speak for the crucial importance of political agency, not its absence.

Accordingly, our key proposition is that within the constraints and opportunities inherent in the international order and in the region's legacies of incomplete modernization and Westernization, East Central Europeans have been eager to take advantage of a unique historical opportunity that has allowed them to shape their future. We contend that their choices have been politically conditioned and politically consequential. On these grounds, the book contributes to broader theoretical debates on the factors and logics of change in capitalist societies with an argument about how transformative vision and action can shape the institutional dynamics of emerging capitalist societies. Chapter 2 develops the argument by exploring the interplay of three groups of factors.

First, we argue that the *initial choices* of transformation strategies by political and technocratic elites helped set directions for divergent paths of regime formation. Such choices were constrained by the legacies of socialist and earlier pasts, and were also shaped by the transformative capacities of states and state-society relationships. However, we take seriously the fact that like other objective constraints, legacies of the past do not act on political outcomes directly. Rather, their influence is mediated by how policy makers and citizens *perceive* these inheritances. Which aspects of the past are likely to cast a long shadow in the aftermath of socialism is then also dependent on human sentiment and vision. In this vein, we contend that the extent to which influential economic and political actors saw the legacy as an asset or a liability or even a threat from the viewpoint of economic development or national sovereignty, had a deep impact on the postsocialist regimes. Perceived legacies and the related initial choices were also crucial for the degree of democratic inclusion, and the different patterns of protest and patience on the paths towards the new orders.

Second, we find that the real-world dynamics of regime formation can only be fully captured once the impact of *uncertainty and crisis* on transformative vision and practice is factored in. That is to say, the neoliberal, embedded neoliberal, and neocorporatist regimes cannot be explained as the direct results of preexisting master plans and resulting purposive action. Instead, these outcomes are better understood as products of Polanyian movements and countermovements and their advocates' political struggles. Under the conditions of radical uncertainty, policies and institutions often evolved as by-products or unintended consequences of solutions to problems that were viewed as more pressing than the pursuit of coherent long-term development agendas. The sense of pressure and urgency was heightened by economic and political fragility that put the popular loyalties upon which the new order's fate ultimately hinged permanently under stress. All this is elaborated in our inquiry into the processes by which alternatives to the actual regime outcomes were first pursued and eventually abandoned, or formerly rejected solutions came to the fore.

Third, we stress that *transnational and international factors and actors* have had a constitutive role in the emergence of regime diversity. We see this influence as twofold. On the one hand, initial choices were informed by the international context in so far as neoliberal reform strategies seemed to be the only game in town. Capitalist diversity in East Central Europe, with the notable exception of Slovenia, is therefore limited to diversity *within* neoliberalism. On the other hand, as a consequence of early choices East Central Europe became increasingly enmeshed in the circuits of European capitalism and its institutions. Interacting with domestic politics, varied types of transnational corporations, international financial institutions, the EU, and subregional cooperation and rivalry have locked the new regimes into paths on which many of the features of these external actors have been reproduced, and others challenged or altered.

Chapters 3 to 5 develop the above logics in empirical detail. Chapter 3 demonstrates the political and policy consequences of the marriage between nationalism and neoliberalism in the Baltic states. Chapter 4 explores the Visegrád regimes' simultaneous pursuit of the costly and contradictory objectives of foreign-led reindustrialization and bloated welfare states financed by only a handful of taxpayers and social security contributors. Chapter 5 demonstrates the ways in which neocorporatism instituted by a capable state in Slovenia, and pervasive state weakness in Bulgaria, Romania, and Croatia, have turned southeastern Europe into the most heterogeneous East Central European subregion in terms of regime variety and stability. Each chapter discusses the ways in which country-specific differences as well as varied regional logics reinforced, or led to divergences from, the original regime paths.

Are these regimes merely transitory phenomena, or are they viable orders able to reproduce key features and consolidate their existence? While there have been signs of consolidation, recurrent crises have posed challenges to regime stability. Comparable to the Great Depression of 1929–33 for its depth and length, an extraordinary recession erupted from the agony of socialism. Neither the front-runners nor the laggards of transformation were spared from its impact. Parallel to the economic crisis, the region was affected by the peaceful or violent processes of (re)building independent nation-states. Hardly had the recovery started, when in the second half of the 1990s a new wave of financial and economic shocks, provoking in some cases massive protests, shook a number of countries. All this turbulence changed the direction of capitalist paths, and paved the way towards transnational capitalist regimes.

From the late 1990s to the mid-2000s the region enjoyed its brief golden age of fast expanding foreign and domestic demand for its products, large foreign capital inflows, and rising living standards. Completed accession to the EU contributed to the spread of optimistic assessments of future economic perspectives. Transnational capitalism seemed to function remarkably well until the late 2000s when it was shaken worldwide.

Soon after the EU enlargement, the fragility of capitalist democracy returned with a vengeance. There have been riots and mass demonstrations, centrist parties have become radicalized and illiberal forces mixing agendas of the right and left extremes of the political spectrum have come to power. Radical programs of new and "real" transformations have gained popularity. The rise of radical voices has coincided with a mass exit of citizenry from formal politics, as evidenced by, among other things, dramatic drops in voter turnout. Opinion polls reveal strong dissatisfaction with democracy and a lack of trust in its institutions. Alas, the striking financial and economic downturn at the end of the first decade of the new millennium has brought with it an ongoing destabilization of political life in many countries of the region.

While leaving socialism and heading toward transnational capitalism appeared to be the solution over the 1990s, by the late 2000s full exposure to the risks of an increasingly strained and unstable global order has become part of the region's problems. As discussed in chapter 6, many of the transformation's front-runners have had to face savage speculative attacks against their national currencies, runs on their banks, capital flight, recession in their foreign-controlled industries, rising unemployment, and growing foreign debt. Hence, there are reasons for new concerns over the viability of some of the most successful postsocialist market societies. Whether the former socialist countries will eventually converge on the affluent, solidaristic, and democratic Western European standards is less clear today than it ever was. Indeed, analysts ought to be prepared for the possibility of backsliding in politics and the economy alike.

In all likelihood, the crisis and ongoing transformative change will reopen old and provoke new debates in the field of comparative capitalism. This book hopes to contribute to these debates by novel insights into the postsocialist Great Transformation, which has brought about institutional differentiation and economic and political progress, but has also revealed many of the system's vulnerabilities and its destructive and irrational tendencies: that is, features of capitalism *tout court*.

1

Capitalist Diversity after Socialism

It was not before the late 1990s that the diversity of postsocialist political economies became a major issue for East Europeanists. Before that time discussions had been dominated by the essential problem of the road toward market economy "without adjectives." As Jeffrey Sachs asserted, "the main debate in economic reform should therefore be about the means of transition, not the ends. Eastern Europe will still argue over the ends: for example, whether to aim for Swedish-style social democracy or Thatcherite liberalism. But that can wait. Sweden and Britain alike have nearly complete private ownership, private financial markets and active labor markets. Eastern Europe today has none of these institutions; for it, the alternative models of Western Europe are almost identical."[1]

As if to corroborate the above sequence, two decades after the breakdown of the socialist system and following sustained attempts at market reform, East European societies seem to have settled on divergent models of capitalism, and transitology has moved on to comparison. Yet notwithstanding important contributions, the existing comparative literature leaves researchers with open questions and tasks concerning all the main issues with which this book is concerned: the success, fragility, and diversity of postsocialist capitalism, the emergence of institutions, and the character rather than merely the varieties of capitalism.

In the debates of the 1990s the front-runners of transformation were distinguished from the laggards by their radical and comprehensive rather than gradual and piecemeal reforms, and by the superior performance attributed to best practices of reforming. This way, success could be measured and

1. Jeffrey Sachs, "Eastern Europe's Economies: What Is to Be Done?" *Economist*, January 12, 1990, 19.

countries ranked by constructing indexes or by studying conventional indicators. We contend, however, that transition index scores, or rates of inflation, employment, and GDP cannot fully describe the state of capitalist democracy in the region. To add substantive meaning to the partial indicators, in this chapter we will introduce a broader and theoretically founded yardstick of success that takes seriously the complex character of capitalist progress including its endemic tensions and the obstacles it encounters.

Analysts have stressed the fragility of capitalism in Eastern Europe as a whole virtually from its birth, and have explained it by the overloaded transformation agenda, the contradictory institutions emerging from half-hearted reforms, or, finally, by the fact that the postsocialist countries formed an especially vulnerable part of the capitalist world to which they returned. Although not denying the salience of these idiosyncratic factors, this chapter suggests an added emphasis on systemic sources of fragility—those that we ascribe not least to capitalism itself and to East Central Europe's deep global economic integration. Driven by its own cycles of expansion, contraction, and recurrent loss of stability, the global economy tends to reward its parts in good times, but may punish them (whether they are advanced or less advanced) in hard times even more than its outsiders.

Although comparativists have proposed several alternative models to capture the varieties of Eastern Europe's new social order, the emerging capitalist system itself has been rarely analyzed in the necessary theoretical breadth and depth.[2] However, we argue, no convincing concept of *capitalisms* can be elaborated without settling first on a theory of *capitalism*. This book adopts Karl Polanyi's notion of market society as its intellectual road map, and characterizes capitalist varieties by the institutions and conflicts that are the focus of *The Great Transformation*.[3]

We see several advantages of a Polanyian framework over alternative approaches. Polanyi has an original concept of capitalism, with multiple analytic levels and institutional dimensions that offer keys to understanding the system's character and factors of rise and demise, and thus readily provide a theoretical background for capturing diversity within systemic unity. Central aspects of the resulting typology can be operationalized and empirically traced in the postsocialist world. Finally, as stated below and demonstrated in greater detail in the book, the approach allows for static and dynamic comparisons alike.

We begin with a brief critical overview of selected earlier and more recent comparisons of East European capitalisms. The review is followed by a

2. However, a few outstanding early studies, most prominently János Kornai, *The Socialist System: The Political Economy of Communism* (Princeton: Princeton University Press, 1992), did contrast socialism with capitalism in the Cold War tradition of social system comparisons.
3. Karl Polanyi, *The Great Transformation: The Political and Economic Origins of Our Time* (Boston: Beacon Press, 1957 [1944]).

presentation of our Polanyian framework, which we then apply to the context of East Central European new regimes. Finally we provide evidence to link our typology to the universe of our empirical cases.

Comparing East European Capitalisms

Gil Eyal, Iván Szelényi, and Eleanor Townsley were among the first to perceive the new capitalism "as a variety of possible destinations...a world of socioeconomic systems with a great diversity of class relations and institutional arrangements."[4] Concretely, they identified a dividing line between East Central Europe, where marketization outpaced the creation of a private propertied class and thus a managers' "capitalism without capitalists" emerged, and the former Soviet republics, which exhibited the opposite mismatch. There, new "capitalists" expropriated state property "without capitalism," that is, before all the core institutions of a market economy were put in place.

Concerning the origins of capitalist varieties, Eyal, Szelényi, and Townsley stressed the role of inherited elite fractions and their new coalitions. In another influential example of early comparative work, David Stark and László Bruszt focused on transformative political choices leading to varied "paths of extrication" from the old social order, and the impact of "recombinant" socioeconomic networks on the new one.[5] Although the contribution of these and other pioneering studies was important, they had little to say about international and transnational influences.

Since the start of the new millennium comparativists have moved in two directions relevant for our inquiry. The first is represented by recent authors in the path dependency tradition, who also pay more attention to the international dimension than their predecessors. Drawing on the concepts of Eyal, Szelényi, and Townsley, Lawrence King observed the existence of "a patrimonial variety dependent on raw material exports which produces 'involution' and a liberal variety that is dependent on capital imports and manufactured exports, and that leads to some development."[6]

Although King's distinction is based only on the Russian and Polish cases, its relevance has been confirmed by other research. It has become widely accepted in the literature to contrast the western rim states of the defunct Soviet empire with their fully fledged market economies and democracies,

---

4. Gil Eyal, Iván Szelényi, and Eleanor Townsley, *Making Capitalism without Capitalists: The New Ruling Elites in Eastern Europe* (London: Verso, 1998), 16, 4–5.

5. David Stark and László Bruszt, *Post-Socialist Pathways: Transforming Politics and Property in East Central Europe* (Cambridge: Cambridge University Press, 1998).

6. Lawrence King, "Postcommunist Divergence: A Comparative Analysis of the Transition to Capitalism in Poland and Russia," *Studies in Comparative International Development* 37, no. 3 (2002): 28.

and the members of the Commonwealth of Independent States (CIS) reminiscent of what used to be called Third World countries for their natural resource dependence, ethnic conflicts, and authoritarian features.[7]

Many states fall, however, in between these extremes. Recently, attempts have been made to map more systematically the various types of capitalism that exist in the postsocialist world. The most comprehensive taxonomy to date has identified five varieties across Russia, Eastern Europe, and Central Asia. Based on different forms of international integration and domestic state structures, Martin Myant and Jan Drahokoupil have distinguished foreign direct investment (FDI)–based and peripheral market economies, oligarchic-clientelistic capitalism, order states, and remittance- or aid-based economies.[8]

Inspired by the Varieties of Capitalism (VoC) approach, a second body of new research explores the diversity of capitalism within East Central Europe. In an influential volume Peter Hall, David Soskice, and their collaborators have developed a powerful account of how different institutional configurations shape firm behavior and national strategies to meet the challenges of the global economy in advanced capitalist states.[9] As is well known, one of their basic configurations, the liberal market economy (LME), is characterized by the prevalence of market relations in the spheres of corporate governance and finance, industrial relations, interfirm contacts, and skills (re)production. This market-generated flexibility is well suited to promoting strategies of radical innovation. LMEs thus compete successfully in high-tech, high-risk sectors. In contrast, Hall and Soskice's coordinated market economy (CME) relies more on consensual and cooperative relations among enterprises, between enterprises and their banks, and between social partners. Although CMEs are less well prepared to foster radical innovation, they rule world markets in sectors where incremental innovation is a key to success.

Some of the authors who have applied VoC to East Central Europe have concentrated on Slovenia and Estonia, and have identified them as cases of CME and LME, respectively.[10] Others have stressed that the region is populated by "mixed" rather than "pure" capitalisms.[11] Yet even if the recent wave of

7. László Bruszt, "Making Markets and Eastern Enlargement: Diverging Convergence?" *West European Politics* 25, no. 2 (2002): 121–40; László Csaba, *The New Political Economy of Emerging Europe* (Budapest: Akadémiai Kiadó, 2005); David Lane and Martin Myant, eds., *Varieties of Capitalism in Post-Communist Countries* (Basingstoke: Palgrave Macmillan, 2007).

8. Martin Myant and Jan Drahokoupil, *Transition Economies: Political Economy in Russia, Eastern Europe, and Central Asia* (Hoboken: Wiley-Blackwell, 2010).

9. Peter A. Hall and David Soskice, eds., *Varieties of Capitalism: The Institutional Foundations of Comparative Advantage* (Oxford: Oxford University Press, 2001).

10. Magnus Feldmann, "Emerging Varieties of Capitalism in Transition Countries: Industrial Relations and Wage Bargaining in Estonia and Slovenia," *Comparative Political Studies* 39, no. 7 (2006): 829–54; Clemens Buchen, "Estonia and Slovenia as Antipodes," in Lane and Myant, *Varieties*, 65–89.

11. Vlad Mykhnenko, "Strengths and Weaknesses of 'Weak' Coordination: Economic Institutions, Revealed Comparative Advantages, and Socioeconomic Performance of Mixed Market Economies in Poland and Ukraine," in *Beyond Varieties of Capitalism: Conflict,*

comparisons has shed light on some patterned differences among postsocialist institutions, the limitations of VoC cast doubt on these studies' usefulness
for understanding capitalist diversity in the aftermath of socialism.[12]

First, the VoC approach has been designed to analyze advanced economies, and derives many of its insights from the German, British, and American
forms of capitalism. But to assume that these models can be readily applied
to less developed market societies seems far too much of a stretch. In other
words, the LME and CME set of varieties underestimates the true diversity
of capitalism, especially once we move from Europe's core to its periphery.

Second, most of the new economic and political institutions were not yet
in place when the postsocialist economies became exposed to global pressures. Therefore, their emergence and consolidation have been much more
influenced by international and transnational factors and actors than was
usual in the Western cases. The latter influences, then, have to be taken more
seriously than in the VoC literature. An adequate approach to the varieties of postsocialist capitalism has to be able to map and carefully assess the
concrete form of international and transnational embeddedness of national
institutions, and the contradictory pressures stemming from this condition.

In a recent article Andreas Nölke and Arjan Vliegenthart try to get beyond these limitations.[13] Departing from a more complex reading of the VoC
literature, they add to the original classification a third one, the dependent
market economy (DME), and demonstrate its presence in the Visegrád area.
Also inspired by earlier work on transnational capitalism in Eastern Europe,
they introduce the DME as a postsocialist mutation of Ben Schneider's hierarchical market economy, elaborated for Latin America.[14]

In Nölke and Vliegenthart's view, the Visegrád economies, coordinated
largely by hierarchical intrafirm relationships within transnational corporations (TNCs), dispose of comparative advantages as export platforms of semi-
standardized industrial goods produced by abundant skilled labor. In line with
the VoC school, Nölke and Vliegenthart trace comparative advantages and superior performance to complementarity across the institutions of investment
finance (via foreign investment and banks), corporate governance (by foreign

Contradictions, and Complementarities in the European Economy, ed. Bob Hancké, Martin Rhodes,
and Mark Thatcher (Oxford: Oxford University Press, 2007), 351–78.

12. For recent critical reviews of the VoC approach and the debates it provoked, see
Dorothee Bohle and Béla Greskovits, "Varieties of Capitalism and Capitalism *Tout Court*,"
European Journal of Sociology 50, no. 3 (2009): 355–86; Wolfgang Streeck, "E Pluribus Unum?
Varieties and Commonalities of Capitalism," Discussion Paper 10/12 (Cologne: Max-Planck-
Institut für Gesellschaftsforschung, 2010); and Jamie Peck and Nik Theodore, "Variegated
Capitalism," *Progress in Human Geography* 31, no. 6 (2007): 731–72.

13. Andreas Nölke and Arjan Vliegenthart, "Enlarging the Varieties of Capitalism: The
Emergence of Dependent Market Economies in East Central Europe," *World Politics* 61, no. 4
(October 2009): 670–702.

14. Ben Ross Schneider, "Hierarchical Market Economies and Varieties of Capitalism in
Latin America," *Journal of Latin American Studies* 41, no. 3 (2009): 533–71.

company headquarters), fragmented industrial relations (firm-level collective bargaining agreements for skilled workers), limited arrangements for (re)training, and the transfer of technology within TNCs' production systems.[15]

Thanks to their interest in the Visegrád economies' strong reliance on TNCs, these authors have made a step forward in understanding an important specificity of the region. At the same time, by allowing only for a single new type of dependent market economy, they downplay the salience of diverse kinds of FDI and production systems for East Central Europe's *varied* forms of dependence. More generally, it seems misleading to reserve this term for the exact handful of countries that due to their peculiar history managed to escape one peril usually attributed to dependency: lasting scarcity of human capital. Conceived the way it is, the DME model cannot cover the majority of dependent economies. Ironically, therefore, it also means a step backward when compared, for instance, to the sophisticated typology of Fernando H. Cardoso's and Enzo Faletto's classic work on patterns of dependency and development in Latin America.[16]

More importantly, all attempts at applying the original or enlarged VoC concept to Eastern Europe suffer from the concept's shortcomings when it comes to understanding the emergence of institutions: a crucial issue in postsocialist economies where the market order has only recently taken shape and its consolidation cannot yet be taken for granted. In the context of the radical change that has occurred across the region, the origins of the postsocialist order must partly be located outside of the realm of existing institutions. Any meaningful conceptualization of the new configurations must therefore include propositions about transformative political agents and their interplay with transnational and supranational actors.

Aware of the salience of agency, Nölke and Vliegenthart urge researchers to explore their model's case-specific relevance and details, and thus put more historical flesh on its bare bones. But we wonder whether this alone would solve the problem of exclusion of politics from the proposed model. This is unlikely, because the VoC framework grants little autonomy to the state and democratic politics. As a consequence, it loses sight of a key dimension of capitalism's systemic profile, namely its tendency to create separate economic and political spheres, and the permanent struggles around its core institutions that occur in both realms.[17]

---

15. Nölke and Vliegenthart, "Enlarging," 680. Bruno Amable defines institutional complementarity as follows: "Two institutions can be said to be complementary when the presence of one increases the efficiency of the other." *The Diversity of Modern Capitalism* (Oxford: Oxford University Press, 2003), 6.

16. Fernando H. Cardoso and Enzo Faletto, *Dependency and Development in Latin America* (Berkeley: University of California Press, 1979).

17. Amable, *The Diversity of Modern Capitalism;* Wolfgang Streeck, *Re-Forming Capitalism: Institutional Change in the German Political Economy* (Oxford: Oxford University Press, 2009).

For all these reasons, we find the VoC approach not quite suitable for our inquiry. Let us now demonstrate how a Polanyian perspective on postsocialist capitalism and its varieties can overcome the shortcomings identified above.

Polanyian Varieties

Closely reading Polanyi's work, we have found the following interdependent aspects of his concept of capitalism. For Polanyi, capitalism is a multilevel (international and national) form of political economy; it can produce immense wealth and freedom at the price of permanent conflict between the "self-regulating market mechanism" and the protective arrangements against its dangers; it expands and contracts in cycles of open-ended differentiation; but it is always exposed to existential risks stemming from the opposition between promarket "movements" of trading classes and protective "countermovements" of landed and working classes, an opposition that is hard to reconcile and thereby keeps capitalism's political life in motion.

As far as the international level is concerned, Polanyi's analysis focused on what he called nineteenth-century civilization and its demise in the interwar period. The economic pillars of the first capitalist world order were free trade and the gold standard. Its political underpinnings included balance among the great powers and the rising liberal nation-states that could act as amplifiers and mediators of international pressures. In the interwar years these foundations crumbled: free trade degraded into protectionism, the gold standard collapsed, the balance of power gave way to rivalry, and nation building bred aggressive militarism.

The rise and demise of the liberal international order is intrinsically linked to what Polanyi famously called the double movement, namely the tension between a constant push towards self-regulating markets and spontaneous resistance to the subordination of society to market forces. It is at the national level that the double movement becomes institutionalized. Polanyi's thoughts on capitalism's defining institutions appear with remarkable clarity already in the first outline of his path-breaking book. Referring to the nineteenth and the first decades of the twentieth century he wrote: "*There was hardly a political or economic institution, a characteristic stress or strain, in this period, which was not either part of the self-regulation of the market-mechanism, or of the protective arrangements against the dangers of such a mechanism, or, finally which was not a direct consequence of their interaction.*"[18]

---

18. "Memorandum concerning the plan of a book on the 'Origins of the Cataclysm. A Political and Economic Inquiry,'" 3. Emphasis in the original. The typed manuscript is kept in the Rockefeller Archive Center, Sleepy Hollow, New York, and is dated 1941 by Richard Swedberg who shared a photocopy with us.

As virtually all of the capitalist order is absorbed or influenced by the institutions of self-regulating markets and social protection, these areas have key importance for understanding the system, while their conflicting interplay gives shape to a third capitalist building block, namely political institutions. Whereas in the above-quoted passage political institutions are seen as being directly shaped by the double movement, in his later work Polanyi also attributes more autonomy to the political sphere: "the legislature, like industry, had its formal functions to perform in society. Its members were entrusted with the forming of the communal will, the direction of public policy, the enactment of long-term programs at home and abroad. No complex society could do without functioning legislative and executive bodies of a political kind."[19] These two slightly different views of the autonomy of the political sphere point to the fact that Polanyi, similar to writers in the Weberian tradition and a number of Marxist authors, sees the tension inherent in capitalist democracies, namely that while political institutions are deeply enmeshed in concrete social interests, to formulate goals for society as a whole they need a degree of autonomy.

From the above it is clear that Polanyi conceptualized the market society as a highly dynamic entity, full of tensions and contradictions. Writing from the vantage point of the Great Depression, Polanyi was also well aware of the destructive potential of these tensions. In a well-known passage he outlines two potentially perilous outcomes of the double movement: "Such an institution [the self-regulating market economy] could not exist for any length of time without annihilating the human and natural substance of society. . . . Inevitably, society took measures to protect itself, but whatever measures it took impaired the self-regulation of the market, disorganized industrial life, and thus endangered society in yet another way."[20] In addition to the social calamity following from excessively "disembedded" markets, and economic disorganization following from overly or perversely "reembedded" markets, the system is also exposed to the risk of political breakdown triggered by the malfunctioning of the polity and/or absent legitimacy. Polanyi's prime example of such a danger is Germany, where in the 1930s the political system became itself a factor of crisis, and where an unmitigated class conflict resulted in the paralysis of state and economic institutions alike.[21]

In Polanyi's view, sustainable social diversity becomes possible only under the condition that societies manage to avoid the above perilous scenarios, which requires removing "the elements of production—land, labor, and money—from the market." He saw this new development coming in the aftermath of the interwar depression, fascism, and World War II: "In effect, the disintegration of a uniform market economy is already giving rise to a *variety*

---

19. Polanyi, *The Great Transformation*, 235.
20. Ibid., 3–4.
21. Ibid., 235.

of new societies. Also, the end of market society means in no way the absence of markets. These continue, in various fashions, to ensure the freedom of the consumer, to indicate the shifting of demand, to influence producers' income, and to serve as an instrument of accountancy, while ceasing altogether to be an organ of economic self-regulation."[22]

This analysis forms the basis of our Polanyi-inspired notion of capitalist varieties. Exposed to the opportunities and risks inscribed in a given international order, and pushed and pulled by contradictory motives, social forces, and institutions toward and away from perilous scenarios, capitalist development involves constant "playing with fire." Hence, all viable varieties, whose number and forms vary with the existing world order, must be anchored in a particular historical moment, and be able to maneuver within a space bordered by social disintegration, economic disorganization, and/ or political breakdown—without coming dangerously close to any of these borders. Accordingly, the viable varieties can be distinguished and compared according to their specific configurations and the coordinating abilities that together enable them to cope with capitalism's conflicts and so ensure its survival across three core institutional areas: marketization of the economy, the opposing goal of protection of society, and the broadly conceived political system.

The resulting classification can be viewed as "ideal-typical" in Max Weber's sense. As he put it: "The theoretically constructed types of conflicting 'life orders' are merely intended to show that at certain points such and such internal conflicts are possible and 'adequate.'" Along these lines, Polanyi's theory allows us to conceive of capitalist models "with a rational consistency which is rarely found in reality. But they *can* appear thus in reality and in historically important ways, and they have."[23]

The implied imperative for capitalism's sustainability of a degree of politico-economic balance is related to the idea of low-level equilibrium proposed by one of us in the late 1990s. This term implied that after the collapse of socialism "democracy and a market economy could be simultaneously introduced only because neither has been fully implemented. Democracy could only stabilize at the costs of some of its qualitative aspects because of the crisis and economic transformation. Economic transformation, in turn, has remained feasible only at a cost of its speed and radicalism, and its many

---

22. Ibid., 252. Emphasis added.
23. Max Weber, "Religious Rejections of the World and Their Directions," in *From Max Weber: Essays in Sociology,* ed. Hans H. Gerth and C. Wright Mills (London: Routledge, 1948 [1920]), 323–24. Emphasis in the original. Our attempt to construct Weberian ideal types of postsocialist capitalism resonates with some of Uwe Becker's ideas. See his *Open Varieties of Capitalism: Continuity, Change and Performance* (Houndsmills: Palgrave Macmillan, 2009), and his "How Comparatively to Map Changing Capitalist Varieties: Methodological Considerations Illustrated by Examples from the BRICs," paper presented at the SASE annual meeting, June 14, 2011. The main differences in our typology stem from the systematic application of Polanyi's theory.

imperfections are due not least to the democratic framework of the change."[24] Our new framework extends the concept by analyzing markets and politics in a dynamic perspective characterized by the interplay and cycles of equilibrating and disequilibrating factors and tendencies.

But is it not the case that Polanyi's double movement dynamic essentially precludes the possibility of balanced situations? We do not think so. Polanyi also distinguished between capitalism's "quiet times" and its critical moments. In his own words, in the 1930s when "normal methods were insufficient, abnormal ones would be tried...which were socialistic...the very hint would suffice to throw markets into confusion and start a universal panic....While a divergence of economic interests would normally end in compromise, the separation of the economic and political spheres tended to invest such clashes with grave consequences to the community."[25]

Against the background of separate economic and political spheres, the main burden of sustaining capitalism is put on the political sphere. As already argued above, this is not an easy task, as capitalist democracies and states are characterized by a fundamental tension. In the words of Fred Block and Margaret Somers: "The added complexity to Polanyi's view rests on the insight that the self-regulating market created a peculiar situation in which...the state...was necessarily both a universal, representing the interests of society against the market, and a class state, pursuing the agendas of the capitalist class, since the reproduction of capitalist relations was necessary to preserve society."[26]

This interpretation is in line with our proposal to consider the political sphere as a part of capitalism's systemic problems as well as a part of their temporary solution. It is on these grounds that we try to capture and operationalize political actors' and institutions' general significance for capitalist development but also the variations in their capacity for successful navigation on the stormy waters of that process.

In turn, bringing politics back in nontrivial and clearly identifiable roles helps create our yardstick of postsocialist success with capitalist democracy. This yardstick is essentially a measure of sustainability rooted in the political capacities, first to combine market efficiency and social protection in viable ways, and second, to gain from such configurations the most in terms of economic freedom, social cohesion, and political liberty. *It is, then, ultimately in the capacities of the political sphere that the secret of capitalist success lies.* We are aware that our yardstick cannot produce as clear and stable rankings of

---

24. Béla Greskovits, *The Political Economy of Protest and Patience: East European and Latin American Transformations Compared* (Budapest: Central European University Press, 1998), 181–87.

25. Polanyi, *The Great Transformation*, 235.

26. Fred Block and Margaret R. Somers, "Beyond the Economistic Fallacy: The Holistic Social Science of Karl Polanyi," in *Vision and Method in Historical Sociology*, ed. Theda Skocpol (Cambridge: Cambridge University Press, 1984), 68.

countries or groups of countries as any partial indicator would do. However, we see our yardstick's added value in highlighting the multiple (complementary and contradictory) dimensions of success, the importance of its differing kinds, not only its varying degrees, and the matrixes of opportunities, risks, and trade-offs that go with and define the stakes of political maneuvering.[27] Let us turn to the task of operationalization.

Postsocialist Regime Concepts

Few scholars would deny that in view of their economic and political achievements the East Central European states should be considered as the success stories of postsocialist transformation. Another often-made claim is that the global capitalist system of the 1990s provided a harsher environment for the newcomers' return to capitalism than the postwar system would have done. To understand why, it is helpful to recall the dynamics of world order in the second half of the century. Incidentally, several important conceptualizations of this order have been inspired by Polanyi's intellectual legacy.

In the final chapters of his book Polanyi envisions a postwar settlement, many aspects of which could be discovered in the international order adopted at the Bretton Woods Conference in 1944. John Ruggie aptly termed this settlement a compromise inspired by "embedded liberalism." Its essence was that "unlike the economic nationalism of the thirties, it would be multilateral in character; unlike the liberalism of the gold standard and free trade, its multilateralism would be predicated upon domestic interventionism."[28] Importantly, embedded liberalism entailed regulated international finance and competitive markets for goods and services but also national-level compromises on "democratic corporatism" and several "worlds of welfare," respectively theorized by Peter Katzenstein and Gösta Esping-Andersen.[29]

Yet if we compare the postwar order with the international context in which capitalism overcame its formidable rival Soviet-type socialism, the contrast could hardly be more striking. The end of the Cold War was both prepared by and resulted in new circumstances marked by a revival of nineteenth century economic liberalism as *neo*liberalism which, according to critical accounts, has put the system's postwar dynamics "into reverse gear."[30]

---

27. These thoughts have been also inspired by Peter J. Katzenstein, *Small States in World Markets: Industrial Policy in Europe* (Ithaca: Cornell University Press, 1985), esp. 27–30.

28. John G. Ruggie, "International Regimes, Transactions, and Change: Embedded Liberalism in the Postwar Economic Order," *International Organization* 36, no. 2 (Spring 1982): 393.

29. Katzenstein, *Small States;* and Gösta Esping-Andersen, *Three Worlds of Welfare Capitalism* (Cambridge: Polity Press, 1990).

30. Mark Blyth, *Great Transformations: Economic Ideas and Institutional Change in the Twentieth Century* (Cambridge: Cambridge University Press, 2002), 6.

In the new era, volatile global finance replaced the Bretton Woods system. Monetarist coordination replaced Keynesian demand management, flexible specialization took over from Fordist mass production. Virtually from its birth, postsocialist capitalism became part and parcel of a new global environment, which in Wolfgang Streeck's succinct formulation not merely boosted the expansion of "markets within states" but squeezed "states within markets," thereby blurring the boundaries of public authority and limiting its chances for protecting society.[31] As a consequence, social protection became subordinated to the cause of global competitiveness. Finally, the former socialist states have had to cope with the risks and threats of an ideological climate forgetful of the interwar calamities. This is the new variant of international capitalist order within which national diversity ought to be conceptualized. The initially largely benevolent but later more controversial impact of the EU must be factored in, too.

While the idea of overall successful response in East Central Europe to the challenges of transformation is commonly accepted, no consensus has yet been reached on its institutional foundations. Several paradigms have been proposed to understand the essence of new capitalism and the factors that made for its viability.

Recognizing that in the first half of the 1990s many of the East Central European states relied on formally established tripartite institutions of social dialogue to generate political support for the transformation, to determine minimum wages, and to manage pension and health care funds, Melanie Tatur labeled them "corporatist," and Elena Iankova "transformative corporatist."[32] David Ost, on the other hand, contended that this corporatism was "illusory" because it was "used to generate neoliberal outcomes," and make labor accept its own weakening and "a radical decline of the welfare state."[33] Adherents to the critical international political economy tradition similarly argued that neoliberalism was the apt term for postsocialist capitalism.[34]

At the same time, the issue of how liberal the new market economies actually were has been controversial. Assessing Eastern Europe's transformation strategies, Peter Murrell concluded that "taken as a whole, this is the

31. Wolfgang Streeck, "'Globalization': Nothing New Under the Sun?" *Socio-Economic Review* 5, no. 3 (July 2007): 540.

32. Melanie Tatur, "Towards Corporatism?—The Transformation of Interest Policy and Interest Regulation in Eastern Europe," in *Industrial Transformation in Europe: Process and Contexts*, ed. Eckhard J. Dittrich, Richard Whitley, and Gerd Schmidt (London: Sage, 1995), 163–84; Elena A. Iankova, *Eastern European Capitalism in the Making* (Cambridge: Cambridge University Press, 2002). These studies confirm Philippe Schmitter's classic work "Still the Century of Corporatism?" *Review of Politics* 36, no. 1 (1974): 85–131.

33. David Ost, "Illusory Corporatism in Eastern Europe: Neoliberal Tripartism and Postcommunist Class Identities," *Politics and Society* 28, no. 4 (December 2000): 504–5, 507.

34. Dorothee Bohle, Hugo Radice, and Stuart Shields, eds., "State, Capital and Labor: The Political Economy of Capitalist Diversity in Eastern Europe," special issue, *Competition and Change* 11, no. 2 (June 2007).

most dramatic episode of liberalization in economic history."[35] In contrast, international advisers of the reformist governments were concerned that liberalization had not gone far enough to produce favorable outcomes, and questioned the idea of a welfare state decline.[36] Sachs, for instance, argued that "it is the high and escalating social spending, not the alleged cuts, that offers us the real insight into the political dynamics of the region."[37]

Without sharing the normative concerns underlying the market-radical perception of insufficient liberalization and welfare overspending, Katzenstein also doubted the region-wide validity of the term neoliberalism. Commenting on the transformative corporatism versus neoliberalism debate, he contended that "to call all of the Central and East European regimes 'neoliberal'...stretches the concept unduly. If we had to choose one label under which to subsume their different experiences, then it would probably be 'European-style welfare capitalism.'"[38]

Our approach helps integrate these paradigms into a single coherent framework. Compatible with the Polanyian triad of core institutions and capacities, each paradigm points to essential logics, which must be present in all models of capitalism but may have different significance in any one of them. Neoliberalism prioritizes the creation of efficient markets, welfare capitalism compensates for the costs of radical socio-economic change, and democratic corporatism foregrounds the three key institutional dimensions of political coordination, as it takes into account the influence of both the electorate and organized business and labor over the policy choices of a capable public authority. Accordingly, postsocialist capitalisms can be differentiated by the changing relative weight of the ideas and institutional implications of neoliberalism, welfare capitalism, and democratic corporatism. Hence, our postsocialist regime definition refers to: (1) types of national political economies that while (2) deeply and variably integrated in the neoliberal global and European order, (3) tend to pursue marketization and transformation cost compensation with different amounts of vigor and in varied forms, and (4) politically govern the pursuit of these conflicting and contested social objectives in different ways and with varied effectiveness.

For illustrative purposes the resulting configurations can be plotted onto a six-dimensional property space demonstrating both the Polanyian origins of our regime concept, and the extensions proposed by us (figure 1.1). Two

35. Peter Murrell, "How Far Has the Transition Progressed?" *Journal of Economic Perspectives* 10, no. 2 (1996): 31.

36. Anders Aslund, "Possible Future Directions for Economies in Transition," in *Transforming Post-Communist Political Economies*, ed. Joan M. Nelson, Charles Tilly, and Lee Walker (Washington, D.C.: National Academy Press, 1997), 457.

37. Jeffrey Sachs, "Postcommunist Parties and the Politics of Entitlements," *Beyond Transition: The Newsletter about Reforming Economies*, 1995, 1, http://www.worldbank.org/html/prddr/trans/mar95/pgs1–4.htm (accessed February 20, 2009).

38. Peter J. Katzenstein, "*Small States* and Small States Revisited," *New Political Economy* 8, no. 1 (2003): 22.

corners of such a hexagonal "diamond" scheme represent the polar extremes of fully fledged markets versus large-scale transformation cost compensation through welfare state benefits or industrial policies, and the highest levels of economic freedom versus social cohesion predicted by these arrangements. A third corner stands for the institutions of effective macroeconomic (fiscal and/or monetary) coordination, and the economic stability they produce. The remaining three corners refer to the institutions which, once in place, define the full potential of the political system for democratic decisionmaking, overall administrative capacity, and neocorporatist social partnership. These corners also indicate the highest possible quality of governance and amounts of political freedom and inclusion the polity can offer.

This way, the edges of the diamond bring together all the economic, social, and political benefits capitalism could ideally bring about, and point to the institutional bases of such common goods. In the East Central European context, the gestalt of capitalism "at its best" can be proxied by a combination of regional top scores on indexes of economic transition, social protection spending, robustness of fiscal and monetary institutions, democratization, negotiated industrial relations, and bureaucratic capacity—as if all these were achievements of a single country or regime.

According to our Polanyian concept the very same scheme also hints at the opposite gestalt of capitalism "at its worst," namely as a source of "common bads." Successful expansion on one or another institutional dimension may sow the seeds of failure, whenever the negative externalities inevitably produced in the process are not counterbalanced or at least mitigated by the impact of other institutions. Evidently, markets bring about economic freedom and efficiency at the expense of human beings and nature, both of which are commodified. Social protection brings about security but when provided in a paternalist manner it can lead to infantilized and pauperized societies. Macroeconomic effectiveness may come at the price of structural inflexibility or high costs of adjustment. Similarly, democracy may bring about political freedom and representation but lead to ungovernability or the tyranny of the majority, whereas corporatism may result in mediation and reconciliation of conflicting interests, but also in the predominance of particularistic over common ones. Finally, the government's challenge is to avoid its accountability degrading into state capture and its administrative capacities turning into overbureaucratization that cripples individual realization.

All this means that given the complexity of the system's endemic tensions and externalities there is no capitalism in which all good (or, for that matter, all bad) things will go hand in hand. Accordingly, particular configurations of institutions and performances, which we term "regimes," tend to occupy more or less permanent asymmetric positions closer to some, but more distant from other edges of the scheme of ideal capitalism. The characteristic shape of the matrixes depicts the complementarities, trade-offs, and challenges typical for each regime family or its members.

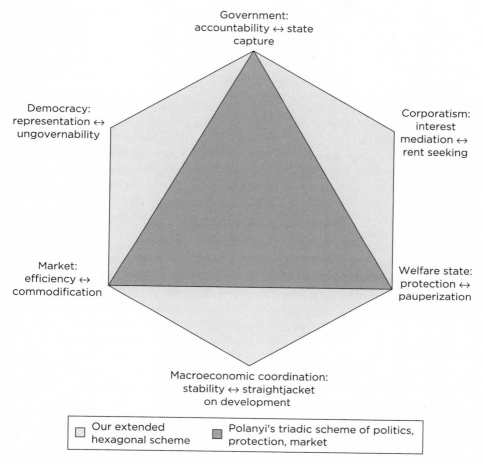

Figure 1.1. Institutional foundations of capitalist democracy's common goods, common bads, and tensions: Polanyi's triadic scheme, and our extended hexagonal scheme

In turn, the range and complexity of social objectives, which each regime aspires (or is able) to pursue and coordinate, can be illustrated by the size of the area covered by their respective matrixes, with the regions closer to the center of the diamond depicting configurations not yet, or no longer, worth the names "capitalist," "democratic," or "order." Note that the two interpretations of figure 1.1 indicate at least two different ways in which societies may fall short of having a viable capitalist democracy. This may be due to their resistance or inability to institute markets, democracy, social protection, or other important building blocks of a capitalist regime, but also to the implosion of their social order following over-expansion in some areas while neglecting others.

Along the above lines, we shall first demonstrate the existence and then explain the emergence of three capitalisms: a *pure neoliberal* type in the Baltic states, an *embedded neoliberal* type in the Visegrád countries, and a *neocorporatist* type in Slovenia. Let us first illustrate these types by adding stylized empirical content to the ideal scheme of figure 1.1, and then briefly explain the three regimes' specificities.

Members of the neoliberal regime family Estonia, Latvia, and Lithuania rapidly instituted market economies, but did little to mitigate businesses' risks and losses or help them by adequate industrial policies to capture promising market niches. Similarly, the Baltic welfare states fell short in providing sufficient protection against inequality and social anomie. The Baltic form of government has, with the exception of Lithuania, not been fully democratic, nor at all corporatist. Rather, the quality of Estonian and Latvian democracies is undermined by de jure exclusion of an important share of the resident population from politics, and by overall low participation rates. Although Lithuanian democracy is not de jure exclusive, political participation there has been as limited as in its Baltic neighbors. Finally, Baltic social partnership is the least institutionalized in East Central Europe (figure 1.2).

After spending most of the 1990s in a situation of economic and political disorder (termed nonregime in figure 1.3), Bulgaria and Romania also ended as neoliberal market societies, but their weak state institutions set them apart from their Baltic counterparts. Another difference is that low levels of political participation do not reflect legal exclusion but rather de facto absence of large social groups in Bulgarian and Romanian politics. At its worst, the neoliberal regime comes close to one of the Polanyian perils, namely social disintegration.

In turn, the Visegrád states opted for a socially and politically more inclusive strategy. The Czech and Slovak Republics, Hungary, and Poland (later followed by Croatia which initially lacked social order of any kind) mobilized substantial resources to compensate for the transformation costs of domestic firms inherited from socialism, and to pamper in their infancy and later assist the expansion of new transnational industries. Relatively generous welfare schemes helped large social groups to avoid or at least slow down decline to underclass status. It is precisely the search for compromises between market transformation and social cohesion that makes the Visegrád states' neoliberalism embedded and distinctive.[39] The Visegrád regime also differs from the Baltic pattern in political terms, as it grants political rights to all citizens.[40] However, the difference is less accentuated when social partnership institu-

---

39. The term "embedded neoliberalism" was coined by Bastiaan van Apeldoorn, *Transnational Capitalism and the Struggle Over European Integration* (London: Routledge, 2002), who used it with a different meaning than here, to characterize the EU's political economy under neoliberal hegemony.

40. Slovakia and Croatia suffered authoritarian backlashes in the early to mid-1990s.

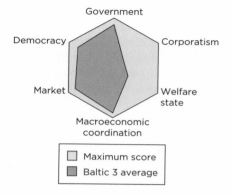

Figure 1.2. Neoliberal regime

Figure 1. 3. Nonregime

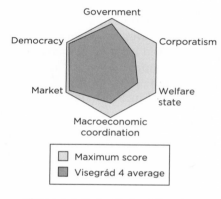

Figure 1.4. Embedded neoliberal regime

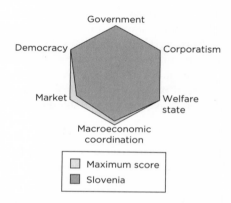

Figure 1.5. Neocorporatist regime

Definitions and sources for figures 1.2–1.5:

Maximum score: Score achieved by any of the 11 East Central European countries on the 6 dimensions in 1998 (or the closest year for which data are available). Regime averages are presented as a percentage of the maximum score. *Government:* Sum of indicators of government effectiveness, regulatory quality, rule of law, and control of corruption. Authors' calculations based on Kaufmann, Kraay and Mastruzzi, "Governance Matters VIII." *Corporatism:* Sum of scores of wage bargaining, the level at which it takes place, and the extension of collective agreements to nonunionized firms. Authors' calculations based on Jelle Visser, *ICTWSS: Institutional Characteristics of Trade Unions, Wage Setting, State Intervention, and Social Pacts* (Amsterdam: Amsterdam Institute for Advanced Labour Studies, 2011), http://www.uva-aias.net (accessed August 15, 2011). *Welfare state:* per capita spending on social benefits in PPS EUR. EUROSTAT, http://epp.eurostat.ec.europa.eu (accessed September 18, 2011). *Macroeconomic coordination:* index of budgeting institutions based on Mark Hallerberg, Rolf R. Strauch, and Jürgen von Hagen, *Fiscal Governance in Europe* (Cambridge: Cambridge University Press, 2009), table 6.1, 144. *Market:* average of 9 transition indexes of the EBRD, http://www.ebrd.com/pages/research/economics/data.shtml (accessed September 20, 2010). *Democracy:* Polity index, Polity IV 2010, http://www.systemicpeace.org/inscr/inscr.htm (accessed August 12, 2011).

tions are considered. While initially relatively well established, the Visegrád states' neocorporatist institutions have largely atrophied over time. Moreover, from the mid-2000s the Visegrád democracies have periodically fallen short in effectively coordinating their transformation agendas. Especially Hungary has faced a combination of policy-related and political symptoms of ill-conceived embeddedness: macroeconomic instability coupled with the ascendance of radical forces, which challenged the economic and political settlements and eventually the governability of embedded neoliberalism (figure 1.4).

Slovenia has adopted the least radical strategy of marketization coupled with the region's most generous and specifically targeted transformation cost compensation efforts. Unlike the Visegrád states' industrial policies which have increasingly favored foreign capital, the Slovenian policy has been geared toward industries inherited from socialism and has nurtured domestic entrepreneurial and managerial talent. However, the foreign-led modernization of certain activities has been able to count on selective state support. The Slovenian welfare state has been far the most generous in East Central Europe. Uniquely in the region, this regime falls closest to Katzenstein's "democratic corporatist" polity where legally enforced negotiated management-labor relationships, extended collective bargaining agreements, and social pacts, which invite business, labor, and the state to act as social partners, have for long enabled the balanced pursuit of an inclusive transformation strategy (figure 1.5).

Let us now point to another Weberian aspect of our typology. In Weber's words, ideal typical constructions "make it possible to determine the typological locus of a historical phenomenon. They enable us to see if, in particular traits or in their total character, the phenomena approximate one of our constructions: to determine the degree of approximation of the historical phenomenon to the theoretically constructed type."[41] Accordingly, our three models make a "distinction of ideal types and empirical cases, with the former as fixed entities and the latter as moving ones," and thus help comparisons across cases and over time.[42]

At any given point in time both the three regime types and the eleven concrete societies populating them are distinguished by the extent to which and the forms in which their economies are marketized; members of society and the economy are compensated for transformation costs; and their political and policy processes are governed by more or less capable state bureaucracies, distinct forms of democracy, and varied degrees of social partnership. This allows for static comparisons of members of different regimes and those belonging to the same regime alike.

In turn, dynamic comparisons become possible when, driven by Polanyian movements and countermovements, societies appear to drift gradually back

41. Gerth and Mills, *From Max Weber*, 324.
42. Becker, "How Comparatively to Map," 5.

and forth between more or less marketized and/or socially and politically inclusive institutional setups within their own regimes, or to shift more radically from one type to another.

Matrixes of Institutions and Performances

The two decades since the collapse of socialism provide a convenient time frame for examining the peculiarities of the three regimes in greater detail. Importantly, such a framework allows comparisons of the social and political dynamics of hard times and good times.[43] Punctuated by major crises, the period 1989–98 includes the historical turning points at which key decisions on the shape of postsocialist capitalism were taken. The following decade of 1999–2007 brought about consolidation, but eventually saw fierce struggles over the distribution of gains and losses.

Below, we shall present evidence on the three core regime dimensions: opening, regulating, and stabilizing markets; compensating for transformation costs in economy and society; and governing through democratic and neocorporatist institutions and practices of capable states. We then map three important related areas of economic and social performance: semicore versus semiperipheral international economic integration, social cohesion versus disintegration and status loss, and the external and domestic aspects of macroeconomic (in)stability. The related indicators are meant to capture the multiple dimensions of successful maneuvering within the space where postsocialist capitalism has proven viable.

Opening, Regulating, and Stabilizing Markets

In 1989–98 the Visegrád states and Slovenia were leaders in achieved levels of marketization, while initially the Baltic states, Croatia, Bulgaria, and Romania lagged behind them. By 1999–2007 the Baltic states had caught up with the Visegrád states, while the Southeastern European states continued to be laggards, although they partly worked off their initial disadvantages.

Nevertheless, although by 2007 the differences in marketization levels became trivial, there has been systematic variation in the radicalism of the reform paths that have led to this outcome. The comparison of annual increases of the transition index of the European Bank for Reconstruction and Development (EBRD), which we use as a proxy for the rate at which market reforms have been introduced and new institutions built, leads us to the conclusion that the Baltic states have been the most radical and Slovenia the least radical in

---

43. In this and many other respects we draw inspiration from Peter A. Gourevitch, *Politics in Hard Times: Comparative Responses to International Economic Crises* (Ithaca: Cornell University Press, 1986).

TABLE 1.1
Performance in opening and regulating markets, 1989–98 and 1999–2007

	Annual advance of reforms (%)[a]	Overall level of reforms (%)[b]	Level of 1st-phase reforms (%)[c]	Level of 2nd-phase reforms (%)[d]
1989–98 averages				
Baltic states	6.6 (1992–98)	54	70	44
Visegrád states	6.2	64	81	53
Slovenia	4.4	59	83	45
Croatia, Bulgaria, Romania	4.5	50	70	38
1999–2007 averages				
Baltic states	1.4	84	99	75
Visegrád states	0.8	87	100	79
Slovenia	0.3	79	98	67
Croatia, Bulgaria, Romania	1.5	78	96	67

Source: Authors' calculations based on EBRD, http://www.ebrd.com/pages/research/economics/data.
shtml (accessed August 11, 2009).
[a] Annual change of the average of 8 transition indexes.
[b] Average level of 8 transition indexes.
[c] Average level of domestic price liberalization, foreign trade and currency liberalization, and small-scale privatization.
[d] Average level of large-scale privatization, competition policy, reform of banking and nonbank financial institutions, and overall infrastructure reform.

adopting the market economy. The Visegrád countries occupy intermediate positions in this respect. Finally, Croatia, Bulgaria, and Romania were slow reformers in the first period but progressed fast during the second period.

Two facts have to be considered to make sense of this variation. Thanks to their long experimentation with market reforms under socialism, Hungary, Poland, and the successor states of former Yugoslavia had relatively liberalized economies already in 1989, and could capitalize on a legacy of market-oriented institutions and practices. The Baltic states, Czechoslovakia, Bulgaria, and Romania were, however, disadvantaged in this respect, as they started building markets largely from scratch. This meant that marketization was a race among contenders who had to cover varied distances between different starting points and the same finish line.

Furthermore, some participants in the race got the start signal later than others, and had to spurt to catch up. As Estonia, Latvia, and Lithuania completed their struggle for independence after August 1991, their comprehensive market reforms started at full speed two years later than was the case in other countries.[44] It was due to their rapid progress with reforms, substantiated

44. See, however, chapter 3, "Origins of the National and Nationalizing Projects," for pre-independence reforms especially in Estonia.

by their having the largest annual advances on the transition index, that by 1999–2007 the Baltic states caught up with the Visegrád group and overtook Slovenia in converging on Western markets' institutional standards.

Focusing narrowly on achieved levels of marketization, some influential accounts ignored the fact that the overall high figures of Hungary, Poland, and Slovenia were not merely due to the fast pace of transformation but rather reflected the cumulated impact of reforms many of which had been initiated before and brought to completion after the end of socialism.[45] This confusion had far-reaching consequences for policy advice. Over the 1990s, the radical paragon Baltic countries performed worse on indicators of growth, FDI, and social cohesion, than the less radical Visegrád states and Slovenia. However, lumping all these countries together under the labels of "fast" or "comprehensive" reformers, and contrasting their superior average performance with that of alleged laggards further south and east provided the dubious backing for the international financial institutions' (IFIs') claim that fast marketization was the key to latecomers' success in the world economy.[46]

As is well known, the process of building markets did not end with the "first phase" reforms of liberalization, deregulation, and small-scale privatization. States also had to design and put into operation the organizational and legal framework of large-scale privatization, firm governance and competition, and new regulation for the financial sector, telecommunications, transport, and utilities. The data in Table 1.1 indicate that notwithstanding regime-specific differences in their pace, building market-conform regulative institutions has been more difficult overall than opening markets via state withdrawal from the economy. Joan Nelson explained this by the fact that these "second phase" measures "require sweeping institutional and legal changes and involve the legislature, the courts, and multiple central and local government agencies.... Moreover, while many of the initial costs of stabilization are temporary and spread over much of the population, sectoral and institutional reforms usually impose permanent losses focused on specific interests. They, therefore, prompt tenacious resistance."[47]

One key area where the varied responses to the above administrative and political challenges can be fruitfully studied is that of market-conform monetary regulation, which has had a major influence on the stable functioning

45. *From Plan to Market: World Development Report 1996* (Washington, D.C.: World Bank, 1997); Stephen Fish, "The Determinants of Economic Reform in the Post-Communist World," *East European Politics and Societies* 12, no. 1 (1998): 31–78. According to our analysis, during 1989–98 only the Czech Republic's reforms progressed as fast as those of the Baltic states. Critics, however, argued that the indexes of large-scale privatization and firm governance far overestimate the radicalism of the Czech reforms.

46. *From Plan to Market*, 9–10.

47. Joan M. Nelson, "Overview: How Market Reforms and Democratic Consolidation Affect Each Other," in *Intricate Links: Democratization and Market Reforms in Latin America and Eastern Europe*, ed. Joan M. Nelson, Jacek Kochanowicz, Kálmán Mizsei, and Oscar Muñoz (New Brunswick: Transaction Publishers, 1994), 14.

of the whole economy. In this field perhaps the most important development has been the emergence, from the transformation of inherited financial systems, of a powerful new institution, the independent central bank with power to define macroeconomic stability as a policy priority, institutionalize it against rival preferences, and shape economic performance in line with its own agenda.

The East Central European countries appear to have been among the front-runners in instituting central bank independence, catching up with Western Europe in this respect already by the mid-1990s.[48] By the time of EU accession, East Central European central bank governors were appointed to their legally well-protected and generously remunerated positions for six years, a period that exceeded the terms granted to elected governments. Governors gained significant albeit varying influence over appointments of their deputies and monetary council members. Professional credentials became a condition for appointments to executive positions. Sizable and internationally well-connected research departments enabled the monetary authorities to become sources of trusted macroeconomic data, analyses, and forecasts. Increasingly, EU-compliant legislation limited and ultimately abolished central banks' role in financing fiscal deficits.

Notwithstanding these similarities, important regime-specific differences prevailed. First, the new monetary authorities differed in the extent to which they retained the traditional functions of a central bank. The currency board mechanism adopted in two of the Baltic states and Bulgaria during the 1990s prevented the central bank from influencing money supply through interest rate policies and from acting as lender of last resort. Instead, money supply has been determined by foreign currency reserves, and the central banks have typically refused to bail out troubled commercial banks and industrial firms. On the other hand, the central banks of the Visegrád states, Slovenia, and Croatia have retained the right to control interest rates and function as lenders of last resort.

Second, there have been differences in central banks' behavior across a variety of policy arenas, especially in their interactions with fiscal authorities, industrial relations regimes, and commercial banks. In particular, independent central banks have acted in tandem with ministries of finance to (re) produce macroeconomic stability through prudent monetary and fiscal policies in the Baltic states and Bulgaria, and also in Slovenia. In contrast, conflicts between monetary and fiscal authorities have repeatedly undermined efficient macroeconomic coordination in several Visegrád states.

Third, diversity in institutional interactions has reflected variations in the degree to which monetary authorities have been sheltered from partisan efforts to exploit or impair central bank power. Accordingly, the paths

---

48. Sylvia Maxfield, *Gatekeepers of Growth: The International Political Economy of Central Banking in Developing Countries* (Princeton: Princeton University Press, 1997).

leading to central bank independence have differed in terms of radicalism and political contestation. In the Baltic states and Bulgaria the divorce of the monetary authority from the political system, and its hegemony in mediating the relationships between the domestic and international economy and the state and society, have rarely been effectively challenged. Central bank independence and its political implications have been more controversial in Slovenia, where initially fierce debates prevailed. Eventually however, a favorable consensus was reached. In contrast, although country-specific differences have been significant, the advance toward central bank independence by most of the Visegrád states and by Romania has been gradual and partial, and has provoked recurrent party-political struggles and bureaucratic rivalry.

All the above configurations have shaped central bank capacity to affect economic performance. Finally, central bank power has also exhibited variation over time. Importantly, the relatively rapid establishment of independent monetary authorities and restoration of macroeconomic stability in 1989–98 contrasts with the reviving political contestation of central bank hegemony and the task of compliance with the Maastricht criteria during the 2000s.

Compensation for Transformation Costs

Opening and instituting markets led to massive social dislocation and threatened disruptive social and political conflict. One way of coping with the challenges was to compensate economic actors and citizens for the costs of transformation, and so elicit their support or at least secure their acquiescence in the face of uncertainty and economic hardship. We define compensation in terms of the policies and political gestures by which states attempt to overcome opposition to capitalist transformation, and to bring and keep together coalitions of interests to make the changes politically feasible and the new order viable.[49] Before characterizing the varied measures adopted, some issues need to be clarified in advance.

First, for our purposes, compensation is a common denominator for widely varying types of state intervention ranging from sheltering inherited domestic and new transnational industries by tariffs, subsidies, and special regulations to social welfare policies, whether they protect the middle class or the most vulnerable poor.[50] Although political discourse tends to contrast industry subsidies with social welfare expenditures on the realistic basis that

---

49. This definition and the following discussion draw on Greskovits, *The Political Economy,* esp. 137–41.

50. Our interpretation resonates with Polanyi's ideas. "A book so stimulating and so deep-probing is bound to excite controversy and to be questioned at various points. ...Some may wish that the different forms of 'protection' against the self-regulating market were given different valuations and they may be a little uneasy that the tariff promoter and social legislator seem to appear as brothers in arms" (Robert M. MacIver's foreword to *The Great Transformation,* xi).

in any given moment spending on one purpose may directly limit spending on the other, the contradiction between these two kinds of compensatory measures might not be wholly antagonistic.

At the macro level, state assistance that helps private actors to save existing jobs or create new ones may substitute for unemployment benefits or early retirement and disability pensions. Conversely, public spending on education and health care can partly be viewed as subsidies to firms that rely on skilled and healthy labor forces. In certain instances businesses' individual preferences can be compatible with such macrosocial solutions. However, the micro-logic of firms is likelier to contradict any macrologic requiring that conflicting social groups take responsibility for each other. Hence the high probability of collective action problems and the need for public intervention to solve them—even if states differ in their ability or willingness to forge commonly accepted solutions.

The second issue is that of winners and losers. As the transformation affected a multitude of social groups in profound, simultaneous, and contradictory ways, it confused actors' own perceptions of their situations, as well as the judgment of politicians who tried to identify prospective winners and losers, and target them by appropriate policies. Rivalry among various groups disadvantaged by the transformation also constrained governments' ability to target the neediest for relief measures.[51]

Indeed, competition for state resources was rarely limited to the losers. Rather, there was nothing to prevent certain groups of actual winners from competing with each other and especially with the losers for public resources. The winners' chances were substantial if they wielded sufficient political power. Accordingly, governments tended to use public resources to mitigate large domestic and transnational corporations' perceived costs and risks, the status anxiety of old and emerging new middle classes, and the concerns of certain elite and middle-class groups over the limits of upward mobility. Frequently those who were more handicapped but less able to derail market reforms or political stability, such as the poor, who were typically overrepresented in ethnic minorities, have had to content themselves with less generous public relief.

From the above it follows that compensation as a strategy for bridging economic efficiency and political legitimacy could easily fail. Incentives meant to reward and encourage the champions of transformation, compensatory payments to those who were disadvantaged but unable to obstruct reform, and the resources absorbed in rents and spoils to supporters would

---

51. Joan M. Nelson, "The Politics of Pro-Poor Adjustment," in *Fragile Coalitions: The Politics of Economic Adjustment,* ed. Joan M. Nelson (New Brunswick: Transaction Publishers, 1989), 95–114.

inevitably mix.[52] Certainly, policy strategists tried to maximize positive signals to efficient firms, to design and disburse compensatory payments with the maximum political payoff, and to minimize rents and spoils. But, in line with our Polanyian framework, their success was far from guaranteed.

Last but not least, compensation does not constitute the entire repertoire of political measures available for overcoming opposition to reforms and targeting those who perceive a loss. In East Central Europe reformist governments frequently aimed at least in part at destroying the economic and political bases of transformation's opponents. Certain privatization policies, purges of bureaucracy, restrictions on unions and political parties, and the selective granting of political freedoms are cases in point. This particular set of measures is to be distinguished from compensation on the basis that it implies deprivation—as opposed to distribution—of economic and political benefits. The main challenge of the latter kind of policies is not in their fiscal burden or the administrative or political difficulty of coordination. Rather, they could be costly in terms of impaired democratic quality and social apathy.

Although the East Central European regimes all adopted various mixes of industrial and social policies, their approach to compensation exhibited marked differences. To capture the diversity of industrial policies, we introduce five proxies: average applied tariff rates, the amount of subsidies provided to firms and households, domestic credit to the private sector, investment incentives offered primarily to TNCs in manufacturing industries, and the scope and quality of services provided to foreign investors by investment promotion agencies (table 1.2).

In 1989–98, contributing to the shock of systemic breakdown, marketization exposed the inherited socialist industries to immense adaptation pressures. Left on their own, they would hardly have coped with such grave challenges. Accordingly, during the decade of crisis ad hoc and temporary damage control measures dominated the industrial policy agenda of East Central European economies. Many but not all postsocialist administrations tried to ease adjustment through varied combinations of some gradualism in phasing out subsidies, partly maintained protective tariffs, and new credits for survival and/or restructuring. While the original focus of industrial policies had been domestic firms, some states had simultaneously laid the groundwork for incentive packages, export-processing zones, and promotion agencies to attract foreign investors. Initially it was only in Hungary and to a lesser extent Poland and Romania that TNCs were targeted by generous compensation for the costs of pioneering investment in high-risk transitory settings.

The banking sectors' foreign penetration, which accelerated during the period, led to two relevant consequences. On the one hand, "foreign

52. John Waterbury, "The Political Management of Economic Adjustment and Reform," in Nelson, *Fragile Coalitions*, 41. See also Katzenstein, *Small States*, 29.

TABLE 1.2
Levels of compensation for economic transformation costs, 1989–98 and 1999–2007

	Average applied tariff rates (%)[a]	Budgetary subsidies and current transfers (% of GDP)	Domestic credit to private sector (% of GDP)	Investment incentives score[b]	Investment promotion agencies score[b]
1989–98 averages					
Baltic states	2.5	1.2	13.9	2.2	1.9
Visegrád states	8.1	4.5	28.7	2.5	2.6
Slovenia	10.6	2.7	26.4	2.7	1.6
Croatia, Bulgaria, Romania	15.7	7.9	18.8	2.3	1.5
1999–2007 averages					
Baltic states	1.7	2.1	33.5	2.7	2.3
Visegrád states	3.6	3.4	35.1	4.1	3.0
Slovenia	5.0	3.4	45.7	2.8	2.7
Croatia, Bulgaria, Romania	7.7	10.9	30.3	2.8	1.7

Sources: Authors' calculations based on the following. *Tariffs:* UNCTAD TRAINS database and WTO IDB data. *Budget, transfers, domestic credit:* EBRD, http://www.ebrd.com/pages/research/economics/data.shtml (accessed June 9, 2009). *Investment incentives, promotion agencies:* Fergus Cass, "Attracting FDI to Transition Countries: The Role and Impact of Incentives and Promotion Agencies," M.A. thesis draft (London: University College London, School of Slavonic and Eastern European Studies, January 2006), appendixes 2a, 2b, 3, 48–50.

[a] Nonweighted percentages.

[b] Average investment incentives scores, data are for 1994–98 and 1999–2005. Minimum value 1, maximum value 4.33, as with the EBRD transition indexes

ownership translated into better bank management and profitability."[53] On the other hand, the overwhelming dominance of large foreign banks in the financial sector led to a bias toward lending to large foreign firms.[54] Understandably, the foreign banks preferred financing established clients to the riskier business of lending to small or medium-sized enterprises. Especially since financial services tailored to small firms' needs evolved very slowly, the small and medium-scale domestic private sector suffered from scarcity of needed finance during the 1990s. Arguably, it was not targeted industrial policies that practically saved the petite bourgeoisie from region-wide extinction, but rather the postsocialist states' incapacity and/or unwillingness to collect taxes and social security contributions, or enforce labor market regulation in the "gray" or "shadow" economy.

In 1999–2007, foreign commercial banks increased the amount of credits offered to private actors, this time including smaller firms as well. At the same time, converging on the EU's standards, the Visegrád states and Slovenia halved tariff rates and subsidies. Most importantly, however, although differences in timing, form, and content were significant, by the early 2000s all the Visegrád states converged on more conscious industrial policy efforts, and designed packages of generous incentives and services to accelerate foreign capital infusion and help the birth and growth of infant transnational industries.[55] Croatia, Bulgaria, and Romania followed suit with some delay and less coherence in shifting from domestically oriented to foreign-focused industrial policies.

The Baltic approach to compensation via industrial policies diverged from that of other countries in both periods. Estonia, Latvia, and Lithuania virtually eliminated tariffs and subsidies already in 1992–98, and were reluctant to shelter enterprises from the impact of collapsing former Soviet markets and supplier networks. Moreover, due to central banks' strict monetary policy under the currency board arrangement, firms faced a credit crunch over the decade of crisis.

Industrial policy vis-à-vis TNCs was similarly minimalist. They were offered overall limited incentives with a focus on low tax rates. Investment promotion agencies were established only after some delay, and their scope of activity and budgets remained relatively modest.[56] Baltic industrial policies did not change significantly in 1999–2007, except that commercial bank credits

---

53. Piroska Mohácsi Nagy, "Financial Market Governance: Evolution and Convergence," in *Enlarging the Euro Area: External Empowerment and Domestic Transformation in East Central Europe,* ed. Kenneth Dyson (Oxford: Oxford University Press, 2006), 245.

54. Slovenia, where the banking sector mostly remained in domestic ownership until the late 2000s, is an exception.

55. Jan Drahokoupil, *Globalization and the State in Central and Eastern Europe: The Politics of Foreign Direct Investment* (London: Routledge, 2009).

56. Fergus Cass, "Attracting FDI to Transition Countries: The Use of Incentives and Promotion Agencies," *Transnational Corporations* 16, no. 2 (August 2007): 77–122.

were much easier to obtain and incentives and services granted to foreign firms started to be more generous. Even so, in terms of attractive incentive packages the Baltic subregion continued to lag behind the Visegrád area.

State aid to threatened domestic firms and industries and later to the transnational agents of reindustrialization has been complemented by public welfare assistance to vulnerable social groups across East Central Europe. In János Kornai's footsteps, who termed the relatively generous Hungarian welfare state "premature," Stephan Haggard and Robert Kaufman found that the internal structure of East Central European welfare expenditures was no less characteristic than their magnitude. Not only had these countries spent much more on social protection than the newly industrializing countries (NICs) of Latin America or Asia, but they far surpassed the latter in terms of pension, family, and housing benefits.[57] Let us add that in the 2000s the postsocialist public sectors still offered about twice as many jobs as those of the NICs. In this respect, the East Central European employment structure approximated that of the Western European small states.

Notwithstanding their similarities, East Central European social policies combined in a patterned way into distinct worlds of welfare capitalism. To highlight the differences, we characterize the postsocialist welfare states by total and per capita expenditures on social protection, GDP shares spent on pensions and education, and, using a broader definition, data on public sector employment (table 1.3).

During the decade of crisis, the Baltic states, Bulgaria, and Romania were set apart from the Visegrád countries and Slovenia by overall significantly smaller shares of GDP devoted to social compensation purposes. On average, the sum of social benefits provided to a Baltic individual amounted to a half of the typical amount a Visegrád country citizen could expect and a third of what a Slovene citizen could count on. The meager relief offered in the Baltic states is especially striking in light of the fact that these economies had been the hardest hit by the transformational recession.

The decade of recovery has not altered this cross-regional pattern significantly. Indeed, in 1999–2007 the discrepancy in social spending shares of GDP increased still more, while the gap in per capita benefits remained roughly the same. This is the more surprising in that by the second half of the 2000s the Baltic states' average per capita GDP approximated that of the Visegrád countries. In 2006 Estonia was second only to the Czech Republic in per capita GDP at purchasing parity standards, and both Latvia and Lithuania were richer than Poland. All in all, then, the Baltic subregion has hardly been the place to live for anybody whose meager living standards depended on state assistance—whether in hard times or good times. In particular, it has not been the right place to be a pensioner.

57. Stephan Haggard and Robert R. Kaufman, *Development, Democracy, and Welfare States: Latin America, East Asia, and Eastern Europe* (Princeton: Princeton University Press, 2009).

TABLE 1.3
Levels of compensation for social transformation costs, 1989–95 and 1999–2006

	Total expenditure on social protection (% of GDP)[a]	Social benefits per head of population (EUR, PPS)	Expenditure on pensions (% of GDP)	Expenditure on education (% of GDP)	Public sector employment (% of 15+-year-old population)
1989–95 averages (for public sector employment 1998 or closest available year)					
Baltic states	15.5	875	6.9	5.9	17.3
Visegrád states	21.1	1,752	9.6	5.1	14.9
Slovenia	24.6	2,929	12.8	4.5	15.1
Bulgaria, Romania	15.5	n.a.	7.9	4.1	14.0
1999–2006 averages (for public sector employment 2006 or closest available year)					
Baltic states	13.7	1,331	7.1	5.5	15.2
Visegrád states	19.7	2,371	9.6	4.7	11.7
Slovenia	23.8	4,021	10.8	6.0	13.7
Bulgaria, Romania	14.6	1,075	7.2	3.8	10.4

Sources: Authors' calculations based on the following. *Social protection*: 1989–95, *Children at Risk in Central and Eastern Europe: Perils and Promises*, Economies in Transitions Studies Regional Monitoring Report 4 (Florence: UNICEF, 1997), 135; 1999–2006, EUROSTAT, http://epp.eurostat.ec.europa.eu (accessed November 18, 2008). *Social benefits*: EUROSTAT. *Pensions, education*: 1989–95, *Children at Risk*, 136–37; 1999–2006, EUROSTAT. *Public sector*: LABORSTA, http://laborsta.ilo.org/cgi-bin/brokerv8.exe (accessed May 22, 2008).
[a] The two data sets might not be fully comparable, but since time series covering the whole period are unavailable, we use them for illustrative purposes.

In terms of the target groups of social compensation three features have distinguished the Baltic countries from the Visegrád states. The former tended to devote lower shares of their GDP to pensions and equal or occasionally higher shares to education, while maintaining higher public sector employment compared with the latter. Thus, the Baltic pattern seems to favor educated young private sector–based and state-dependent middle classes versus the elderly and the unemployed.

In turn, the Visegrád welfare states tend to be biased in favor of the temporarily, partly, or wholly "nonproductive" groups of society who had nevertheless earned a respected social status through work or otherwise— including the army of "under-age" pensioners in early retirement (especially in Hungary and Poland,) and young mothers with children (in Hungary).[58] Slovenia was East Central Europe's top spender on pensions and education alike, and was in between the Baltic and Visegrád countries as far as the share of public sector employment is concerned. Bulgaria and Romania lagged behind other countries in all of these aspects.[59]

In sum, over the periods of crisis and recovery, the Baltic states have been the least and Slovenia the most willing to compensate for the transformation costs of economic actors and members of society. The Visegrád countries fell in between these extremes, and also differed among themselves in terms of prioritizing compensation through industrial or social policies. The first preference is exemplified by the Czech Republic and the second by Poland. Finally, Bulgaria and Romania tried to compensate economic actors more, while in terms of the GDP share and generosity of welfare state benefits they lagged behind the Visegrád group.

Let us finally note that the Baltic and Visegrád worlds of welfare also differ in how they mitigate the risk of impoverishment across various groups defined by age and ethnic origin. (See more details on these aspects in chapters 3 and 4.)

Democracy, Social Partnership, and State Capacity

Threats of protest, political destabilization, and social disintegration, resistance to public regulation of private activity, and immense coordination tasks across policy areas have marked the politics of postsocialist regime formation. How could the new governments maneuver among the implied risks and opportunities? More specifically, in what ways have democratic

58. See for an insightful analysis of these countries' "abnormal pensioner booms," Pieter Vanhuysse, *Divide and Pacify: Strategic Social Policies and Political Protests in Post-Communist Democracies* (Budapest: Central European University Press, 2006).

59. Comparable evidence on Croatia is scarce. The data that exist give the impression that over 1999–2007 Croatia fell closest to the Visegrád states in terms of generous welfare spending and large public sector employment. For an explanation see chapter 5, "Neocorporatist Balancing versus Crisis-Driven Path Corrections."

and neocorporatist institutions constrained and/or enabled the reformist authorities of various regimes?

A brief comparative reference to forms of government in other known success stories of economic transformation and development helps understand the relevance of democracy for diverse pathways to capitalism. The Asian and Latin American NICs are cases in point. Some of these states are still authoritarian or at best partially free, and those that democratized did so after and not before their economic transformation brought fruits. Has authoritarianism helped them to put in place the institutional vehicles of smooth international integration and fast economic growth? This is a complicated question to which contradictory answers have been proposed.[60]

Nevertheless, since most countries of East Central Europe achieved political freedom immediately after the breakdown of socialism, their leaders have had to content themselves with the possible advantages of democratic government from the viewpoint of successful transformation and development. One of these advantages is pointed out by Dani Rodrik, who views "participatory political institutions as meta-institutions that elicit and aggregate local knowledge and thereby help build better institutions."[61]

In this perspective democracy facilitates choice and thus leads to a greater diversity of institutions than other systems in which political decisions are the privilege of a few. Moreover, since democracy favors dialogue between state and society, it is ideally suited to the purposes of fine-tuning institutions through experiments and feedback as well as correcting mistaken decisions or altering unpromising paths. Needless to stress, these properties also hinge upon the forms in which and the degree to which society is represented and/or actually participates in key political decisions and policy choices. Overall, the institutional output of less participatory and representative democracies should be inferior, since such systems' capacity to elicit and aggregate society-wide local knowledge is relatively limited.

Katzenstein suggested a different possibility for linking institutional outcomes with participatory political institutions. Assuming that "fiscal effectiveness can be interpreted as an indirect, economic-outcome measure of the coordination of diverging political objectives across different policy sectors," he suggested that participatory institutions are likely to coordinate better.[62] He supported this claim with evidence on the Western European small states, in which democratic corporatism delivered the balancing acts required for the implementation of complex policy agendas.

---

60. For a summary see Stephan Haggard, "Institutions and Growth in East Asia," *Studies in Comparative International Development* 38, no. 4 (Winter 2004): esp. 57–64.

61. Dani Rodrik, "Institutions for High-Quality Growth: What They Are and How To Acquire Them?" *Studies in Comparative International Development* 35, no. 3 (Summer 2000): 14.

62. Katzenstein, *Small States*, 93.

In what way could participatory political institutions have affected state capacities to experiment with, fine-tune, modify, and effectively coordinate policies—and so avoid risking capitalism's viability in East Central Europe? Our suggestions (examined in detail in chapters 3 to 6) are based on proxies of democratic quality such as measures of the new systems' popular acceptance (see table 1.4), institutional-procedural features, propensities to elicit participation whether by political or neocorporatist forms of inclusion, and finally indicators of quality of governance. All these measures show large variation across cases and over time.

First, citizens' approval of the democratic form of government is compared with their approval of communist authoritarianism in retrospect. Neither of these political systems is entirely rejected, but East Central Europeans generally prefer democratic to communist one-party government. However, while in 1989–98 democracy's net approval was only marginal in the Baltic states, citizens in other countries valued democracy significantly more than communism. In the more consolidated countries, by and large, net approval of democracy co-varied with the amount and quality of political rights and civil liberties granted to the citizenry. Accordingly, the Baltic states initially lagged behind the Visegrád countries and Slovenia in terms of democratic quality— witness the difference in the Freedom House indexes.[63] More surprisingly, net approval of democracy was the highest in the Southeastern European states, which had had the lowest Freedom House scores in the 1990s.

We measure the actual extent of democratic political participation by two indicators. When opting for these particular measures we concur with the authors of a recent large-N study of democratic quality who contend that: "It is not enough that citizens have a right to participate. To make democracy meaningful and different from other governance systems, citizens must actively exercise that right."[64] From our viewpoint, their most interesting finding is that "participation is a key component of democracy not only because it makes democracy more complete at present, but also because it makes it more likely to endure and even progress in future."[65]

Measured by turnout in national parliamentary elections, the Baltic democracies stand out as the least and the Slovenian system as the most participatory, while the Visegrád states and a few Southeastern European democracies fall in between these polar extremes. The second indicator of actual participation, electoral volatility, was very high in the Baltic states in

63. The same variation is confirmed by Polity IV, *Political Regime Characteristics and Transitions, 1800–2010,* http://www.systemicpeace.org/inscr/inscr.htm (accessed September15, 2009).

64. Bruce E. Moon, Jennifer H. Birdsall, Sylvia Ciesluk, Lauren M. Garlett, Joshua J. Hermias, Elizabeth Mendenhall, Patrick D. Schmid, and Wai H. Wong, "Voting Counts: Participation in the Measurement of Democracy," *Studies in Comparative International Development* 41, no. 2 (Summer 2006): 6.

65. Ibid., 18.

TABLE 1.4
Indicators of democratic government, 1989–98 and 1999–2007

	Net approval of democracy (%)[a]	Freedom House scores	Turnout at national parliamentary elections (%)[b]	Electoral volatility[c]	Voice and accountability score[d]
1989–98 averages (for voice and accountability 1996–98)					
Baltic states	2	2.4	59	77	0.71
Visegrád states	17	2.0	72	42	0.86
Slovenia	19	1.8	80	28	0.91
Croatia, Bulgaria, Romania	21	3.2	76	39	−0.03
1999–2007 averages (for voice and accountability 2000–2005)					
Baltic states	4	1.4	51	54	.95
Visegrád states	10	1.3	62	29	1.03
Slovenia	5	1.2	67	34	1.06
Croatia, Bulgaria, Romania	−7	1.9	63	46	0.46

Sources: Authors' calculations based on the following. Net approval: Richard Rose, "Diverging Paths of Post-Communist Countries: New Europe Barometer Trends Since 1991," Studies in Public Policy 418, (Aberdeen: Centre for the Study of Public Policy, 2006), 22–23. Freedom House scores: Freedom House, Freedom in the World 2007, www. freedomhouse.org, (accessed December 7, 2008). Turnout: IDEA Database, at http://www.idea.int/vt/country_cfm (accessed December 18, 2008). For missing years, voting age populations are estimated from LABORSTA data, http://laborsta.ilo.org/cgi-bin/brokerv8.exe (accessed May 22, 2008). Volatility: Conor O'Dwyer and Branislav Kovalcik, "And the Last Shall be First: Party System Institutionalization and Second-Generation Economic Reform in Postcommunist Europe," Studies in Comparative International Development 41, no. 4 (2007): 3–26. Election results are from Sten Berglund, Joakim Ekman, and Frank H. Aarebrot, eds., The Handbook of Political Change in Eastern Europe (Cheltenham, UK: Edward Elgar, 2004), and Wikipedia. Voice and accountability: Kaufmann, Kraay, and Mastruzzi, "Governance Matters VIII."

[a] Data are for net endorsement of "current system governing with free elections and many parties" versus "the former Communist regime," averages for 1991–98 and 2001–4.

[b] Percentage is of voting age population.

[c] Following our source, we calculate volatility as follows. V = 0.5sum (vpt–vpt₋₁), where vp_t = vote share of party in election t, and vp_{t-1} = its vote share in the previous election. Splits and mergers count as new parties.

[d] Index values range from –2.5 (minimum) to 2.5 (maximum) of voice and accountability.

1989–98, whereas voters overall were somewhat more loyal to their preferred parties in the majority of Visegrád states and Slovenia.

By the second period, net approval of democracy was on the decline in most countries of the region, although in the Baltic states there was a marginal increase in democracy's reputation. This development is the more surprising in that it occurred despite overall improving Freedom House scores. Less surprising, waning net approval of democracy coincided with a large drop in electoral participation. Notwithstanding the procedural-institutional convergence on Western standards during the decade of recovery and growth, a growing army of East Central European citizens opted for vacating the newly erected democratic edifices.

The regime-specific differences that evolved in 1989–98 seem to have been reproduced in the economic golden age between the late 1990s and the mid-2000s, since the figures of democracy's net approval, procedural-institutional quality, and participation in formal politics were lower, while those of electoral volatility were higher, in the Baltic states than in the Visegrád countries and Slovenia. These measures signal a rising democratic deficit that seems to be the largest in the Baltic states followed by the Southeastern European and Visegrád countries. Slovenia's democracy continues to perform best.

Against this background it is puzzling that voice and accountability, considered by the World Bank's analysts to be one of the six composite indicators of their quality of governance index, have been by and large stable in East Central Europe throughout the whole period of 1996–2007.[66] In light of the region-wide declining trends of formal political participation and democracy's net approval, it is far from clear whose voice is being heard, or to whom exactly the postsocialist governments are accountable in the new millennium.

Accountability to organized workers, for instance, is unlikely to be the right answer, as participatory labor relations have gone through a similar brief cycle of rise and decline to that of participatory democracy. Consistent with other scholars' observations, our evidence indicates that the short career of organized workers' collective action peaked amidst the decade of crisis but was largely over by its end. We consider levels and trends of trade union density, workers' collective protest, coverage rate of collective bargaining agreements, and coordination of wage bargaining, as indicators of the collective action capacities critical for institutionalized and participatory social partnership arrangements. These indicators show an almost uniform region-wide trend as well as intraregional variation (table 1.5).

In 1989–98 East Central Europe's industrial relations systems still appeared to be relatively labor-inclusive, at least in formal institutional terms.

---

66. David Kaufmann, Aart Kraay, and Massimo Mastruzzi, "Governance Matters VIII: Aggregate and Individual Governance Indicators 1996–2008," Policy Research Working Paper 4978 (Washington, D.C.: World Bank, June 2009).

TABLE 1.5
Trends in social partnership institutions, 1989–98 and 1999–2007

	Union density rate (%)	Industrial union density rate (%)	Workers involved in strikes[a]	Collective bargaining coverage rate (%)	Coordination of wage bargaining[b]
1989–98 averages					
Baltic states	35	n.a.	0.0	26	1.0
Visegrád states	55	n.a.	3.8	55	2.4
Slovenia	56	n.a.	n.a.	100	3.1
Bulgaria, Romania	47	n.a.	2.9 (Romania)	n.a.	3.7
1999–2007 averages					
Baltic states	17	5	0.6	18	1.0
Visegrád states	23	19	1.2	40	2.2
Slovenia	41	52	n.a.	100	4.0
Bulgaria, Romania	29	n.a.	2.1 (Romania)	25	2.7

Sources: Authors' calculations based on the following. *Union density, industrial union density, collective bargaining coverage rate, coordination of wage bargaining*: Jelle Visser, Institutional Characteristics of Trade Unions, Wage Setting, State Intervention, and Social Pacts (ICTWSS), an international database, (Amsterdam: Institute for Advanced Labour Studies, AIAS 2008), http://www.uva-aias.net. (accessed November 9, 2009). *Strikes*: LABORSTA, http://laborsta.ilo.org/cgi-bin/brokerv8.exe (accessed May 22, 2008).

[a] Workers involved in strikes per year standardized for 1000s of working-age (15+) population.

[b] Coordination of wage bargaining index: minimum value "1" indicates fragmented company level coordination and maximum value "5" indicates economy-wide bargaining.

After the breakdown of socialism workers' rights to organize and strike were legally guaranteed. Inherited communist unions were dissolved or reformed, new unions were founded and allowed to have a measure of influence over the course of restructuring and privatization as well as issues of employment, wages, and work conditions. In a number of countries organized labor got institutionalized representation in the boards of newly established health care and pension funds. National-level tripartite councils were set up all over the region.

These were the grounds for Iankova to characterize the interplay of actors, institutions, and policies that drove the process of systemic change toward peaceful and sometimes efficient ends as transformative corporatism.[67] Although more skeptical about the actual role of corporatism, Ost confirmed that "if mimicry is the greatest form of flattery, East European countries would seem to be quite enamored of West European–style corporatism. In the years after 1989, all postcommunist countries in Eastern Europe invested heavily in tripartism."[68]

Subsequent trends, however, signaled the rapid decline of social partnership arrangements and indicated that transformative corporatism was a temporary and exceptional rather than a permanent and general feature of the region. By 1999–2007, trade union density rates had dropped drastically in most countries. Although the public sector stayed relatively organized, the emerging private sector became almost union-free. Accordingly, in the manufacturing industries exposed to global competition, strike activity has come to a halt. Overall, the postsocialist countries have diverged from Western Europe's small corporatist states, as they ended up having decentralized and less coordinated patterns of wage bargaining and collective agreements with typically much lower coverage.

Within this general trend, Baltic labor seems to have suffered the most devastating defeat as evidenced by its region-wide lowest level of organization and weak capacity for collective action. Labor's organizational power and militancy deteriorated dramatically in most of the Visegrád countries too. In contrast, in Slovenia labor power has been firmly established and institutionalized. This pattern is further confirmed by the variation in coverage rates of collective bargaining as well as its centralization.

To summarize, in respect of the constraints and opportunities provided to transformative states by participatory political institutions, the latecomer small countries of East Central Europe bore the strongest resemblance to their democratic corporatist Western European counterparts at a time when the economic institutions of these two country groups were still very different. Conversely, the postsocialist economies' institutional convergence on Western European standards coincided with the opening of a gaping chasm

---

67. Iankova, *Eastern European Capitalism.*
68. Ost, "Illusory Corporatism," 503–4.

TABLE 1.6
Levels of state capacity, 1996–98 and 2000–2008

	Government effectiveness	Regulatory quality	Rule of law	Control of corruption
1996–98 averages				
Baltic states	0.28	0.97	0.49	−0.08
Visegrád states	0.75	0.71	0.76	0.54
Slovenia	0.82	0.95	0.97	1.06
Croatia, Bulgaria, Romania	−0.28	0.04	−0.22	−0.43
2000–2008 averages				
Baltic states	0.77	1.09	0.69	0.46
Visegrád states	0.78	0.98	0.71	0.46
Slovenia	0.96	0.81	0.91	0.95
Croatia, Bulgaria, Romania	0.12	0.36	−0.12	−0.04

Source: Authors' calculations based on Kaufmann, Kraay, and Mastruzzi, "Governance Matters VIII."
Note: Index values for each of the four indexes range from -2.5 (minimum) to 2.5 (maximum) of voice and accountability.

regarding the functioning and quality of negotiated management-labor relationships, tripartism, and participatory democracy.

To be sure, the symptoms of "hollowing of democracy" and weakening corporatist structures have lately been observed in older EU member nations, including also the democratic corporatist small states.[69] Nevertheless, these symptoms' strength and simultaneous occurrence signal that both processes have developed faster and advanced further in East Central Europe. Accordingly, over time the governance of postsocialist regimes has been less and less backed and/or constrained by the original broad array of organized social interests and democratic electorates.

Let us finally consider the best available direct proxies of states' administrative capacity and quality of governance, which combine the indexes of government effectiveness, regulatory quality, rule of law, and control of corruption (table 1.6).

For the 1990s, these measures show similar variation to that of the above indirect indicators of the capacities of the political system. The Slovenian state appears to have been the most capable followed by the Visegrád and Baltic states, in that order. The other Southeastern European states did not seem to have much capacity in this period. During the 2000s, while these regimes' overall ranking did not change, the differences became smaller.

69. Peter Mair, "Ruling the Void? The Hollowing of Western Democracy," *New Left Review* 42 (November–December, 2006): 25–51; Colin Crouch, "The Euro and Labour Market and Wage Policies," in *European States and the Euro*, ed. Kenneth Dyson (Oxford: Oxford University Press, 2002), 276–304.

Indeed, on average the Baltic states outperformed the Visegrád states (although not Slovenia), while the Southeastern European states acquired modest capacities.

Since the first decade of the 2000s was also the period of preparation for and completion of EU accession, which implied massive state (re)building (see chapter 2, "Returning to the West"), it is interesting to note that while the capacities and quality of governance radically improved in the Southeastern European and Baltic countries, they all but stagnated in the Visegrád area and, most surprisingly, declined somewhat in Slovenia. EU accession, then, appears to have enhanced stateness in neoliberal but less so in embedded neoliberal or neocorporatist regimes. No less interesting is the fact that while both the procedural-institutional quality and accountability of the political system have apparently improved in the course of EU enlargement, the downward trends of participatory political and industrial democracy are in contrast with the former developments. (We will return to this issue in chapter 6.) Let us now complete the characterization of the three regimes by providing evidence on some key performance areas in which neoliberalism, embedded neoliberalism, and neocorporatism have fared differently.

International Economic Integration: Semicore and Semiperipheral Profiles

We introduce five indicators to establish the postsocialist market societies' more or less promising paths of international economic integration: output and employment of complex industries as a share of total manufacturing data, exports of complex goods relative to total goods exports, FDI stock accumulating in complex industries as a percentage of total FDI stock, and unit labor cost in complex industries relative to Austrian labor cost. Complex industries are distinguished by their intensity of physical and human capital, that is, complex equipment and technology, productive infrastructure, intensive research and development (R&D), and a skilled labor force. In light of statistical evidence, starting from largely similar situations the East Central European capitalisms became characterized by varied performances on all these dimensions.

In the early 1990s, complex industries turned out about a quarter of manufacturing output and provided a third of all manufacturing jobs all over East Central Europe. Although the Visegrád countries and Slovenia inherited somewhat larger manufacturing sectors, the initial differences between the former and the Baltic states, Bulgaria, Romania, and Croatia were trivial. It was only during the decade of crisis that these two groups' paths started to diverge radically. In 1989–98, industrial restructuring in the Baltic and two of the Southeastern European states occurred through deskilling. They all suffered substantial losses of complex-manufacturing output, employment, and exports. In contrast, both the Visegrád and the Slovenian economies

TABLE 1.7
Semicore and semiperipheral profiles of international economic integration, 1989–98 and 1999–2007

	Complex-manufacturing output[a,b]	Complex-manufacturing employment[a,b]	Complex-manufacturing exports[b,c]	FDI stock in complex manufacturing[d]	Complex-manufacturing unit labor cost[e]
1989–98 averages					
Baltic states	18 (−8)	26 (−6)	27 (−1)	7 (51)	48
Visegrád states	31 (−1)	35 (−3)	37 (−5)	17 (231)	25
Slovenia	37 (−3)	31 (0)	42 (−4)	24 (351)	53
Croatia, Bulgaria, Romania	27 (−1)	30 (−2)	29 (−3)	n.a.	38
1999–2007 averages					
Baltic states	16 (−3)	17 (0)	28 (−5)	4 (222)	56
Visegrád states	44 (−9)	35 (−2)	54 (−8)	17 (1,045)	33
Slovenia	44 (−7)	33 (−2)	50 (−6)	25 (880)	66
Croatia, Bulgaria, Romania	25 (−1)	26 (0)	29 (−4)	13 (541)	50

Sources: Authors' calculations, based on the following. *Output, employment: wiiw* Industrial Database Eastern Europe (Vienna: The Vienna Institute for International Economic Studies, 2008). *Exports:* United Nations TRADECOM DATABASE, various years, http://comtrade.un.org/db/. *FDI stock, unit labor cost: wiiw* Foreign Direct Investment Database Central and Eastern Europe (Vienna: The Vienna Institute for International Economic Studies, 2008).

[a] Percent of manufacturing total value at 2002 prices. Includes chemicals, machinery, electrical and optical, and transport equipment (NACE codes DG, DK, DL, DM, respectively).

[b] Data in parentheses: 1989–98, difference between the averages and the earliest year for which data are available in %; 1999–2007, difference between the averages and the latest year for which data are available in %.

[c] Percent of total value of goods exports in current prices. Complex export products are chemicals and machinery and equipment (SITC 1 digit codes 5 and 7, respectively).

[d] Percent of total inward FDI stock. Data in parentheses are volumes per capita of working age (15+) populations, in euros.

[e] Percent of Austria's complex-manufacturing unit labor cost.

weathered the hard times with more moderate contraction of their complex industrial establishment.

The variation is in large part due to the operation of TNCs, without which, especially for latecomers, capturing complex-manufacturing production segments and market niches is no longer possible. Table 1.7 shows that in 1989–98 the infusion of FDI in the complex industries of the Visegrád countries and Slovenia exceeded in per capita terms the Baltic figure by a factor of 5. It is unsurprising, then, that the Visegrád states' unit labor costs were half of those of the Baltic group notwithstanding the latter countries' much lower wages.

The processes of divergence were reinforced during the fast growth period. In 1999–2007 the share of complex-manufacturing industries in the Visegrád and Slovenian economies was double that of the Baltic and Southeastern European countries—whether output, employment, or exports are considered. Earlier differences in complex industry FDI stock and unit labor cost proved to be persistent too. Data on employment in knowledge-intensive services indicates similar variation. In the early 2000s, merely 2.3 percent of total service employment occurred in the knowledge-intensive services in the Baltic states, in contrast to 6.5 and 7.9 percent in the Visegrád states and Slovenia. In this respect even Croatia, Bulgaria, and Romania performed better than the Baltic states.[70]

The above facts allow propositions concerning the strengths, weaknesses, and further prospects of East Central Europe's paths of international economic integration. The Visegrád countries and Slovenia (and to a much lesser extent Croatia) have integrated into circuits of European and global systems of production and commerce in similar roles to those of the advanced industrial economies, including the small Western European states.

At the other end of the spectrum, Bulgaria and Romania have become locations of many export-oriented sweatshops producing textiles, clothing, and footwear for Western European markets. They combine this specialization with exports in low-tech and medium low-tech heavy industries, such as iron, steel, and nonferrous metals. Traditional light and heavy export industries, especially food, textiles, and wood and metal products are also important in the Baltic states.

All in all, the Visegrád and Slovene economies seem to have adopted features of a *semicore* profile of international economic integration. Despite the apparent similarities with the core countries' specializations, we find this mixed term, which paraphrases Immanuel Wallerstein's world systems terminology without necessarily sharing all of his assumptions and predictions, suitable for characterizing the developmental status of some of the East Central European countries for two reasons.[71]

---

70. EUROSTAT, http://epp.eurostat.ec.europa.eu (accessed November 18, 2008).

71. Immanuel Wallerstein, *The Capitalist World-Economy* (Cambridge: Cambridge University Press, 1979). For the original distinction and empirical substantiation of semicore and

First, while these economies have been relatively rich in experienced and skilled labor, and have even displayed a degree of local managerial and entrepreneurial talent, they have had to rely on the advanced economies in their needs for capital, technology, and global entrepreneurial skills, such as design, worldwide input sourcing, and marketing access and knowledge. Consequently, their newly achieved competitiveness in complex sectors has been inextricably linked to foreign input. Second, notwithstanding recent progress in technological upgrading, the actual productive roles of the complex-manufacturing industries of the Visegrád economies still exhibit overall lower levels of autonomy, sophistication, and skills than the activities concentrated in the Western segments of the same transnational industries.

In contrast, as indicated by the less robust appearance of complex-manufacturing industries and products, the Bulgarian, Romanian and Baltic economies fall short of semicore status and are more properly viewed as *semiperipheral*. Nevertheless, the Baltic economies are also distinguished by a shared characteristic. As the westernmost enclave of the former Soviet Union now within EU boundaries, these states still earn a good part of their living from services related to Russian transit trade in oil and other resources (and goods imported by Russia). Consequently, some features of entrepôt economies, such as openness, orientation toward services, dependence on large economic hinterlands, and vulnerability to economic and political external shocks might apply to their profiles.[72]

Last but not least, in terms of international economic integration, none of the East Central European states appear to us as fully *peripheral*. Such a characterization seems to be more adequate to the situation of the majority of former Soviet republics, as oil, gas, metals, cotton, or food constitute the bulk of their exports, while complex industrial products account for less than 10 percent. Russia's case does not strike us as an exception. Although some authors characterize Russia as semiperipheral, its resource-based specialization seems to rather confirm the patronizing tone of early Western narratives of the sudden collapse of the once fearful rival. The Soviet Union was not a modern industrial society. It was rather, as the *Times* of London noted, "a Third World country with First World weapons."[73]

All in all, then, the neoliberal program of adopting a market economy has so far helped the East Central European states to avoid a decline to peripheral status. Yet only neoliberalism's embedded variant seems to combine well with core-like manufacturing specializations. In light of the overwhelmingly optimistic expectations concerning the impact of radical market opening on

semiperipheral profiles see Béla Greskovits, "Leading Sectors and the Varieties of Capitalism in Eastern Europe." *Actes de Gerpisa* 39 (2005): 113–28.

72. Stephan Haggard, *Pathways from the Periphery: The Politics of Growth in the Newly Industrializing Countries* (Ithaca: Cornell University Press, 1990).

73. Jane J. Kirkpatrick, "Beyond the Cold War," *Foreign Affairs* 69, no. 1 (1990): 5.

FDI, industrial restructuring, and technological upgrading, this outcome is a surprise.

Social Cohesion, Material Loss, and Existential Stress

The data on income inequality, unemployment, and poverty do not paint an excessively gloomy picture of the magnitude of social stress accompanying the transformation. Although the risks of total and long-term unemployment and impoverishment have been high in East Central Europe (table 1.8), the old EU member states themselves did not escape these dangers during 1989–2007.[74]

This said, the true extent of social shock cannot be conceived without factoring in the dramatic speed at which life amidst high risk and uncertainty has become a state of normality for people in the region after long decades of full employment and low wage disparity under socialism despite losses of economic efficiency. Writing about the social limits to change in earlier contexts Polanyi insisted that an overly radical rate of progress was likely to turn "the process itself into a degenerative instead of a constructive event. For upon this rate, mainly, depended whether the dispossessed could adjust themselves to changed conditions without fatally damaging their substance, human and economic, physical and moral."[75]

But has postsocialist marketization really posed a serious threat to social cohesion? Neoliberals questioned this. Sachs cited facts of fast improving social situations: "The living standards of the population did not really drop, if one examines actual household consumption behavior (rather than changes in crude indexes of real wages, which do not give a picture of the shortages prevalent in the old regime)."[76] Similarly, Anders Aslund traced the "march of folly to bad policies" such as unwarranted welfare spending, to distorted official statistics, and to public sentiments aroused by faulty analysis and negative publicity. In this vein he claimed: "The alleged misery in postcommunist transformation is primarily the delayed revelation of the true costs of communism."[77]

Apparently, the neoliberals of the 1990s did not have much to add to their nineteenth-century predecessors' views, who had claimed that the Industrial Revolution had improved rather than undermined the material living standards of the population. However, Polanyi contended that the social calamity of the Industrial Revolution "is primarily a cultural not an

74. This observation is confirmed by other indicators of inequality, such as the income quintile ratio. EUROSTAT, http://epp.eurostat.ec.europa.eu (accessed November18, 2008).
75. Polanyi, *The Great Transformation*, 37.
76. Sachs, "Postcommunist Parties," 1.
77. Anders Aslund, "The Myth of Output Collapse after Communism," Working Paper 18 (Washington D.C.: Carnegie Endowment for International Peace, Post-Soviet Economies Project of the Russian and Eurasian Program, March 2001), 17–18.

TABLE 1.8
Levels of social cohesion, material loss, and existential stress, 1990s and early 2000s

	Gini coefficients of income	Total unemployment rate (%)[a]	Long-term unemployment rate (%)[b]	At-risk-of-poverty rate after social transfers (%)	Losses/gains of male life expectancy at birth[c]
1990–98 averages (2000 for at-risk-of-poverty rates)					
Baltic states	0.343	12.7	6.5	17.0	–2.3
Visegrád states	0.253	9.9	4.5	13.5	–0.8
Slovenia	0.253	7.9	3.4	11.0	–1.2
Croatia, Bulgaria, Romania	0.327	11.2	2.4 (Romania)	15.5	0.0
1999–2006 averages (2001–7 for at-risk-of-poverty rates)					
Baltic states	0.359	11.4	5.5	19.5	–0.1
Visegrád states	0.280	12.2	6.7	13.0	–3.6
Slovenia	0.243	6.3	3.4	12.0	–4.1
Croatia, Bulgaria, Romania	0.342	12.0	6.8	16.8	–1.9

Sources: Authors' calculations, based on the following. *Income, total unemployment, life expectancy:* Transmonee Database UNICEF Innocenti Research Centre, www.unicef-irc.org, various release dates. *Long-term unemployment, at-risk-of-poverty rate:* EUROSTAT, http://epp.eurostat.ec.europa.eu (accessed November 18, 2008).

[a] LFS, percent of labor force.

[b] Longer than 12 months, % of active population.

[c] Number of years relative to 1989.

economic phenomenon that can be measured by income figures and population statistics.... The economic process may, naturally, supply the vehicle of the destruction, and almost invariably economic inferiority will make the weaker yield, but the immediate cause of his undoing is not for that reason economic; it lies in the lethal injury to the institutions in which his social existence is embodied. The result is loss of self-respect and standards."[78]

Following Polanyi, we identify emerging capitalism's main threat to social cohesion not in terms of pure economic hardship, but above all in its damaging impact on felt security, self-respect, dignity, social usefulness, and perceived status across broad social strata. This interpretation opens the floor for a substantive understanding of compensation that focuses on its role in mitigating even more fundamental anxieties than the ones stemming from declining "objective" standards of material well-being. We are aware of the difficulty (and perhaps impossibility) of quantifying and measuring the impact of deep anxiety. Neither can we precisely assess the extent to which various compensatory policies can mitigate this impact. Yet we believe that data on spreading social anomie do at least indicate the magnitude of the existential rather than purely material shocks suffered by East Central Europeans after 1989.

The dramatic rise of infant mortality, addiction, and crime, and the unparalleled drop in total fertility are cases in point.[79] Faced with a rapid and deep decline in male life expectancy (which may be another indicator of a disintegrating social fabric) even some of the most self-confident neoliberal analysts admitted bewilderment.[80] There is no doubt that the data in table 1.8 indicate a characteristic, albeit not always purely regime-specific pattern in the regional distribution of social stress—whether manifested in material loss or existential anxiety.

In 1989–98 the Baltic neoliberal regimes (followed by some of the Southeastern European states on many but not all dimensions) performed consistently worst in terms of inequality, unemployment, long-term unemployment, risk of poverty, as well as male life expectancy. Slovenes have suffered the least severe social shock, while the embedded neoliberal Visegrád regimes fell in between the polar cases in every respect except inequality, which in Poland grew close to Baltic levels.

Although by the golden age male life expectancy had improved overall, the intraregional pattern of the early transformation years persisted during the decade of growth as well. Male life expectancy failed to recover before the early 2000s in Estonia, Latvia, and Bulgaria, while in 2006 it was still below

78. Polanyi, *The Great Transformation*, 157.
79. We are indebted to Éva Fodor for drawing our attention on the region-wide free fall of total fertility rates and their slow or virtually absent recovery in a number of countries even during the region's brief golden age.
80. Aslund, "The Myth," 16.

its 1989 level in Lithuania. Likewise, weighted down by unfavorable Polish and Slovak data, the average performance of the Visegrád states fell behind that of the Baltic states and Romania in long-term unemployment.

Macroeconomic (In)stability

Overall, sustaining macroeconomic stability has been difficult for the new capitalist regimes. Thus, the risk of economic disorganization has been as serious as the threat of social disintegration. Again, Slovenia is exceptional in that until the late 2000s, it successfully strove for balance in external debt, current account deficit, inflation, budget deficit, and state debt. The rest of East Central European countries varied both in the origins of their macroeconomic instability and in their success in keeping these disturbances under control.

In 1989–98, the agenda of macroeconomic stabilization was crowded with serious, albeit different, problems left behind by the socialist system that needed to be solved. The inheritance of the Baltic states, Slovenia, and Croatia included galloping inflation. At the same time, these new nation-states did not assume responsibility for the debt burden of the former Soviet Union and Yugoslavia, and could start their transformations without crippling foreign indebtedness. Within the Visegrád group, Poland was plagued by both galloping inflation and a large foreign debt, Hungary only by the latter, while Czechoslovakia (and later the Czech and Slovak Republics) by neither. Finally, during the decade of crisis Bulgaria and Romania suffered from recurrent high inflation cycles. Bulgaria, in particular, also rapidly amassed large foreign debts.

Over time, many of the East Central European countries have partly succeeded in macroeconomic stabilization, although they have had to face recurrent backlashes and to combat destabilization with draconic austerity programs. The new nation-states accomplished the challenging tasks of disentangling the national monetary authority from quasi-federal structures, ending galloping inflation, and introducing new convertible and stable national currencies that replaced the multiple-currency regimes of Soviet rubles, Yugoslav dinars, German marks, and U.S. dollars. Poland and for some time Hungary could, albeit in different ways, manage their inherited foreign debt, while Bulgaria continued to be a critical case for most of the 1990s.

Interestingly, by 1999–2007, the tables were turned in the sense that some of the initially debt-free states caught up with or even surpassed the original large-scale borrowers, and accumulated huge and mainly private debts. Their heavy dependence on foreign loans both followed from and perpetuated their ballooning current account deficits, which reflected in part a characteristic weakness of the Baltic and Bulgarian economies, namely limited export capacities and in part also the lending strategies of these countries' transnationalized commercial banking sectors. Conversely, despite much worse

TABLE 1.9
Levels of macroeconomic (in)stability, 1989–98 and 1999–2007

	External debt (% of exports of goods and services)	Current account balance (% of GDP)	Annual average change of consumer prices (%)[a]	General government balance (% of GDP)	General government debt (% of GDP)
1989–98 averages					
Baltic states	60.8	–4.1	192.3	–1.9	11.7
Visegrád states	118.5	–3.3	40.4	–3.7	47.0
Slovenia	47.8	1.7	52.0	0.4	24.6
Croatia, Bulgaria, Romania	117.0	–3.3	199.8	–3.1	71.5
1999–2007 averages					
Baltic states	124.8	–9.9	3.4	–0.6	13.1
Visegrád states	94.3	–5.2	4.9	–5.1	42.4
Slovenia	93.7	–1.8	5.4	–2.2	27.4
Croatia, Bulgaria, Romania	131.2	–7.3	10.3	–2.2	37.7

Source: Authors' calculations, based on EBRD *Transition Report*, various years.
[a] Previous year=100%.

initial positions, during the years of recovery the Baltic states and Bulgaria outperformed the Visegrád group (except Poland) in price stability and fiscal performance alike. It was not before the abrupt end of their rapid expansionary period in 2008–9 that these overheated catching-up economies had to pay a price in terms of the EU's worst inflation rates and rapidly deteriorating fiscal balances.

Puzzles of the Small State Pattern

Analogies and contrasts with two relevant country groups, the small states of postwar Western Europe and the late industrializers of the nineteenth and twentieth centuries, help highlight some further fascinating aspects of East Central Europe's divergent development. Commenting on their path Katzenstein suggested that "in the period of great crisis the small states of Central and Eastern Europe responded in some, though not in all, ways that were consonant with the behavior of the small Western European states half a century earlier."[81]

Structural factors, such as experiences of massive social dislocation in the inter- and postwar years and after the Cold War, similar challenges of bridging "the divergent requirements of international competitiveness and political preference," and the powerful influences stemming from the liberal world economy and European integration, make Katzenstein's proposition that the latecomer small states could learn from and emulate the experiences of their predecessors sound convincing indeed.[82]

Yet the varied extent to which the East Central European paths appear to be in line with the small state model is surprising. As demonstrated above, only Slovenia exhibits all the features of democratic corporatism. Why so? Surely the Visegrád countries or Croatia also share similarities with the Western European small states, in particular economic openness and generous compensation to those who lose from this. But how to make sense of the simultaneous weakness of these states' neocorporatist institutions, which could have helped them "adjust to economic change through a carefully calibrated balance of economic flexibility and political stability"?[83] And the most puzzling aspect of the dissimilar Baltic pattern is its political feasibility. Where to trace the sources of capitalism's survival if democratic leaders turn a blind eye to the anxiety of its losers?

From the standpoint of the small state model, then, the larger puzzle is in the fact that despite similarities in historical context, size, requirements of adjustment, and international influences, only half of the East Central

81. Katzenstein, "*Small States* and Small States," 22.
82. Katzenstein, *Small States*, 29.
83. Ibid.

European countries have opted for strategies that share a degree of similarity with the choices of their Western European counterparts? Why have the rest followed other models?

To complicate things further, the adoption of some key features of the far more advanced Western European small states makes East Central Europe's late development effort appear unique when compared with other earlier and contemporary success stories of breaking out of backwardness. Famously, Alexander Gerschenkron argued that "in every instance of industrialization, imitation of the evolution in advanced countries appears in combination with different, indigenously determined elements....What can be derived from a historical review is a strong sense for the significance of the native elements in the industrialization of backward countries."[84]

The Gerschenkronian perspective on belated development, then, all but reverses the previous puzzle. What becomes surprising is the relatively large number of postsocialist countries that have partly emulated the advanced small states' institutions, notwithstanding the large disparity between the two groups' economic wealth.[85] The following chapters will address these and other puzzling aspects of capitalist diversity.

---

84. Alexander Gerschenkron, *Economic Backwardness in Historical Perspective* (Cambridge: The Belknap Press of Harvard University Press, 1976 [1962]), 26.

85. In 1999, average GDP per capita in Katzenstein's small states—Austria, Switzerland, Belgium, the Netherlands, Denmark, Norway, and Sweden—was almost triple that of the East Central European small states. In 2006, the ratio was still well above double. EUROSTAT, http://epp.eurostat.ec.europa.eu/tgm/ (accessed November23, 2008).

Paths to Postsocialist Capitalism

The significance of postsocialist capitalism's diversity cannot be fully understood without capturing how it came to be that way. The emergence of new regimes raises complex questions about the possibilities of transformative agency within the constraints of the international environment and past legacies. How far could the East Central European states influence the direction of their postsocialist history? How would we know whether they were active shapers of their fortunes or misfortunes in the first place? One way to substantiate that their paths were indeed chosen by the small states— rather than externally imposed, overdetermined by their past, or purely accidental—is to identify some originality, innovation, or at least deviation from known patterns in their ideas and institutions.

Echoing an earlier debate on whether small states can be considered more than the playthings of powerful external forces, scholars have pointed to the overwhelming influence of IFIs, TNCs, and the EU on the emerging new order.[1] While there has been much dispute on whether deep internationalization and Europeanization lock postsocialist market societies into promising paths or trap them in dependency, authors in the Europeanization literature

---

1. For the earlier debate, see the position of Alexander Gerschenkron, according to whom, "the economy of a small sovereign country may be so much enmeshed in the economy of another, more advanced, country as to be virtually an integral part of the latter area. Its economic evolution may therefore proceed...simply mirroring the course of events in the larger country." Gerschenkron, *Economic Backwardness*, 361. See also Barrington Moore, Jr., *Social Origins of Dictatorship and Democracy: Lord and Peasant in the Making of the Modern World* (Boston: Beacon Press, 1993 [1966]), xix. It is against this intellectual background that Katzenstein's study of small states that had been both dependent on and capable of economic and political innovation laid the groundwork for further inquiry into small countries' strategies in the world economy.

tend to agree with critical political economists on the region's limited political and economic autonomy.[2]

Other analysts have stressed the long shadow cast by the past on Eastern European development after 1989. Socialist and presocialist legacies are frequently invoked to account for postsocialist failures, successes, and regime diversity. Advocates of such explanations argue that structural, institutional, and power configurations that precede crucial choices of the early transformation period create specific constraints and opportunities for reformers, and thus shape the likelihood of institutional choices leading to successful transformation. Authors in this tradition differ in how much structural power they accord to legacies. While only a few go so far as to claim that the peculiar Eastern European legacies undermine any attempt at building stable regimes, most analysts see reform choices constrained by the past.[3]

We do not question that after the breakdown of socialism past legacies and powerful external influences have narrowed the room for transformative vision and action. Yet the emerging varied institutional landscape in the region and the ongoing struggles around key institutions speak for the importance of political agency, not its absence. Accordingly, our approach to capitalist diversity rests on the premise that the historical turning point of the early 1990s enabled East Central Europeans to make politically consequential decisions about their future.

This chapter spells out the building blocks of our argument on the emergence, reproduction, and limits of regime diversity. Adapting Polanyi's notion of the double movement to postsocialist conditions, we stress the centrality of political and technocratic elites and state-society relations for shaping capitalist orders. To explore the chances and limits of strategic action, we take a

2. For the literature on the powerful external forces shaping the region's path and the limited domestic capacities to filter these influences see, e.g., Frank Schimmelfennig and Ulrich Sedelmeier, eds., *The Europeanization of Central and Eastern Europe* (Ithaca: Cornell University Press, 2005); Milada A. Vachudova, *Europe Undivided: Democracy, Leverage, and Integration after Communism* (Oxford: Oxford University Press, 2005); Alice H. Amsden, Jacek Kochanowicz, and Lance Taylor, *The Market Meets Its Match: Restructuring the Economies of Eastern Europe* (Cambridge, Mass.: Harvard University Press, 1994); Iván T. Berend, "Alternatives of Transformation: Choices and Determinants—East Central Europe in the 1990s," in *Markets, States, and Democracy: The Political Economy of Post-Communist Transformation*, ed. Beverly Crawford and Arendt Lijphart (Boulder: Westview Press, 1995), 130–49.

3. For legacy approaches see, e.g., Stark and Bruszt, *Post-Socialist Pathways*; Eyal, Szelényi, and Townsley, *Making Capitalism without Capitalists*; Herbert Kitschelt, Zdenka Mansfeldová, Radoslaw Markowski, and Gábor Tóka, *Post-Communist Party Systems: Competition, Representation, and Inter-Party Cooperation* (Cambridge: Cambridge University Press, 1999); and Grzegorz Ekiert and Stephen Hanson, eds., *Capitalism and Democracy in Central and Eastern Europe: Assessing the Legacy of the Communist Rule* (Cambridge: Cambridge University Press, 2003). The radical position that legacies undermine any attempt at stable new regime building has been taken by Kenneth Jowitt, "The Leninist Legacy," in *Eastern Europe in Revolution*, ed. Ivo Banac (Ithaca: Cornell University Press, 1992), 207–24; Claus Offe, "Capitalism by Democratic Design? Democratic Theory Facing the Triple Transition in East Central Europe," *Social Research* 58, no. 2 (Winter 1991): 865–92.

closer look at the paradigm that guided policy reforms in the early 1990s, and the broader sources of popular support political elites could tap into when implementing these reforms.

We identify two ways of generating support, with compensatory policies and identity policies, and trace the varied degrees to which concerns over welfare and identity entered the politics of transformation back to how political actors perceived the socialist and presocialist legacies. Further, to better understand the relationship between the anticipated and actual regime outcomes, we consider the impact of radical uncertainty during transformation.

Our focus on transformative domestic agency does not negate the importance of transnational and international factors and actors. On the contrary, we argue that since the transformation has advanced through deep global and European integration, these processes have played a constitutive role in regime diversity. Once again we can draw on Polanyi's theory of capitalism as a multilevel political economy and his related idea "that particular moments in the organization of the international economic regime provide particular kinds of opportunities for states to act, and the degree of freedom or unfreedom open to the state."[4]

The contemporary international regime has had several channels to influence the postsocialist states' choices in such a way that they remain compatible with the neoliberal paradigm. Western policy ideas and particularly the Washington consensus[5] have profoundly influenced the East Central European reform efforts. Moreover, Western policymakers and advisers have built transnational "advocacy coalitions"[6] with their Eastern colleagues who have shared their preference for rapid and comprehensive marketization over any other transformation strategy. When competing for power over policy, these coalitions were also backed by the practice of IFIs to make financial assistance conditional on compliance with their own recommendations. It is not by accident, then, that with the sole exception of Slovenia all the East Central European countries have settled on regime variants within the confines of neoliberalism.

Even more important, the region ended up being deeply integrated in the European political economy and its institutions, which implied new opportunities but also pressures for convergence on a striking array of EU norms, rules, and regulations. Accordingly, in interaction with domestic actors and factors, the EU and various types of TNCs have locked the new regimes into paths able to reproduce many of their features in the short run, while also contributing to the new order's fragility in the long run.

---

4. This formulation is from Block and Somers, "Beyond the Economistic Fallacy," 73.

5. On the Washington consensus on policy reform see John Williamson, ed., *Latin American Adjustment: How Much Has Happened* (Washington, D.C.: Institute for International Economics, 1990).

6. Paul A. Sabatier, "Toward Better Theories of the Policy Process," *Political Science and Politics* 24, no. 2 (1991): 147–56.

Leaving the East

After socialism broke down, the East Central European societies and their political elites were united in their wish to "leave the East" and "return to Europe," which have emerged as the two largely uncontroversial main interpretive frames of transformation. Varied national projects pairing both agendas could be tapped as sources of support and legitimacy by centrist and populist politicians of the Left and Right alike, especially given that the two visions combined historically rooted and future-oriented elite and mass appeals. As Joseph Love noted, throughout centuries for the region's "leaders and intellectuals...with the exception of those who saw the Soviet Union as the Second World alternative, progress was a road, rough but not impassable, leading to Europe, the First World."[7] Similarly, many ordinary East Central Europeans shared the view of Europe as a place abundant in all those features that their own region lacked in the late 1980s and before: an efficient economy, generous public welfare provision, political freedom, and respected national sovereignty.

Economic reforms took pride of place in the region's disentanglement from the East. This is not by chance. The socialist system's popular acceptance rested largely on its capacity to bring about economic progress and social cohesion. Despite the fact that Soviet-type socialism took root in less advanced societies, it was the West not the Third World that provided the standards of comparison. Thus, socialism's ultimate failure to match Western capitalism, and even worse, its obvious falling back after the 1970s, was a chief factor in its breakdown. Almost all initial economic reform blueprints opted for strategies in line with the neoliberal policy paradigm. Neoliberalism claims the superiority of markets and competition over state-governed mechanisms of social and economic organization. To foster markets and competition, governments were to be limited, property rights strengthened, state enterprises privatized, strictly controlled markets deregulated, and money kept stable.[8]

Neoliberalism, which, as we shall see below, also formed an important tenet of the European order to which East Central Europe sought to return, proved an attractive policy choice for reformers. Its agenda of a radically altered relationship between states and markets fell on fertile ground in countries that had struggled with reforming the socialist system without ever being able to prevent its deepening economic crisis. Moreover, its decidedly

7. Joseph Love, *Crafting the Third World: Theorizing Underdevelopment in Rumania and Brazil* (Stanford: Stanford University Press, 1996), 5–6.

8. On neoliberalism, see, e.g., Dieter Plehwe, Bernhard Walpen, and Gisela Neunhoeffer, eds., *Neoliberal Hegemony: A Global Critique* (New York: Routledge, 2005). We use the term "policy paradigm" to denote templates and hierarchies of goals guiding economic policies, and the instruments relied on to effect the latter, following Peter A. Hall, "Policy Paradigms, Social Learning, and the State: The Case of Economic Policy Making in Britain," *Comparative Politics* 25, no. 3 (April 1993): 275–96.

antipolitical orientation seemed to offer the right remedy against the ubiquitous presence of politics (read the state) under socialism.[9]

It was only Slovenia that consciously and substantially diverged from the Washington consensus. The architects of that country's initial economic strategy opted for gradualism in liberalization and privatization alike, and maintained a significant role of the state in the economy.

When designing economic reforms, initially the political elites did not have clear ideas in mind about where these would take them. The capitalist diversity identified in this book as the outcome of transformation certainly did not inspire their initial choices. Even if competing concepts of "efficient laissez-faire capitalism; worker self-managerial participation in a 'Sozialpartnerschaft' Scandinavian Socialism; a mixed economy and ownership; and an East European populist 'Third Road' between capitalism and socialism" existed, these were, as Iván T. Berend noted, "rather uncertain and foggy."[10] Thus, notwithstanding the superficial similarities between some of these models and the actual outcomes of regime formation, for a number of reasons the former could hardly offer much guidance for the latter.

Leading representatives of neoliberal reform elites and their foreign advisors expressed aversion to projecting concrete capitalist varieties as the end goals of transformation. Some architects of the new order rejected the discussion of road maps to concrete forms of capitalism on philosophical grounds. Being Friedmanite and Hayekian by self-definition, these reformers saw their mission as respecting and allowing freedom of choice and not paralyzing society's creativity by "artificial" templates. As the leading reformers of Czechoslovakia put it, the principles of liberalism "go against the thinking of individuals who have dirigistic and constructivist ambitions (the typical case of 'socialist' intellectuals), who prefer to be guided by visible and foreseeable 'concrete' purposes and who want things to be done now, immediately, because these purposes are evident to them."[11]

In the triumphant atmosphere following socialism's demise the liberating tone found its way to the IFIs, such as the EBRD, whose first *Transition Report* issued in 1994 suggested that "transition is not only an intermediate goal contributing to economic development. It may also be regarded as an ultimate objective in itself. The market economy...gives, in principle, the

---

9. The origins of neoliberal reform elites and the content and the political contexts of their blueprints have been extensively analyzed in the literature. See e.g. Eyal, Szelényi, and Townsley, *Making Capitalism;* Béla Greskovits, *The Political Economy;* Dorothee Bohle, *Europas neue Peripherie: Polens Transformation und transnationale Integration* (Münster: Westfälisches Dampfboot, 2002); Johanna Bockman and Gil Eyal, "Eastern Europe as a Laboratory for Economic Knowledge: The Transnational Roots of Neoliberalism," *American Journal of Sociology* 108, no. 2 (September 2002): 310–52; and Jerzy Szacki, *Liberalism after Communism* (Budapest: Central European University Press, 1995).

10. Berend, "Alternatives of Transformation," 130.

11. Václav Klaus and Tomás Jezek, "Social Criticism, False Liberalism, and Recent Changes in Czechoslovakia," *East European Politics and Societies* 5, no. 1 (Winter 1991): 28.

individual the right to basic choices over aspects of his or her life.... The right to these choices may be seen as a basic liberty and as a fundamental aspect of standard of living. Thus the transition is also an end in itself."[12]

Foreign advisers also had political reasons to urge the new democratic governments to put market economies in place without delay. It was argued that lengthy disputes over the new system's details would allow populists, communist bureaucracies, and the managers and workers of state-owned enterprises (SOEs) to block marketization.[13]

Furthermore, reformers' negative stance toward emulating precise models may have been due to their concern that this would impair latecomers' chances of rapid development.[14] Recognizing that the Visegrád countries were "adopting much of the Western European model," Anders Aslund expressed worries about the implied "danger of limited economic growth and the entitlement trap most clearly developed in Sweden as a result of taxes that are too high and social transfers that are too large." He seems to have been less concerned over the prospects of other former socialist countries, such as Estonia, Latvia, Lithuania, Moldova, Georgia, the Kyrgyz Republic, and Kazakhstan, which opted "for a new liberal economic model with low taxes, limited social transfers, few regulations, an open economy, and far-reaching privatization." [15]

Last but not least, Czechoslovak Minister of Finance Václav Klaus questioned the scientific value of distinctions between various types of market economy.

No third way in economy, no attempts at a symbiosis of various state regulating mechanisms of the market, and no civil initiatives can lead to a modern European state.... Trade unions' interference in management is incompatible with the idea of economic reform.... Putting adjectives in front of the term 'market economy' is useless. A market economy is a real market economy and obeys market laws and nothing else.... In my intensive comparative studies of economic systems, I have not found any distinction between various types of a market economy. There is

---

12. *Transition Report 1994* (London: EBRD, 1994), 3. Hence the remarkable continuity with the original liberal utopia that had assisted capitalism's birth. As Polanyi summarized it: "To the typical utilitarian economic liberalism was a social project which should be put into effect for the greatest happiness of the greatest number; *laissez-faire* was not a method to achieve a thing, it was the thing to be achieved." Polanyi, *The Great Transformation,* 139.

13. Jeffrey Sachs, "Eastern Europe's Economies."

14. This was the gist of Leszek Balcerowicz's criticism of Germany's social market economy that "[f]rom the start of the 1970s appears to have been distinctly 'oversocialized,' which affected the rate of its development, and more recently contributed to the crisis in its public finances. Therefore, the *soziale Marktwirtschaft* does not seem to be the most appropriate model for the latecomers who want fast growth in order to catch up." Leszek Balcerowicz, *Socialism, Capitalism, Transformation* (Budapest: Central European University Press, 1995), 233.

15. Anders Aslund, "Possible Future Directions," 468.

only one model. There is only one serious economic science for which Nobel Prizes are awarded. We are drawing from this science today.[16]

What this all adds up to is that neoliberal technocrats presented their reform agenda as the only way to transition to a capitalist society. The ultimate goal of transition, however, was perceived broadly enough to embrace many of the existing varieties of capitalism—at least rhetorically. At the same time, alternatives to neoliberal reforms rarely crystallized in more concrete terms and coherent programs. As noted, for instance, by the architect of Poland's transformation, Minister of Finance Leszek Balcerowicz, although the term social market economy "has made a fine career for itself in Poland...few people know exactly what it means, but just about everyone is blissfully convinced that it means some sort of better market economy."[17]

In light of the above, the actual outcome of transformation, namely, to borrow Balcerowicz's term, "oversocialized" market economies in about half of the countries and neocorporatism in at least one of them, seems surprising. Sharply criticized and rejected by leading economic reformers, these variants could hardly be traced to preexisting master plans. Rather, as if to corroborate Polanyi's famous distinction between the features of processes leading to market expansion versus social protection, it appears that "*laissez-faire* was planned; planning was not."[18]

To clarify our point: over the 1990s the neoliberal paradigm scored a major victory in the region, and played a formative role in the emergence of postsocialist capitalism. The early liberal thinkers, most prominently Adam Smith, as well as their influential followers Friedrich A. von Hayek and Milton Friedman, became the acclaimed heroes of many reformers. Ten out of eleven East Central European countries did embrace some variant of economic neoliberalism. At the same time, the capitalist regimes on which these states eventually settled have also significantly diverged from the neoliberal agenda, notwithstanding their leading advocates' professed reliance on liberating philosophy and serious economic science. It appears that neoliberalism could not triumph in "pure" form except in very specific circumstances. In line with the argument developed in chapter 1, our explanation of this outcome is essentially political.

16. Interview with Vaclav Klaus by Branislav Janik, place and date not given; "Politics on the Razor's Edge: Will 1991 Be the Alpha and Omega of Our Existence?" *Narodna Obrona,* FBIS-EEU-90–012 (January 17, 1990), 15–16.

17. Balcerowicz, *Socialism,* 233. It is interesting to note, however, that Poland was one of the few countries in the region where opposition forces also had elaborated a non-neoliberal reform program, which could have served as an alternative to the Balcerowicz plan. See Tadeusz Kowalik, "The Ugly Face of Polish Success," in *Poland in the New Millenium,* ed. Grazyna Blazyca and Rychard Rapacki (Cheltenham: Edward Elgar, 2001), 33–53.

18. Polanyi, *The Great Transformation,* 141.

As we learn from Peter Gourevitch, "good ideas do not always win. Many interesting and powerful theoretical constructs have been developed, be it in economics or other domains, which have had little or no impact on policy. To become policy, ideas must link up with politics—the mobilization of consent for policy. Politics involves power."[19] Accordingly, we argue that the pure neoliberal, embedded neoliberal, and neocorporatist regimes grew out of conflicts and compromises between the reform elites' radical economic agendas, which became integral (but not necessarily dominant) parts of most party programs, and the new rulers' efforts to mobilize consent for their policies and maintain legitimacy despite adverse circumstances.

Mobilizing Consent

Mobilizing consent for the chosen economic strategies was by no means a simple task. After a short honeymoon between the technocratic elites' and the populations' aspirations, the "seductive force of neoliberalism" has faded away.[20] Nonetheless, those who approved or rejected the new economic system seem to have judged its performance by more complex yardsticks than rates of growth or even wages and consumption.

When popular approval of the market economy is compared with approval of the socialist economy in retrospect, the former tends to be on the losing side in both hard times and good times. Although overall perceptions improved during the brief expansionary period of the 2000s, even then only Estonians and Czechs expressed significantly more satisfaction with the market system than with the socialist economy. Similar to the case of democracy, in 1989–98 the new economic order was least popular relative to the old one in the Baltic states, followed by the Southeastern European and the Visegrád countries, and Slovenia, in that order. [21]

Yet it would be wrong to conclude on these grounds that East Central Europeans refused to value individual economic freedom altogether. Consider the unexpected development that in the early to mid-1990s the electorate brought back to power Communist successor parties that increased social outlays but typically did not stop market reforms. Witnessing

19. Peter A. Gourevitch, "Keynesian Politics: The Political Sources of Economic Policy Choices," in *The Political Power of Economic Ideas: Keynesianism across Nations,* ed. Peter A. Hall (Princeton: Princeton University Press, 1989), 87. By this quote we do not want to imply that radical neoliberalism was a good idea.

20. Dorothee Bohle and Gisela Neunhoeffer, "Why Was There No Third Way? The Role of Neoliberal Ideology, Networks and Think Tanks in Combating Market Socialism and Shaping Transformation in Poland," in Plehwe, Walpen, and Neunhoeffer, *Neoliberal Hegemony,* 89–104.

21. Richard Rose, "Diverging Paths of Post-Communist Countries: New Europe Baromenter Trends since 1991" (Glasgow: Centre for the Study of Public Policy, University of Strathclyde, 2006), 32–33.

this trend, Sachs noted: "Generally speaking, most East Europeans want *both* a market economy and the security of an extensive social safety net."[22]

Polanyi would not have been surprised by the fact that once East Europeans realized that a fully fledged market system might not satisfy their simultaneous "desire for opportunity and...need for security,"[23] they rapidly changed their political loyalties. Rather, he would have explained the early shift in the fortunes of postcommunist parties by the epochal dynamics of market society, whereby "the market expanded countinuously but this movement was met by a countermovement checking the expansion in definite directions."[24] The new countermovements, like those in nineteenth-century Europe, were provoked by liberals' relentless quest for a sharp break with the past on a whole range of historically ingrained human motifs and practices in a situation where people would rather fall "back on the familiar in order to cope."[25]

More similarity with the original Great Transformation is revealed by the fact that although the postsocialist countermovements had a common origin in the uncertainty and insecurity of society in general, the demand for protection was advanced "under the most varied slogans, with very different motivations [by] a multitude of parties and social strata...in a series of countries."[26] The social and political forces that in various periods supported the movements and countermovements, and their impact on politics and policy, will be characterized in greater detail in chapters 3 to 6.

The last and perhaps most important common feature of the two transformations is the centrality in both cases of the political system. Just like the liberal state of the late nineteenth century, the postsocialist transformative state of the twentieth century became "the crystallization of the contradictory impulses of...development."[27] The new governments acted on behalf of capitalist expansion and its beneficiaries at the same time as they were also "in charge of the general interests of the community,"[28] ordinary citizens and new entrepreneurs alike, who wanted enhanced market access but from relatively protected and secure socio-economic positions.

The conflicts between these contradictory popular expectations and between their advocates in the political arena could not have been preempted or resolved without embedding the neoliberal reforms in a broader transformation agenda that appealed to what in a different context David Landes

22. Sachs, "Postcommunist Parties and the Politics of Entitlements," 2.

23. The formulation is from Wolfgang Streeck, "Response," in the discussion forum on his *Re-forming Capitalism, Socio-economic Review* (2010): 18.

24. Polanyi, *The Great Transformation*, 130.

25. Valerie J. Bunce, "Leaving Socialism: A 'Transition to Democracy'?" *Contention* 3, no. 1 (Fall 1993): 45.

26. Polanyi, *The Great Transformation*, 147.

27. Block and Somers, "Beyond the Economistic Fallacy," 68.

28. Polanyi, *The Great Transformation*, 154.

called "sentiments of wider resonance" among the citizenry. Recognition of attachment to social status acquired in the past regime and of "collective commitment to nationhood...and independence"[29] became the typical ways in which politicians tried to mobilize consent to their painful economic strategy. To the extent that elites disposed of the will and skill to tap into these sources of legitimacy, their maneuvering and compromises were likely to lead to viable varieties of neoliberal capitalism characterized by different structures of political opportunities, risks, and trade-offs.

Materialist and Idealist Political Arenas

Intervention into the process of market expansion was triggered by two distinct but related processes of dislocation—status decline within the transforming societal hierarchy and atomization due to disintegration of inherited social ties—both of which could provoke fierce resistance to reforms and reformers, whether by anti-incumbent voting or other forms of protest. Among the remedies available to politicians, compensation for transformation costs stood out as the main measure to mitigate vulnerability to status decline, while policies strengthening collective identity could take the lead in mitigating the fear of atomization.

The substantive justification for compensation is central to Polanyi's theory, and remains illuminating in the postsocialist context too:

> Even when money values were involved, they were secondary to other interests. Almost invariably professional status, safety and security, the form of a man's life, the breadth of its existence, the stability of his environment were in question.... Customs tariffs which implied profits for capitalists and wages for workers meant, ultimately, security against unemployment, stabilization of regional conditions, assurance against liquidation of industries, and, perhaps most of all, the avoidance of that painful loss of status which inevitably accompanies transference to a job at which a man is less skilled and experienced than at his own.[30]

In turn, to combat fears of atomization within a horizontally disintegrating "social fabric," which have been no less deep-seated than fears of degradation along the vertical axis of social hierarchy, identity politics could be invoked. The national idea's ability to nurture emotionally powerful attachments has been highlighted by Benedict Anderson: "Regardless of the actual inequality and exploitation that may prevail in each the nation is always

---

29. David Landes, "Does it Pay to be Late?" in *Between Development and Underdevelopment*, ed. Jean Batou (Geneva: Publications du Centre D'Histoire Économique Internationale de L'Université de Genève, 1991), 49.
30. Polanyi, *The Great Transformation*, 154.

conceived as a deep horizontal comradeship. Ultimately it is this fraternity that makes it possible, over the past two centuries, for so many millions of people not so much to kill, as willingly to die for such limited imaginings."[31]

Since Communists in their quest for ideological monopoly oppressed people as members of nations and religious believers, many East Central Europeans, and particularly those whose national existence or religious life had been most severely undermined by incorporation into the Soviet empire, have felt true satisfaction over their regained freedom to "imagine" and actually craft such communities, and so escape atomization. This, however, means that nurtured collective commitment to nation or religion could have a profound and varied impact on how governments were able to cope with other felt vulnerabilities, such as fears of declining social status.

To summarize, over the first decade and a half of transformation, there were two typical ways in which East Central European governments could implement market reforms while appealing to broader sources of legitimacy. One was the appeal to identity politics, which was pursued in the most thoroughgoing fashion in the Baltic states; the other was that of material compensation for the costs of marketization, which predominated in some of the Visegrád countries. A third group of countries—and especially the new nation states of the Czech and Slovak Republics and Slovenia—combined the two approaches.

Why have political leaders capitalized on so different sources of consent and legitimacy, and what explains the dominance of identity politics versus compensation policies (or vice versa) in specific cases? How have politicians' choices influenced their capacities to reform and the paths of regime formation? In order to answer these questions, we will now turn to the issue of legacies.

Unfinished Tasks

The distinctive socialist and presocialist legacies that made the East Central European countries the likeliest candidates for successful transformation among all the former Soviet bloc countries have been well established in the literature.[32] These economies had the longest history of industrial development in the Soviet bloc. Although the industrial breakthrough occurred mostly under socialism, the beginnings of industrialization predated that period. As socialist industrialization (albeit only to a limited extent) built on previous specializations and product mixes, the western rim countries

31. Benedict Anderson, *Imagined Communities: Reflections on the Origins and Spread of Nationalism* (London and New York: Verso, 1991), 7.

32. The case for the longer-term cumulative advantages of many of the East Central European countries has been forcefully made by Herbert Kitschelt, "Accounting for Postcommunist Regime Diversity: What Counts as a Good Cause?" in Ekiert and Hanson, *Capitalism and Democracy*, 49–86.

of the Soviet empire and the northwestern members of the Yugoslav federation could develop the system's most advanced and complex industries. They were also the first that entered into commercial relations with the capitalist world after cautious experiments with liberalization in the 1970s.

Equally important, presocialist legacies of state and nation building and democratic experiences provided most of the eleven countries with unique resources to draw on in the period of democratic breakthrough. Geographic proximity to the West, finally, is also often mentioned among these states' specific resources. In contrast to other socialist states, here presocialist development was inseparably bound up with that of Prussia, Germany, and the Habsburg Monarchy. Western Europe had been the reference point for East Central European elites ever since the early nineteenth century. Even under socialism, Western Europe remained important as a benchmark against which to measure performance, and as source of alternative economic development strategies (such as market socialist experiments with a kind of mixed economy). Such a source of benchmarks and alternatives was out of reach for most other socialist countries.[33]

Broadly, legacy-centered approaches highlight the importance of presocialist and socialist efforts for convergence on the structural and institutional characteristics of the West. Once socialism collapsed, these accomplishments provided the eleven postsocialist states with valuable resources for democratic and capitalist transformation. Can the legacies also account for the differences in outcomes among our cases, and if so, how?

Past legacies, of course, did have an impact on initial resources and expectations, and helped actors clarify their interests and select the means and ways to pursue goals. But like other "objective" constraints, legacies do not act on political outcomes directly. Rather, their impact is mediated by how policymakers and citizens perceive them.[34] To pursue this idea one step further, although the legacies themselves are hardly a matter of choice, the perception of them can well be such, especially if the former are complex and controversial and leave ample room for alternative interpretations.

In order to come to terms with the complexity of interaction among legacies, choices, and perceptions, our argument stresses two major factors that get less attention than they deserve in existing legacy-centered perspectives. These are the multitude of unfinished tasks reformers were confronted with after socialism, and the ambivalence stemming from repeated attempts at catching up with the West. Both of these aspects are crucial, as they point to possibilities of choices within constraints and the role of perceptions in informing the choices.

---

33. Iván T. Berend, *History Derailed: Central and Eastern Europe in the Long Nineteenth Century* (Berkeley: University of California Press, 2003).

34. See Katzenstein, "*Small States* and Small States," 11, for the importance of perceived vulnerability in the emergence of democratic corporatism.

The multitude of unfinished tasks offered political elites the choice of whether to prioritize some tasks over others, or tackle all of them simultaneously. These decisions—which were typically made in response to broader popular movements and countermovements—were crucial for the emerging materialist, or rather idealist structures of political support and contestation. The choices of initial tasks were important in yet another way. They shaped reformers' interpretation of concrete aspects of socialist and presocialist legacies, and the elements that were taken on board or rejected.

Our stress on the significance of perceptions is also informed by the region's historical experiences with nonlinear, incomplete, and reversible attempts of catching up with the West, which did not easily lend themselves to straightforward interpretations as either assets or liabilities. Below, we first briefly recall the region's peculiar and ambivalent legacies. Then we show in greater detail how decisions about major tasks created specific opportunity structures for consent and contestation, how certain legacies were turned into assets or threats for transformation, and how this all impacted on capitalist regime formation.

Let us start our elaboration on the specific modernization legacies with a reference to Peter Katzenstein's account of Austria's markedly different historical path from that of other Western European small states. "If we picture Austria and the other small European states as trains and history as a set of switches, the Austrian train was at every branch switched in a direction opposite from the other small European states."[35] East Central Europe, then, we argue, can be depicted as the Austrian train taken to an extreme destination by history. The history of these countries was the most dissimilar to that of Western Europe's accumulated experiences.

Unfinished and Conflict-Ridden Nation-States

The region's countries share with Austria the experience of "wrong" sequencing of state formation and nation building. In most of Western Europe, including many small countries, building a territorial state occurred before the national idea became influential, and provided the framework for nationalism's consolidation. In East Central Europe the nationalist ideology became influential within the fluid political structures of the Ottoman, Russian, and Habsburg empires. This gave nationalism in the region its distinct character. On the empires' peripheries it was a project of liberation from foreign domination, of unification based on ethnicity, language, or religion, rather than on civic rights. Nation building had to be realized simultaneously with and through state building.[36]

---

35. Katzenstein, *Small States*, 188.
36. Valerie J. Bunce, "The National Idea: Imperial Legacies and Post-Communist Pathways in Eastern Europe," *East European Politics and Societies* 19, no. 3 (2005): 406–42.

The late nation- and state-building attempts of the nineteenth century, and in the aftermath of World War I, brought with them a host of tensions and problems, and resulted in traumatic defeats. Congruence between the new political units and the nations they sought to represent was far from perfect, as most new states made territorial claims based on precedents of glorified but long-faded historical precursors, rather than on existing distributions of ethnolinguistic groups. All new nation-states thus had sizable minorities, who ended up being second-class citizens of "nationalizing states," and were neglected and urged to assimilate at best, and at worst outright discriminated against and persecuted. The minorities themselves often fought for their own national liberation from the new states. Conflicts became especially severe if, as in the case of Germany's *Deutschtumspolitik* in the interwar period, "external national homelands" interfered on behalf of minorities.

As a consequence of accumulated tensions between nationalizing states, national minorities, and external homelands,[37] Hungary and Bulgaria lost substantial territories and populations after World War I. Reversing the losses was one of the major reasons that both countries joined the Axis powers in World War II. The German annexations and occupations in Poland and Czechoslovakia originated partly in similar tensions and conflicts. In almost all East Central European countries the first attempts at state and nation building resulted in defeats of enormous proportions. In none of these countries was the national question settled at the end of World War II. To the contrary, multiple occupations, territorial changes, the annihilation and forced movement of millions of people, and economic devastation played havoc with the foundations of nation-state building. Before any of these traumatic experiences could be digested and lessons drawn, the region's countries fell once again under the domination of the Soviet empire either as its satellite states or its occupied territories.

A number of authors point to the fact that integration into the Soviet empire filled the process of nation-state building in East Central Europe with new life.[38] The satellites remained semisovereign nation-states. Within the Soviet Union nationhood was institutionalized on the substate level. Each of the fifteen republics was based on a nation whose name it bore. On paper at least, the union republics had far-reaching powers, including the right to secede. Even if their political and economic autonomy was limited, they could secure

37. These terms are borrowed from Rogers Brubaker, *Nationalism Reframed: Nationhood and the National Question in the New Europe* (Cambridge: Cambridge University Press, 1996). He analyzes the consequences of the nineteenth- and early twentieth-century nationalist projects in East Central Europe as a triadic relationship between three types of nationalisms, those of nationalizing states, national minorities within these states, and the external homelands to which the latter "belonged." Nationalizing states are "of and for a particular ethnocultural 'core nation' whose language, demographic position, economic welfare and political hegemony must be protected and promoted by the state" (ibid., 105).

38. Ibid. See also Valerie J. Bunce, *Subversive Institutions: The Design and the Destruction of Socialism and the State* (Cambridge: Cambridge University Press, 1999).

a measure of cultural autonomy, and protect their national languages and education systems. Indeed, the republics were often governed by national rather than supranational elites. As a result of Soviet (and Yugoslav) ethnofederalism, nationhood could to some extent be consolidated and national identities strengthened under the post–World War II settlement. As Valerie Bunce puts it: "What communism provided to many of the nations of Eastern Europe, in short, were resources [institutionalization of nationhood] and resentment [against Soviet oppression and the socialist system]—precisely what social movement theorists suggest as the key building blocks of political protest."[39]

At the end of the 1980s, liberation from empire was once more formulated in national terms in East Central Europe. While nation-state building advanced under the socialist rule, it remained an unfinished task nevertheless. Some of countries had to reestablish, or establish themselves for the first time, as independent nation-states. Many of them remained plagued by the lack of congruence between state borders and the nations they sought to represent. Despite the huge territorial and population changes during and after World War II, sizable national minorities were still left in nationalizing states, allowing external homelands to continue making claims on their behalf. The unfinished legacy of nation-state building was thus the first to create constraints and opportunities for postsocialist policy makers.

Belated Foreign-Led Industrialization

Timing and form of industrialization brought about another divide between East Central and Western Europe with important consequences. East Central Europe industrialized late, even when compared with some of the Western European latecomers such as Denmark, Sweden, and Norway. Apart from the Czech lands, the region was still predominantly agricultural in the 1930s, with industrial employment rates mostly below 20 percent. Moreover, these economies depended heavily on FDI for industrialization.[40] Foreign influence was not limited to capital imports. In contrast to Western Europe, domestic social groups on which to base industrialization were also largely absent. Early modern times brought the emergence of merchant capital and commercial farming in large parts of Western Europe, but East Central Europe stepped back toward renewed feudalism and a "second serfdom." It was only in the second half of the nineteenth century that "serfs were liberated, noble privileges were abolished, and feudal institutions were mostly eliminated."[41]

39. Bunce, "The National Idea," 430. See also Mark R. Beissinger, *Nationalist Mobilization and the Collapse of the Soviet State* (Cambridge: Cambridge University Press, 2002).

40. Berend, *History Derailed,* 134–42, and 157–58; David Turnock, *The Economy of East Central Europe 1815–1989: Stages of Transforming a Peripheral Region* (London: Routledge, 2006), 206.

41. Berend, *History Derailed,* 184.

The region's arrested development all but prohibited urbanization, the emergence of free labor, or proto-industrialization. When industrial development started to take off in the nineteenth century, it did so under the political and economic dominance of the landed aristocracy. Although some landlords turned into capitalists, industrialization relied mostly on foreign entrepreneurship and the import of skilled workers. Many pioneers of capitalist business in the region, including the most advanced Czech lands, were German, Austrian, British, or Swiss. A substantial part of the skilled workforce originated from Germany or Austria.[42] Drawing on earlier scholarship, Berend argues that as a consequence of late industrialization without breakthrough, the sustained significance of the landed aristocracy, and the importance of ethnic minorities in the urban classes, these societies were characterized by dualistic features, in which each domestic social class was supplemented by minorities.[43]

Through the Holocaust of the Jews, and the migration and expulsion of millions of Germans after World War II, formerly important urban middle-class groups were eliminated, and many East Central European countries once again had to face the challenge of insufficient entrepreneurship, capital, and professional expertise.

In reaction to dependence and backwardness, nationalist protectionism and state interference in the economy had been constant companions of the region's industrialization. Generally, industrialization took off behind the protective walls of the respective empires. Even within the empires, nascent nationalism spread to the economic sphere. In Hungary and the Polish Kingdom, associations for "buying national products only" were established, and Hungary sought protection against Austrian and Czech competition by promoting its own industrialization through subsidies, tax exemptions and preferential railway rates. Independent Bulgaria and Romania also passed industrial laws, "offering indirect tax, and import tariff exemption, free land, railway rebates and some state purchases of production."[44]

The socialist system provided peculiar solutions to East Central Europe's problems of partial and dependent industrialization and the lack of a domestic bourgeoisie and urban labor force. First, it continued the regional tradition of industrialization behind protective walls. Second, the institutions

---

42. Ibid., 136, 200, Wilfried Schlau, "Der Wandel in der sozialen Struktur der baltischen Länder," in *Die Baltischen Nationen*, ed. Boris Meissner (Cologne: Markus Verlag, 1991), 357–59. For the significance of Jewish, German, and Austrian immigrants in Romanian industrialization see John R. Lampe, "Varieties of Unsuccessful Industrialization: The Balkan States before 1914," *Journal of Economic History* 35, no. 1 (1975): 79–80.

43. Iván T. Berend, "The Historical Evolution of Eastern Europe as a Region," in *Power, Purpose and Collective Choice: Economic Strategy in Socialist States*, ed. Ellen Comisso and Laura D'Andrea Tyson (Ithaca: Cornell University Press, 1989), 165.

44. See Lampe, "Varieties of Unsuccessful Industrialization," 81, and 80–83 on economic nationalism in the Balkans. On economic nationalism in Congress Poland and Hungary, see Berend, *History Derailed*, 140–42; and Turnock, *The Economy of East Central Europe*.

of central planning and state ownership originating in Stalinist industrialization and war preparation eventually led to breakthroughs. State ownership and public investment compensated for the limited availability of capital and entrepreneurship.

As is well known, Soviet-type industrialization focused on heavy industry, especially the development of iron, steel, and traditional engineering sectors, thereby copying the Western model of the late nineteenth and early twentieth centuries. Initially this made it possible to catch up with the West, but from the 1970s the region started again falling behind. In contrast to the West, socialist institutions were not capable of shifting from an extensive "heavy metal"–centered growth path to one characterized by flexible specialization, the expansion of services, and the microelectronic revolution.[45] Socialist industrialization had additional shortcomings beyond its anachronistic industrial structures. It was highly inefficient in utilizing both labor and investment, caused tremendous environmental damage, and produced low-quality goods.

While the physical legacies of heavy industrialization were not conducive to successful reindustrialization after socialism, some of the major social changes that went hand in hand with socialist industrial development were. In the socialist system masses of peasants were forcefully turned into urban workers. One major albeit often overlooked function of the socialist mobilization machine was to familiarize—through membership in a wide variety of mass organizations—large peasant masses with the skills and values of workers, such as regular work attendance, skill and quality improvement, and cooperative behavior with peers.[46]

In addition, through what Berend calls a "belated educational revolution,"[47] the socialist system significantly improved general education and workers' specific skills. It introduced comprehensive preschooling, as well as extended primary and generalized secondary education. Secondary education and higher education alike were dominated by vocational-oriented training, endowing large parts of the population with specific, industry-related skills.

All in all, late industrialization presented the East Central European states with a second set of specific legacies. Socialism left behind an outdated and

45. Iván T. Berend, *Central and Eastern Europe, 1944–1993: Detour from the Periphery to the Periphery* (Cambridge: Cambridge University Press, 1996); Charles Maier, "The Collapse of Communism: Approaches for a Future History," *History Workshop* 31 (Spring 1991): 34–59.

46. In the early 1970s, "an absolute majority of workers in Hungary, Yugoslavia, Bulgaria and Romania …were people who had grown up in peasant families. Only in Poland, Czechoslovakia and, presumably the GDR did 'hereditary proletarians' constitute a bare majority of the blue-collar ranks (and in Poland this threshold evidently had only very recently been crossed)." Paul M. Johnson, "Changing Social Structure and the Political Role of Manual Workers," in *Blue Collar Workers in Eastern Europe,* ed. Jan F. Triska and Charles Gati (London: George Allen and Unwin, 1981), 33–36.

47. Berend, *Central and Eastern Europe,* 204.

distorted industrial infrastructure, and its breakdown reproduced the historical challenge of how to substitute for absent domestic capitalists. Unlike
in the interwar period and before, however, all of East Central Europe had
accumulated significant manufacturing experience and an abundant pool of
disciplined and skilled workers.

Paternalist Welfare States

In contrast to its lag in industrialization, East Central Europe kept pace with
the development of welfare states in the rest of Europe—at least to some degree.[48] As shown by Tomasz Inglot, the region's most advanced welfare states
had imperial roots. The Austrian and Hungarian parts of the Habsburg
Empire were the first in Europe to follow the Bismarckian reforms of the
1880s, albeit to a more limited extent, and these systems continued in the
successor states. Poland's former German territories had the most encompassing welfare arrangements of the time.

During the interwar period, welfare state development became an integral part of nation-state building projects across the region. Welfare state
expansion resulted from the aim of elites to create loyalty to the new states,
and to some degree also from the pressure of tiny, but radical and mobilized working classes. An important characteristic of interwar East Central
European welfare systems was their state-paternalist character.

After World War II, socialism put in place encompassing systems of social
protection including pension, sickness, and disability benefits as well as generous family policies and public health care provision. As full employment
was a major pillar of the socialist system of welfare, social insurance reached
nearly universal coverage. In addition, governments heavily subsidized consumption of food, housing, and energy. However, social assistance and unemployment insurance were practically nonexistent.

In addition to budget-financed social services, a second pillar of social
policies was enterprises themselves, as direct providers of health services,
kindergartens, vocational education, and vacation homes. In some estimates
"Russian enterprises spent around 3–5 percent of GDP on social provision,
and...East European firms spent about half this amount....Large Russian
enterprises provided up to 40% of social expenditure."[49] Accordingly, Claus

---

48. Our summary draws on Branko Milanovic, *Income, Inequality and Poverty during the
Transition from Planned to Market Economy*, World Bank Regional and Sectoral Studies (Wash-
ington, D.C.: World Bank, 1998), 12–22; Dena Ringold, "Social Policy in Postcommunist
Europe: Legacies and Transition," in *Left Parties and Social Policy in Postcommunist Europe*, ed.
Linda J. Cook, Mitchell A. Orenstein, and Marilyn Rueschemeyer (Boulder: Westview Press,
1999), 11–46; Linda J. Cook, *Postcommunist Welfare States: Reform Politics in Russia and Eastern
Europe* (Ithaca: Cornell University Press, 2007), 35–45; and Tomasz Inglot, *Welfare States in East
Central Europe, 1919–2004* (Cambridge: Cambridge University Press, 2008), 25, 54–195. For a
global comparison see Haggard and Kaufman, *Development, Democracy, and Welfare States*.

49. Cook, *Postcommunist Welfare States*, 39–40.

Offe describes the socialist welfare state as a type centered on the productive worker, to whom benefits were allocated in a largely paternalistic way qua status rather than as a social right.[50]

Hence a third important legacy replete with risks and opportunities for East Central European politicians was the existence at the onset of transition of mature welfare states that had emerged from long decades of paternalistic policies, rather than from pressures of strong working classes. The welfare state legacy confronted politicians with contradictory issues. First, existing welfare systems had to be adapted to a new set of problems, such as massive unemployment and the emergence of poverty. Second, similar to the advanced capitalist states, the transforming countries faced financial constraints on their major social programs, especially pension systems. Finally, as East Central Europeans were strongly attached to the public provision of social security, politicians had to take this feeling into account.[51]

Western Betrayal

A last legacy that is important for understanding the postsocialist trajectories is these countries' contradictory, ambivalent, and frequently strained relationship with Western culture and the international community. Ironically, while substantial local elite groups have for long been Western-oriented, neither have they fully believed in their own societies' "Westernness," nor have they trusted the West itself. On the one hand, Love rightly claims that (unlike most other world regions) East Central Europe can be viewed as "quasi-Europe" or "epigonal Europe" in "its formal cultures...legal codes, high art forms, and dominant religious traditions.... [Its] elites' aspirations, sometimes their self-deluding perceptions of local societies, certainly their desire to impress foreigners, all tended to focus on the degree of Westernization. This is not to deny the vigorous search for authentic local roots in some circles, much less the frequently felt ambivalences or even societal self-depreciation."[52]

On the other hand, a common *fil rouge* woven through East Central European perceptions of history is the feeling of repeated betrayal by Western, in particular Western European, powers.[53] Examples abound, as each coun-

---

50. Claus Offe, "The Politics of Social Policy in East European Transitions: Antecedents, Agents, and Agenda of Reform," *Social Research* 60, no. 4 (Winter 1993): 619–83.

51. "Surveys for Russia, Poland and Hungary at various points from the early 1990s through 2000 show that large majorities of respondents—in many cases more than 80 percent—favored state guarantees for jobs, health care, education, pensions, and social benefits." Cook, *Postcommunist Welfare States*, 42.

52. Love, *Crafting the Third World*, 5–6.

53. Whether betrayal is real, and how far the region's "misery" is also due to its own failures, is not our primary concern here, as even perceived betrayal has a great potential to shape politics. However, see the brilliant analysis of István Bibó on how the West's major and faulty policy decisions overshadowed the region's own grave mistakes, leaving behind a pervasive

try can tell from its own painful experience. As is well known, Poland became a victim of German (and Austrian and Russian) expansion at least five times during its history. Hungary's attempt at creating an independent state in 1848 ended with military intervention of the Austrians (and Russians) and the support of Great Britain and France for the uprising of non-Hungarians within Hungarian territory. Seventy years later, due to the territorial reordering after World War I, Hungary lost two-thirds of its territory and 60 percent of its population including many ethnic Hungarians who became stranded as minorities in Romania, Ukraine, Czechoslovakia, and Yugoslavia.

The greatest Czech trauma was, of course, the Munich Agreement of 1938, in which the major European powers gave in to Nazi Germany's aggressive expansion plans, and allowed the annexation of Czechoslovakia's Sudetenland. Western powers could also not prevent the incorporation of East Central Europe in the Soviet bloc, and failed to stand up against Soviet intervention in 1956 in Hungary, and in 1968 in Czechoslovakia.

Just like other important presocialist and socialist legacies, the belief in repeated Western betrayal has influenced the region's most recent attempt to return to Europe. On the one hand, elites' longing for admittance to the "Land of Promise" was overshadowed by the fear that their own societies lacked the ability to follow them, and the suspicion that, ready for a new betrayal, the EU was unwilling to fully integrate East Central Europe, and rather wanted to keep the region at arm's length. On the other hand, while European integration might be seen as "a kind of reassurance against excessive reliance on Berlin-Bonn," and the postsocialist small states might have emulated their Western European counterparts' earlier strategy by "shelter[ing] their bilateral dependence on Germany in multilateral European arrangements,"[54] for East Central Europe the past holds more complicated lessons. Policymakers had to face difficult decisions on whether to trust Western Europe or to turn to the United States for guarantees of independence. Indeed, the general topic of settlement of Western Europe's historical debt toward its East Central European neighbors has been more or less permanently on the agenda of intellectual and foreign policy debates in the region.

Within a European context, then, East Central Europe's legacies are unique in three ways: they are marked by a deep impact of great powers and their conflicts; they reflect permanent preoccupation and frustration with the "unfinished business" left behind by the past; and they exhibit a mixture of regime-specific and region-specific successes and failures, assets and liabilities.

---

sense of betrayal. István Bibó, "A kelet európai kisállamok nyomorúsága" [The misery of East European small states], in *Válogatott tanulmányok* [Selected studies], vol. 2, ed. István Vida and Endre Nagy (Budapest: Magvető Könyvkiadó, 1986 [1946]), 185–266.

54. Peter J. Katzenstein, "Germany and Mitteleuropa: An Introduction," in *Mitteleuropa between Europe and Germany*, ed. Peter J. Katzenstein (Providence: Berghahn Books, 1998), 3.

Interpreting the Historical Legacies

This overview allows us to revisit the key conceptual issues of the emergence of specific political opportunity structures of consent and contestation, and their contribution to regime formation. We borrow this concept from social movement theory. Sidney Tarrow defines political opportunity structures as "consistent—but not necessarily formal or permanent—dimensions of the political environment that provide incentives for people to undertake collective action by affecting their expectations for success or failure."[55]

While inspired by Tarrow's notion, our interpretation is specific in three ways. We put the stress on those dimensions of the political environment that were able to structure the fortunes of transformative policies at the crucial turning point of systemic collapse when uncertainty magnified the opportunities and risks involved in political action. Relatedly, our focus is on historical legacies, that is, the more permanent constituents of the emerging political arena. Finally, we consider opportunity structures' potentials to orient and constrain conventional and nonconventional politics, democratic party competition, and social movement activism alike. Along these lines, our argument is as follows.

First, a multitude of unfinished business and the related historical ambivalences allowed reformers to pick and choose the tasks on which to settle and in what order. A major dividing line across our cases runs among those countries that inherited independent nation-states and those that did not. It would therefore be logical to assume that the latter would prioritize nation-state building over other issues. Actual decisions, however, did not follow such a straightforward logic, as it was only in the Baltic states and Croatia that national independence enjoyed unequivocal priority over any other goal of the early transformation agenda. National independence there was an end in itself, worth any economic and social pain.[56]

In contrast, for Slovak and Slovene reformers independence was a means to achieve broader socio-economic goals that could not be realized within

55. Sidney G. Tarrow, *Power in Movement* (Cambridge: Cambridge University Press, 1994), 85. See, for a pioneering attempt at capturing postsocialist transformative politics by the terms and concepts of social movement theory, Sidney G. Tarrow, "Understanding Political Change in Eastern Europe," *PS: Political Science and Politics* 3 (1991): 12–20. For a thorough review and analysis of the concept of political opportunity structures in its varied uses by social movement scholars see David S. Meyer and Debra C. Minkoff, "Conceptualizing Political Opportunity," *Social Forces* 82, no. 4 (June 2004): 1457–92.

56. Rawi Abdelal, *National Purpose in the World Economy* (Ithaca: Cornell University Press, 2001). For Croatia see Ivo Bićanić and Vojmir Franičević, "Understanding Reform: The Case of Croatia," The wiiw Balkan Observatory Working Papers 033 (Vienna: Vienna Institute for International Economic Studies, 2003), 4, http://www.wiiw.ac.at/balkan/Files/GDN_Croatia.PDF.UnderstandingReform (accessed May 6, 2008).

their respective federations. Slovak political actors tried to preserve some of the social and economic achievements of socialism. The fact that the social consequences of Czech-led economic transformation hit their country earlier and harder than the Czech lands is a more plausible explanation of Slovak leaders' eventual preference for a "velvet divorce" than preexisting collective commitments to independent nationhood. Premier Vladimír Mečiar's government first tried to negotiate favorable terms within Czechoslovakia, and its demands for secession intensified only after this attempt failed.

Slovenia was the most advanced republic within the Yugoslav federation, and it gained most from the economic decentralization of the mid 1970s. It took the danger of recentralization and increasing resource transfer to less developed republics as well as the fear of falling behind the more dynamically transforming Visegrád states to convince political elites that national independence was indispensable for continuing Slovenia's socio-economic success story.

Let us in this context recall a widely cited passage from Max Weber's introduction to the *Economic Ethics of the World Religions:* "Not ideas, but material and ideal interests directly govern men's conduct. Yet very frequently the 'world images' that have been created by 'ideas' have, like switchmen, determined the tracks along which action has been pushed by the dynamic of interests."[57]

Accordingly, we argue that the "switchman" setting the Baltic countries on the neoliberal track was the idea of national independence. It legitimated the economic and social costs of transformation as the price of autonomy from the Soviet Union. All the more so as nationalism was not only what Anderson calls "official—i.e. something emanating from the state, and serving the interests of the state first and foremost"[58]—but it had a strong popular base as well, at least initially.

The idea of national independence acted as switchman in Croatia too. In contrast to the Baltic states, however, nationalism derailed the country from undertaking economic and political reforms. As Ivo Bićanić and Vojmir Franičević argue, "When the federal prime minister started proposing radical economic reforms, nationalists' agendas had already filled a political space and became too powerful to be successfully contested by the political message of the program, even when it became clear that it has a potential of being a real alternative, not only to nationalism, but to communism too."[59] As we will further elaborate below, in the Croatian case nationalism and war also weakened state capacity to implement economic reform decisions, which made that country the regional laggard in its transformation towards democracy and capitalism.

---

57. Max Weber, "The Social Psychology of the World Religions," in Gerth and Mills, *From Max Weber,* 280. We are indebted to Richard Swedberg for this reference.

58. Anderson, *Imagined Communities,* 159.

59. Bićanić and Franičević, "Understanding Reform," 4.

In contrast, in countries whose national existence had been less truncated or threatened under (or right after) socialism, or in which the idea of national independence was only one among several main purposes of transformation, combating social vulnerabilities through satisfaction of popular material interests proved more salient in mobilizing consent for reform policies.

The initial tasks transformative elites set themselves also provided the lenses through which they viewed socialism's and earlier historical periods' legacies. To generate support for the core tasks chosen by the Visegrád group and Slovenia, namely long-overdue economic modernization projects, reformers emphasized a degree of continuity with the past. In particular, their citizens were promised that while returning to Europe they did not have to leave the East empty-handed. Instead, the ruins of socialism, whether institutional practices, human skills, or acquired welfare status, were to be used as building blocks of the new capitalist order.[60] Such "bricolage," however, implied that policymakers would tame the "destructive" potential of market forces and foster their "creativity,"[61] which was the main promise of embedded neoliberalism.

In contrast, politicians in the Baltic states saw the new institutions' main advantages in their sharp discontinuity with the remnants of the Soviet past. They stressed the need for leaving the East as fast as possible, emphasized the merits of a clear break with socialism's worthless or outright dangerous legacies, and belittled the economic and social losses caused by neoliberal restructuring. With more resolve and passion than leaders in other countries, Baltic politicians tended to depict Russia as non-European,[62] and interpreted European integration as a return to "normality." If in 1940 the Baltic states had been conquered and "Sovietized" by the Red Army, which meant a break with normality, then rooting out the Soviet period's legacy could rightly be termed normalization.[63]

Generally, the above perspectives differed in the extent to which and forms in which they integrated the socialist past (and earlier periods) into the flow of national history. More specifically, these perceptions also served as interpretive frames for many concrete elements of inheritance: witness the sharply conflicting views of the performance of the socialist economy and of the skills and social status of its workers and pensioners.

The economic output of the socialist system, as measured by GDP, was assessed differently by politicians in various countries. During the 1990s there was no expert consensus on this matter, and the uncertainty about the

60. See for the original argument Stark and Bruszt, *Post-Socialist Pathways*.

61. Joseph A. Schumpeter, *The Theory of Economic Development: An Inquiry into Profits, Capital, Credit, Interest, and the Business Cycle* (Cambridge: Harvard University Press, 1968 [1942]).

62. Valerie J. Bunce, "The Visegrad Group: Regional Cooperation and European Integration in Post-Communist Europe," in Katzenstein, *Mitteleuropa*, 241.

63. Mart Laar, *Estonia: Little Country That Could* (Bury St. Edmunds: St Edmundsbury Press, 2002).

objective figures allowed wildly diverse opinions. In turn, the varied perceptions of inherited economic potential fundamentally shaped the views of
postsocialist dynamics and the impact of liberalization, and ultimately influenced the extent to which the new order's superiority could be substantiated
by data on actual economic performance.

At the onset of transformation reformers viewed "economic performance
in Czechoslovakia... [as] tolerable if unpromising. The silent majority of its
citizens during the last two decades obtained 'automobilism' and a 'weekend-
house culture,' labor effort is not very high, and in spite of various shortages and bottlenecks we are living 'a life of ease.' "[64] Their perception was
grounded on estimates that put initial Czech per capita GDP close to EU
levels. According to anecdotal evidence, Minister of Industry and Trade
Vladimír Dlouhý "insisted, against more 'pessimistic' estimates, that Czech
GDP per capita was not much behind Austria's."[65] Since leaders were convinced that Czechoslovakia was relatively well endowed with inherited assets,
and economic actors needed a grace period to adapt, they opted for "looking
for a non-crisis scenario."[66]

Estonian politicians had very different perceptions. Assessing the economic legacy, Premier Mart Laar attributed to the socialist economy a strikingly high proportion of " 'pure socialist output,' meaning that part of total
output which could be maintained, if at all, only under a socialist economic
order." Under "normal" (i.e. capitalist) conditions such production was "unwanted," not demanded by anyone. Were pure socialist output deducted
from national accounts, "the fall in the GDP at the time of economic reform
would be smaller."[67] Laar's perception had its roots in the view, shared by
many international advisers, that the socialist industrial plant was a site of
"sheer value detraction" rather than value creation. If this was indeed the
case, then radical marketization could not be all that destructive, as ceasing
unwanted production did not imply real losses.[68]

The decision on accepting or rejecting the socialist economy as an integral part of the region's past development crystallized in no less divergent perceptions of the skills, status, and general social standing of its

64. Klaus and Jezek, "Social Criticism," 39.
65. Drahokoupil, *Globalization and the State,* 71.
66. Klaus and Jezek, "Social Criticism," 39.
67. Laar, *Estonia,* 24–25.
68. Scandalized by the colossal waste produced by the socialist economy, Anders Aslund
claimed that "Soviet fishermen caught excellent fresh fish. But rather than sell it on the market, they processed it into (often inedible) fish conserves, reducing the fish's value to almost
zero. This value detraction was recorded, incorrectly, as value added in national accounts
and thus included in the GDP. ...Proper national accounts should thus exclude most of the
'production' of consumer goods and processed foods, and any elimination of such value detraction is positive for real output." He hoped that such correction was going to "alter the
perception of post-communist transformation," as regrettably "absurd official statistics herald
non-reforming and miserable [*sic*] Belarus as far more successful than, say, reforming Latvia
and Lithuania." Aslund, "The Myth," 6, 17.

employees—whether still active or already retired. To cite a Czech example, Jan Amos Havelka, former CEO of the investment promotion agency Czechinvest, kept the following memory from a promotion trip to Asia: "We...made the point that an investor can find cheap but unqualified labor in many places—but not in the Czech Republic. There you get a trained worker for very low cost. Klaus learned about that. He started to lecture me: 'How can you talk like this?...You cannot do that. We are not bushmen or monkeys. We should be compared to Denmark or to the Netherlands.' "[69]

Unlike Czech leaders, who credited workers with the capacity to adapt to the high standards of sophisticated production, Estonian politicians were less optimistic about the quality of inherited labor forces. Criticizing employees in state administration, Premier Laar commented that it "is not possible to teach an old dog new tricks. People who worked in the Soviet system and made a career for themselves find it hard to adapt to the requirements set by society. If you have based your entire career not on honest work but on lies and deceit, then it is unrealistic to expect that you will now start to change."[70]

Latvian politicians were similarly skeptical about the actual value of inherited skills. Juris Dreifelds observed that, although confirmed by census data, "the higher educational achievement rate of Russians in particular has created psychological problems for most Latvians... [who] do not accept the veracity of the 1989 data...in the spring of 1992 the Minister of Education of Latvia explained the 'anomaly' as arising from misreporting on census forms, especially by [Russian] officers' wives who considered some 'insignificant' diploma as the equivalent of a university degree."[71] By the same token, diverging perceptions of the value created and skills accumulated during a working life back in socialism led to contrasting views of the social rights acquired in its course, such as the right to pensions that would help avoid pauperization of the elderly. (For the contrasting examples of Latvia versus Hungary or Poland see chapter 3, "Nationalist Social Contracts," and chapter 4, "Welfarist Social Contracts.")

69. Interview conducted by Jan Drahokoupil on 30 December 2005 in Prague; Drahokoupil, *Globalization and the State,* 70.

70. Laar, *Estonia,* 168. Negative perceptions of the work habits and skills of socialist workers are also widespread in scholarly accounts. For instance, comparing the situation of Polish workers under communist rule with that of English laborers under the ill-conceived Speenhamland welfare regime of 1795 analyzed by Polanyi, Maurice Glasman wrote that both the former and the latter "led to the pauperization of the self-sufficient, the erosion of personal morality and the destruction of work skills vital to the health of the body politic. ...The effects of paternalism on the 'substance' of the common culture were so devastating that anything seemed better in comparison. In time the victims of the new regime either passively acquiesced in, or actively supported, market utopianism as a way of rescuing their freedom and dignity." Maurice Glasman, "The Great Deformation: Polanyi, Poland and the Terrors of Planned Spontaneity," in *The New Great Transformation? Change and Continuity in East-Central Europe,* ed. Christopher Bryant and Edmund Mokrzycki (London: Routledge, 1994), 198.

71. Juris Dreifelds, *Latvia in Transition* (Cambridge: Cambridge University Press, 1996), 159.

None of the bombastic generalizations that socialist manufacturing equaled value detraction, that the products of food industry were inedible,[72] that workers were paupers with useless skills, and that working lives were short of accomplishments, strikes us as convincing. Nevertheless, the inaccuracy of these views (or of the opposite kind of exaggerations, for that matter) is not our concern here. Our point is rather that partly in disregard of its objective features, the socialist legacy was perceived either as a source of assets or as worthless and dangerous, and could be related to the "utopias" of the market and Europe either in pragmatic terms or by the contrast of its "pathological" aspects. In a different context, scholars argued that "utopias and pathologies supply the raw material for political debates about the paradigms they express."[73] Accordingly, when skillfully deployed, the above interpretations could help politicians mobilize consent for initial policy choices and seek legitimacy.

A basic proposition of the argument presented so far is that transformative political actors could choose among possible tasks, and had the capacities to implement the policies following from their choices. In three countries, however, this does not seem to have been the case. Romania and Bulgaria are well known for their "stop and go" policies, and in Croatia the priority of achieving national independence in the context of Yugoslav secession wars derailed the country's progress toward democracy and capitalism. All three countries initially also shared questionable democratic credentials.

Two of these countries are distinguished by their patterns of state formation and economic development before and under socialism, which set them apart from the rest of East Central Europe, and place them closer to the postsocialist countries further east and south. According to Herbert Kitschelt and his co-authors, the Romanian and Bulgarian regimes had started the transformation as successors of "patrimonial communism," so that they were characterized by little past experience with formal bureaucratic rule, and persistent strong networks of patronage and clientelism.[74]

Weak transformative state capacities suggest that the initial choices of political elites were much less consequential in these states than elsewhere in East Central Europe. Economic reforms were only reluctantly attempted, were often slowed or watered down, and fell victim to pervasive corruption. Achieved liberalization tended to escape the control of public authority. The

---

72. *De gustibus non disputandum.* Yet in our recollection, and contrary to Aslund's skepticism about the meager culinary value of socialist food products, while Riga sprats, Szeged salami, Prague ham, Thuringian bratwurst, Yerevan cognac, or Pilsner beer were not always easy to come by, they were perfectly edible and drinkable. Indeed, once upon a time Hungarian tomatoes still tasted like real tomatoes—in contrast to the imported Dutch produce that replaced them in the course of EU integration.

73. Ellen Commisso, Steven Dubb, and Judy McTigue, "The Illusion of Populism in Latin American and East Central Europe," in *Flying Blind: Emerging Democracies in East-Central Europe,* ed. György Szoboszlai (Budapest: Hungarian Political Science Association, 1991), 27.

74. Kitschelt et al., *Postcommunist Party Systems,* 23–24, 39–41.

emerging capitalisms exhibited features of growth driven by particularistic domestic interests, rather than the impact of coordinated public efforts to build a new order.

In Bulgaria, Romania and Croatia, it took the devastating crises of the second half of the 1990s to eventually move them past the threshold of democratic government, and settle on their own variants of pure or embedded neoliberalism, respectively. For all these reasons, notwithstanding superficial similarities between the Baltic states' and Bulgarian or Romanian neoliberalism on the one hand, and the Visegrád states' and Croatia's embedded neoliberalism on the other, these regimes, which at first glance look like two variants of a similar species, are thus qualitatively different. In contrast to the "state-crafted" capitalist regimes of most countries of the region, Southeastern European capitalisms originated in weak state capacities, limited party competition, and strong reliance on patronage politics and corruption.

The First Phase of Regime Formation: Summary

Let us recapitulate the argument we have put forward so far. To understand the emerging economic order, we first took a closer look at the paradigm that guided economic reforms in the early 1990s. With the exception of Slovenia, all countries of the region that had the capacity to choose their reform paths did embrace some form of economic neoliberalism. Given the severe social dislocations that the neoliberal strategy entailed, as well as its meager performance, governments needed to draw on broader sources for support. To this end, they could either resort to identity politics or try and mitigate the deleterious social impact of marketization by compensating for (some of its) costs.

It was the political opportunity structures emerging with the disintegration of the socialist system that shaped the likelihood of identity or material welfare issues, and the implied distinct cleavages and social contracts, dominating the arena within which political struggles over economic reforms were staged. At the same time, as the disintegration of socialism confronted reformers with many unfinished tasks, political elites had both a choice of and a decisive and politically motivated say in which tasks to prioritize. In all those countries that did not inherit nation-states from socialism, a stronger case for the priority of nation building could be made, and identity politics could be more relied on as a source of political support. However, the actual extent to which this opportunity was used, and national independence viewed as an end in itself or rather as a means to achieve broader socioeconomic goals, crucially depended on political decisions.

The degree to which concerns over social welfare entered reform politics shaped the embeddedness of the new economic order. This was so because in the political arenas where above all material interests acquired a formative role, politics was more likely to feed demands for social welfare and industrial

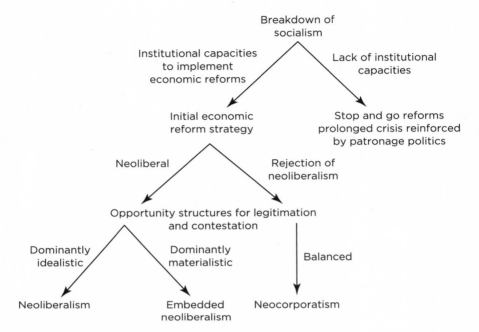

Figure 2.1 Postsocialist regime formation: The first phase

protection back into the economic reform process. For the same reason, re-formers were also likelier to work with the remnants of socialism, rather than turning their backs on them.

Even though economic reforms were fused with nationalism, or their so-cial impact was mitigated by compensatory policies, or consent was mobi-lized by a combination of both, domestic resources alone eventually proved insufficient to create solid support for the new order. In the second half of the 1990s, popular patience with reforms started to wear out. At this point, however, international actors and markets came to the rescue of the fragile new regimes. The manifold ways in which the international context shaped regime paths are discussed in the rest of this chapter.

Returning to the West: Transnationalization and European Integration

A further building block in our argument about regime formation and con-solidation in East Central Europe is the key importance we attribute to the role played by transnational actors, institutions, and markets. Via economic liberalization and market-oriented institution building, the East Central

European countries have also integrated into the systems of production, commerce, and finance of global and European capital, while their return to Europe has made them part and parcel of a broader regional integration project. From the early 2000s onwards, scholars have recognized the initially ignored salience of transnational aspects of East Central European transformations.

The major contention of the Europeanization and transnationalization literature is accurately summarized by Mitchell Orenstein and his collaborators:

> "A quadruple transition framework suggests that the projects of nation-state building, democratization, and marketization have been embedded within transnational agendas and pressures, most importantly but not limited to those of the EU.... The quadruple transition framework rests on the observation that transnational integration limited the scope for disruptions and disjunctures that had been theorized between the various transition projects. At first ignored, transnational actors turned out to be the dark matter that held the various aspects of postcommunist transition together in Central and Eastern Europe."[75]

To understand how transnationalization and Europeanization have contributed to East Central European regime formation and stability, we draw on the framework proposed by Wade Jacoby to capture external influences on domestic institutional change in postsocialist Europe.[76]

Forms of External Influence

Based on a review of numerous studies devoted to the issue, Jacoby distinguishes three forms of external influence. "Inspiration" is the least interventionist among them. It refers to ideas about ultimate goals or concrete steps in reform programs. As opposed to inspiration, "substitution" is the most interventionist form of influence. It is characterized by direct external intervention with the aim to push certain reforms and institutions. Examples are military occupation or economic sanctions.

Finally, in the "coalition" approach, external actors seek to actively influence domestic reforms by building coalitions with domestic social forces. Jacoby stresses that the coalition approach often strengthens "minority" traditions within countries, and has the effect of empowering like-minded reformers: "In particular, the coalition approach emphasizes that outsiders may lengthen PCRs' [postcommunist reformers] time horizons such that

75. Mitchell A. Orenstein, Stephen R. Bloom, and Nicole Lindstrom, ed., *Transnational Actors in Central and East European Transitions* (Pittsburgh: University of Pittsburgh Press), 6.

76. Wade Jacoby, "Inspiration, Coalition, and Substitution: External Influences on Postcommunist Transformations," *World Politics* 58, no. 4 (July 2006): 623–51.

they are willing to trade off short-term gains against longer-term benefits that may flow from better policies. Outsiders can also broaden the circle of interested reformers and even help them deter domestic opponents."[77]

Jacoby's typology provides a useful starting point for tackling the problem of how the international context has shaped regime formation and contributed to stability in East Central Europe. Thus, while we earlier stressed the attraction of neoliberalism in a postsocialist context, it is of course also the case that international actors have had a decisive role in its region-wide diffusion. The East Central European countries have (re)joined the West at a specific historical juncture. The crises of the Fordist production regime and Keynesian regulation in the 1970s triggered a phase of experimentation with diverse strategies of how to restore growth and productivity, and settle on macroeconomically more viable paths. By the time communism collapsed, neoliberalism had become the most influential policy paradigm around the world. Initial policies, in Jacoby's terminology, were thus "inspired" by the hegemonic paradigm. That is, international advocates of existing best practices advised East Central European reformers on "the end state of particular institutional or policy reforms or how to execute such reforms."[78]

As discussed above, however, neoliberalism did not lend itself as a basis for clear-cut ideas about the eventual outcome of policy reforms, nor had international actors conceived a blueprint for transformation. Instead, the dramatic collapse of socialism took them no less by surprise than their counterparts in the countries concerned. Accordingly, they were uncertain about what exactly was to be done. In the early 1990s, numerous international missions were climbing steep learning curves about where the region had been coming from and where it was heading.

Nonetheless, external advisers were eager to repeat the general mantra of stabilization, liberalization, and privatization, and to stress the need for speed in reforming. They were also active in propagating ideas about how to execute specific reforms, although different advisory teams' proposals were sometimes at odds with each other. For instance, the Estonian government was visited by a group of international advisers led by Sachs that promoted the idea of the currency board at the same time that members of an IMF mission cautioned against it (see chapter 3, "The Politics of Early Economic Reforms"). All in all, international inspiration was part of transformative policymaking from the early 1990s, but it was largely up to domestic political forces to let themselves be inspired. Slovenian policymakers were clearly the least impressed.

77. Ibid., 629. Jacoby's trinity has important antecedents. See especially Barbara Stallings, "International Influence on Economic Policy: Debt, Stabilization, and Structural Reform," in *The Politics of Economic Adjustment: International Constraints, Distributive Conflicts, and the State*, ed. Stephan Haggard and Robert R. Kaufman (Princeton: Princeton University Press, 1992), 41–88.

78. Jacoby, "Inspiration, Coalition, and Substitution," 628.

The nature of inspiration has changed over time. On the one hand, experiences with the policy packages adopted throughout the region made international actors more certain about the factors affecting the chances of economic success and failure. On the other hand, regional success stories started to be held up as models for laggards. Take the Estonian example: once their reforms became acknowledged as a road to success, currency boards and flat taxes started to appear in the IMF's recommendations to all postsocialist countries that were threatened by currency crises or lacked the capacity to attract FDI. In the laggard countries Bulgaria and Romania, inspiration turned at times into outright conditionality. Even so, the degree to which transnational inspiration affected institution building depended largely on domestic political factors all over East Central Europe.[79]

From the second half of the 1990s, the EU stepped in as a central actor with a strong influence on the region's reform processes. The form of EU influence is best captured by the coalition pattern. Domestic forces were fervently pushing for EU membership all over East Central Europe, while EU actors used the accession process to lock in local commitments to a liberal-democratic order.

Empowerment of reformers, which was crucial for the coalition pattern to work, occurred through several mechanisms. First, the perspective of EU membership bestowed transformation with a concrete goal and a road map to get there. There is no doubt that accession conditionality made it more rewarding for policymakers to follow the roadmap. Importantly, it lengthened the time horizons of political actors.

In this respect the EU could exert the strongest influence on regime formation in those countries that had initially not settled on coherent development paths. In the "electoral revolutions" of Bulgaria, Romania, and Croatia international influences, including those of the EU, helped tip the balance in favor of promarket, prodemocratic, and pro-European actors. The perspective of EU membership led domestic politicians to be more open to the demands of other international actors as well. These countries' paths of joining the East Central European success stories with a delay and more by "default" than design, has thus reflected greater international influences.[80]

Second, one of the major efforts of the EU in the region was directed toward advancing administrative, institutional, and regulatory capacities. This was in line with the key role attributed to effective regulation by the EU's

79. For Romania and Bulgaria see Grigore Pop-Eleches, *From Economic Crisis to Reform: IMF Programs in Latin America and Eastern Europe* (Princeton: Princeton University Press, 2009).

80. Vachudova, *Europe Undivided*. On electoral revolutions, see Valerie J. Bunce and Sharon Wolchik, "International Diffusion and Postcommunist Electoral Revolutions," *Communist and Post-Communist Studies* 38, no. 3 (September 2006): 283–304. A fourth candidate country in which an electoral revolution set pro-European forces in the driving seat was Slovakia. In contrast to the Southeastern European states, Slovakia's economic reform path under Vladimír Mečiar was not incompatible with the EU's requirements. For more detail on the Slovak case see chapter 4.

policymaking bodies. As argued by Giandomenico Majone, the *acquis communautaire* governing the internal market and the common policies has been an exercise in regulatory state building on multiple levels of European governance. Majone defines the regulatory state as a state where "rule making is replacing taxation and spending."[81]

The rise of the regulatory state is in direct relationship to the neoliberal turn Western European economies have taken since the 1980s. It is characterized by the delegation of policymaking power to regulatory agencies, and by the growing influence of nonmajoritarian institutions and courts. In consequence, policymaking is being shifted away from parliaments, parties, and civil servants to regulators, experts, and judges. European integration has contributed to the depoliticization of policymaking by removing crucial policy areas from the realm of national decisionmaking.

Regulatory capacity building associated with the accession process has helped to stabilize the nascent East Central European regimes. Importantly, it has strengthened effective government, and this way increased the new order's legitimacy. Effective government is particularly salient in this region, where the popular component of democracy is overall weakly institutionalized. The electorate is unstructured, volatile, uncertain, and only partially mobilized. Parties are predominantly elite-based with weak links to civil society. Party competition, however, is fierce, as the electorate is up for grabs in each election, decision load is high, and the rules of the game fall short of being settled.[82]

Under these conditions, legitimacy based on governments' responsiveness to the electorates' preferences—in Fritz Scharpf's words "input legitimacy,"—is hard to achieve. Governments can, however, aim to achieve "output legitimacy" stemming from their capacity to solve problems of the governed.[83] The required skill and will have been enhanced by EU conditionality with its stress on depoliticization, regulation, administrative capacity building, and rule by experts. With a reform blueprint in place, EU accession has also put a limit on party competition over substantive issues. Instead, mainstream parties have begun to compete over their competence for administering the challenging reform agenda.[84]

While all of this worked well during the accession process, the narrow focus on output legitimacy and restricted party competition over substantive

81. Giandomenico Majone, "From the Positive to the Regulatory State: Causes and Consequences of Changes in the Mode of Governance," *Journal of Public Policy* 17, no. 2 (1997): 139; see also László Bruszt and Gerald A. McDermott, "Transnational Integration Regimes as Development Programs," forthcoming in *Review of International Political Economy*.

82. Peter Mair, *Party System Change: Approaches and Interpretations* (Oxford: Oxford University Press, 1997), 175–98.

83. Fritz Scharpf, *Governing in Europe: Effective and Democratic?* (Oxford: Oxford University Press, 1999).

84. Anna Grzymala-Busse and Abby Innes, "Great Expectations: The EU and Domestic Political Competition in East Central Europe," *East European Politics and Societies* 17, no. 64 (2003): 66–67.

policy alternatives has had its drawbacks. This has become more obvious with full membership in the EU when, notwithstanding the facts that the desired goal was attained and conditionality ceased to work, the EU has still kept pressuring new members for further reforms in order to ensure compliance with the Maastricht convergence criteria of Economic and Monetary Union (EMU) enlargement. The ongoing reform drives have lacked popular support in the embedded neoliberal countries, where further convergence on the EU requirements has entailed a rush for monetary and exchange rate stability, fiscal discipline, and welfare state retrenchment. Especially the latter issue has maintained high political prominence on the national level, and popular disenchantment with the ongoing reform drive has led repeatedly to the defeat of pro-Western reformist political forces, and the rise of radical illiberalism or radicalization of formerly moderate centrist parties.

It follows that far from challenging regime diversity, EU accession and full membership have in fact reinforced it while also pushing the whole region toward further (neo)liberalization. The EU's focus on regulatory state building and fiscal discipline has had a differentiated impact across the region. Due to the affinity between the neoliberal regimes' core institutions and the regulatory state model, EU accession and membership have helped consolidate this regime cluster. It has also helped the effort of the laggard states to catch up by strengthening their reform capacities. In contrast, it has exacerbated tensions around the macroeconomic and fiscal policies characteristic of the embedded neoliberal regimes. While not immune to the pressures for fiscal consolidation and welfare state retrenchment, neocorporatist institutions have made Slovenia better able to comply with the requirements of EMU accession while keeping political legitimacy.

Two caveats are, however, in order. Accession conditionality has also corrected some of the most "deviant" institutional and policy choices of the latecomer countries. By monitoring minority rights the EU has contributed to broadening democratic accountability in the two exclusionary democracies Estonia and Latvia. It has also cut back on some of the wilder forms of market freedom by pressuring the neoliberal paragons toward a degree of deliberalization. Conversely, the least neoliberal state, Slovenia, has been pushed toward further marketization and transnationalization. Moreover, as we will argue below, the EU accession process has opened the door for deeper transnationalization of all of the East Central European political economies.

Foreign-Led Reindustrialization, and Deindustrialization

While the Europeanization literature in general and Jacoby's framework in particular help us understand how international institutions interacted with domestic agents, these were not the only forces that mattered for East Central Europe's transnational integration. Early on, TNCs played a major role in shaping the region's diverse development paths.

The EU's decision to start entry negotiations with selected candidates greatly increased the region's attraction for FDI. This was because the perspective of full EU membership amounted to a seal of approval on previously undertaken reforms, and served as a guarantee for further efforts. In addition, accession conditionality entailed privatizing economic infrastructure, most importantly the banking sector. This laid the foundations for a far reaching transnationalization of the financial systems in the region. In what ways have the inflows of transnational capital shaped regime formation and consolidation? To answer this question, we will first offer an interpretation of the different attractions for and impacts of transnational industrial capital in the region.

As Jonas Pontusson argues, capital enjoys " 'systemic power' embedded in the institutional substructure of the economy.... Perhaps the simplest way to think about the systemic power of business is in terms of 'exit options.' "[85] This general concept can be tailored to fit the context of East Central European transformation. First, given the scarcity of capital in the region, it is unsurprising that TNCs became the leading sector of emerging business communities. Second, these firms disposed of systemic power before entering the region's economies: this stemmed from the option to refuse to enter and invest. Third, after FDI materialized, the whole dynamics of Albert Hirschman's "exit, voice, and loyalty"[86] came fully into play, and shaped, depending on foreign firms' strategies and cross-border mobility, the actual form and degree of their power vis-à-vis national governments.

How have TNCs responded to the signals of public authorities? How much have they invested and what have they invested in? In chapter 1 we showed that divergence among regime performances in industrial transformation coincided with variation in FDI inflows into complex industries. How did this variation come about, and what have been the consequences? In the mainstream view FDI is endogenous to the advance of market reforms. For this view, the meager achievements of the Baltic states and Bulgaria and Romania in attracting complex industry FDI and the resulting deskilling of these economies' exports should present a puzzle.

Why have these states proved so ineffective in attracting the main drivers of industrial upgrading if they have been so capable of creating many of its alleged conditions: radically reformed and stabilized economies, low taxes, political stability, and national security? Why have complex industry transnational corporations consistently preferred Visegrád locations over the Baltic area, Bulgaria, and Romania? Our answer is that foreign firms' location choices responded to incentives stemming from a dynamic interplay

85. Jonas Pontusson, *The Limits of Social Democracy: Investment Politics in Sweden* (Ithaca: Cornell University Press, 1992), 233.

86. Albert O. Hirschman, *Exit, Voice, and Loyalty* (Cambridge: Harvard University Press, 1970).

between inherited and restructured production profiles, inherited and newly built market institutions, and special subsidy packages.

To account for transnational corporations' motivation we adapt Raymond Vernon's product cycle theory,[87] and on this basis we argue that export-oriented, complex industry FDI had to flow first to those former socialist economies whose initial production profiles (captured in chapter 1 by the data on manufacturing output, employment, and total goods exports of the late1980s to early 1990s) had been relatively complex (i.e., intensive in technologically sophisticated physical capital and human skills).

As a consequence, the Visegrád countries, which specialized in the automobile, machinery or electronics industries during late socialism, could rightly expect larger inflows of industry-specific FDI than other states (such as those of central Asia) where this sector was virtually absent. However, the main attraction of the Visegrád economies has not been in industry-specific plant, equipment, or infrastructure. All these components needed significant modernization, renewal, and upgrading, tasks that were rapidly undertaken by foreign investors. Rather, the region's advantages in locational competition stemmed above all from inherited complex-manufacturing experience. According to Alice Amsden, manufacturing experience is a "stock of knowledge that passes through a specific historical and institutional filter... [and] emerges as a necessary condition for postwar industrial expansion given that no successful latecomer country managed to industrialize without it."[88]

Similarly, extensive experience with complex manufacturing has been a necessary albeit not a sufficient condition for the successful export-oriented development of the East Central European countries in the aftermath of socialism. In respect of inherited experience, the Baltic and Southeastern European states, which by the last decade of socialism increasingly exchanged technology and skill-intensive goods against natural resources from other parts of the empire or the Third World,[89] were not particularly handicapped relative to the Visegrád countries and Slovenia. Given that on the basis of their production profile initially all East Central European countries seem to have had broadly comparable attractions as new locations for transnational complex export production, product cycle theory alone cannot account for the diverging path taken by the Visegrád and the Baltic and Southeastern European states. How then did investors choose among them?

For an answer we have to consider that even similar production profiles may fail to raise investors' interest if institutional and policy barriers hamper access to the required local factors of production. It follows then, that

87. Raymond Vernon, *Sovereignty at Bay: The Multinational Spread of U.S. Enterprises* (New York: Basic Books, 1971).

88. Alice H. Amsden, *The Rise of "the Rest": Challenges to the West from Late-Industrializing Economies* (Oxford: Oxford University Press, 2001), 15, 21.

89. László Csaba, *Eastern Europe in the World Economy* (Cambridge and Budapest: Cambridge University Press and Akadémiai Kiadó, 1990).

countries which, by the time investors were ready and able to cross the former Cold War borders, advanced furthest in removing entry barriers and rebuilding their institutions and policy regimes were better able to attract FDI.

The evidence presented in chapter 1 confirms that in the first half of the 1990s the Visegrád states outcompeted all other East Central European states, which could start their quest for institutional convergence with the West only with a delay and (except for Croatia) had few if any reformist legacies to build on. In the first phase of the transformation, then, in the context of rather similar production profiles, institutional advantages tilted the balance of investors' preferences in favor of the Visegrád countries. The level of complex industry FDI inflows depended on the levels of marketization inherited and achieved by the early to mid-1990s.

The interplay of structural and institutional factors seems to have fully reversed, and the dependence of complex industry FDI on marketization levels failed to materialize after the mid-1990s. The Baltic states and later Bulgaria and Romania gradually worked off their institutional disadvantage, and by the mid-2000s arrived at a high degree of institutional similarity with their regional rivals and the West. However, their institutional catching up does not seem to have been appreciated by transnational complex industry investors.

What seems to explain these states' inability to attract complex industry FDI after the mid-1990s is that their institutional convergence—the pace of which was dramatic in the Baltic cases—has been achieved at the expense of increasing divergence from the rest of East Central Europe. In the late 1990s, in the context of increasing institutional similarity among the region's countries, transnational corporations continued to prefer the same Visegrád area locations mainly because of their enhanced structural similarity with the West, whereas the Baltic and Southeastern European countries might have lost out due to their different production profiles.

Initial investor preferences, motivated by a combination of structural and institutional factors, seem to have launched both virtuous and vicious cycles of foreign-led capital accumulation. The driving forces included the contrasting trends of industry upgrading versus deindustrialization; the tendency for many more foreign firms to "follow the leader"—their rivals and buyers—to the initially preferred Visegrád locations; the concomitant clustering of complex industries in the same areas; and lastly the generous subsidy packages offered by the Visegrád states to transnational complex industry investors.

Through FDI, the complex industries of the Visegrád states gained access to much-needed tangible and intangible factors of production, upgraded their activities, and developed competitive strengths in the demanding single market. In contrast, deprived of the above advantages and—equally importantly—of compensation for their transformation costs that could have helped their survival in a period of capital scarcity, in the Baltic countries, Bulgaria, and Romania these same industrial sectors could not stand the intense global competition. Instead, they all but lost their markets, factors of production, and policy influence. Moreover, the Baltic course of radical liberalization, rather than breaking the vicious circle, accelerated the atrophy and collapse of complex industries. An entirely different production profile soon emerged with traditional light and resource-based industries and services at its core.

Transnational corporations usually follow their competitors and clients to new production locations, while the first investors try to fend off rivals who follow them, not least by enlarging their already existing facilities.[90] This strategy, observed in all Visegrád countries, further contributed to virtuous cycles of accumulating complex industry FDI. In contrast, the Baltic and Southeastern European states, due to the increasing divergence of their production profiles from that of Western Europe, could neither establish dense linkages to the Visegrád cluster, nor attract adequate FDI to build their own complex-manufacturing growth points.[91]

The competition for complex industry investors through generous incentive packages, which has intensified within the Visegrád group from the first half of the 2000s, has made it even more difficult for outsiders to acquire new investments in these industries (see chapter 4, "Rival Manufacturing Miracles"). The resulting bidding war in incentives has magnified the overall cost of complex FDI inflows and exacerbated the competitive disadvantages of countries outside the cluster, especially if they were structurally handicapped too, like the Baltic and some of the Southeastern European states. Slovenia has been a peculiar participant in this competition, since its complex industries have been attractive for TNCs despite the lack of generous incentives (see chapter 5, "Postsocialist Capitalism in Strong and Weak States").

Foreign Banks and Financialized Growth

Although the neoliberal regimes were largely bypassed by complex-manufacturing investors, this does not mean that their economies were less shaped by TNCs than those of their embedded neoliberal counterparts. FDI in the former countries was heavily concentrated in the banking and real estate sectors. As we noted earlier, the Baltic states' banking sectors have become even more foreign-penetrated than those of other East Central European countries. The region's early and latecomer pure neoliberal regimes have provided particularly fertile ground for finance-led development. Because of inherited backwardness and the governments' harsh stance when facing

90. Raymond Vernon and Louis T. Wells Jr., *Economic Environment of International Business* (Englewood Cliffs: Prentice Hall, 1981), 16–18.
91. On how similar processes of foreign capital accumulation led to increasing disparities between Hungary's fast-growing developed regions and its laggard ones, see David L. Brown, Béla Greskovits, and László Kulcsár, "Leading Sectors and Leading Regions: Economic Restructuring and Regional Inequality in Hungary since 1990," *International Journal of Urban and Regional Research* 31, no. 3 (September 2007): 522–42.

the banking crises of the 1990s, the Baltic states' financial sectors lagged behind those of the Visegrád countries. Until the end of the 1990s, Baltic firms and populations were deprived of access to commercial credits.

This changed with EU accession. The adoption of the institutional and regulatory standards of a sound financial system was part of the EU entry requirements. Fast convergence with the EU standards contributed to a credit boom. In 2000–2004 alone, the average annual credit growth in Bulgaria and the three Baltic countries was 20 percent. This is in contrast to Poland, the Czech Republic and Slovakia, where annual credit growth was below 5 percent. The rest of the region fell in between the two extremes. Credit growth even accelerated after EU accession, and came to a halt only when the global financial crisis hit.

Foreign banks took the lead in generating the credit boom. In the Baltic states, it was Swedish banks for which eastward enlargement provided a great opportunity to expand internationally. Swedish banks, similar to their Austrian, German, and Italian competitors, were motivated by the promise of high returns. They were also actively involved in developing new market segments, and could easily tap into sources of credit expansion via borrowing from their parent banks.[92] To understand the specific significance of credit-financed growth in the neoliberal regimes, it is important to recapitulate the social implications of this path.

Radical reforms, deindustrialization, and meager welfare states have resulted in depressed wages, widespread poverty and wide inequality. Inclusion in labor-intensive transnational production chains has further exacerbated social disparities. Light industry TNCs, rather than significantly investing in local facilities, have usually subcontracted production to a multitude of small or medium-sized domestic firms. While less demanding in terms of generous incentive packages or infrastructure development, these TNCs expected from their hosts above all to keep labor markets flexible, wages, taxes, and social security contributions low, and workers docile. This stands in contrast to the Visegrád countries and Slovenia, where foreign businesses relied more on high-skilled workers whose demands were more easily accommodated than those of the low-skilled labor forces employed in the region's sweatshop economies.

Under these circumstances, credit could expand the purchasing power of struggling (mainly state-dependent) middle classes, and low-wage manufacturing industry workers. This explains the fact that in East Central Europe's

---

92. See for the credit boom and the role of foreign banks Calin Arcalean, Oscar Calvo-Gonzales, Csaba Móré, Adrian van Rixtel, Adalbert Winkler, and Tina Zumer, "The Causes and Nature of the Rapid Growth of Bank Credit in the Central, Eastern, and South-Eastern European Countries," in *Rapid Credit Growth in Central and Eastern Europe*, ed. Charles Enoch and Inci Ötker-Robe (Basingstoke: Palgrave Macmillan, 2007), 23–24; and Katharina Pistor, "Into the Void: Governing Finance in Central & Eastern Europe," Columbia Law and Economics Working Paper 355 (New York: Columbia University, 2009).

pure neoliberal regimes household lending and mortgages constituted the overwhelming share of overall credit growth. As a consequence, the growth pattern of the region's neoliberal cluster mimicked to some extent that of the advanced liberal market economies. In both contexts, a virtuous circle of consumer credits, mortgage lending, and a construction and housing boom reinforced each other. While this circle allowed for spectacular growth rates, it also fueled inflation which, under the fixed exchange rate regime, put more strain on export competitiveness. In short, while financialized growth allowed the Baltic and some of the Southeastern European countries to address social questions that became more pressing in the 2000s than in the 1990s, by the same token it reinforced their specific weaknesses in terms of global competitiveness.

The Second Phase of Regime Formation: Summary and Outlook

The second phase of East Central European regime formation brought about increasing exposure to the influence of transnational actors, and accompanying opportunities and risks. In line with Jacoby's framework we have identified three major forms of external influence: inspiration for reform steps and desirable goals stemming from the broader international context; the emergence of linkages and coalitions between domestic and European actors; and finally the constraints and opportunities brought about by TNCs and world markets. All of these influences have in our view reinforced rather than challenged regime diversity across the region. How could that be the case?

Our answer is that the neoliberal policy paradigm is no *pensée unique*. Its overall preferences for markets over states, private over public actors, and elite policymaking over mass participation allow for a broad range of diversity, and for ideological debates and political conflicts when it comes to concrete institutional design and the ways to get "from here to there." Therefore, East Central European reformers could let themselves be inspired by different ideas and actors, and pick their allies among those who came closest to sharing neoliberal priorities. They were even free to reject major tenets of the paradigm, as was the case in Slovenia.

EU membership was appealing enough to sweep political forces into power that were willing to implement the union's agenda of market making and regulatory state building. Especially by strengthening the candidate governments' effectiveness, EU accession helped stabilize and legitimize the new order across all regimes. At the same time, its impact differed according to the particular varieties of capitalism that were evolving in the region.

Due to the affinity between the neoliberal regimes' core institutions and the regulatory state model, EU accession and membership was most helpful

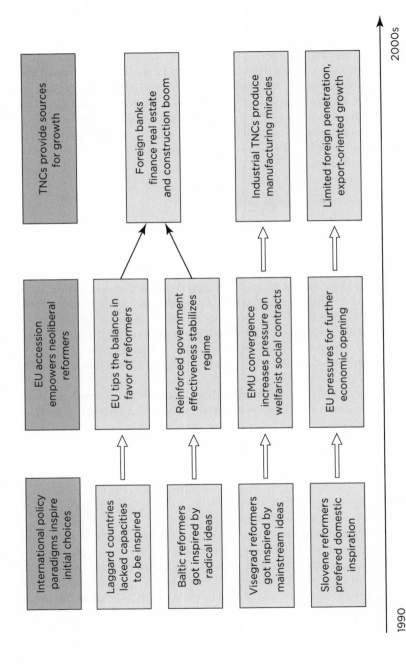

Figure 2.2 Postsocialist regime formation: International factors

in consolidating this particular regime cluster. It also helped the catch-up efforts of the laggard Southeastern European states by strengthening their reform capacities. In contrast, the EU's overall impact on government effectiveness was less pronounced in the Visegrád group where state institutions and administrative capacities had already been developed well before accession. At the same time, the postaccession stress on macroeconomic and fiscal stability put the Visegrád countries under much stronger pressure than the rest of the region.

Finally, transnational capital has played a major part in reinforcing different economic roles and specializations. Legacies of complex manufacturing and advantages in early institution building allowed the Visegrád countries and Slovenia to attract an increasing inflow of FDI in complex-manufacturing industries. While this boosted their export competitiveness, it also put their states under stress. In order to attract and keep FDI, they had to offer generous investment incentives.

The Baltic states, and to a lesser degree Bulgaria and Romania, lost out in the competition for complex-manufacturing TNCs, as radical reforms or an extended period of postsocialist disorder, respectively, all but destroyed their complex-manufacturing sectors. In the 2000s, however, these states benefited from an increasing inflow of FDI into their banking, real estate, and construction sectors, which allowed for credit-fueled growth of the economy.

From all of this it follows that while the processes of EU accession and integration into transnational circuits of manufacturing and financial capital have provided ample opportunities for all regimes, they have also added to their specific vulnerabilities. High export dependency and fierce political conflicts around fiscal consolidation in the Visegrád group are cases in point, as much as the Baltic states' and Romania's and Bulgaria's loss of export competitiveness and dependency on credit. With the global financial crisis, these vulnerabilities have taken center stage. Chapters 3 to 5 will spell out the regime-specific and country-specific interplay among legacies, political choices, international actors, and transnational capital. Chapter 6 is devoted to the analysis of East Central Europe's vulnerabilities in light of the global financial crisis, and to these countries' coping strategies.

Nation Builders and Neoliberals

The Baltic States

The Baltic states stand out for their convergence on radical neoliberal macroeconomic, structural, and social policies. Fast liberalization of foreign trade and investment, fixed exchange rate regimes, tight monetary policies, and rapid privatization have been the hallmark of their transformation strategies. Although the Baltic countries have experienced some of the most severe transformational recessions, they have done little to mitigate the accompanying social hardship. They have also been barely concerned with protecting inherited industries. As a consequence, their industrial capacities have greatly diminished. In contrast, financial, real estate, transport, and communication services have boomed and have attracted the bulk of inward FDI.

Reform radicalism in the subregion has been intrinsically tied to the agenda of nation-state building. Baltic elites saw national independence as their highest priority. They were united in considering Russia's economic and political influence as the biggest threat to their national sovereignty and security. Their transformation strategies aimed at a radical departure from the past, responded to perceived needs of independent statehood, and served the purpose of forging national identities. Due to the shared belief in the urgency of (re)building their nations, Baltic elites were less constrained by the economic and social costs of radical transformation than was the case in other East Central European countries.

Although all three Baltic states have been champions of neoliberalism, they have differed with respect to the speed and coherence of reforms. Estonia has implemented the most comprehensive strategy and has been the first mover in major reform areas, thereby influencing the other two countries. Typically, Latvia has come in a close second, while Lithuania has tended to lag behind. Moreover, in important instances Lithuania has chosen neoliberal solutions only as a result of prolonged political struggles. We see three sets of factors that account for the differences amidst the similarities of neo-liberalism in the Baltic states.

First, while political elites in all three countries have been engaged in the process of nation-state building cum decolonialization, which has provided the rationale for overall radical strategies, Estonian and Latvian power hold-ers have in addition pursued a nationalizing project to reverse the effects of the massive influx of Russian speakers in Soviet times. Nationalizing, as Rogers Brubaker has put it, aims at "a state of and for a particular ethnocul-tural 'core nation' whose language, demographic position, economic wel-fare and political hegemony must be protected and promoted by the state."[1] The nationalizing projects also shaped the party systems in both countries, as they prevented the emergence of parties or governments—in Estonia and Latvia, respectively—that would propose alternatives to the adopted reform paths.

Second, the form and speed of transnational integration can account for some of the differences among the three countries. Estonia was picked early on by Finnish and Swedish investors as a preferred location, which gave it a head start over the two other countries in attracting FDI. In contrast, Latvia banked more heavily on its role as an entrepôt economy for the Russian hinterland by delivering intermediary services for Russia in its transactions with the European economy. Lithuania stands out for its initially limited ac-cess to Western capital and its most protracted reliance on domestic sources and continuing trade relationships with Russia and other parts of the former Soviet Union. The initial difference between Estonia and the two other coun-tries was later acknowledged by the EU, which originally picked Estonia as the single Baltic state to join the first wave of countries to start entry negotia-tions. Thus, in Estonia the nationalizing project that undermined opposition to neoliberalism, and relatively favorable terms of transnational integration, conspired to produce the most consistent neoliberal reform path.

Finally, there has been a regional rationale for neoliberal regime forma-tion, best described by a follow-the-leader logic. Estonia has been considered as the pace-setter for reforms, and its advances have often served as models for the other two Baltic states.

This chapter presents the policy packages chosen by the Baltic govern-ments to master the transformation, and explains the domestic, regional, and international dynamics that account for the specificities. Furthermore, we shall elaborate on the social and economic consequences of these strate-gies, and on the sources of their support despite the hardships they imposed on the Baltic populations. Both the similarities and the differences among the Baltic states will be discussed.

---

1. Brubaker, *Nationalism Reframed*, 105. For a similar interpretation see James Hughes, "'Exit' in Deeply Divided Societies: Regimes of Discrimination in Estonia and Latvia and the Potential for Russophone Migration," *Journal of Common Market Studies* 43, no. 4 (2005): 739–62.

Origins of the National and Nationalizing Projects

When at the end of the 1980s Baltic historians challenged the official Soviet account of their countries' incorporation in the USSR, they heralded a crucial turning point in Soviet-Baltic relations.[2] The subsequent political mobilization against this unlawful action boosted the quest for Baltic national independence, and paved the way for an official and popular reinterpretation of communism as a period in which the republics had been subject to illegal foreign occupation. Reformers in the three countries agreed upon the need to regain the Baltic states' "Europeanness" undermined by Russia, which they defined as a non-European power.[3] Their view invoked the memory of a golden presocialist past, which would serve as a guideline for the postsocialist future, and stressed an inherent right to national self-determination. Reflecting variations in their history under the Soviet empire, however, they differed in their perceptions of how much the changes inflicted by Soviet occupation had put major features of their national identities at risk. Two issues stand out.

First, under Soviet rule both Latvia and Estonia recorded a massive immigration of Russian-speaking workforce. Thus, whereas in 1945, some 95 percent of the Estonian population belonged to the titular nation, in 1989 the proportion was only 61.5 percent. The respective numbers for Latvia were more than 80 and 52 percent. This stands in contrast to Lithuania, where the share of the titular nation was 79.6 percent in 1989. In 1989, Eastern Slavic groups (most importantly Russians, but also Belorussians and Ukrainians) made up 35 percent of the Estonian, 42 percent of the Latvian, and 11.5 percent of the Lithuanian population.[4] These trends were even more accentuated in the capital cities. By 1980, the share of ethnic Estonians in Tallinn had dropped to slightly more than 50 percent, the share of Latvians in Riga to barely 40 percent, whereas the share of Lithuanians in Vilnius increased from 33 percent in 1959 to 47 percent in 1980.[5]

These trends were cited by Estonian and Latvian radical nationalists when they defined the Russian minorities as threats to the mere survival of their nations. An official of the Latvian People's Front entitled an appeal to the

---

2. According to the official Soviet interpretation "Stalin's motives for signing the Non-Aggression Pact with Hitler in 1939 were purely intended to secure peace, and…the peoples of the Baltic states welcomed their incorporation into the Soviet Union as an alternative to the continuation of the authoritarian rule in their own respective republics." Graham Smith, "The Resurgence of Nationalism," in *The Baltic States: The National Self-Determination of Estonia, Latvia and Lithuania*, ed. Graham Smith (New York: Macmillan, 1994), 132.

3. Abdelal, *National Purpose*, 10–11, 84.

4. Ole Norgaard, Dan Hindsgaul, Lars Johannsen, and Helle Willumsen, *The Baltic States after Independence* (Cheltenham: Edward Elgar, 1996), 172–73.

5. Romuald J. Misiunas and Rein Taagepera, *The Baltic States: Years of Dependence, 1940–1990* (Berkeley: University of California Press, 1993), 216.

world in 1990: "The Latvian Nation and the Genocide of Immigration."[6] In a similar vein, the head of Estonia's first freely elected government and architect of the country's radical reforms, Mart Laar, commented: "The Nazi 'General Plan Ost' had envisaged 520,000 German colonists to reside in the Baltic States by 1965. Instead, by that date, the Baltic countries had received over a million Russian colonists. Soviet reality surpassed Nazi plans."[7]

Second, during socialism, Lithuania had been much more successful in building up a national ruling elite than Latvia and Estonia. Its Communist Party leaders were native Lithuanians, who consciously packed the republic's top posts with members of the indigenous population. Communist Party rank and file were predominantly Lithuanian too. In contrast, the Latvian and to a lesser degree the Estonian Communist Party leadership and top administration had been in the hands of ethnic Russians, or Latvians and Estonians born and/or educated in Russia. Party membership was also less frequent among ethnic Latvians and Estonians.[8]

As a consequence of these different legacies, Estonian and Latvian reform elites more than those of Lithuania perceived their newly independent states as "unrealized" nation-states, and actively tried to reverse the former trends, which they saw as having led them away from their paths towards nation building. Premier Laar expressed this aspiration well with his suggestion that "transition is somehow some kind of 'return to the future.' Transition turns these countries back to the point at which their normal development was stopped by forceful sovietization."[9] Rather than just building nation-states, political actors in these two countries became engaged in nationalizing projects. The nationalizing agendas have left their most distinctive traces on the new democratic institutions, leading to exclusionary democracies in Estonia and Latvia, in contrast to Lithuania's inclusive democracy. In turn, the different systems of democratic governance have influenced economic and welfare policies, and the management of related social and political tensions.

Exclusionary and Inclusionary Democracies

One of the first crucial choices the nationalist movements in the Baltic republics had to make concerned the question of who would constitute the new states' citizenry. As is well known, ultimately both the Estonian and Latvian movements embraced a legal restorationist solution. According to this interpretation, the Baltic republics differed from other parts of the Soviet Union

6. Quoted in Dreifelds, *Latvia in Transition*, 144.
7. Laar, *Estonia*, 37.
8. Misiunas and Taagepera, *The Baltic States*, 204–8, 274–81, 359–60; Anton Steen, "The New Elites in the Baltic States: Recirculation and Change," *Scandinavian Political Studies* 20, no. 1 (1997): 91–112.
9. Laar, *Estonia*, 22.

similarly engaged in struggles for more autonomy, reforms, and ultimately independence, since these states had been unjustly occupied and thus had the right to restore their independence fully and immediately. Concomitant to this, legal restorationism also claimed that citizenship could only be granted to citizens of the republics prior to occupation and their descendants, thus excluding all Soviet-era immigrants.

The Estonian Supreme Council embraced the legal restorationist doctrine in 1991. Specific policy implications of the principle were confirmed in a referendum in 1992. As a consequence, about 40 percent of the inhabitants of Estonia were denied citizenship. In Latvia, a similar decision by the Supreme Council left roughly 25 percent of the resident population without Latvian citizenship.[10] Over the 1990s, both countries adopted naturalization laws establishing the procedures by which Russian speakers could acquire Baltic citizenship. Restrictive language laws, frequent amendments, and procrastination in passing these laws have, however, led to slow progress in naturalization. In Estonia after 1993–96 the initial wave of naturalization ebbed. In 2003, some 12 percent of the resident population still did not have any citizenship at all, and around 7 percent had opted for Russian citizenship.[11] Progress was even slower in Latvia. The first significant wave of naturalization occurred as late as in 1999–2001. Even so, in 2003 22 percent of Latvian residents were still noncitizens. A second wave of naturalization coincided with Latvia's EU membership from 2004.[12]

Notwithstanding the large size of the minority population in Estonia and Latvia, the restrictive stance on the citizenship issue was not a foregone conclusion but a matter of choice emerging from political conflicts. Anatol Lieven describes the exclusion of non-Baltic Soviet citizens from the new states as a result of a "protracted duel between the proponents of the First and Second Republic," that is, between the legal restorationists and those who believed that the new states should be built on existing realities and thus should include all residents. Initially, the popular fronts in both countries adopted a moderate stance, with some fractions supporting a "zero option" that would base citizenship on territorial rather than ethnic attributes. This was the choice made in Lithuania. During the independence struggle, however, radical nationalists organized in the Citizen Committees emerged as

---

10. Norgaard et al., *The Baltic States* (1996), 65, 69. The relatively low number of Russians denied citizenship in Latvia is due to the fact that a significant share of the Russian-speaking population had already held citizenship in the interwar state.

11. Mikko Lagerspetz and Henri Vogt, "Estonia," in *The Handbook of Political Change in Eastern Europe,* ed. Sten Berglund, Joakim Ekman and Frank H. Aarebrot (Cheltenham: Edward Elgar, 2004), 75–76; and Estonia.eu. Official gateway to Estonia. Citizenship, http://estonia.eu/about-estonia/society/citizenship.html (accessed August 1, 2011).

12. Hermann Smith-Sivertsen, "Latvia," in Berglund, Ekman, and Aarebrot, *The Handbook,* 102–3; Minister of Foreign Affairs of the Republic of Latvia, "Citizenship in Latvia" (May 21 2010), http://www.mfa.gov.lv/en/policy/4641/4642/4651/ (accessed August 1, 2011).

powerful contenders to the more moderate forces in Estonia and Latvia, and ultimately their restorationist position prevailed.[13]

The denial of citizenship to large sections of the Russophone population had important repercussions for Estonia's and Latvia's democracies. It transferred political power to an overwhelmingly ethnic Baltic citizenry, and excluded a large share of the resident population from the right to participate in the democratic polity, as "non-citizens cannot form political parties, run for political office or vote in national elections."[14] This exclusion has undermined the capacity of the party system to represent popular interests. While the literature has been divided on the issue of how far postcommunist party systems are at all able to shape cleavages and represent voters, there is little doubt that Estonian and Latvian parties are among the least representative in terms of encompassing all of their territorial populations. Two combined and closely interrelated factors can account for this.

First, the restrictive citizenship laws greatly diminished the electoral base for parties representing industrial labor's interests. Russian speakers, many of whom worked in the inherited socialist industries, were overall more supportive of left-wing parties than their ethnic Baltic counterparts.[15] However, the electoral chances of the pro-Russian and left-oriented parties have been severely impeded, as most Russians could not vote while ethnic Baltic citizenry did not turn out in great numbers to support such parties. Moreover, different stances on the issue of independence divided Latvia's two pro-Russian parties. In addition to artificially limiting the core constituency for left-wing parties, issues of nationality and independence have more generally constrained formation of parties that would compete on a Right-Left scale. As Hermann Smith-Sivertsen writes: "Party names tell a story too. In Latvia, not a single party claiming to be socialist, social democratic, workers' or representing the underprivileged or defrauded won significant support in the 1993 and 1995 elections."[16] Instead, parties often chose names evoking patriotic sentiments.

13. Anatol Lieven, *The Baltic Revolution: Estonia, Latvia, Lithuania, and the Path to Independence* (New Haven: Yale University Press, 1993), 216, 274; Graham Smith, Adne Aasland, and Richard M. Mole, "Statehood, Ethnic Relations and Citizenship," in Smith, *The Baltic States,* 181–205; and Vello Pettai and Klara Hallik, "Understanding Processes of Ethnic Control: Segmentation, Dependency and Co-optation in Post-Communist Estonia," *Nations and Nationalism* 8, no. 4 (2002): 505–29.

14. Hughes, " 'Exit,' " 745. In Latvia noncitizens can be members of political parties.

15. Survey data from the New Baltic Barometer give ample evidence that Russian speakers in Latvia and Estonia are stronger inclined to vote for social democratic or left-wing parties than ethnic Balts: see Richard Rose, "New Baltic Barometer V: A Pre-enlargement Survey," Studies in Public Policy 368 (Glasgow: Centre for the Study of Public Policy, University of Strathclyde, 2002), 30; Richard Rose, "New Baltic Barometer III: A Survey Study," Studies in Public Policy 284 (Glasgow: Centre for the Study of Public Policy, University of Strathclyde, 1997), 41–43.

16. Smith-Sivertsen, "Latvia," 99. More precisely, the electoral alliance "Equal Rights" won 5.8 percent of the vote and entered parliament with seven seats in 1993. They were generally

Second and closely related, the Communist Parties collapsed in Estonia and Latvia. In this way, the only parties that had a membership to speak of were wiped out from the emerging party systems. As a consequence, even more than was the case in other postsocialist states, the new Estonian and Latvian parties originated from elite circles representing at best only a section of civil society. They barely had members, and have not been capable of undertaking or willing to undertake efforts to build up stronger organizational links with the electorate. By way of example, Latvia's Way—a party that played a crucial role in forming and sustaining Latvian governments during the first decade of independence—had only 173 members in 1994. What is more, the party was "created specifically for the purpose of unifying the Latvian elite" with the aim of representing elite interests in efficient policy-making unhampered by lengthy parliamentary debates.[17]

Following Richard Katz and Peter Mair, it can be said that a party of the above kind will inevitably emphasize the tasks of a "party in public office" versus those of a "party on the ground."[18] But more precisely, what Estonian and Latvian parties seem to be all about is to serve as vehicles to transfer "persons in public office." In both countries, the party landscape has been in constant flux because of the " 'political tourism' practiced by organizationally disloyal postcommunist politicians," or newcomers to politics, who have been constantly engaged in party switching, fusion, fission, or start-ups.[19]

Iconic leaders of the independence movement and early reformers, central bankers, successful businessmen and "oligarchs," as well as maverick émigrés, have all been among party builders. Competition for office has been intense—the more so that it has occurred in a highly uncertain and unstructured context, within which virtually anybody could cherish hopes of victory. Rather than reflecting solid ideological polarization, competition has been driven by barely concealed personal ambitions for power. Conversely, coalition governments have not been built on programmatic harmony but oftentimes on alliances against rival personalities.[20]

The specificities of the Estonian and Latvian party systems come to the fore when compared to that of Lithuania, which has not suffered from the

seen as the remnants of the pro-Moscow Communist Party and as struggling for the socialist legacy. Moreover, even when the group was reorganized into the Socialist Party in 1995 it won 5.6 percent and five seats.

17. Ole Norgaard, Lars Johannsen, Mette Skak, and Rene Hauge Sorensen, *The Baltic States after Independence* (Cheltenham: Edward Elgar, 1999), 79.

18. Richard Katz and Peter Mair, "The Ascendancy of the Party in Public Office: Party Organizational Change in Twentieth-Century Democracies," in *Political Parties: Old Concepts and New Challenges,* ed. Richard Gunther, Jose R. Montero, and Juan Linz (Oxford: Oxford University Press, 2002), 113–36.

19. Marcus Kreuzer and Vello Pettai, "Patterns of Political Instability: Affiliation Patterns of Politicians and Voters in Post-Communist Estonia, Latvia, and Lithuania," *Studies in Comparative International Development* 38, no. 2 (2003): 77–78.

20. Axel Reetz, *Die Entwicklung der Parteiensysteme in den baltischen Staaten: Vom Beginn des Mehrparteiensystems 1988 bis zu den dritten Wahlen* (Wittenbach: Wilhelm Surbir, 2004), 185–90.

birth defect of disenfranchisement of social groups most negatively affected by transformation. Lithuania adopted the "zero option" in respect of citizenship. Leaders of the Sajudis, the Lithuanian popular front, saw this as a means to "harness the support of the non-indigenous population" to the cause of independence. Although it was made clear that this solution did not invalidate prewar Lithuanian citizenship, "thereby acknowledging the fact that the Republic of Lithuania was a restored and not a new state," president of Sajudis Vytautas Landsbergis resisted the radical nationalist voices for a referendum on citizenship during the struggle for independence.[21] Lithuania's language law also demonstrates the country's commitment to a multiethnic polity. For example, the law stipulates that in communities with populations more than a third of which is non–Lithuanian-speaking, public institutions are obliged to conduct their business in the minority as well as the majority language.[22] Concomitant to this, Lithuania's democratic polity lacks the exclusive features so characteristic of the two other Baltic countries.

Lithuania's Communist Party successfully transformed itself into a new democratic labor party, the Lithuanian Democratic Labor Party (LDDP) early on. In turn, the challenge of the postcommunist party's inherited organizational and membership strength forced its major contender, Sajudis, to reorganize itself as a political party, the center-right Homeland Union. In terms of membership, the Homeland Union was to overtake the LDDP by the mid 1990s. While differences in party membership across the Baltic states remain trivial, initially the Lithuanian party system was somewhat more structured than that of its neighbors. At least in the first decade after independence, only a few parties mattered for politics and the party system remained highly polarized rather than excessively fragmented. Further, elections have produced clear majority governments enabling partisan political choices.[23]

As we will see below, the initial differences among the Baltic democracies and party systems have affected the politics of reform. In Lithuania, crucial institutional and economic decisions did not become depoliticized from the outset, but were only taken after protracted political debates. They also reflected partisan preferences, and to some degree the influence of party constituencies. This has resulted in a somewhat more open and gradual transformation path than was the case in the other two countries.

21. Smith, Aasland, and Mole, "Statehood," 183.
22. Ibid., 192. The Estonian Constitution technically allows the use of minority languages in government administration in areas with more than half of whose population belongs to minorities, but this stipulation has never been formally enacted.
23. Hermann Smith-Sivertsen, "Why Bigger Party Membership Organisations in Lithuania than in Latvia 1995–2000?" *East European Quarterly* 38, no. 2 (2004): 215–59; Ingrid van Biezen, Peter Mair, and Thomas Poguntke, "Going, Going …Gone? The Decline of Party Membership in Contemporary Europe," *European Journal of Political Research* (2011), onlinelibrary.wiley.com/doi: 10.1111/j.1475–6765.2011.01995; Kreuzer and Pettai, "Patterns of Political Instability." It is interesting to note that party membership in Estonia increased over the 2000s due to a change in the party finance law.

The Politics of Early Economic Reforms

Parties and governments in the Baltic states faced a significantly larger problem load than the political leaderships of many other countries, as they had to master all the challenges of what Claus Offe called a "triple transformation" to nation-state, market economy, and democracy.[24] The combined impact of the problem load and the overarching purpose of transformation—national independence interpreted as decolonization—have created ample incentives as well as opportunities for reformers to choose radical and seemingly simple solutions. Not only did these options contribute to the extraordinary depth of the transformational recession, but they have also tied the hands of politicians ever since.

National Money and Stability Culture

The single most important policy choice in this respect was the rapid introduction of national currencies, viewed as foundations for economic independence, powerful symbols of national identity and sovereignty, and the related institutionalization of the independence of newly established central banks with their powers curtailed in Estonia and Lithuania by the establishment of currency boards. The currency reforms occurred against the background of increasing monetary chaos in the final years of the Soviet Union, which forced many ex-Soviet republics to leave the ruble zone even before its final collapse in the summer of 1993. Yet the Baltic states were the first to unambiguously and enthusiastically endorse the idea of introducing national currencies. Estonia (re)introduced the kroon in June 1992, Latvia followed with the lats in March 1993, and Lithuania with the litas in June 1993.[25]

Estonia had prepared for monetary reforms long beforehand, and moved ahead in the most determined fashion. As early as September 1987 a group of economists published a reform proposal that aimed at transferring as many economic powers as possible to the republic. Called IME (the acronym for self-management but also meaning "miracle" in Estonian), the program proposed republican management of taxes, budgets, and property; the authorization of different forms of property including foreign ownership; and more independence in financial and monetary policies. The document also included the suggestion of introducing a national currency. In 1990, the Estonian Supreme Council (re)established the Bank of Estonia. A Monetary Reform Committee was formed, led by Premier Edgar Savisaar. Its mandate was to decide together with the central bank about the necessary steps toward transition to an independent currency. These two institutions became home

---

24. Offe, "Capitalism by Democratic Design?" 865–92.
25. Lieven, *Baltic Revolution,* 357; Abdelal, *National Purpose,* 46–49.

to Estonia's most ardent promarket forces, including a group of émigrés residing in Sweden, the United States, and Canada.

The committee eventually settled on a currency board regime, a highly restrictive fixed exchange rate arrangement.[26] Currency board regimes de facto rule out the mediating role central banks assume between external and domestic monetary requirements. Control over monetary policy is placed in the board, which operates separately from the central bank. Its mandate is to convert all national currency offered to it into the reserve currency (and vice versa) at a fixed rate. The domestic money supply is regulated by foreign exchange, as it can only be changed in connection with changes in foreign currency reserves. Discretionary monetary policy is thus precluded. The central bank cannot offer credit to enterprises and the government, and only in exceptional circumstances is it allowed to lend to banks. Thus, it cannot assume the role of lender of last resort.

Estonia also invented a strong protective device against possible future temptations to devalue its currency by issuing futures contracts guaranteeing the same exchange rate for up to eight years ahead. Any devaluation of the currency would, therefore, come at extremely high cost. Estonia decided to peg the kroon to the deutschmark, allowing fluctuation within a 3 percent margin. Initially, it backed its currency mostly with gold reserves deposited in Western banks before 1940 and transferred back to Estonia after independence.

From an international political economy perspective it could be questioned whether the adoption of the currency board followed a domestic economic rationale. From this viewpoint it would seem that these measures were the result of Estonia's and the other Baltic states' quest for international creditworthiness, reinforced by advocacy on the part of the central bankers' transnational epistemic community. In this vein, Juliet Johnson argues that across East Central Europe the process of rapidly instituting national currencies and refashioning the inherited authorities as independent central banks or currency boards "by and for international actors...occurred without the need to build extensive domestic support for the new institutions."[27]

Although considerations of international creditworthiness certainly played a major role, neither the suggested overwhelming importance of foreign pressures nor the assumption of lacking domestic political support sits

---

26. On the introduction of the currency board in Estonia see Seiga Lainela and Pekka Sutela, "Introducing New Currencies in the Baltic Countries," in *The Transition to Market Economy: Transformation and Reform in the Baltic States,* ed. Tarmo Haavisto (Cheltenham: Edward Elgar, 1997), 66–95; Adalbert Knöbl, Andres Sutt, and Basil Zavoico, "The Estonian Currency Board: Its Introduction and Role in the Early Success of Estonia's Transition to a Market Economy," IMF Working Paper WP/02/96 (Washington, D.C.: International Monetary Fund, 2002).

27. Juliet Johnson, "Post-Communist Central Banks: A Democratic Deficit?" *Journal of Democracy* 17, no. 1 (2006): 91.

well with the evidence of the Baltic countries' strict adherence to the "stability culture."[28] First, initial support for the new currencies and monetary policy institutions could not mainly stem from international backing, as in Estonia crucial decisions were taken in 1992, even before massive external pressure or assistance could materialize. Indeed, Premier Laar recalled that during the spring of 1992 the IMF "initially urged Estonia to postpone monetary reform until its technical capabilities were more advanced."[29] Second, as to the often noted presence and pressure of émigré policy advisers, the fact that Estonia's exclusive Monetary Reform Committee included Jeffrey Sachs's former student Ardo Hansson (who, holding a very fresh Ph.D., hardly could be viewed as a senior representative of global academic and financial circles at the time), seems less a proof of powerful external influences than of a preexisting domestic consensus favoring radical solutions.

Third, at the turn of the 1990s, the currency board arrangement still seemed to be an outdated remainder of a distant past. While currency boards had once been common in the colonies of the nineteenth-century British empire, they all but vanished with decolonization.[30] At the time of its adoption in Estonia, the institution had just started to get more attention in the international neoliberal policy community. It was first adopted in the 1980s in Hong Kong, to reassure investors in light of the territory's return to China, and then made its way to Argentina where a currency board was seen as a possible solution against hyperinflation. In both cases, members of the neoliberal Mont Pelerin Society (MPS) were instrumental in bringing this institutional solution about. Society members Steve Hanke and Kurt Schuler developed a blueprint for monetary stability in Argentina, and subsequently also for Yugoslavia and the former Soviet Union.

It is interesting to note that Kurt Schuler had just started his Ph.D. thesis on the issue when the socialist system broke down. His advisor was George Selgin of Georgia University, who, together with Lawrence White, was a key person advocating "free banking," a system of competitive note issue by private banks. In the nineteenth and early twentieth centuries, free banking had been supported by some liberals against the emergence of central banks and the gold standard. In the 1970s the idea was famously invoked by Friedrich August von Hayek, who advocated the elimination of national currencies in

28. We take the term from Geoffry Underhill, "Global Integration, EMU, and Monetary Governance in the EMU: The Political Economy of the 'Stability Culture,'" in Dyson, *European States and the Euro*, 31–52.

29. Laar, *Estonia*, 114.

30. For the history of currency boards, see John Williamson, *What Role for Currency Boards? Policy Analyses in International Economics* (Washington, D.C.: Institute for International Economics, 1995), 7; Anna Schwartz, "Do Currency Boards Have a Future?" Occasional Paper 88 (London: Institute of Economic Affairs, 1992); Dieter Plehwe, "Transnational Discourse Coalitions and Monetary Policy Reform in Argentina: The Limited Powers of the 'Washington Consensus,'" *Critical Policy Studies* 5, no. 2 (2011): 127–48.

order to "protect money from politics."[31] Free banking was the most radical neoliberal vision of a depoliticized and denationalized currency system. From the vantage point of free banking advocates, currency boards (albeit still short of an optimal regime) presented at least a middle-of-the-road solution between the disapproved central bank arrangement and the cherished but still unavailable system of private bank currencies.[32]

One of the Estonian reformers' main reasons for settling on the currency board solution was precisely the feature that even if tied to national currency, this institution went furthest in isolating money from politics. Moreover, institutional insulation of monetary policy resonated well with the more general nationalist sentiment that the cause of national independence ought to be removed from the everyday struggles of democratic politics. This symbolic connection was also important because the technicalities and risks of the new monetary authority and instruments had been hardly intelligible for politicians, let alone ordinary citizens. On this aspect Premier Laar recalls that "The fact that politicians that outwardly supported the currency board were at the same time sure that after monetary reform the central bank would continue to deliver 'cheap credits' to inefficient factories and collective farms indicates that many politicians probably never understood exactly what they supported."[33]

In a similar vein, the enthusiastic reception of the stable kroon elevated the symbolic status of the monetary authority and enhanced the popularity of central bankers as nation builders. It was on these grounds that the Bank of Estonia's governor in 1991–95, Siim Kallas could build political capital around his role as "father of the national currency." In 1994, while still in office at the Bank of Estonia, he founded the Reform Party which came in second in the 1995 parliamentary elections and later became Estonia's most influential political party.

The currency board's echo of the gold standard has further contributed to its attraction. Indeed, Kallas was originally attracted "to the transparency and high degree of confidence associated with the gold standard, under which Estonia had achieved a period of monetary stability during the period 1927–33." However, recognizing that in the new international environment the gold standard was impractical, Kallas opted for the currency board as its closest substitute, which he "associated with the same transparency and

---

31. Friedrich August von Hayek, *Denationalization of Money—The Argument Refined* (London: Institute for Economic Affairs, 1990), quoted by Eric Helleiner, "Denationalising Money? Economic Liberalism and the 'National Question' in Currency Affairs," in *Nation-States and Money: The Past, Present and Future of National Currencies*, ed. Emily Gilbert and Eric Helleiner (London: Routledge, 1999), 148.

32. For a discussion of the advantages of a currency board over free banking in the post-Soviet context, see Steve H. Hanke and Kurt Schuler, "Currency Boards and Currency Convertibility," *Cato Journal* 12, no. 3 (1993): 699–701.

33. Laar, *Estonia*, 121–22.

high degree of confidence."[34] More generally, the currency board solution represented a close match with the program of Premier Laar's nationalist-neoliberal government which sought a decisive break with the communist past through the fast implementation of far-reaching reforms. Reform speed as well as the institutionalization of nonmajoritarian institutions was crucial to prevent possible resistance and backlashes against reform. Institutional choices also had to respond to the lack of local expertise in complex fields such as monetary, fiscal, and macroeconomic policies. The currency board was an ideal match for all these needs. In institutional terms it was relatively simple, it did not require extensive administrative capacity, and it could be put in place fast.

Latvia (re)established its own central bank in 1990. After independence the Bank of Latvia became a full-fledged central bank with the right to issue its own currency. The Latvian central bank was modeled on the German Bundesbank. Among its most important objectives was to ensure price stability, an objective that was pursued with great vigor under one of the founders of the Latvian National Independence Movement, Einars Repse, who was the Bank of Latvia's president from 1991 to 2001. As with the impressive career of Kallas, in the 2000s Repse also founded a party and as a democratic politician capitalized on his previous role as nation-building central banker.

This institutional choice was inspired by memories of Latvia's successful monetary policies of the 1920s and 1930s. Latvia's interwar stabilization had been singled out as a complete success in a study commissioned by the League of Nations in 1936.[35] It had been achieved by "rigid economies in the sphere of public expenditure," by pegging the new currency to gold, and by observing the principle that the central bank should hold sufficient gold or foreign exchange reserves to offset any temporary disturbance in the balance of payments.[36] This experience provided a resource for the postsocialist Latvian central bank presidents to draw on.

In contrast to Estonia, the Latvian central bank decided to first issue an interim currency, the Latvian ruble. It aimed to bring inflation under control before introducing its permanent currency in order to ensure confidence.

---

34. Knöbl, Sutt, and Zavoico, "The Estonian Currency Board," 7, 11. Laar gives a similar justification for his currency regime preference. According to him, economic prosperity in the interwar period was associated with the introduction of the kroon. "The economic turnaround occurred with the introduction of currency reform in 1928. The Estonian national currency, the kroon, was established with the aid of a loan from Great Britain and for the next 10 years the value of the kroon remained stable." It seems of minor importance that the economic turnaround of 1928 was soon to be interrupted by the Great Depression, which forced Estonia to go off the gold standard after only five years, to devaluate its currency, and to join the sterling bloc.

35. Brian van Arkadie and Mats Karlsson, *Economic Survey of the Baltic States* (New York: New York University Press, 1992), 158.

36. Royal Institute of International Affairs, Information Department, *The Baltic States: Estonia, Latvia, Lithuania* (London: Oxford University Press, 1938), 131, 171–75.

The bank was indeed highly successful in stabilizing the Latvian ruble before it introduced the lats in 1993. The lats was initially allowed to float; in 1994 it was pegged to IMF special drawing rights; and in 2002, the peg was changed to the euro. Although Latvia did not opt for a currency board, its central bank policies so closely paralleled the operation of such an institution that an IMF report concluded that "there has been little difference in practice between the CBA [currency board arrangement] in Estonia and the peg in Latvia in recent years, as foreign reserves usually exceed the monetary base in Latvia."[37]

Both countries thus settled on institutional solutions that, albeit different, took monetary policy as far out of the political sphere as possible. There was little public debate in either country over this choice. This was in contrast to Lithuania, which only settled on a currency board after prolonged and intensive political fights; indeed, the currency board has remained at the center of political debate ever since.[38] Like the other two Baltic countries, Lithuania (re)established its central bank in 1990, and prepared to launch its own currency. Before 1993, when the litas was introduced, Lithuania issued an interim currency, the talonas, to cope with a ruble shortage. After launching the litas, the government still brooded for nine months over the final design of the institution that would regulate it. It was only in 1994 that the parliament passed a law introducing the currency board.

The idea of a currency board had long lacked support in Lithuania. Interestingly, the first proposal for such an institution in the postcommunist world was made to Lithuania rather than Estonia, on the occasion of a visit by Schuler and Selgin in 1990. The two economists, joined by Joseph Sinkey, a professor of finance at Georgia University, paid another visit to Lithuania in 1991, and repeated their recommendation. However, the Sajudis government under Gediminas Vagnorius rejected the proposal. Stabilization was not as high on the priority list of the central bank as it was in Latvia.

The currency board idea gained momentum only under the left-wing government of Adolfas Šleževičius in late 1993. The prime minister hoped that it would contribute to the stabilization of the litas and back the international opening of Lithuania's economy. He was supported in this view by the IMF, which was worried about Lithuania's lax monetary policy, as well as by the Lithuanian Free Market Institute. The latter's director, Elena Leontjeva, served as economic adviser to various left- (and right-) wing governments. She was also a close collaborator of Schuler and Hanke.

    37. Knöbl, Sutt, and Zavoico, "The Estonian Currency Board," 20.
    38. On the Lithuanian currency reform see Lainela and Sutela, "Introducing New Currencies"; Jerome Blanc, "Les conditions d'établissement d'un *Currency Board:* L'exemple Lituanien, 1990–1994," *Revue d'Études Comparatives Est/Ouest* 35, no. 3 (2004): 119–45; and Jerome Blanc and Jean-Francois Ponsot, "Crédibilité et *Currency Board:* Le cas Lituanien," (GdR Économie Monétaire et Financière 0098 du CNRS, 19èmes Journées Internationales d'Économie Monétaire et Bancaire, Lyon, June 6, 2002).

Subsequently, the issue of the currency board became the object of intense political struggle between the government, the governor of the central bank, the opposition, and the president. Among central bankers, the currency board was seen as a sign of mistrust of their monetary policy and the achievements of the Bank of Lithuania in bringing down inflation. The right-wing opposition was mostly concerned about the constraints put on monetary sovereignty by the institution's automatic features. Moreover, the opposition represented the interests of industrial exporters, who preferred a weak currency to boost their competitiveness. Finally, President Algirdas Brazauskas—allegedly under pressure from commercial bankers who feared that an important part of their revenue would disappear under the currency board—also opposed the project. Thus it was only under the threat of Premier Šleževičius' s resignation that the parliament passed the "Law on the Credibility of the Litas."

The struggle over the currency board continued even after its introduction. The right-wing opposition took the law to the Constitutional Court, claiming that it violated the exclusive right of the central bank to issue banknotes.[39] The court upheld this view, but the law had meanwhile been amended, so that the court's decision had no impact. With the return to power of a right-wing government under Premier Vagnorius in 1996, a second attack on the currency board was staged. The government prepared a plan for a rapid exit. The IMF, however, about to issue a major loan to Lithuania, opposed the plan. In addition, the central bank favored a more gradual exit from the currency board. The central bank's plan finally prevailed, although it was never fully implemented. As a result, at the end of the 1990s, Lithuania had a currency board whose restrictions on monetary policies were slightly lifted, without however affecting the fixed exchange rate and the foreign exchange cover for base money.

Regardless of the different political paths along which national currencies were introduced and of the varying concrete forms in which monetary stability was institutionalized in the three states, the strength of the popular feeling aroused in the process is indicated by Baltic citizens' hopes and fears about the euro in the second half of the 2000s. Eurozone entry, which requires giving up monetary policy autonomy and national currencies, is clearly less compatible with national agendas than the achievement of monetary sovereignty had been. Accordingly, public opinion polls reveal strong attachments to the national currencies. To a larger extent than in other East Central European countries, Baltic citizens' hopes for protection from international crises and strengthened European identity resulting from the changeover to euro seem

---

39. The law initially stipulated that the decision over the official exchange rate and the anchor currency should be taken by the government in coordination with the central bank. This was seen as an unconstitutional constraint on the emission of banknotes by the central bank. Blanc and Ponsot, "Crédibilité et *Currency Board*," 7.

TABLE 3.1

Hopes and fears about the euro: Baltic and other East Central European countries, mid-2000s

	Hopes to feel more European	Fears losing national identity
Estonia	43	48
Latvia	51	66
Lithuania	41	51
Baltic average	45	55
Other East Central European average	56	34

	Hopes better protection from international crises	Fears losing national policymaking autonomy
Estonia	38	36
Latvia	31	51
Lithuania	31	37
Baltic average	33	41
Other East Central European average	46	29

	Trusts EU institutions for reliable information on the euro	Trusts national central bank for reliable information on the euro
Estonia	64	83
Latvia	59	79
Lithuania	67	73
Baltic average	63	78
Other East Central European average	76	84

Sources: Authors' calculations based on Gallup Europe Flash Eurobarometers: various polls conducted in 2006–8, http://ec.europa.eu/public_opinion/flash/fl183-en.pdf (accessed July 11, 2009).
Note: Data shown as average percent of citizens polled.

to have been overshadowed by worries about losing national policymaking autonomy and national identity. Similarly, for reliable information on the euro Estonians and Latvians (but not Lithuanians) appear to trust their national central banks more than EU institutions. Their preference for the national monetary authority is stronger than in other new member nations.

Flat Tax Regimes

The Baltic states' inclination to adopt radical and seemingly simple policy solutions also showed in their choice of tax regimes. As in the case of the currency board, Estonia pioneered a maverick solution to the problem of tax reforms by adopting a flat tax in 1994, once more sidestepping the IMF, which advised an increase of taxation rates in the existing system.[40] Until

40. On the flat tax, see Anthony J. Evans, "The Spread of Economic Theology: The Flat Tax in Romania," *Romanian Economic and Business Review* 1, no. 1 (2006): 47–59; Anthony J. Evans

Estonia's bold step, only a few places, such as Hong-Kong, Guernsey, Jersey, and Jamaica, and some subnational governments in the United States had levied a flat tax. Although marginal in the real world, since the 1980s the flat tax idea was becoming popular among radical neoliberals. The first to speak in favor of such a tax were August Friedrich von Hayek in *The Constitution of Liberty*, and Milton and Rose Friedman in *Free to Choose*. Among its most influential advocates was MPS member and Hoover Institution Fellow Alvin Rabushka, who became fascinated with Hong Kong's tax model. Together with Robert Hall in 1983 he published *The Flat Tax*, advocating "a combination of a cash-flow income tax on business income, and a tax on workers' income, both levied at the same, single rate."[41]

It has to be said that in practice, the term flat tax has been used loosely, characterizing tax systems with a single marginal tax rate on labor income. Hall's and Rabushka's work was most influential in the United States. Yet when Estonia put the idea into practice, it earned international acclaim for its pioneering role: "Simplicity itself. At the stroke of a pen, this tiny Baltic nation transformed itself from backwater to bellwether, emulated by its neighbors and envied by conservatives in America who long to flatten their own country's taxes."[42] For the Estonian government, the flat tax was appealing because it promised to be easy to administer, restrict the size of government, and provide a signal to the outside world that the country was serious about market reforms. The government settled on a 26 percent personal income tax rate, which was broadly midway between the lowest and highest prereform marginal rates, and also lowered the corporate income tax from 35 to 26 percent.

Lithuania followed suit with its flat tax reform, likewise implemented in 1994. The major difference was that it set its marginal tax rate at 33 percent, which was the upper level of the rates imposed prior to the reform. As a consequence, revenues from personal income taxes increased. Lithuania's corporate tax rate was maintained at 29 percent. Latvia introduced its flat tax regime in 1997, replacing a degressive rate structure with a marginal rate of 25 percent. The corporate tax rate was set at the same level.

In all three countries, the flat tax reforms were later followed by other steps to decrease corporate taxation rates. In Estonia in 2000, the second Laar government completely abolished taxation of undistributed profits.

---

and Dragos P. Aligica, "The Spread of the Flat Tax in Eastern Europe: A Comparative Study," *East European Economics* 46, no. 3 (2008): 49–67; Michael Keen, Yitei Kim, and Ricardo Varsano, "The 'Flat Tax(es)': Principles and Evidence," IMF Working Paper WP/06/218 (Washington, D.C.: International Monetary Fund, 2006); and Alexander Baturo and Julia Gray, "Flatliners: Ideology and Rational Learning in the Diffusion of the Flat Tax," IIIS Discussion Paper 210 (2007), accessed November 29, 2009 at SSRN: http://ssrn.com/abstract = 980704.

41. Keen, Kim, and Varsano, "The Flat Tax(es)," 5.

42. "Special Report. Simplifying Tax Systems: The Case for Flat Taxes," *Economist*, April 16, 2005, 63.

Lithuania and Latvia both reduced their corporate income tax rates to 15 percent in 2002 and 2004, respectively. The overall effect of the new tax regimes on government revenues was limited. All three states had experienced a sharp decline of their revenues already in the early 1990s. Whereas under socialism revenues roughly equaled 50 percent of GDP, they dropped to between 30 and 38 percent around 1993–94, a level at which they stabilized. Flat tax reforms, however, led to a shift away from direct toward indirect taxation.[43]

The currency and tax reforms are emblematic for the Baltic states' early institutional choices. They show a clear preference for encompassing, radical and simple institutions that restrict the space and resources for politics proper. While the design of these institutions typically originated in radical neoliberal epistemic communities, they found their way to the Baltic states first through the decisions of Laar's entrepreneurial government, whose ambition was to administer a sharp break with communist legacies, exploit the enthusiasm of national rebirth and the nationalizing project in domestic politics, and also signal to the West the seriousness of the regime shift undertaken in the country.

Nationalist Social Contracts

The currency regimes chosen by the Baltic states are often analyzed and understood in terms of their significance for political and economic independence. However, more has been at stake. As Emily Gilbert and Eric Helleiner argue, national currencies have emerged and largely prevailed since the nineteenth century because of their contribution to binding state and nation. They increased nation-states' capacity to raise taxes, contributed to the formation of national identities, and allowed the realization of a "broader political project which called for inhabitants of a territory, in their new role as 'national citizens' to make diverse claims on the state to provide certain political rights and economic benefits."[44]

Much of the struggles of the twentieth century over national currencies and central banking did indeed involve competing visions of the right of national citizens to make these claims, and of the duty of the state to deliver in political, economic, and social terms alike. The argument here is that because of the extremely restrictive currency board arrangements (or their functional equivalent, the Latvian independent central bank), the Baltic

43. See *Baltic States: A Regional Assessment* (Paris: OECD, 2000), 83; Hans Aage, "Public Sector Development: Difficulties and Restrictions," in Haavisto, *Transition*, 96–118.
44. Emily Gilbert and Eric Helleiner, "Introduction—Nation-States and Money: Historical Contexts, Interdisciplinary Perspectives," in Gilbert and Helleiner, *Nation-States and Money*, 1–20.

states were only able to offer their citizens a nationalist rather than a welfarist social contract.

The Baltic monetary regime acted as a straightjacket for fiscal, industrial, and social policies. They locked in the goal of monetary stability notwithstanding the implied social costs. Under the currency board arrangements, options for fiscal policy were limited, as governments could not borrow from central banks but had to rely on private actors instead. Since private savings were nonexistent in the early transformation, and external sources of financing insecure, the currency regime imposed strict budgetary discipline. At the same time, the low flat taxes limited public spending from the revenue side. Far from viewing strict fiscal discipline as a harmful restriction on governments' room for maneuver, Laar praised its advantages: "The stringent financial restraints made it easier for the government to decide what to do."[45]

Under the conditions of imposed fiscal discipline financing of welfare states has posed a specific challenge. All three Baltic states inherited from the socialist system "fully articulated, mature systems of social security that carried extensive financial obligations to their populations. These included old age pensions and sickness, disability and survivor benefits covering most workers and their families and financed from state budgets partly through taxes on enterprises, usually with no direct worker contribution."[46] Welfare states were largely financed from the central budget. With their extrication from the Soviet Union, the Baltic states had to find new financial sources for their social systems. In order to provide for independent social insurance budgets all three states introduced high payroll taxes amounting to 33 percent in Estonia, 38 percent in Latvia, and 31 percent in Lithuania. They also established social insurance funds separate from the general budgets. At the same time, they took great pains to limit their expenditures on social protection. This was most striking in the area of pensions.[47]

Pauperizing the Elderly

Pension benefits amounted to more than two-thirds of total social transfers, and were thus the social protection item that was most likely to drive expenditures up. Nevertheless, the first pension acts of the early 1990s, which the Baltic states still issued as republics of the Soviet Union, aimed at more

45. Mart Laar, "The Estonian Economic Miracle," *Backgrounder* (Heritage Foundation), no. 2060 (2007): 4.

46. Cook, *Postcommunist Welfare States*, 35.

47. On the Baltic pension reforms see Elaine Fultz, ed., *Pension Reform in the Baltic States* (Budapest: International Labour Office, 2006); Katharina Müller, "Old-Age Security in the Baltics: Legacy, Early Reforms and Recent Trends," *Europe-Asia Studies* 54, no. 5 (2002): 725–48; Jolanta Aidukaite, "The Formation of Social Insurance Institutions of the Baltic States in the Post-socialist Era," *Journal of European Social Policy* 16, no. 3 (2006): 259–70; and Bernard Casey, "Pension Reforms in the Baltic States: Convergence with 'Europe' or 'the World'?" *International Social Security Review* 57, no. 1 (2004): 19–45.

generous pension systems than the existing ones. They sought to provide more favorable terms to a wide group of people, establish stronger ties between pensions and earnings, and merge the different schemes of farmers and workers into a single unified system with universal coverage. After independence, however, these laws were quickly replaced by much more restrictive provisions. The newly adopted formulas resulted in highly compressed pension distribution.

In fact, Lithuania was the only Baltic country that integrated individual earnings into its new system of the early 1990s, thus explicitly acknowledging the entitlements earned in the Soviet past. Policymakers in Estonia and Latvia resisted such a calculation on the grounds that it would be "a throwback to the Soviet legacy."[48] Ironically, however, the earnings-related component created severe problems for a number of Lithuanians, as many enterprises accumulated huge wage arrears and failed to pay the social insurance contributions. Overall, pension benefits in Lithuania stayed as meager and flat as in the two other countries.

The fact that the three states effectively managed to keep pensions low and their cost contained during the transition period is truly outstanding in a broader comparison. As Branko Milanovic observes:

> The Baltics started the transition with a low pension-wage ratio (under 40 percent), while Poland, Hungary, Slovenia and former Czechoslovakia had pension-wage ratios between 45 and 60 percent. Four years into the transition, the ratios for the Baltics have gone further *down*, while those in Central European countries, with the exception of the Czech Republic, have stayed the same or gone up.... Since the wage (the denominator in our pension-wage ratio) declined even faster in the Baltics, the real cut in the pensions in the Baltics was even more substantial than indicated by the pension-wage ratio alone. Between 1987–88 and 1992–1993, the average pension and pension spending in the Baltics were cut by 45 percent.[49]

The minimal pensions in the Baltic states were associated with a dramatic loss of status for people who had made most of their careers under socialism. In the stark formulation of Daina Eglitis and Tana Lace, the elderly in Latvia were in essence sentenced to become "human waste" that had to bear fully the consequences of their "wasted lives."[50] That this was not purely by

48. Laurie Leppik and Andres Vörk, "Pension Reform in Estonia," in Fultz, *Pension Reform*, 47.
49. Branko Milanovic, "Poverty, Inequality, and Social Policy in Transition Economies," Policy Research Working Paper 1530 (Washington, D.C.: World Bank, 1995), 32–33. Emphasis in the original.
50. Daina S. Eglitis and Tana Lace, "Stratification and the Poverty of Progress in Post-Communist Latvian Capitalism," *Acta Sociologica* 52, no. 4 (2009): 336–38.

accident is clearly revealed by the following statement by a Latvian minister of welfare, who addressed the pensioners as follows: "You do not need big pensions, because you worked under the Communist regime, and your work accomplished nothing."[51]

There were, of course, less harsh and outspoken narratives of the new contract. Contrasting Latvia with Hungary, the World Bank praised the former: "State pension spending is to be reduced by abolishing favorable treatment for special groups and by paying lower benefits to people who retire earlier and higher benefits to people who defer retirement and continue to contribute.... In essence, Latvia's older and younger generations have made a deal. Pensioners have agreed not to press for larger benefits, and workers have accepted the burden of higher contributions in the hope for greater security for themselves in old age."[52] However, data on the distribution of risk-of-poverty rates across age groups reveal that while the Hungarian solution saved many pensioners from such a risk, the Latvian "deal" has effectively pauperized workers by the time they become elderly. Old people run the highest risk of becoming poor in Estonia as well, a feature that is particularly striking in comparison with the Visegrád states (see chapter 4, "Welfarist Social Contracts").[53]

What were the political and policy processes that led to this outcome? The Baltic states were also among the first to embrace the new international "pension orthodoxy," which, concerned with the long-term sustainability of spending, advocated funded schemes and partial privatization.[54] Latvia, being hardest hit by the transformational recession, struggled more than the other two countries with balancing its expenditures. It was therefore the first country to look for more radical solutions. The issue of pension privatization was first brought up under the right-wing government of Valdis Birkavs (1993–94), which included many representatives of financial and business circles. Premier Birkavs appointed Jānis Ritenis, an émigré Latvian who had worked for private insurance companies in Australia, as minister of welfare.

Ritenis advocated a pension system based on a private insurance model, and sought cooperation with the World Bank, which invited a Swedish team

51. Quoted in Milanovic, "Poverty, Inequality, and Social Policy," 33.

52. *From Plan to Market*, 79.

53. With the harsh fiscal austerity programs of 2007–9, the risk of old age poverty became even greater in the Baltic states.

54. The term "new pension orthodoxy" was coined by Lo Vuolo, "Reformas Previsionales en América Latina: El Caso Argentino," *Comercio Exterior* 46, no. 9 (1996): 692–702, quoted in Katharina Müller, "The Political Economy of Pension Privatisation in the Baltics," in Fultz, *Pension Reform*, 402. Since the early 1990s, the World Bank has advocated radical pension reforms in Latin America and Eastern Europe. In its 1994 report *Averting the Old Age Crisis* (Washington, D.C.: World Bank), the bank encouraged partial privatization and individualization of pensions. The World Bank recommended a three-pillar model, which includes a first, state-managed pay-as-you-go tier; a privately managed, mandatory and prefunded second tier; and a third, privately managed voluntary tier.

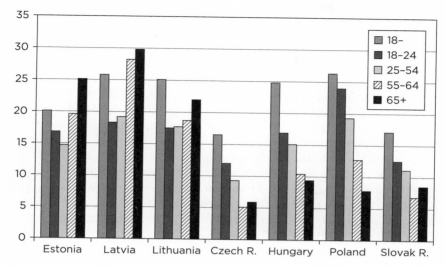

Figure 3.1 At-risk-of-poverty rate after social transfers by age group, percent in 2006. Authors' calculation based on EUROSTAT, http://epp.eurostat.ec.europa.eu (accessed August 8, 2011). At-risk-of-poverty rate refers to the share of persons with an equivalized disposable income below the risk-of-poverty threshold, which is set at 60 percent of the national median equivalized disposable income after social transfers.

to support his reform efforts. The Swedish experts eagerly embraced this opportunity, and de facto used Latvia as a testing ground for their recently launched reforms back home. As a result, Latvia was the first East European country to introduce a multi-pillar pension system as advocated by the World Bank. It went beyond that, however. The first, pay-as-you-go (PAYG) pillar was based on the Swedish template of a notional defined contribution scheme, a system that "mimic[s] a lifetime contribution based pension that would be offered by an insurance company."[55] This scheme is meant to impose discipline on contributors, and sends strong incentives to delay retirement, as retirement benefits are entirely dependent on an individual's contribution.

A key issue of the transition to the notional defined contribution scheme was how to calculate the initial pension "capital" from the old system. The government decided to credit insurance periods up until 1995 based on past

55. Louise Fox and Edward Palmer, "Latvian Pension Reform," Social Protection Discussion Paper 9922 (Washington D.C.: World Bank, 1999), 9. The notional defined contribution (NDC) scheme is a method that emerged in the 1990s to record earnings-related benefits in the public pension system. Pension contributions are recorded in individualized accounts, and future benefits take into account past contributions, the "rate of return," which is typically linked to the growth of the wage sum, and the life expectancy of the cohort to which the beneficiary belongs. In contrast to private funded schemes, the money is not invested. Under NDC the pension scheme remains a pay-as-you-go system.

service years, but at current earning levels. Moreover, contributions rather than actual wages were taken into account. The transition formula had major distributional consequences. It disadvantaged all those with a long employment record who were unemployed, held inferior jobs, worked in state-owned enterprises, or were employed in firms where wage arrears or underreporting had prevailed during the crucial years of 1996–99. At the same time, those in the private sector who understood the new system and were in a position to manipulate their earnings for the relevant period became major winners of the reform.[56]

In Estonia, the second wave of pension reforms started when the incoming centrist minority government under Prime Minister Mart Siimann set up a Social Security Reform Commission in 1997, with the mandate to prepare a reform outline. Siimann appointed Hansson (previously a member of Estonia's Monetary Reform Committee) as chair of the commission. The commission included experts from the National Social Insurance Board and the Ministry of Finance. After only a month of deliberation, the commission proposed the introduction of the World Bank's multipillar system. At the same time, it favored a low replacement rate for reasons of financial viability. It also gave a highly unfavorable opinion on recalculating the pensions on the basis of previous earnings. The commission's pension proposals laid the foundations for the subsequent pension reforms.[57]

In Lithuania, the gateway to more radical pension reforms was the deficit accumulated by the Lithuanian Social Insurance Fund from 1996 onward. Because of the prolonged crisis, the substantial decrease in economic activity, and the large number of companies defaulting on their social insurance contributions, the fund's income did not keep up with the expenses. While the magnitude of the deficit was small—it amounted to 0.1 percent of GDP in 1996–98, and could easily have been covered by a slight increase in the contribution rate—it spurred a heated media campaign against the fund.[58]

The conservative government under Premier Vagnorius (1996–99) started to prepare for radical reforms. However, it got in the line of fire between the divergent privatization models advocated by the Confederation of Industrialists and the Free Market Institute. The latter was also backed by the World Bank. As a result, the 1999 Pension Funds Law remained an ambiguous piece of legislation. Although it provided the legal framework for funded pensions, it did not stipulate mandatory participation, and never even mentioned private

56. Inta Vanovska, "Pension Reform in Latvia," in Fultz, *Pension Reform,* 181.

57. Leppik and Võrk, "Pension Reforms"; Aidukaite, "The Formation of Social Insurance." For a comparison between the Estonian and Latvian pension reforms see Margit Tavits, "Policy Learning and Uncertainty: The Case of Pension Reforms in Estonia and Latvia," *Policy Studies Journal* 31, no. 4 (2003): 643–60. In light of the findings in other literature, Tavits seems to slighty overstate the coordinated, deliberative, and endogenous character of the Estonian pension reform.

58. Romas Lazutka, "Pension Reform in Lithuania," in Fultz, *Pension Reform,* 306.

pensions explicitly. All in all then, as was the case with the currency board, Lithuania only half-heartedly embraced the option of pension privatization.

Generally, pension benefits in all the Baltic states remained low and their distribution compressed. The reforms that were carried out reflected an overall concern with macroeconomic stability rather than social compensation. They aimed at ensuring medium- and long-term affordability of the pension system, improving its transparency, reducing redistribution, and increasing the contribution of welfare to economic growth and development. Not only pensions, but also unemployment insurance and social assistance exhibited similar features.[59]

Ethnic Aspects of Social Policy

The social losses resulting from radical marketization and economic restructuring disproportionately burdened Estonia's and Latvia's mostly Russian-speaking manufacturing labor force. Manufacturing workers' high occupational status under Soviet rule had manifested itself in privileged access to firm-based social provisions, but with the collapse of inherited industries not only did they lose their job-related benefits, but they also suffered more frequent and longer periods of unemployment and losses of employment quality—such as wage arrears and compulsory unpaid holidays—than members of the ethnic majorities.[60]

However, protective industrial policies were not adopted to slow down the process of disruption of the predominantly Russian labor force's life, nor were adequately funded unemployment benefit and retraining programs offered to ease the resulting social stress. Indeed, while the refusal of state assistance to troubled industrial firms—such as in the form of subsidies and grace periods for restructuring—had been justified by the requirements of fiscal discipline and monetary stability, identity politics helped to cement the hegemony of the stability-oriented agenda in yet another way.

On the one hand, denial of industrial protection could be more easily justified on grounds of perceived vulnerability of the national economy to postcolonial influences. In the case of Estonia, in Premier Laar's words, after 1940 a "large Soviet military garrison and the continued influx of Russian speaking colonists who acted like a 'civilian garrison' replaced the lost population. In order to effect colonialization, rapid industrialization was launched by Moscow."[61] By implication, after independence, radical deindustrialization could be perceived as a means of decolonization.[62]

---

59. Aidukaite, "The Formation of Social Insurance."
60. See Adne Aasland, "Citizenship, States and Social Exclusion in Estonia and Latvia," *Journal of Baltic Studies* 33, no. 1 (2002): 57–77.
61. Laar, *Estonia*, 37.
62. For a formulation focusing on the general impact of systemic change rather than on the ethnically patterned variants of social exclusion, see Eglitis and Lace, "Stratification

TABLE 3.2
Ethnic aspects of social dislocation, 1993

	Ethnic Estonians	Estonian Russians	Ethnic Latvians	Latvian Russians	Ethnic Lithuanians	Lithuanian Russians
Initially enjoyed firm-based benefits[a]	24	43	22	34	24	33
Currently unemployed	6	11	10	15	8	10
Loss of employment quality in the past year[b]	24	38	27	33	26	22
Very worried about losing job	10	43	39	53	48	49

Source: Richard Rose, William Maley, Vilmorius Lasopec, and EMOR, "Nationalities in the Baltic States," A Survey Study, Studies in Public Policy 222 (Glasgow: University of Strathclyde Center for the Study of Public Policy, 1994), 6–8, 10.
Note: Data shown as percent of affirmative answers.
[a]Enjoyed at least one of the following job-related benefits: food, meals, housing, consumer goods, care for children, holiday facilities, medical care.
[b]Experienced at least one of the following: unemployment, short-time pay, compulsory holiday without pay.

The imminent atrophy of business and labor organizations has not been viewed as too painful a loss, even if it led to highly fragmented industrial relations that impaired the prospects for more socially embedded monetary coordination. Led in part by similar fears of Russia's continuing economic influence, by the abrupt withdrawal of public assets, and by the desire to set strict prudency standards, the Bank of Estonia urged the liquidation of banks that allegedly laundered revenues of Russian organized crime. The monetary authority also encouraged acquisitions by Western commercial banks that rapidly emerged as market leaders.[63]

On the other hand, passive and active labor market policies fell short of compensating for the ethnic bias in social losses, especially given that social spending has been overall meager in the Baltic states in comparison with the Visegrád countries and Slovenia, let alone many older EU member nations. Furthermore, not all Estonian and Latvian social policies have been blind to ethnicity.

---

and the Poverty of Progress," 336: "The most apparently superfluous category of the population in the post-Soviet context is the classic icon of Soviet progress and productivity, the heavy industrial worker." For the way workers' role after socialism has been discursively redefined see David Ost, *The Defeat of Solidarity: Anger and Politics in Postcommunist Europe* (Ithaca: Cornell University Press, 2005) for the Polish case, and Daina Eglitis, "Class, Culture, and Consumption: Representations of Stratification in Post-Communist Latvia," *Cultural Sociology* 5, no. 3 (September 2011): 423–46, for the Latvian context.
    63. Laar, *Estonia,* 191–93.

To the contrary, the welfare states in these countries have been more generous in those areas that could be linked to the nationalizing projects. Relative to GDP they have spent as much or even more on education, and also employed a higher share of the workforce in the public sector, than many of their East Central European peers. In Estonia and Latvia, the latter policy has reinforced an inherited ethnically divided labor market, and protected the ethnic Baltic populations somewhat better than the Russian speakers from adverse market shocks. At the onset of the transformation, non-Balts in Estonia and Latvia were overrepresented in the industrial, transport, and maritime sectors, whereas ethnic Balts were concentrated in agriculture, education, and the state bureaucracy.[64]

Independence gave members of the titular nation the opportunity "to use the institutional structure of their ethnic republic in order to take over 'the state' more effectively and thus turn society more rapidly towards an ethnic Estonian direction"[65]—as was also the case in Latvia. By means of restrictive language and citizenship laws, both societies limited the access of the Russophone population to career opportunities in government, public administration, the professions, and many categories of the economy at large. Latvia developed the most discriminatory regime, with "more than 33 separate categories of employment barred for non-citizens."[66] Satisfactory command of the majority language was required for employment in both the public and several branches of the private sector, with the required degree of fluency varying according to the employee's position. Remarkably, industrial workers were de facto exempted from language requirements.[67]

As a consequence, the new states' public sectors became more "Estonianized" and "Latvianized" as the 1990s wore on. According to a survey carried out by Richard Rose and his collaborators in 2000, at the beginning of the 1990s, 31 percent of employed ethnic Latvians and 32 percent of ethnic Russians had jobs in the public sector. In 2000, 35 percent of the former and a mere 21 percent of the latter were employed in public services. The developments in Estonia were similar. Whereas at the beginning of the decade, 22 percent of ethnic Estonians and 25 percent of ethnic Russians reported employment in the public sector, by 2000 27 percent of the former and only 16 percent of the latter claimed to have jobs in this sector. In contrast, the share of Lithuanian Russians working in public service increased slightly from 35 to 38 percent, although not as much as that of ethnic Lithuanians for whom the numbers were 30 and 37 respectively.

---

64. Colin W. Mettam and Steven W. Williams, "Internal Colonialism and Cultural Divisions of Labour in the Soviet Republic of Estonia," *Nations and Nationalism* 4, no. 3 (1998): 383–88; Pettai and Hallik, "Understanding Processes," 515; Norgaard et al., *The Baltic States* (1996), 174.

65. Pettai and Hallik, "Understanding Processes," 516.

66. Hughes, " 'Exit,' " 745.

67. Norgaard et al., *The Baltic States* (1996), 179–81; Pal Kolsto, *Political Construction Sites: Nation-Building in Russia and the Post-Soviet States* (Boulder: Westview, 2000), 105–16.

On the other side of the coin, the private economy became "Russified": in 2000 47 percent of employed ethnic Latvians and 57 percent of ethnic Russians found occupation in privatized or newly founded private firms. The respective numbers for ethnic Estonians were 54 percent and for ethnic Russians in Estonia 62 percent. In Lithuania, a similar proportion of both groups was employed in the private sector.[68]

What is more, in Estonia and Latvia, Russophones were almost entirely removed from top public and partly even from top private positions. In a study of elite change in the Baltic countries after independence, Anton Steen found out that by 1993–94 the core institutions of the state, and the top state bureaucratic positions in Estonia and Latvia were almost entirely in the hands of the majority nation. The picture of the economic elites is somewhat more mixed: in Latvia, Russians constituted 13 percent of the elites in state enterprises, and 30 percent of the elites in private enterprises. In Estonia, the respective numbers were 15 and 6 percent.[69]

Related to the above, it is interesting to observe that nation builders though they were, neither Estonian nor Latvian neoliberal reformers experimented much with the kind of privatization techniques that led to various (albeit transitory) forms of national capitalism in many other East Central European states. In the latter countries both insider-dominated methods allowing management employee buyouts (MEBOs) on a massive scale, and outsider-oriented voucher privatization programs promoting the emergence of masses of small owners based on citizenship rights had been initially popular. The sole exception was Hungary, where the service of crippling foreign debt made it almost imperative for the state to secure large hard currency inflows by selling firms mostly directly to foreign strategic investors. As none of the Baltic states assumed responsibility for former Soviet debt, they were less constrained than Hungary when choosing among methods of privatization. Yet in contrast to Slovenia, Croatia, and Romania (or even Hungary or Poland where to a lesser extent MEBOs were also used) Estonia and Latvia opted for direct sales to foreigners as the primary, and vouchers as secondary, technique.[70]

Beyond efficiency considerations, these decisions might have reflected nationalizing concerns too. Permitting massive management-employee buyouts, especially in the privatization of large enterprises, would have inevitably empowered ethnic Russian managers and workers, while Western strategic owners were seen as less of a threat to sovereignty. Vouchers limited the entry

---

68. See for these and other data on the social consequences of the ethnic divide Richard Rose, "New Baltic Barometer IV: A Survey Study," Studies in Public Policy 338 (Glasgow: Centre for the Study of Public Policy, University of Strathclyde, 2000), 5, 14.

69. Steen, "The New Elites," 103–8.

70. *Transition Report 2000* (London: EBRD, 2000), 160, 184, 188; OECD, *Baltic States*, 125–33. It is interesting to note that the early privatization schemes before independence favored insiders.

of residents without citizenship into the ranks of the new propertied class. In light of the above, it is unsurprising that Lithuania, with its first preference for vouchers and initially only limited use of direct sales, was an outlier in this respect as well.

All in all, then, the Baltic states have offered their population a nationalist rather than a welfarist social contract (the latter being the version of the Visegrád states, to be discussed in chapter 4, "Welfarist Social Contracts"). Under this contract spending on forms of social protection accessible to citizens and noncitizens alike—health care, pensions, and active and passive labor market policies—has been subject to strict controls. At the same time, in the few areas where Baltic welfare generosity has stood out—namely, spending on higher education and certain kinds of state employment—access has been controlled via citizenship requirements or language proficiency tests administered in the official language. Hence, the Estonian and Latvian welfare states' overall relatively meager performance should also be judged against the yardstick of the nationalizing project in which these countries' elites have been engaged—that is the project of building a state for the core titular nation. In Lithuania, the nationalist social contract has remained symbolic, as it has not offered much shelter or opportunities for selected groups.

Exclusionary democracies and nationalist social contracts go a long way toward accounting for the relatively limited challenges to radical neoliberal policies in the Baltic countries.[71] Still, the economic transformation has had grave social consequences. Workers in the Baltic states suffered a dramatic loss of income in the early transformation period. Real wages fell by as much as two-thirds in 1990–99, and even with the recovery thereafter, by the end of the millennium they only reached between 40 and 60 percent of their 1989 levels.[72] Employment levels decreased sharply, leading to significantly lower labor force participation and high unemployment. The transformation has also been accompanied by a significant increase in income inequality, especially in Latvia, where the Gini coefficient increased by 17 percentage points between 1990 and 1994. In Estonia and Lithuania, it increased by 10 and 11 points respectively.[73] Income differentials widened particularly among the poorer segments of the population. Parallel with rising unemployment and income inequalities, poverty also became widespread.[74]

To account for the relative societal quiescence and unchallenged neoliberalism in light of these grave social dislocations, factors other than

71. See Vello Pettai, "Political Stability Through Disenfranchisement," *Transitions* 3, no. 6 (4 April, 1997): 21–23, on how the ethnopolitical aspects of Estonian and Latvian politics minimized resistance to the neoliberal economic reforms.

72. OECD, *Baltic States*, 151.

73. Peter K. Cornelius and Beatriz S. Weder, "Economic Transformation and Income Distribution: Some Evidence from the Baltic Countries," IMF Staff Papers 43.3 (Washington, D.C.: International Monetary Fund, 1996), 587–604.

74. Milanovic, *Income, Inequality and Poverty*, 68–71.

exclusionary democracies, fragmented and nonrepresentative party systems, and nationalist social contracts have to be factored in. In this respect, it certainly helped that in time, the pains of transformation started to bear some fruit. Out of the deep transformational recession, first the Estonian "rising star of the Baltics," and then the Baltic tigers emerged.

Constructing the Estonian Success Story

One of the most remarkable aspects of the Baltic states' transformation is how fast these countries could change their image as fragile, backward, ethnic conflict–ridden post-Soviet successor states into internationally acclaimed models of democratic capitalist success. A conjuncture of ideational, structural, domestic, and international factors made this happen.

The Baltic success story took its origin in Estonia, and it owed its existence as much to a powerful narrative of success as to the fact of Estonia's relatively satisfactory economic performance. Arguably, the most influential interpreter of the Estonian transformation is two-time Prime Minister Laar whose radical reform package is said to have laid the foundations for Estonia's rise from the ruins of communism. Laar spent considerable efforts at promoting Estonia internationally. In the early 1990s, his government sponsored an international media campaign to draw attention to the "Estonian miracle." One of its offshoots was *Newsweek*'s label for Estonia as "A little country that could." Laar later used this as the title for his own book on the reforms, which was published and promoted by the Center for Research into Post-Communist Economies, a neoliberal think tank founded by members of the Institute of Economic Affairs and the Atlas Economic Research Foundation. Laar also gave many interviews to mostly neoliberal and libertarian journals and newspapers.

Laar's narrative of the Estonian transformation has a number of ingredients. He is adamant in his rejection of any socialist legacy. Even more than the physical legacies—the ruins of Soviet industrialization and infrastructure—he deplores the mental legacies, and stresses the need for changes in people's attitudes. He relentlessly underlines the need for radical and speedy reforms as the only way to do away with inherited liabilities. The issue of national vulnerability looms large. Estonia is invariably presented as a small country that has again and again been a battlefield of big powers. Yet, out of foreign occupation and dominance, Estonians have come unaltered in their cultural identity and their craving for freedom. In particular the period of the first independence is a source for pride and also inspiration, the more so as many of the challenges of the interwar period are seemingly repeating themselves after the breakdown of communism.

Among the most striking elements in Laar's narrative is his stress on the country's and its leaders lack of preparedness for the tasks that initially faced them and, hence, the improbability of success. "It is very fortunate that I was not an economist," Laar says in an interview.

> I had read only one book on economics—Milton Friedman's *Free to Choose*. I was so ignorant at the time that I thought that what Friedman wrote about the benefits of privatisation, the flat tax and the abolition of all customs rights, was the result of economic reforms that had been put into practice in the West. It seemed common sense to me and, as I thought it had already been done everywhere, I simply introduced it in Estonia, despite warnings from Estonian economists that it could not be done. They said it was as impossible as walking on water. We did it: we just walked on the water because we did not know that it was impossible.[75]

This narrative, then, is built on the notion that even under the most unlikely circumstances, success could happen. This is nothing short of a miracle. What is this success? In Laar's account, it is the fast economic recovery made possible by radical reforms. Recovery is being built on foundations very different from those of the socialist system. It is characterized by the creation of an ultraliberal business-friendly environment that helps attract large amounts of FDI; a balanced budget and strict monetary policy that give Estonia a strong reputation as a reliable borrower; a fully open trade regime that has led to a rapid reorientation of foreign trade; and a social protection system "inspiring people to assume responsibility for their own future."[76]

In this context, the rapid deindustrialization so characteristic for the Baltic states (see table 1.7) is not seen as problematic. Industrial legacies are identified with wasteful, useless, and unwanted production, built up by the Soviets with the aim to colonize the country. While Estonia lost most of its complex industries in the process of deindustrialization, and this sector's recovery has mostly been carried by traditional industries, Laar takes pride in the fact that Finnish investments have transformed some segments of the machinery and electrical equipment industries, which now contribute significantly to exports.

In a similar way, some of the disastrous social consequences of the multiple shocks inflicted on the Estonian economy are interpreted in a favorable way, as they have led to a change of attitude among the people, and especially among the Russian community, who were made to understand that they could not rely on the state any more to help them out, but had to take their fate in their own hands. In this sense, the Estonian way of

75. Mart Laar, quoted in "Walking on Water," *Brussels Journal*, August 27, 2005, http://www.brusselsjournal.com/node/202 (accessed November 23, 2009).

76. Laar, *Estonia*, 271.

resolving the ethnic question has also turned out to be a success. While it was necessary to deny Russian speakers the right to vote in parliamentary elections and referendums, as they were not supportive of radical reforms, the very success of these reforms has given Russians hope for upward mobility as well. With the new individualistic values flourishing, ethnic tensions are disappearing.

A major ingredient of Laar's account of Estonia's success finally is that the country has been pulling itself up by its own bootstraps. Resolutely going its own way, more often than not defying the advice of IFIs and Western advisers, and consciously cutting Estonia off from international sources that provided "aid rather than trade" was the hallmark of "the little country that could."[77]

There is overall ample evidence that in a comparative (Baltic) perspective, Estonia's economic performance is superior. Dissenting voices have, however, pointed to a number of factors other than reform radicalism that may have contributed to this relative success. Two accounts deserve attention here. The first alternative interpretation challenges the perception of legacies being merely obstacles to reform.[78] It argues that Estonia had privileged initial conditions, as it had served as an economic laboratory for economic experiments ever since the 1960s. Estonian experiments often provided models for broader reforms throughout the Soviet Union. Under Mikhail Gorbachev's perestroika, Estonian reform plans became more ambitious. As soon as it was possible, Estonia encouraged the establishment of semiprivate "people's enterprises" as well as joint ventures with foreign companies, initiated small-scale privatization, and gradually liberalized its prices. Moreover, as mentioned above, in September 1987 leading economists published a reform proposal that anticipated many of the reforms that were to be implemented after independence.

What this adds up to is that "Estonia 'hit the ground running' once the communist system collapsed, and did not waste valuable time in the early days of the transition."[79] Further, the country also had inherited structural advantages vis-à-vis its peers that made its reform tasks less daunting. Its share of light industry was higher than that of the two other republics, and as light industries had remained under regional rather than centralized control, the number of all-union enterprises with centralized decisionmaking was significantly lower in Estonia than in Latvia and Lithuania.[80] While this interpretation of Estonian success does not challenge the overall representation of

---

77. Ibid., 248.
78. See, e.g., Ritsa A. Panagiotou, "Estonia's Success: Prescription or Legacy?" *Communist and Post-Communist Studies* 34 (2001): 261–77. For a discussion of Estonia's reform legacies, see Van Arkadie and Karlsson, *Economic Survey;* Misiunas and Taagepera, *The Baltic States.*
79. Panagiotou, "Estonia's Success," 273.
80. John Hansen and Piritta Sorsa, "Estonia: A Shining Star from the Baltics," in *Trade in the New Independent States,* ed. Constantine Michalopoulos and David G. Tarr (Washington, D.C.: The World Bank/UNDP, 1994), 115–32; Norgaard et al., *The Baltic States* (1999), 143–46.

Estonia as a radical reformer, it qualifies that view to some degree by pointing to the legacies the early postindependence reformers could build on. It also suggests that Estonia could become more successful than its peers only as a result of these favorable legacies.

A second interpretation of Estonia's transformation is much more critical when it comes to the structural changes that have been taking place, and thus qualifies the notion of success. This interpretation—much in line with our own analysis—points to the fact that radical liberalization of trade and investment and limited support for industrial restructuring destroyed much of the basis for innovation and competitiveness, as it led to "wiping out the most knowledge- and technology-intensive industries of the relatively less competitive economy."[81] It also sheds a more critical light on Estonia's industrial sector of pride—its export-oriented machinery and electrical equipment industries. A large share of this sector's output is reexported either directly or following some processing. In terms of value added, Estonian "high-tech" production occurs mostly in the lowest segments of the sector, typically in assembly subcontracting operations.[82]

Moreover, some authors also point to another important source of revenue that is quite consistently downplayed in most narratives of the Estonian success, namely transit of Russian oil and oil products as well as other commodities. With the Soviet collapse, Estonia—like the other two Baltic republics—could charge world prices, payable in hard currencies, for transit and loading fees. Managing transit of Russian oil and oil products thus became a profitable industry, contributing—depending on the estimates—between 4 to 10 percent to the country's GDP.[83] Estonia's dependency on transit trade does not fit particularly well with the dominant narrative of success, as it involves continuing dependency on Russia and on a particular sector that had previously been firmly controlled by Soviet authorities. Consider the following statement by Lagle Parek, chairwoman of the Estonian National Independence Party and Estonian interior minister in 1992–93:

81. Marek Tiits, "Industrial and Trade Dynamics in the Baltic Sea Region—the Last Two Waves of European Union Enlargement from a Historic Perspective," Working Paper 1 (Tartu: Institute of Baltic Studies, 2006), 23.

82. Niels Mygind, "The Internationalization of the Baltic Economies," BRIE Working Paper 130 (Berkeley: BRIE, 1997); Robert Burgess, Stefania Fabrizio, and Yuan Xiao, "The Baltics: Competitiveness on the Eve of EU Accession," Country Report 3/114 (Washington, D.C.: International Monetary Fund, 2004); Uwe Dullek, Neil Foster, Robert Stehrer, and Julia Wörz, "Dimensions of Quality Upgrading in CEECs," wiiw Working Paper 29 (Vienna: Wiener Institut der Weltwirtschaftsforschung, 2004); Marek Tiits, Rainer Kattel, and Tarmo Kalvet. "Made in Estonia," Working paper, (Tartu: Institute of Baltic Studies, 2006), 17–18, 52–53; Tiits, "Industrial and Trade Dynamics," 23.

83. David J. Smith, *Estonia: Independence and European Integration* (London: Routledge, 2002), 123; Andreas Saarniit, "Estonia's Transit Trade," *Kroon and Economy* 1 (2006): 43–48; Juhani Laurila, "Determinants of Transit Transports between the European Union and Russia," BOFIT paper 1 (Helsinki: Bank of Finland, Institute for Economies in Transition, 2002).

[In our party] we do not in fact want Estonia to become "a new Hong Kong." That way, we might become richer economically, but Estonians do not fit that role, because spiritually they are closer to the soil. As a people we have always aspired to education and culture, even amidst the greatest difficulties, so we deserve today something a bit better than the role of a Hong Kong. I hope that in the course of time... Estonia will be a country that creates values, and does not mediate them; because true joy comes from making something, not just circulating or processing it."[84]

The qualifications and alternative interpretations of Estonia's success notwithstanding, major elements offered by Laar's narrative became cornerstones of the dominant view. This was partly because they resonated well with the outlook of influential international actors. As Laar recalls in the above-cited interview, the world started to notice that something was happening "in 1994 when people first started to talk about the Estonian economic miracle. Then this reputation began to grow. Of course we always tried to find new things to add to this reputation and to really be successful. We have been quite good in this. After a first wave of reforms we had a second and a third wave too."[85]

Not surprisingly, Estonia's economic miracle and the policies that allegedly made it possible initially drew most attention among radical neoliberal and libertarian circles. However, increasingly Estonia also became a poster child of more mainstream international organizations. Several factors account for this.

First, some of Estonia's early policy innovations actually anticipated an emerging international consensus. This was the case with the currency board. The early Washington consensus on exchange rate regimes, formed after the Latin American debt crisis, favored fixed or managed exchange rate regimes. After the Mexican currency crisis of 1994, however, a new policy consensus started to emerge that favored regimes that adjusted automatically, that is without government interference in market forces. In a world characterized by high capital mobility, only currency board or fully flexible exchange rate regimes were seen capable of averting currency crises.[86] By this time, the Estonian experience could already serve as an example of the advantages of currency boards. From then on, the IMF recommended this institution to all postsocialist countries that faced currency crises. Currency boards, once a maverick solution, thus started to expand to other countries of the region.

Second, there might have been a need on part of international and supranational organizations to highlight the possibility of success beyond the

84. Quoted in Lieven, *Baltic Revolution*, 331.
85. Laar interview, "Walking on Water," 2005.
86. Dominick Salvatore, James W. Dean, and Thomas D. Willett, eds., *The Dollarization Debate* (Oxford: Oxford University Press, 2003), 3.

Visegrád group. This became most apparent in the decision of the EU to include Estonia in the first round of applicants with whom entry negotiations were started. The road to Europe has been bumpier for all three Baltic states than for most of the Visegrád countries and Slovenia. These countries' belated start with economic and political reforms, as well as concerns about relations with Russia and the fate of the Russian minorities in Estonia and Latvia, made the EU more hesitant in its commitment. The EU's stance changed after its northern enlargement, with the Scandinavian countries supporting the Baltic states' membership.

Nonetheless, it was far from obvious that any of the Baltic states would qualify for immediate entry negotiations, as they fell short of meeting the Copenhagen criteria. This notwithstanding, both Estonia and Lithuania assumed that they were in a better position than their peers. Whereas Estonia pointed to its economic reform credentials, Lithuania referred to its track record with respect to political and minority rights.[87] The choice to include only Estonia sent two important signals to the Baltic region. On the one hand it made clear that despite their Soviet past, these countries had the same chances for joining the EU as any other former communist country, provided that they established a good record of reforms. On the other hand, the EU decision signaled that priority was being given to economic transformation. While the commission had an issue with the treatment of Russian-speaking residents, it was the fact that it regarded Estonia "as a functioning market economy, able to cope with the competitive pressure and market forces within the Union"[88] that tipped the balance in its favor.

Third, the consolidation of neoliberalism that took place over the 1990s and 2000s also contributed to spreading the specific interpretation of Estonian success internationally. One manifestation of this was the proliferation of international rankings related to "economic freedom" and economic competitiveness. These rankings typically seek to promote specific and standardized understanding of a single best economic practice, allow for easy regime comparisons, and single out particular successful countries that constitute models to follow. The rankings are often built on the perceptions of members of the international business community. Estonia invariably comes up in a top position among its peers.[89]

87. Norgaard et al., *Baltic States* (1999), 171.
88. "Agenda 2000—Commission Opinion on Estonia's Application for Membership of the European Union," European Commission DOC/97/12 (Brussels, July 15, 1997).
89. See, e.g., the World Economic Forum's ranking of progress toward implementing the aims of the Lisbon agenda, in which Estonia always tops the list among the accession countries, e.g., *The Lisbon Review 2010: Towards a More Competitive Europe?* (Geneva: World Economic Forum, 2010), http://www3.weforum.org/docs/WEF_LisbonReview_Report_2010.pdf (accessed March 1, 2011); the WEF's global competitiveness ranking, e.g., *The Global Competitiveness Report 2011–2012* (Geneva: World Economic Forum, 2011), http://reports.weforum.org/global-competitiveness-2011–2012/ (accessed August 15, 2011); and the World

In contrast to Estonia, neither Latvia nor Lithuania succeeded during the 1990s in presenting themselves as successful transition economies. In Latvia, the idea of becoming a "new Hong Kong" offering offshore banking and trade services for the Russian hinterland fell on more fertile ground than in Estonia. Especially the government under Andris Šķēle (1995–97) has attempted to boost the role of transport and the port economy, trying to build on Latvia's locational advantage as the main transport corridor for East-West trade. It created free port areas and special economic zones, including tax reduction for investors. In addition to transport, Latvia's financial sector has also sought to strategically exploit the country's specific geographical location. Parex Bank, Latvia's first private bank, founded in 1988, built its strategy around attracting deposits from the former Soviet Union. In the early 1990s, Parex advertised its services with the slogan "We're closer than Switzerland." Indeed, for Russian depositors Latvia offered a good mix of a place relatively easy to go to that at the same time offered better legal guarantees than banks back home.[90]

Yet it was hard to sell the new Hong Kong as a success story. First, ambivalences related to dependence on Russia loomed large, and not all governments shared Premier Šķēle's enthusiasm for exploiting the specific opportunities of port cities. It did not help matters that Russia repeatedly used its economic position to interfere in Latvia's domestic policies. For instance, oil transports were interrupted several times in order to influence Latvia's treatment of the minority population. Second, the Russian hinterland itself was repeatedly subject to economic troubles that had serious repercussions on the transport and financial sectors. Russia also tried to decrease its dependency on Baltic transit by playing the three countries against each other, expanding its own port capacities, and undertaking pipeline projects aimed at bypassing the Baltic states. As a consequence, transit traffic has not grown nearly enough to compensate for the economic decline in other areas.[91]

Third, the entrepôt economy provided a fertile soil for corruption. Thus, international actors repeatedly accused Latvia's banking sector of money laundering. Also, the three men most often referred to as Latvian oligarchs— the long-term mayor of the oil port of Ventspils, Aivars Lembergs, former Prime Minister Andris Šķēle, and Transport Minister Ainārs Šlesers—are thriving on the transit economy. It is also telling that the list of the ten richest

Bank's *Doing Business* rankings, http://www.doingbusiness.org/EconomyRankings/ (accessed November 8, 2009).

90. Eiki Berg, "Where East meets West? Baltic States in Search of New Identity," in *Regions in Central and Eastern Europe: Past and Present,* ed. Eiki Berg (Hokkaido: Slavic Research Center, 2007), 49–67; Lieven, *Baltic Revolution,* 363–65; Pauls Raudseps, "Latvia: Bridge Collapse," *Transitions Online,* no. 3 (December 2008), www.tol.org (accessed November 9, 2009); "Latvian Banks Serve as Transit for Russian Money," *Baltic Times,* November 1, 2004.

91. Laurila, "Determinants"; Alf Brodin, *Baltic Sea Ports and Russian Foreign Trade: Studies in the Economic and Political Geography of Transition* (University of Göteborg, Department of Human and Economic Geography, 2003).

people in the Baltics is headed by Latvians who are involved in either banking or the transit economy. The only Estonian who made it to the group is also a "transit businessman."[92]

Lithuania, finally, was mostly perceived as unstable and struggling in the 1990s. It was identified as being the least thoroughgoing in following the "Baltic way" of radical reforms, thus achieving the least impressive economic results. It was also much less able to compensate for deindustrialization by reliance on the transit sector, having smaller port facilities than Latvia and no border with Russia except for the Kaliningrad enclave. Yet in the new millennium the initial laggard Baltic states caught up with Estonia, and this way a "Baltic miracle" was in the making. We will now turn to the factors behind this outcome.

Internationalization, European Integration, and the Baltic Economic Miracle

The Baltic economic miracle of the 2000s owes its existence to a number of important changes in the international environment. Over the 1990s, international actors and factors mostly acted as constraints on these countries' economies. The collapse of the Russian economy and later the Russian financial crisis sent shockwaves through the Baltic states, while their production profiles were too weak to successfully compete on Western markets. As to the IFIs, as argued above, Estonia did not always heed the advice it got from them. Moreover, as its attempts at going it alone seemed to bear fruits, international actors were increasingly prepared to give Estonia a vote of confidence on whatever further steps it planned to undertake. This was not the case with Latvia and Lithuania whose economic recovery was much more troubled. International organizations held these countries on a shorter leash.

At some point, however, things started to change. The specific conjuncture of the EU accession process and a world economy in which credit was becoming abundant allowed for a paradoxical development. While many of the original institutions and policies of the Baltic states were reinforced, there was no need for correcting the model's drawbacks, as the global credit economy was effectively sidelining external constraints stemming from a decline in international competitiveness.

EU accession provided the reform paths undertaken since the 1990s with a specific purpose and a definite time horizon, and thus empowered reform-minded political actors that might otherwise have backtracked. It also contributed to Latvia's and Lithuania's catching up with the Estonian reform

---

92. The list of the richest people was drawn by the *Baltic Times* in 2003–4, http://www.baltic-course.com/archive/eng/index.htm-read = 381.htm (accessed November 28, 2009).

effort. The EU's agenda in the subregion was broad and encompassing, ranging from improving the political situation for minorities, through a general reinforcement of the privatization and restructuring agenda, to very specific sectoral policy reforms. Arguably, one of major efforts of the EU was directed towards advancing administrative, institutional, and regulatory capacities. This approach was in line with the central position of regulation in the EU's policymaking. At its core, the *acquis communautaire* governing the internal market and the common policies has been an exercise in regulatory state building on multiple levels of European governance.[93]

There is a clear affinity between the Baltic states' reform choices and a regulatory state model. As their most interventionist state institutions had been under central control, the disentanglement from the Soviet Union allowed for an easier dissolution of some of them. Moreover, Baltic reformers rejected the features of a "positive" state, such as high taxation, redistribution, and direct production of goods and services. For that reason, their institutions were, from the beginning, geared to regulating rather than otherwise intervening in the economy. The Baltic states also shared the socio-economic vision institutionalized in the EU: preference for market-enhancing competition policy over excessive state aid, for assistance to new domestic start-ups over subsidies to huge foreign firms, and for reformed social policies that reintegrated people into the workforce over pension-dominated welfare provisions.

In this context, it is of great significance that EU accession helped the Baltic states to develop regulatory capacities. Capacity building has been supported by a variety of programs and has received an important amount of technical and financial assistance. However, the overall record is mixed. Whereas the new EU member states, including the Baltics, have an excellent record of transposing EU directives into national law, there is some doubt as to whether they also have developed the ability to implement directives, and to expand beyond core EU areas. Even so, the Baltic states perform better than most other new members when it comes to (administrative) capacity building. In a number of fields—transposition of EU directives into national law, fiscal discipline, investment climate, and innovation in public management—they have laid stronger foundations than their peers. They also have a better record in making use of monetary transfers stemming from EU funds. Moreover, in contrast to other countries, their reform efforts continued at full speed even after EU accession.[94]

---

93. Majone, "From the Positive to the Regulatory State"; Bruszt and McDermott, "Transnational Integration Regimes," forthcoming.

94. See "EU-8: Administrative Capacity in the New Member States: The Limits of Innovation," Report 36930-GLB (Washington, D.C.: World Bank, 2006). For the crucial field of public service reforms, see Jan-Hinrik Meyer-Sahling, "Sustainability of Civil Service Reforms in Central and Eastern Europe Five Years after EU Accession," (Gov/Sigma Paper 44, (Paris: OECD, April 2009); and for country differences in the degrees of politicization of

Another area in which EU accession significantly reinforced the economic path embarked on earlier by the Baltic states concerns economic restructuring. While privatization and enterprise restructuring had been on these countries' agendas early on, it was in the course of EU accession that they completed large-scale privatization. The EU paid particular attention to the restructuring, privatization, and regulation of infrastructural sectors, such as energy, telecommunications, and the financial sector. Especially in the latter two it encouraged foreign ownership, assuming that selling off these sectors to outsiders would greatly enhance their efficiency. Foreign investment indeed started pouring in, and as a result, foreign banks took over the local banking systems. In Estonia and Lithuania, more than 90 percent of bank assets were transferred into foreign ownership. Latvia still kept one important financial institution, Parex Bank, in domestic hands, but even so, 60 percent of that country's banking assets was in foreign hands. Bank ownership was very concentrated, with two Swedish banks, Swedbank and Skandinaviska Enskilda Banken (SEB), being the major players.

At the same time, some drawbacks of Baltic policies were also reinforced during the accession process. This was especially true of the limited attention paid to the social costs of transformation. The limited formal competence of the EU in social affairs, an emerging workfarist orientation underlying EU initiatives in the field of social policies, and the existing social *acquis communautaire* all combined to strengthening selected institutions and individual social rights, without tackling substantive problems of social equality and integration. Thus, during the accession process new labor codes and tripartite or bipartite institutions and laws strengthening gender equality, antidiscrimination, and occupational health and safety were implemented. With the exception of unemployment, however, the massive social problems in the Baltic states were not dealt with in the accession negotiations. Pension reforms as well as health care reforms were monitored by the EU. Yet the major concern was not with fostering the well-being of pensioners, but with the connections of these social issues to public finances, and financial markets.

In this situation, however, global and European market actors came to the rescue of the Baltic populations, compensating them for the meager public welfare provisions. Indeed, during the 2000s, the three Baltic states turned into the fastest-growing economies of the continent. While the impressive economic growth did not reduce social inequalities, it nevertheless provided for rising living standards and a brighter economic outlook for most. Baltic growth during the early to mid-2000s relied almost entirely on domestic demand, fueled by high investment and rising consumption particularly in the construction and real estate sectors. Foreign bank ownership

the civil service, Jan-Hinrik Meyer-Sahling and Tim Veen, "Governing the Post-Communist State: Government Alternation and Senior Civil Service Politicization in Central and Eastern Europe," *East European Politics* (forthcoming).

greatly facilitated the availability of credit. Helped by the massive credit inflow from their parent companies, Nordic banks started to set nominal interest rates at the same levels as in their home countries. As inflation was higher in the Baltic states than in Western Europe, real interest rates became at times even negative. The foreign-owned banks also promoted euro-denominated borrowing at low costs. Against the background of euro-pegged national currencies and the preparations for EMU membership this practice was not considered overly risky. As a consequence, private loans increased dramatically, and within them, the share of euro-denominated loans soared (see table 6.1).

The banks aggressively lobbied for and marketed new financial products for households and enterprises. Among the most important was mortgage lending. Governments and foreign banks collaborated to set off a mortgage boom of unprecedented proportions. As usual, Estonia's second Laar administration took the lead, introducing a number of tax provisions favorable to home ownership in 2000. These included tax deductibility of mortgage interest payments, provision of housing loan guarantees and subsidies, and abolition of corporate tax on reinvested profits. The latter measure encouraged enterprises to invest their profits in the booming real estate sector. Latvia and Lithuania followed with similar measures.[95] Encouraged by state policies that sought to foster mortgage loans and by the overall bright economic outlook, which was also reflected in a strong increase of real wages, banks tended toward increasingly risky lending practices. The enormous expansion of mortgage lending set off unprecedented construction booms and house price increases. Nominal house prices in 2002–6 surged annually by 24 to 36 percent in the Baltic states—growth rates "unseen in the industrial world."[96]

Building on the work of Colin Hay and his co-authors on the Irish mortgage boom after EMU entry, as well as of Colin Crouch, this device can be dubbed "privatized house price Keynesianism."[97] The origin of the Irish

95. For the housing and mortgage boom, see Baudoin Lamine, "Estonia: Analysis of a Housing Boom," *ECFIN Country Focus* 6, no. 5 (2009): 1–7; Sebastian Leitner, "Baltic States: Perils of a Boom-Bust Scenario Ahead," *WIIW Monthly Report* 4 (2007): 1–8; Zuzana Brixiova, Laura Vartia, and Andreas Wörgötter, "Capital Inflows, Household Debt and the Boom-Bust Cycle in Estonia," William Davidson Institute Working Paper 965 (Ann Arbor: The William Davidson Institute at the University of Michigan, 2007); Balázs Égert and Dubravko Mihaljek, "Determinants of House Prices in Central and Eastern Europe," BIS Working Paper 236 (Basel: Bank for International Settlements, 2007).

96. Égert and Mihaljek, "Determinants," 4. These authors do not provide data for Latvia, but according to all available sources, Latvia was at the high end of the housing boom in the Baltic countries.

97. Colin Hay, Jari M. Riiheläinen, Nicola J. Smith, and Matthew Watson, "Ireland: The Outlier Inside," in *The Euro at 10: Europeanization, Power, and Convergence*, ed. Kenneth Dyson (Oxford: Oxford University Press, 2008), 182–203; Colin Crouch, "What Will Follow the Demise of Privatised Keynesianism?" *Political Quarterly* 79, no. 4 (October–December, 2008): 476–87.

housing boom lies in the difference between the interest rates set within the euro area and those that should have prevailed in Ireland to combat its inflation which was higher than the EMU reference. The lower euro interest rates made mortgage loans and their repayment cheaper, while the concomitant increase of house prices allowed owners to obtain ever higher mortgages. A similar mechanism was at play in the Baltic countries, where the availability of low-interest loans, especially in euros, made credit in general and mortgages in particular advantageous.

In both cases, moreover, it was private banks that exploited the opportunities stemming from transnationalization. House price Keynesianism thus assumed a privatized form. As Crouch argues, privatized Keynesianism involves a shift from countercyclical state policies to secure income and employment in times of recession to the growth of private credit markets for low- and middle-income groups, which compensates for stagnating salaries and job insecurity and maintains consumer confidence.

A specific (and un-Keynesian) aspect of the Baltic states' privatized Keynesianism was that it occurred simultaneously with rising wages. High growth rates brought unemployment significantly down in all three countries, thereby producing increasing labor shortages. In addition to the market-induced decrease of unemployment, the Baltic populations also made use of their newly acquired right to emigrate when their countries joined the EU. According to a Eurobarometer survey of 2005, between 7 and 8 percent of the Baltic (and Polish) populations anticipated moving to another EU country. This was by far the highest share in all EU member states, old and new. Among the reasons for individuals' wish to migrate, factors related to work—higher household incomes and better working conditions—played a crucial role.[98]

Baltic (and Polish) would-be emigrants carried through on their intentions. Estonian analysts estimated that between 2004 and 2007 average gross emigration from Estonia, Latvia, and Lithuania amounted to more than 5, 8, and 12 percent of the population, respectively. That meant that after 2004, annually 7,100 Estonians, 19,800 Latvians and 42,300 Lithuanians left for EU-15 countries.[99] The same study found that "the average emigrant from Estonia was most likely a young person between 15–34 years of age, a blue-collar worker and male. Contrary to evidence from other countries and earlier time periods, employees with a low level of education were more likely to emigrate than highly educated workers."[100] Most migrants came from the

98. Tom Vandenbrande, ed., *Mobility in Europe: Analysis of the 2005 Eurobarometer Survey on Geographical and Labour Market Mobility* (Dublin: European Foundation for the Improvement of Living and Working Conditions, 2006), 23–25.

99. Martii Randveer and Tairi Rõõm, "The Structure of Migration in Estonia: Survey-Based Evidence," Working Paper 1 (Tallinn: Eesti Pank, 2009), 23.

100. Ibid., 2.

private rather than the public sector, and the share of non-Estonians among migrants was slightly higher than their share in the labor force. Emigration also affected Tallinn less than Estonia's northeast and south.

Judging from scattered evidence, migration patterns from Latvia seem to be similar to those from Estonia. There is also evidence that the government of Aigars Kalvītis welcomed the beneficial effects of out-migration on Latvian labor markets. The state employment agency provided job seekers with information about opportunities abroad. Some media even commented that the agency was more engaged in identifying foreign than Latvian employment opportunities.[101] In contrast, Lithuanian migration seems to somewhat deviate from the Estonian and Latvian patterns. According to the OECD, in Lithuania highly skilled nonmanual employees and skilled workers form almost 40 percent of the emigration outflow.[102]

Overall, the economic boom and the credit economy greatly improved the living conditions of the less internationally mobile portions of the Baltic populations, while EU accession offered better possibilities for those willing to move.[103] It is remarkable that this could be achieved without governments having to change their priorities for balanced budgets and market solutions. As in the first postsocialist decade, during the 2000s governments stayed committed to prudent fiscal policies. High growth rates made it easier to reconcile pension and public sector wage growth with fairly balanced budgets. Moreover, the availability of consumer credit extended by foreign banks provided a market device for raising living standards of the population way beyond what their actual wage increases—impressive as they were—would have permitted.

The unfolding economic miracle, finally, also led to an increase of the Baltic populations' satisfaction with democratic and economic regime performance. Satisfaction with the political system, the support for which had been quite shaky during much of the 1990s, rose significantly in all three countries, with the most marked increase coinciding with the EU accession process. Among all accession countries, the rise in satisfaction with democratic regime performance between 1992 and 2004 was highest in Lithuania and Estonia, followed by Latvia in fourth place. The level of regime satisfaction in 2004 was highest in Estonia, followed by Lithuania. In contrast, Latvians' satisfaction with democratic regime performance, although it rose significantly, was still very low. Satisfaction with the economic performance of the regime also improved over time, the biggest increase, once more, coinciding with the EU accession period. Estonians were, however, consistently more

101. Emigration of Latvian workers continues to increase; Eurofound report, http://www.eurofound.europa.eu/eiro/2005/12/feature/lv0512104f.htm (accessed November 28, 2009).

102. SOPEMI-OECD, *International Migration Outlook 2008*, http://www.oecd.org/dataoecd/57/11/41255896.pdf (accessed November 28, 2009).

103. Guglielmo Meardi, "More Voice after More Exit? Unstable Industrial Relations in Central Eastern Europe," *Industrial Relations Journal* 38, no. 6 (2007): 503–23.

satisfied with the functioning of the economic system than either Latvians, who stayed mostly negative, or Lithuanians, who only started to positively evaluate the system in 2004.[104]

104. Richard Rose, "Diverging Paths of Post-Communist Countries: New Europe Barometer Trends Since 1991," *Studies in Public Policy* 418 (Glasgow: Centre for the Study of Public Policy, University of Strathclyde, 2006), 23; Piret Ehin, "Political Support in the Baltic States, 1993–2004," *Journal of Baltic Studies* 38, no. 1 (2007): 1–20.

4

Manufacturing Miracles
and Welfare State Problems

The Visegrád Group

The embedded neoliberal regimes of the Visegrád group differ from Baltic nationalist neoliberalisms in important respects. The four economies integrated into the EU's single market by transforming themselves into one of Europe's largest transborder clusters of complex-manufacturing export industries. To attract TNCs, eventually all these states adopted generous incentive packages, created investment promotion agencies, and launched expensive infrastructure development programs. At the same time, they also kept in place relatively generous systems of social protection uniquely geared to the temporarily, partly, or wholly "nonproductive" groups of society.

The simultaneous pursuit of costly and contradictory social objectives financed by only a handful of taxpayers and social security contributors made the coordination of fiscal and monetary policies exceedingly difficult. Hence the peculiar third aspect of the Visegrád regimes lies in contested and ineffective institutions of macroeconomic coordination, an aspect that is most striking in Hungary. Last but not least, since the transformation led to the atrophy of initially established neocorporatist institutions, it has remained solely the democratic system's task to pursue the embedded neoliberal agenda, cope with the conflicts among varied policy issue areas, and bear the political consequences.

The four countries arrived at similar new regimes through varied and repeatedly modified paths, and their experimentation with institution building reflected both similarities and differences in external constraints, past legacies, and elite visions of how to reconcile the capitalist and democratic aspects of transformation with the effort to rebuild sovereign nation-states amidst processes of thorough internationalization. In this chapter, we seek explanations at three levels of politics, and the interplay among the processes at these levels.

We explore how struggles in domestic democratic arenas shaped policy responses to the challenges of transformation. Further, we argue that the legacies in combination with new external factors contributed to the transition of the Visegrád region from a purely geographic term or organizing myth into an important political and policy level, the dynamics of which proved significant for regime formation. However, the driving force of the Visegrád area's regionalization was not reminiscent of the Baltic states' follow-the-leader logic, nor could it be easily traced to shared identity and attitudes to integration observed in other European regions. Paradoxically, integration and policy convergence within the Visegrád space has mainly advanced through rivalry among peer nations that partly appealed to their citizens' identities, and partly acted as if they were competing private businesses rather than purely nation-states. Finally, we consider the ways in which transnational and supranational pressures stemming from TNC preferences and the EU's major integration projects, in particular the EMU, have impacted the Visegrád paths.

Our conclusion is that even if the new regimes so far have been able to preserve many of their features, their future survival is not more guaranteed than their emergence has been. Democratic competition, regional rivalry, and global and European pressures seem to have the power to reinforce but also undermine the institutional core of embedded neoliberalism. Indeed, our Polanyian approach predicts macroeconomic and/or political destabilization once the regime's maneuvering capacity is overstrained.

The likelihood of gradual drifts or radical shifts between more or less marketized and socially and politically inclusive setups seems to depend on the macroeconomic sustainability of the initial patterns in the face of domestic and external pressures, and on reform elites' will and skill to mobilize political support for a reorientation of policy strategies.

Unsuccessful Experiments and Double-Edged Inheritances

The common factors in the Visegrád success stories of building democratic market societies—relatively high initial levels of economic development and social welfare, geographic and cultural proximity to the West, and presocialist experiences with democracy and the market—are often mentioned in the literature. However, we shall focus on some important differences that indicate that the region's eventual convergence on the embedded neoliberal model was anything but a foregone conclusion. The correctness of tracing the new Visegrád regimes merely to past legacies or preexisting master plans is thrown in doubt by the gap between the new institutional setups anticipated by reformers and the actual outcomes. Indeed, in light of the reform elites' initial preferences, the new regimes' features appear as not just unexpected but in some cases even unwanted.

Take the example of export-oriented manufacturing miracles, and their underpinnings in privatization and industrial policies.[1] No politician has risen to leadership by campaigning on the plank of allowing overwhelming foreign control of the national economy, let alone revealing the public costs of attracting TNCs. Rather, initially politicians advocated various forms of national capitalism that would offer fair chances for the emergence of a domestic bourgeoisie and a middle class including employee-owners. In this vein, Czech Premier Václav Klaus asserted that "foreign capital involvement is appreciated, but foreign capital should not be preferentially treated vis-à-vis domestic capital. The role of foreign advisers and consultants should be minimized."[2] Surprisingly, by the late 1990s the initially laggard Czech Republic caught up with Hungary and Poland in the generosity of incentives and extensiveness of services offered to TNCs, and soon became the regional leader in attracting FDI.

Similarly, all Visegrád countries had their "social democratic" or "social liberal" moments that brought about institutionalization of social partnership and other achievements for labor. Last but not least, the reformers seemed to be prepared to break with the legacy of paternalist welfare states. As Klaus put it with reference to Europe at large: "We are—all of us—confronted with the excesses of welfare state paternalism, with overregulation, with overly ambitious programs to subsidize producers as well as consumers, with corporatist and syndicalist tendencies.... They are not part of a coherent ideology. They 'just happened,' and it is difficult to get rid of them. The transforming countries have a historic opportunity not to let them dominate the lives of their citizens."[3]

Against this background, the fact that after experimenting briefly with national capitalism and instituting national-level social partnership the Visegrád states abandoned both, and instead embarked on the path of embedded neoliberal and transnational capitalism, is surprising. The resilience of relatively generous welfare states also poses questions. Below we shall demonstrate that varied experiences under socialism and in its aftermath were essential backgrounds against which dramatic events forced elites to make or alter crucial decisions.

Three differences appear the most significant. In Hungary and Poland economic and political liberalization had advanced relatively far under socialism, while Czechoslovakia had to transform a centrally planned economy and a rigid one-party system. The former two countries inherited huge

1. "Manufacturing miracle" is a term applied to successful NICs. Gary Gereffi and Donald L. Wyman, eds., *Manufacturing Miracles: Paths of Industrialization in Latin America and East Asia* (Princeton: Princeton University Press, 1990).

2. Václav Klaus, *Renaissance: The Rebirth of Liberty in the Heart of Europe* (Washington, D.C.: Cato Institute, 1997), 48.

3. Ibid., 56–57.

external debt and macroeconomic imbalances. Again, this is in contrast with the Czechoslovak economy, which was neither unstable nor indebted at the onset of transformation. Finally, while Hungary's and Poland's nations and states survived socialism (even if Soviet power heavily restricted their autonomy) and could be relatively easily restored in its aftermath, in 1993 Czechoslovakia dissolved into the newly founded Czech and Slovak states providing a whole new set of political risks and opportunities.

Attempted National Capitalisms

Hungary and Poland differed from Czechoslovakia in having implemented significant economic and political reforms in the last decades of socialism. The fact that they did not have to build their market democracies from scratch has been viewed as an advantage by many analysts. It was argued that influential elite groups that either actively supported or at least did not oppose the turn to democratic market society, were crucial for the success and relatively peaceful dynamics of regime change in both cases. These groups included pragmatic and cooperative prodemocratic oppositions, internationally linked and oriented financial and policymaking technocrats, and the procapitalist wing of the postcommunist elite.

Although the Hungarian opposition lacked the massive force of Solidarity which fought for political liberalization in Poland, here as well relatively strong civil and political groups emerged with the liberalization during the last decades of János Kádár's regime. Following their Polish peers, Hungary's prodemocratic parties had been pragmatic enough to cooperate against (and occasionally negotiate and cooperate with) the Communists and coordinate at the 1989 national Round Table negotiations to design the country's new democratic system. Subsequently, after the founding elections, the victorious Hungarian Democratic Forum (MDF), a conservative Christian Democratic party, entered a quasi power-sharing arrangement with its main competitor, the liberal Alliance of Free Democrats (SZDSZ), which was the leading force of the parliamentary opposition, and thus, on the same lines as in Poland, marginalized the ex-Communist Hungarian Socialist Party (MSZP) for the coalition's entire term in power.

In both countries, the democratic opposition had also influenced preparation and discussion of far-reaching economic reform plans years before the breakdown of the system. In Poland it was the shock of martial law that led opposition forces to focus on economic rather than political reforms, and gave the emerging neoliberal groups and think tanks a competitive advantage over advocates of democratic market socialist ideas.[4]

---

4. See, e.g., Szacki, *Liberalism after Communism*; Andrzej Walicki, "Notes on Jaruzelski's Poland," in *Crisis and Reform in Eastern Europe*, eds. Ferenc Fehér and András Arató (New Brunswick: Transaction Books, 1991), 335–93.

Two other elite groups for whom capitalism paid off and democracy was acceptable deserve mentioning. The first was the reform bureaucracy, with its powerful policymaking and financial apparatus. By the 1980s, market-oriented economic reforms and external openness, and—ironically, the management of huge foreign debts accumulated by both countries' Communist leaderships—had served to integrate these bureaucracies into international financial networks. Fellowships, conferences, debt negotiations, lobbying for new financial resources, education and training grants and programs were as important in fostering these international linkages as Hungary's and Poland's early membership in the IMF and the World Bank from 1982 and 1986, respectively.

New skills were developed during the integration process, such as dealing with the IFIs' staff and policy programs, statistical and analytical capacities, and negotiating and bargaining with foreign creditors and investors, skills that were even more badly needed after 1989. One consequence was that in contrast to many other postsocialist states Hungary's and Poland's transformation strategies could be relatively organic, gradualist, and homegrown in the sense that albeit reflecting the transnational consensus on the desirability of neoliberal reforms, in the concrete design Hungarian and Polish reformers could rely on ideas, skills, and plans developed in domestic intellectual workshops.

The strong external ties of these elites did not mean they were left without potential allies in the changing domestic political arena. SOE managers (especially those connected to Western trade and industry) became another influential group possessing valuable experience with mixed formal/informal, state/market strategies and the skills needed to conduct international operations. These capabilities gave them competitive advantages over their domestic rivals and made them attractive partners for foreign investors.

All in all, such elites formed a less corrupt and more entrepreneurial nucleus of a domestic bourgeoisie, which has been more willing to share with foreign capital the opportunities presented by privatization, than for instance the Russian or Ukrainian oligarchs. Considering the impact of the inherited private sector, János Kornai predicted that "the greater the extent to which both the formal and informal private sector has managed to develop, the faster the advance of the private sector will be after the change of the system." More doubtfully though, he also voiced hope that the democratic system will be more able than "the old party-state to induce real market behavior in state-owned firms."[5]

Alas, Hungary and Poland also shared an inherited liability, namely huge external debts whose service magnified their transformation costs. However, their different credit histories and varied choices of debt management had an

5. Kornai, *The Socialist System*, 460, 512.

impact on their actual burden. During the last decade of socialism Hungary had been keen on servicing its debt in a disciplined manner, and was viewed as a reliable debtor, while in the 1980s Poland defaulted on its payments.

Furthermore, at the onset of transformation the Polish government negotiated a debt relief agreement while the Hungarian government did not. Hungary probably could not have followed the Polish road because its debts were owed mostly to private commercial banks, while Poland's creditors were largely governments. In addition, Hungary was politically less important for the West than Poland. That said, the Hungarian government did not even ask for debt relief. These decisions had crucial implications for the two countries' emerging ownership structures and transformation at large.

In particular, while negotiated debt rescheduling and relief initially offered Poland the opportunity to consider a national capitalist path of transformation, Hungary barely had the same option and essentially adopted foreign-led capitalism from the start. Because of its reformers' preference for disciplined debt service Hungary was highly dependent on hard currency cash receipts available only from exports and privatization. Thus, foreign debt and its management appeared among the main determinants of Hungary's strong export orientation and policy of privatization through massive direct sales to foreigners. At the same time, its reliable debtor status made Hungary an attractive location for FDI. Moreover, in the 1990s the country was the leader in terms of the generosity of incentives and quality of services offered to foreign investors not only in the Visegrád area but in the whole postsocialist world.[6] A secondary privatization method consisted of MEBOs favoring the most entrepreneurial managers of state-owned firms more than the workers.

In contrast, the fact that Poland was partly relieved from crippling debt service proved to be a double-edged sword. Even if Poland's FDI incentives had not fallen far behind those of Hungary, foreign investors, initially distrusting the less stable and less reliable debtor country, adopted a "wait and see" stance. At the same time, the emerging domestic business elite became more politicized and assertive in its acquisition strategies than Hungarian managers. The recurrent political conflicts—also exacerbated by the Solidarity legacy and the polarization of society—ultimately resulted in a more gradual and less foreign-dominated privatization process.

Until 1993, the emergence of Polish national capitalism occurred more by default than according to any blueprint. Originating in Solidarity, several successive governments—although accepting relatively substantial workers' ownership within small and medium-sized firms—were reluctant to sell strategic industries and large firms to either "political capitalists,"[7] the partly

6. Cass, "Attracting FDI," 48.
7. Jadwiga Staniszkis, "Political Capitalism in Poland," *East European Politics and Societies* 5, no. 1 (Winter 1991): 127–41.

nomenklatura-based top management of state firms, or workers. However, other domestic business groups and foreign investors were in short supply. The overall result was that in 1990–93 the share of the private sector in GDP expanded slower in Poland than in the other Visegrád states.

After 1993, the new coalition government formed by the postcommunist Alliance of the Democratic Left (SLD) and the Peasant Party (PSL), opted for more conscious attempts at building national capitalism and strengthening domestic business elements. Revitalizing and rebuilding its links to former nomenklatura business circles, the administration used state programs of centralization, concentration, and subsidized restructuring to support the emergence of "hybrid" forms of property, and of the nuclei of a domestic bourgeoisie.[8] Thus, inherited constraints, opportunities, and choices played equal roles in shaping the features of Poland's attempted national capitalism. Even if ultimately direct sales to foreigners became Poland's primary privatization technique too, MEBOs there prevailed longer and contributed more strongly to the emergence of the new propertied class than was the case in Hungary.[9] In consequence, for Poland it took longer to become integrated with the West through foreign trade and FDI.

Not burdened by excessive debt and macroeconomic instability, Czechoslovakia was the most free to choose among the models of national versus foreign-led capitalism, and among privatization techniques empowering particular groups of "expectant" capitalists. Accordingly, Premier Klaus stressed that "the government's objective is or should be complete economic transformation rather than maximization of proceeds from the sale of government assets."[10] Czechoslovakia's privatization also diverged from the Hungarian or Polish pattern because, sharing Hayek's negative stance toward any form of mixed economy, the Czech premier put his faith in the advantages of starting from scratch. In his view, pretransition market reforms merely complicated "the genuine transformation of an economy."[11] Premier Klaus was no less critical of the political transformation of neighboring countries, which consisted of making a deal with Communists and then banning the party. He viewed liberalizing the political environment and ensuring free entry to new political actors as sufficient for pushing the unreformed Czechoslovak Communist Party to the sidelines.[12]

In the Klausian vision, the emergence of a market economy needed just about the same conditions as the rise of a democratic polity, namely

---

8. Bohle, *Europas neue Peripherie*, chapter 6: 144–76.

9. Ibid. See from the recent literature Károly A. Soós, *Rendszerváltás és privatizáció: Elsődleges és másodlagos privatizáció Közép-Európában és a volt Szovjetunióban* [System change and privatization: Primary and secondary privatization in Central Europe and the former Soviet Union] (Budapest: Corvina Kiadó, 2009).

10. Klaus, *Renaissance*, 71.

11. Ibid., 168.

12. Ibid., 19.

unconstrained free entry and a level playing field for a plethora of competing new agents. It was above all a free market in state assets that Klaus sought to create by his voucher privatization scheme. In contrast, he rejected the MEBO method on the grounds that managers would inevitably collude and block acquisition of state property by other new owners.[13] For similar reasons he was against the dominance of foreign ownership, fearing that the disorganized state of the transforming Czech economy would allow TNCs too easy access to its undervalued assets.

As well known, Czech mass privatization through vouchers, rather than creating clear-cut private property relations, de facto prolonged state ownership of the economy through privatization investment funds founded by the main domestic banks. It also created distorted industrial-financial relations, with banks supporting large numbers of unprofitable enterprises listed in their funds' portfolios. Moreover, minimal governmental regulation and weak corporate governance structures encouraged asset stripping and rampant corruption. These by-products of Czech privatization finally caught up with economic performance in 1996–97, plunging the country into a recession. It was in the context of the crisis that the Czech project of national capitalism was abandoned, to be replaced by foreign-led economic restructuring.[14]

The Slovak national capitalist model was of a different nature, exhibiting the most nationalist features among all the Visegrád countries. Privatization under three-time Prime Minister Vladimír Mečiar allegedly sought to create a national entrepreneurial class that would conduct business in Slovakia's interest. In this endeavor, he built on the legacy of Gustáv Husák's regime, which had restored and consolidated Czechoslovak communism after the debacle of the Prague Spring of 1968. Husák gave priority to developing Slovakia over the Czech lands, thereby securing the acquiescence of Slovaks to the new regime. As a consequence, the Slovak population caught up with the Czechs in terms of industrial output, wages, and living standards under communism.

The Czech-led transformation of the early 1990s seemed to threaten these accomplishments, with the recession showing disproportionately in Slovak unemployment and industrial output figures. After the federation split, Mečiar revived important aspects of the Husák legacy: welfare paternalism,

---

13. Hillary Appel and John Gould, "Identity Politics and Economic Reform: Examining Industry-State Relations in the Czech and Slovak Republics," *Europe-Asia Studies* 52, no. 1 (January 2000): 111–31.

14. For perceptive analyses of the Czech privatization strategy see Mitchell A. Orenstein, *Out of the Red: Building Capitalism and Democracy in Postcommunist Europe* (Ann Arbor: University of Michigan Press, 2001); Hillary Appel, *A New Capitalist Order: Privatization and Ideology in Russia and Eastern Europe* (Pittsburgh: University of Pittsburgh Press, 2004). On the rise and demise of Czech national capitalism see Martin Myant, *The Rise and Fall of Czech Capitalism: Economic Development in the Czech Republic since 1989* (Cheltenham: Edward Elgar, 2003); and Drahokoupil, *Globalization and the State.*

subsidies and protective regulation for inherited industries, and national-ism. His government canceled the second wave of voucher privatization, and instead built entirely on insider deals by selling enterprises directly and at favorable terms to political friends and loyal enterprise managers. Massive infrastructure investments and sectoral industrial policies geared to heavy industry complemented Slovakia's national capitalist model of development. Although the model showed signs of economic stress from the second half of the 1990s, its downfall owed more to the political opposition to Mečiar's in-creasingly open authoritarian methods of defending capitalism Slovak-style.[15]

All in all, then, by the end of the 1990s, the attempts at building national capitalism—be it by default in the case of Poland or by design in the Czech Republic and Slovakia—had to be abandoned. Consequently, all four coun-tries converged on a foreign-led capitalist model. Before we analyze this in greater detail, we first turn to the institutions shaping the Visegrád states' industrial relations.

Rise and Demise of Social Partnership Institutions

Exposed to the immense adjustment pressures of the early 1990s, trade unions in East Central Europe were forced to redefine their roles from so-cialist "transmission belts" to organizations representing the interests of employees. A peculiar feature of the Visegrád countries is that while all of them had their "social democratic" or "social liberal" moments involving attempts at building democratic corporatist institutions, eventually all of them proved reluctant to make these institutions permanent features of their economic governance.[16]

The momentum for cooperation between governments and trade unions—employer organizations being embryonic at best—was strongest at the beginning of the transformation when the former, fearing social unrest in light of the reform measures they were about to take, sought to enlist the latters' support.

In the Czechoslovak case, governments at all levels initially were ready to support the institutionalization of genuine tripartite concertation, a step that was backed by a trade union movement eager to find its new role. In October 1990, Councils of Economic and Social Agreement (RHSD) were formed at the federal and national levels, including representatives of unions, govern-ment, and the nascent employer organizations. The first General Agreement,

15. Appel and Gould, "Identity Politics"; John Gould, "Out of the Blue? Democracy and Privatization in Postcommunist Europe," *Comparative European Politics* 1, no. 3 (2003): 277–311.
16. These terms are used by András Tóth, "The Failure of Social-Democratic Unionism in Hungary," in *Workers after Workers' States: Labor and Politics in Postcommunist Eastern Europe*, ed. Stephen Crowley and David Ost (Lanham: Rowman & Littlefield, 2001), 37–58; and Mitchell A. Orenstein, "Václav Klaus: Revolutionary and Parliamentarian. A Retrospective," *East European Constitutional Review* 7, no. 1 (Winter 1998): 46–55.

signed in 1991, was the high point of tripartite concertation. It included a "low-wage and low-unemployment" compromise, and unions got social policy concessions counterbalancing the negative impact of low wages. The RHSD negotiated union-friendly legislation and strong employment protection, and was also involved in active labor market policies.

While the agreement was to be binding for all partners, it soon turned out that the government was unable to live up to its promise of preventing a major drop in wages. Subsequently, it adopted a more ambivalent attitude toward tripartism, arguing that it could not be forced into binding agreements as its primary responsibility was to the parliament. From then on, the RHSD on the federal and the Czech national level developed into a mere consultative body. Although General Agreements were still concluded, they amounted to little.

The split of the federation was a further blow to the Czech RHSD, as subsequently the government threatened to weaken it on several fronts. Premier Klaus sought to reduce the government's role in the body and to prevent it from sponsoring sectoral collective bargaining agreements. The opportunity of the first major strike against pension reforms was used to break off discussions in the RHSD, and to change the status of the body into an "organ...for consultation on selected questions of social significance with the aim of approaching an agreement or a viable solution in the interest of social peace." Gone was its role as "agreement-seeking and initiative taking" institution. [17]

It was only the crisis of 1997 that made Klaus change his mind on tripartism once again. Faced with increasing social unrest, dwindling support for his government, and a worsening macroeconomic situation requiring austere policies, Klaus sought to strengthen his relations with the trade unions and to reverse some of the damage previously done to the tripartite forum. The unions, however, refused to cooperate on crucial policy issues.

The Social Democratic minority government that replaced Klaus's coalition was committed to social dialogue. Neither this nor subsequent governments, however, returned to the early attempts at institutionalizing binding tripartite concertation. As a result, while the Czech Republic maintained an effectively working consultation mechanism on major economic, social, and legal affairs, it fell short of establishing genuine corporatist relations. [18]

After the "velvet divorce," Slovak tripartism followed its own path. In contrast to the Czech situation, initially Premier Mečiar's government and trade unions had developed fairly friendly relations. In the first years of independence, tripartite negotiations "approached the form of a distinct mode of

17. Martin Myant, Brian Slocock, and Simon Smith, "Tripartism in the Czech and Slovak Republics," *Europe-Asia Studies* 52, no. 4 (June 2000): 731.

18. Ibid. On Czech tripartism see also Sabina Avdagic, "State-Labour Relations in East Central Europe: Explaining Variations in Union Effectiveness," *Socio-Economic Review* 3, no. 1 (2005): 25–53; and Anna Pollert, "Labor and Trade Unions in the Czech Republic," in Crowley and Ost, *Workers after Workers' States*, 13–36.

governance, at least in relation to industrial relations and social policy."[19] The main actors were able to agree on a number of crucial issues concerning labor laws, incorporation of fundamental international conventions, and wage development, issues that remained unresolved in the Czech Republic. The Slovak RHSD also agreed on independently administered health and pension funds that included representation of labor, business, and the state, and created a supplementary pension scheme. The forum was also more involved in collective bargaining than its Czech counterpart, as it could extend collective agreements to enterprises that had not been part of the negotiations.

Yet Mečiar's increasingly open authoritarianism ultimately prevented neocorporatism from sinking deeper roots in Slovakia. The premier frequently overrode the RHSD's decisions as well as labor-friendly legislative proposals coming from his own government. Generally, Mečiar's view of corporatism sat uneasily with the idea of independent trade unions. As a reaction to a conflict over wage controls in 1997 the government, in cooperation with employers, started to build up rival trade unions in one of Slovakia's most important enterprises, the Košice steel works. It also tried to build up a new tripartite body with much more limited competences, from which the main labor umbrella organization, the Confederation of Trade Unions (KOZ) would be excluded.

The premier's unilateral imposition of wage controls and his attempt to build up rival labor representation made KOZ withdraw from tripartite negotiations altogether, and join the political alliance that finally defeated Mečiar in the 1998 elections. In return for the electoral support received from the unions, the first government of Mikuláš Dzurinda adopted a Law on Economic and Social Partnership in 1999. The law established "tripartite 'social dialogue' within a formal and enforceable framework of rules rather than leaving its status prone, as it had been since 1990, to shifting interests and the political will of successive governments."[20]

However, the impact of tripartite negotiations remained ambiguous. The unions continued to support some of the government's reform measures, such as an increase in minimum wages and the initial formulation of a new labor code, elaborated by the left-wing minister of labor. Nevertheless, the negotiations within the RHSD were overshadowed by a fast-deteriorating macroeconomic situation, to which the government reacted with a tough austerity package and fundamental structural reforms. In consequence, relations between the unions and Premier Dzurinda's conservative party began to change to the worse. The second Dzurinda government, solely formed by center-right parties, saw no need to come to agreements with the unions.

19. Myant, Slocock, and Smith, "Tripartism," 733.
20. Jonathan Stein, "Neocorporatism in Slovakia: Formalizing Labor Weakness in a (Re) democratizing State," in Crowley and Ost, *Workers after Workers' States*, 59.

Relations between government and the unions deteriorated to the point that in 2004, the government declared it was no longer interested in social dialogue, at least according to the rules of the 1999 law.[21]

Early tripartism in Hungary also entailed the possibility of developing into full-fledged neocorporatism but, as in the neighboring countries, it ultimately failed to do so. During the first turbulent period of postsocialist transformation, the Interest Reconciliation Council (ÉT), founded by the last Communist government in 1988 and revived by the conservative coalition government under József Antall in 1990, proved an important instrument for economic and political crisis management. When in 1990 the Antall government tried to impose an austerity package to tackle the country's grave macroeconomic imbalances, it met fierce resistance in the form of a blockade of Budapest streets by taxi drivers lasting for several days. The conflict was settled at the ÉT during a televised emergency meeting, which helped to underscore the importance of dialogue among the social partners.

The successful settlement of the country's first major crisis after the fall of socialism endowed the ÉT with broad legitimacy and prestige. In subsequent years, the government found it important to elicit the body's support for major reform steps. In 1993, the government adopted the ÉT's most important agreement on income policies. Trade unions were able to get significant concessions from the government in respect to wage controls, wage development in the public sector, and the minimum wage. Moreover, the government withdrew a controversial bill on union elections and the division of union property. The latter helped to stabilize the Communist successor federation, the National Federation of Hungarian Trade Unions (MSZOSZ), which faced competition from its splinter organizations as well as from newly established unions.

Tripartism, however, took a turn for the worse under the Socialist-liberal government coalition that swept to power in 1994. Although the Socialists campaigned in the 1994 elections with a call for a new social pact, they failed to deliver. A deteriorating macroeconomic situation led to intense negotiations within the ÉT. Profound differences among the positions of trade unions, government, and employers, as well as rivalries among leading politicians within the ruling Socialist party, prevented an agreement. Soon after, the government introduced the most severe austerity program thus far in the country's postsocialist history. The "Bokros package"—named after its architect, Minister of Finance Lajos Bokros—was prepared in secrecy. Neither the administration, nor the legislature as a whole, nor social interest associations were involved in its preparation.

---

21. On Slovak tripartism, see Myant, Slocock, and Smith, "Tripartism"; Stepan Jurajda and Katarina Mathernova, "How to Overhaul the Labor Market: Political Economy of Recent Czech and Slovak Reforms," Background paper prepared for the World Bank, *World Development Report 2005*; and Stein, "Neocorporatism in Slovakia."

Even so, tripartite negotiations were not entirely abandoned under the Socialist-liberal government. In 1996 an agreement was reached that helped to facilitate public sector reforms, and a year later ÉT concluded an agreement on pension reforms. Tripartism received a more devastating blow from the national-conservative government coalition of Premier Viktor Orbán during 1998–2002. The government dissolved ÉT and replaced it by two new bodies with more limited formal rights. The new administration changed the composition of the tripartite institutions governing the health care and pension funds as well, and amended the Labor Code to further restrict the role of unions in the workplace. It also sought to decentralize public sector wage negotiations.

Some of the damage done to tripartism was reversed under the Socialist-liberal government of Péter Medgyessy that came to power in 2002. The new government reinstated the ÉT with the earlier far-reaching competences, and amended the Labor Code with the aim of strengthening unions at the workplace and withdrawing some of the measures for flexible labor markets introduced by its conservative predecessor. Overall, however, tripartism remained weakly institutionalized, and major austerity packages were consistently administered without social consultation.[22]

Poland's experience differed in some crucial aspects from that of its peers. Most importantly, the first government stemming from the Solidarity movement considered it neither desirable nor necessary to engage in formal concertation with the trade unions. While negotiated pacts had a strong tradition in Poland—with the Gdańsk agreements of 1980 and the Round Table agreements of 1989—the government of Tadeusz Mazowiecki sought rather a sharp break with this past. Especially Minister of Finance and Vice Premier Leszek Balcerowicz saw negotiated agreements as one of the causes of the half-hearted and ultimately failed economic reforms of the 1980s.

Moreover, there was no need to establish a formal social dialogue with the then most important trade union, Solidarity, since the union spearheaded the movement that brought victory for the new reformist government. Solidarity leaders considered the political turnabout and the perspective of encompassing reforms as more important than bread-and-butter issues, and agreed to downgrade their role to that of providing a "protective umbrella" to economic reforms.

With this move, however, Solidarity miscalculated the social dissatisfaction radical reforms were to bring about. Already in 1992, huge strike waves erupted, forcing the government, led that time by Premier Hanna Suchocka to negotiate a multisector social dialogue. In 1993, the Pact on the Transformation of State Enterprises was signed, according to which labor

---

22. On tripartism in Hungary see, e.g., Lajos Héthy, "Social Dialogue in Hungary: Its Rise and Decline," *South-East Europe Review of Labour and Social Affairs* 1 (2001): 55–70; and Tóth, "The Failure of Social-Democratic Unionism."

representatives were to help design enterprise privatization strategies, workers would receive a share in their enterprises' stock, and union representatives would sit on the boards of privatized companies. In addition, the pact also included provisions for collective bargaining agreements, employee wage protection, and company social funds.

The next government formed by the postcommunist SLD, instituted in 1994 a Tripartite Commission on Socio-Economic Issues. Over the subsequent years, there were several important attempts at coming to binding agreements within the Tripartite Commission. In 1996 a strongly committed minister of labor, Andrzej Bączkowski, tried to invigorate the commission, but he passed away before reaching a breakthrough. In the early 2000s, SLD Minister of Labor Jerzy Hausner, an advocate of neocorporatism, tried but failed to forge an agreement on reforms of public finance, employment, health care and labor law.

The social pact idea was also popular in Jarosław Kaczyński's national-conservative coalition of 2005–7. Aiming to sideline the Tripartite Commission, Kaczyński proposed a pact under the title "economy-work-family-dialogue," involving selected social groups. Yet, like the earlier attempts, this initiative failed to replicate the success of the early pact on state enterprises. The reasons of the failure to establish corporatist interest mediation in Poland include fierce interunion competition and union politicization; governments weakened at the decisive moments of forging compromises; newly emerging groups of capital hostile to negotiations; and an increasingly more limited scope for negotiations.[23]

Against the above background of the contradictory dynamics of tripartism, we conclude that despite differences in their political histories and the strength of their union movements, ultimately all of the Visegrád states converged on a similar pattern of limited labor inclusion and, when needed, outright exclusion. Even though formal institutions of policy concertation were in place from the end of socialism onward, and were reinforced during EU accession, formal labor inclusion did not automatically generate real competences. Rather, genuine inclusion of labor typically depended on governments' willingness.

Although during the hard times at the onset of transformation trade unions were still valued for their skills in managing conflict, later governments' willingness to count on them was much reduced. Although this depended to some extent on the political orientation of governing coalitions, with left-wing parties more supportive than their right-wing counterparts, labor inclusion usually ended when governments launched sweeping

---

23. On tripartism in Poland, see Juliusz Gardawski and Guglielmo Meardi, "Keep Trying? Polish Failures and Half-Successes in Social Pacting," in *Social Pacts in the European Union*, ed. Philippe Pochet, Maarten Keune, and David Natali (Brussels: ETUI/REHESS, 2010), 371–94; Tatur, "Towards Corporatism?"; Ost, "Illusory Corporatism."

reforms. Typically, major austerity packages have been prepared and implemented as "coups." Organized interests have been bypassed rather than taken into account. The limited concessions that were all that was granted to unions in light of radically changing economic environments took their toll on union strength as well: union membership declined dramatically in all four countries.

There was, however, a single concession to labor, namely a generous welfare state, that proved to be more effective and persistent than either partial inclusion through employee ownership schemes in national capitalist experiments or formal inclusion through tripartism with limited real competences.

Welfarist Social Contracts

The author of an unmatched study of welfare state legacies and reforms in the Visegrád group, Tomasz Inglot, highlights an important contradiction in these countries' socio-economic policies: "During the early 1990s, Poland and, to a lesser degree, Hungary...defied conventional wisdom when the government combined aggressive pro-market economic policies with extremely generous social transfers that brought the welfare state to the brink of financial collapse."[24] While this pattern is most evident in these two countries, welfare state development in the Czech Republic equally defied the government's strong promarket stance, and contributed to a fiscal crisis later in the 1990s. Only the development of Slovakia diverged. Here governments took more consistent stances in either rejecting or embracing both the neoliberal reforms of economy and the welfare state. Hence the reasons for our interest in both the factors of the Visegrád group's welfarism and of its deviation from the regional pattern. In what follows, we shall demonstrate the Visegrád welfare states' generosity in general and in regard to pension policies in particular, and assess the overall political and economic challenges stemming from these efforts to embed neoliberalism.

Pensioners' Welfare States

In a regional comparison, the Visegrád countries converged on an intermediate position between the Baltic states on the one hand and Slovenia on the other with regard to social and political inclusion and exclusion. Their related decisions go far to explain both their success in weathering the early hard times, and the recurrent contestation of embedded neoliberalism. Differences among the cases notwithstanding, the Visegrád countries' welfarist social contracts stand out for their continuity over the period of

24. Inglot, *Welfare States*, 265.

systemic change, and for the protection against social hardship they have granted those who acquired a satisfactory social status through work under socialism.

Much more than the reformers of the Baltic countries, policymaking elites in the Visegrád group built on existing welfare state legacies. They drew heavily on the expertise of socialist social policymakers and bureaucrats, and kept a high degree of continuity in the institutional setup of the welfare states. For instance, in the Polish case, Jacek Kuroń, minister of labor and social affairs in the first governments formed by Solidarity, relied on the advice of social policy bureaucrats who convinced him that the Polish social system had served well in the past to overcome major crises, and, if kept intact, would do so again. In addition, "the inherited decision-making mechanism that centered on the powerful office of the labor ministry and the Social Insurance Institution (ZUS) remained in place as the main backbone of the postcommunist welfare state, creating a formidable structural barrier against any accelerated change."[25] ZUS proved to be especially powerful in the early days of transition, as the new minister was basically "flying blind."[26]

In the Czech Republic, the first postcommunist team of social policy experts included Igor Tomeš, who previously was the Prague Spring leader Alexander Dubček's adviser, and designed his package of welfare state reforms before he was forced to work in the steel industry when the movement for "Socialism with a Human Face" was crushed. The fact that policymakers drew on this distinctive "social democratic" reform legacy helps explain some of the differences between the Czech welfare state and those of the neighboring countries. These specificities include stronger egalitarianism of the pension system, early abolition of privileged occupational categories, and an overall greater concern with preventing unemployment rather than compensating for job loss. The social democratic reformers also merged two social policy bureaucracies into a single new Social Security Agency. However, as in the past, the social policy budget remained under the supervision of the executive branch.[27]

Slovakia clearly had the least expertise and institutional resources to draw on. Its social policymakers, however, partly made up for the lack of home-grown expertise by keeping constant informal contact with Czech social policy experts.[28]

25. Ibid., 254.

26. Jacek Kuroń, *Moja Zupa* [My soup] (Warsaw: Polska Oficyjna Wydawnicza BGW, 1991).

27. Mitchell A. Orenstein, "Transitional Social Policy in the Czech Republic and Poland," *Czech Sociological Review* 3, no. 2 (1995): 179–96; Mitchell A. Orenstein and Martine R. Haas, "Globalization and the Future of the Welfare State in Post-Communist East-Central European Countries," in *Globalization and the Future of the Welfare State*, ed. Miguel Glatzer and Dietrich Rueschemeyer (Pittsburgh: University of Pittsburgh Press, 2005), 130–52; Inglot, *Welfare States*, 224.

28. Inglot, *Welfare States*, 254, 247.

Built on existing policy and institutional legacies, the Visegrád countries' welfare states stand out in the region for the generosity of their provisions—including education, health care, pensions, labor market policies, family and child care and social housing—whether measured by the social spending share of GDP or by the absolute volume of benefits (table 1.3). The Visegrád countries also accumulated, until the late 2000s at least, a fair record in maintaining a degree of social cohesion against destabilizing market forces. Indeed, around the mid-2000s these states (with the exception of Poland) did not seem to suffer from dramatically larger poverty or inequality than many old member states of the EU (table 1.8).

Socially protective as they are, the Visegrád welfare states are also shaped by the paternalist legacies of socialist and presocialist times (see chapter 2, "Mobilizing Consent"). Embracing these legacies and their political lessons, postsocialist reformers by and large continued to offer compensation from above with little involvement of civil society groups, and to award benefits selectively to strategically important sectors of the population. In general, these welfare states have been biased in favor of temporarily, partly, or wholly "nonproductive" social groups that nevertheless earned a respected status through work or otherwise—including the army of "under-age" pensioners in early retirement (especially in Hungary and Poland), and mothers with small children (in Hungary). In turn, the youth and the poorer strata have tended to be neglected. These biases produce a peculiar pattern of redistribution of risk of poverty across age groups. While children and youth run high risks of becoming poor in all four countries, the at-risk-of poverty rate gradually declines with age, and is lowest in the oldest cohort (figure 3.1).

The emergence of a fully fledged "pensioners' welfare state" is a novelty of postsocialism that is in contrast with the situation in late socialism where pensioners were more prone to poverty than the rest of population.[29] In the first years of transformation, an opposite development took place: whereas wages dropped dramatically, pensions were kept more stable. One of the reasons for this peculiar development is that Visegrád reformers, while aware of the fact that market reforms would bring about social hardship, and committed to provide for a minimum safety net for their populations, were uncertain about the social groups that would most suffer under reforms. Perceiving pensioners as the most vulnerable, and out of fear of their power in democratic politics, transformative elites tried to protect pensioners' income.[30]

Equally important is that reformers recognized the contributions and skills accumulated during a working life under socialism, and the social rights acquired in its course. This was perhaps most clearly stated by Polish Minister of Labor and Social Affairs Kuroń: "I believe that you cannot take away certain social rights from people, you can modify them, change the

29. Vanhuysse, *Divide and Pacify*, 76–84.
30. Inglot, *Welfare States*, 258.

method of implementation, make them more rational...but to simply say you are not entitled to them any more cannot be done."[31] In a similar vein, for Hungary's first democratically elected premier, József Antall, "pension is a right acquired by work; the security of pensioners can only be guaranteed in a renewed insurance system....All those who are powerless and disadvantaged should be able to count on society's and the state's help by means of a social safety net."[32]

Finally, there might also have been a Machiavellian calculus underlying the pro-pensioner policies. This is the core of Pieter Vanhuysse's interpretation of the pensioners' welfare states: according to him, state elites clearly understood the potentially explosive social situation and strategically drew on existing social policy devices in order to "divide and pacify" the working population. In particular, the better-educated and potentially more vocal groups of elderly workers were pacified with generous early retirement or disability pension benefits for job losses. In contrast, younger workers made redundant were left with relatively meager unemployment benefits instead.[33]

Vanhuysse's argument accounts in particular for what he calls the "great abnormal pensioner boom," that is for the masses of people taking out disability pensions or being allowed to retire early. Thus, in 1989–96, "the number of disability pensioners increased by 11 percent in the Czech Republic, by 22 percent in Poland and by a staggering 49 percent in Hungary." The number of pensioners, including those who retired early, increased over the same time by 5 percent in the Czech Republic, 20 percent in Hungary, and 46 percent in Poland.[34] Early retirement was significant in Slovakia too. Whereas in 1990, only 3 percent of new pensioners retired early, in 1994 it was almost 80 percent.[35]

To some extent all Visegrád countries' welfare states experienced "abnormal pensioners booms," but the above figures show that such booms were more sizable in Hungary and Poland than in the Czech Republic and Slovakia. This difference is due to the fact that the former two countries used their pension systems as buffers against unemployment. In contrast, Czech reformers initially prevented layoffs by subsidizing employers, and by active labor market policies.[36] An important consequence of the abnormal pension boom is that early retirees and people on disability pensions allied

31. Ibid., 211.

32. Quoted by Júlia Szalai, *Nincs két ország ... ? Társadalmi küzdelmek az állami túlelosztásért a rendszerváltás utáni Magyarországon* [Are there no two Hungaries? Redistributive struggles in Hungary after the system change] (Budapest: Osiris Kiadó, 2007), 131.

33. Vanhuysse, *Divide and Pacify,* chap. 5: 73–95.

34. Ibid., 88.

35. Maria Svorenova and Alexandra Petrasova, *Social Protection Expenditure and Performance Review: Slovak Republic* (Budapest: International Labour Organization, 2005), 127.

36. Vanhuysse, *Divide and Pacify,* 7–95; Michael J. G. Cain and Aleksander Surdej, "Transitional Politics or Public Choice? An Evaluation of Stalled Pension Reforms in Poland," in Cook, Orenstein, and Rueschemeyer, *Left Parties,* 145–74.

with "normal" pensioners to defend their entitlements, thus making welfare state retrenchment politically difficult. Finally it is also worth noting that in all countries apart from the Czech Republic, initially many privileges granted under the old system for special professional groups, such as miners, policemen, firefighters, and railroad and steel workers were kept.

As a consequence of all of this, the pension spending share of GDP increased everywhere. In the extreme case of Poland, it increased (including on early retirement) from a mere 6.5 to a stunning 14.7 percent between 1989 and 1992.[37] At the same time, because of deteriorating dependency ratios, the slump in wages, and massive tax evasion, the existing pension systems seemed increasingly in danger. While initially all four countries tried to respond to the challenge by incremental adjustments, for instance by temporarily suspending pension indexation, selectively tightening some eligibility criteria, or trying to gradually increase retirement age, looming pension crises gave fresh impetus for more radical reforms from the second half of the 1990s.

Poland and Hungary started off with a more fundamental overhaul of their pension systems. In both countries, major pension crises brought about protracted struggles among the ministries of welfare, social policy experts, and the ministries of finance. Especially the latter advocated the multipillar model as recommended by the World Bank (see chapter 3, "Nationalist Social Contracts"). In both countries the basic conflict was finally settled in 1996, with radical reformers coming off best. The overall design of the new pension systems was quite similar, combining a first pillar with a newly created, fully funded private pillar. The Polish reform of the first pillar was more radical than the Hungarian, as it included a switch to a notional defined contribution system in order to create a stronger link between benefits and paid contributions. Hungary kept its first pillar as a PAYG system with defined benefits.

It is interesting to note the similarities between the Polish and the Latvian pension reforms (on the latter, see chapter 3, "Nationalist Social Contracts"), which were due to the fact that Swedish reform teams were invited to advise both countries. In comparison to Latvia, however, the two Visegrád frontrunners in pension reforms look more gradual on several accounts. In both countries, the second pillar is only being built up very slowly, and its overall size is smaller than in Latvia. In Hungary, moreover, the plan to gradually increase the size of the funded pillar was later given up. Also, people who

---

37. "Children at Risk in Central and Eastern Europe: Perils and Promises," Economies in Transitions Studies Regional Monitoring Report 4 (Florence: UNICEF, 1997), 137. One reason for the disproportionately high share of pensions in GDP is the relaxation of eligibility criteria for farmers, who made ample use of the new opportunity. See, e.g., Inglot, *Welfare States*, 255–58.

initially opted voluntarily to switch to the funded pillar were allowed to move back to the PAYG system afterward.

Governments in both Poland and Hungary were also much concerned with protecting the benefits and privileges of those already in retirement. In Poland, early retirement provisions were maintained for all those who had been covered by the old system, and both a low retirement age for women and heavy subsidies for farmer pensions were kept. Finally, reformers were consistently more committed to stabilizing replacement rates than was the case in Latvia. As a result, pensions in both countries are still far more generous than in the Baltic states.[38]

To be sure, as argued by Júlia Szalai for the Hungarian case, it has not been the generosity of pensions per se that has helped to save many of the Visegrád states' elderly from impoverishment. Rather, early retirement has offered able-bodied under-age pensioners a degree of material security that allowed reintegration into formal or informal markets from relatively safe positions and further accumulation of means through working in or running family businesses or moonlighting.[39]

Slovakia was the third country in the group to embark on radical pension reforms. The Mečiar regime had systematically used the pension system to consolidate its nationalist coalition by catering to traditionally privileged occupational groups, such as state employees, the military, railway workers, police, and firefighters, and by extending privileges to new professional groups. Slovakia also kept in place the pension indexing that was originally introduced in Czechoslovakia in 1991. However, because of the frequent occurrence of state-imposed wage controls, pension benefits for the majority of the population deteriorated steadily, especially from the mid-1990s.[40]

In spite of its largely unreformed system and the accumulation of new privileges, Slovakia has in fact not encountered a fiscal crisis of the pension system comparable to that of Hungary or Poland. However, the economic recession and the austerity package implemented by the first Dzurinda government after 1998, as well as massive tax evasion, led to a gradual decline in contribution revenues from the end of the 1990s onwards. The deficit was more visible than in the neighboring Czech Republic, because Slovak authorities had created a separate pension fund financed by employers' and employees' contributions rather than by the central budget. Even so, on the eve of the radical overhaul of the pension system, expenses exceeded revenues

---

38. Inglot, *Welfare States*, 263–64, 285. For pension reforms in Poland and Hungary, see also Katharina Müller, "Pension Reform Paths in Comparison: The Case of Central-Eastern Europe," *Czech Sociological Review* 7, no. 1 (1999): 51–66, Elaine Fultz, ed., *Pension Reform in Central and Eastern Europe*, vol. 1: *Restructuring with Privatization: Case Studies of Hungary and Poland* (Budapest: International Labour Organization, 2002); and Orenstein and Haas, "Globalization and the Future of the Welfare State."

39. Szalai, *Nincs két ország*, 121–25.

40. Inglot, *Welfare States*, 248.

only by half of 1 percent of GDP.[41] In Slovakia, therefore, the step to move toward a multipillar pension model was as much motivated by the neoliberal outlook of the second Dzurinda government as by the actual problems encountered by the Social Insurance Fund.

The Slovak pension reform bill was passed in April 2003, reforming the first pillar in 2004 and introducing a mandatory second, private pillar from 2005. The second pillar is significantly larger than that of Hungary or Poland. The government "has also been aggressive about allowing external investment in the pension funds, which should promote higher returns."[42] To this end, it provided the most liberal regime for investment in this area by foreign firms. The government also eliminated the minimum pension, leaving redistribution to social assistance. Finally, the two-year transition period from the old to the new system was very short, and the scheme saw few exemptions based on existing rights. For the PAYG system this meant that pensions awarded under the new system would be 10 percent lower than in the old system. Thus, not only by Visegrád standards has the Slovak pension reform stood out for its strong commitment to the new model. What is more, the pension reform was only one element within a radical overhaul of the entire welfare and tax regime.[43]

In contrast to Slovakia, which since the early 2000s has seemed ready to defect, as it were, from core patterns of the welfarist contract, the Czech Republic stayed more firmly committed to the contract than any of its peers. The crisis of 1997 brought the issue of pension sustainability to the fore, as growth, employment, and concomitantly revenues for social security, dropped substantially. The increasing fiscal burden of the pension system, however, did not prove enough of an incentive to reform the existing system substantially. Although policymakers debated the privatization of pensions along the multipillar model, this was ultimately rejected. Several reasons account for this.

First, more than in other countries, policymakers in the Czech Republic were worried that the transition costs associated with the move away from the first pillar would worsen the fiscal balance further. Second, while the international community had some leverage on Poland and Hungary because of their indebtedness, and on Slovakia because of the Dzurinda governments' desire to repair the damage done to the country's reputation under the Mečiar regime, similar sources of influence were largely absent in the Czech case. Third, in contrast to Poland and Hungary, the governing social democratic party was opposed to pension privatization, a stance also shared

41. World Bank, *Slovak Republic: Pension Policy Reform Note. Main Report* (Washington, D.C.: The World Bank, 2004), 1.

42. Ibid., 19.

43. Ibid., esp. 17–20, 38–39. For other reforms, see, e.g., Conor O'Dwyer and Branislav Kovalcik, "And the Last Shall Be First: Party System Institutionalization and Second-Generation Economic Reform in Postcommunist Europe," *Studies in Comparative International Development* 41, no. 4 (2007): 3–26.

by trade unions and pensioner groups. Finally, there was a common sense among Czech policymakers that the existing model had worked reasonably well, which made a radical overhaul unnecessary.

Pension reforms in the Czech Republic were thus incrementally pursued before as well as after the crisis of 1997. It should be noted, however, that pension privatization there had itself been part of incremental pension reforms. Already in the early 1990s, while leaving state benefits largely intact, the Klaus government had built up voluntary private social insurance opportunities for the middle classes, including a supplementary third pension tier.[44]

Economics, Politics, and Welfarism

Bearing all this in mind, we are now in a better position to define the Visegrád contract's core features. Under these Visegrád countries' welfarist social contract, welfare spending was originally intended to mainly protect beneficiaries against social decline due to material deprivation and status loss, and was generous or meager in proportion to the threatened groups' demonstrated or anticipated ability to resist changes that might injure them, whether by social protest or massive anti-incumbent vote.

However, rather than terminating the welfarist contract when the hardest times were over, the Visegrád states extended and consolidated the related measures. Thus, while initially welfarism in the region did not appear as a permanent "contract" worth the name, it seems to have acquired a more systemic character over time. As late as in the mid-2000s (and in Hungary even beyond) governments still tried to generate consent through extensive welfare provisions, such as liberalized access to disability and early retirement, benefits for the unemployed and families, and encompassing schemes of public health care and education. While some of these schemes were designed to relieve the better-off and more vocal, and others to help less resourceful workers, typically the former could enter or exit the labor market under more advantageous conditions than the latter.[45]

Importantly, the Roma, representing a sizable share of the total population of Slovakia, Hungary, and the Czech Republic (in that order), were deprived of sufficient protection against the threat of further decline to underclass status—witness the meager spending on active and passive labor market policies and the unconvincing performance of Roma integration programs region-wide. Late socialism's efforts to integrate this ethnic group had been partially successful at best, since even if eventually many Roma had been absorbed by the expanding SOEs, temporary employment in low-skilled occupations fell short of earning them a respected social status. As demonstrated by Szalai's

---

44. Inglot, *Welfare States*, 232; Katharina Müller, "Beyond Privatization: Pension Reform in the Czech Republic and Slovenia," *Journal of European Social Policy* 12, no. 4 (2002): 294–306.
45. Vanhuysse, *Divide and Pacify*.

excellent study on Hungary as well as János Ladányi's and Iván Szelényi's cross-regional comparative work, after the breakdown of socialism the Roma (and other vulnerable groups) lost out in the rivalry with politically more vocal beneficiaries of the welfare state. Roma poverty is above all to be traced to extremely high rates of long-term unemployment or nonemployment.[46]

In sum, under the Visegrád states' welfarist social contract relatively afflu-ent, status-rich, and vocal groups more often than not have pushed their poor, powerless and (partly but not exclusively) Roma competitors for public wel-fare provision to the sidelines. Even so, by preventing the impoverishment of large middle-class groups, these welfare states were relatively successful, albeit hardly efficient, in keeping social disintegration at bay. However, they could do so only at the expense of recurrent macroeconomic instability driven by fiscal overspending and in the Hungarian case by a critical increase of foreign debt.

As to the sustainability of the Visegrád group's social budgets, the essence of their problem is well captured by Martin Rhodes' contention: "If you want to have a large and sustainable welfare state, you have to be able to pay for it."[47] The same applies to generous public aid granted in abundance to "sun-set" or "sunrise" industries and services in the Visegrád area. As collection of social security contributions and taxes in the needed amounts and structures has been a serious challenge for the Visegrád states, their social protection systems have repeatedly been on the verge of bankruptcy, and their state budgets in high debts and deficits (table 1.9).

True, in the hard times of transformation welfare expenditures and willy-nilly tolerated noncontribution of fiscal revenues kept disruptive social pro-test and political radicalism at bay. However, the coexistence of large budgets with a large informal economy eventually threatened to trap the Visegrád states in a vicious circle. Rampant evasion of tax and social security payments spurred legal workers and firms (which found their own tax burdens climb-ing as so many opted out around them) to begin looking for ways to avoid their own obligations.[48]

These symptoms, which in Martin Rhodes's and Maarten Keune's view reveal a whole complex of "pathology," shed light on a grave coordination problem and the related overload of the Visegrád group's democratic insti-tutions. Lacking the support of established social partnership frameworks, over the 2000s these institutions were left alone to face the task of balancing among the costs of social welfare and industrial policies, and the require-ments of macroeconomic stability.

---

46. Szalai, *Nincs két ország;* János Ladányi and Iván Szelényi, *A kirekesztettség változó formái* [Changing forms of exclusion] (Budapest: Napvilág Kiadó, 2004).
47. Martin Rhodes, "Why EMU Is—or May Be—Good for European Welfare States," in Dyson, *European States and the Euro,* 309.
48. Martin Rhodes and Maarten Keune, "EMU and Welfare States in East-Central Europe," in Dyson, *Enlarging the Euro Area,* 284.

Crucial initial choices to generate consent and legitimacy through mitigating the social and economic costs of transformation, locked political parties in a peculiar pattern of democratic competition that reproduced pensioner-biased welfarism and fiscal overspending—and reflected the general dominance of short-term political motives behind policy decisions. Being aware of the popularity of social programs, pensioners' voting power, and the crucial importance of attracting FDI, centrist parties went into debt to keep up spending on welfare and industry despite negative macroeconomic consequences. Yet, as is often the case with compensation from above, the consent mobilized this way was partial and elusive.

Especially given that the social programs provided were insufficient relative to needs, it is hardly surprising that the Visegrád electorate soon learned how to protest through the vote. The more citizens felt "sentenced to patience" in between elections, the more eagerly they sought to punish incumbent parties at the polls, holding these parties responsible for their deprivations. In Poland not once over the period 1990–2010 was an incumbent government returned to office. Instead, forces of the Right and Left alternated in power in predictable sequence. Moreover, terms in power have usually led incumbents not merely to defeat but even to disintegration. In Hungary it was not until the spring election of 2006 that MSZP and the SZDSZ were given a second consecutive term. In the Czech and Slovak Republics the Left-Right alternation has occurred at two-term intervals, with the second term usually being one of a weakened minority government of the Left or the Right. These experiences underline that the Visegrád regimes have remained politically highly contested.

We found that domestic politics mattered for the rise of the embedded neoliberal regimes in the Visegrád area. But is democratic national politics the only important factor? After all, these regimes have not emerged in closed national economies. Consequently, all of the relevant opportunities and constraints might not operate at the level where democratic national politics rules. In fact, although domestic politics has not lost its significance, by the late 1990s it had become increasingly constrained and driven in new directions by intraregional rivalry, the preferences of transnational corporations, and the pressures of the EU.[49]

Rival Manufacturing Miracles

The accession to the EU and the shift from national capitalism to foreign-led development paths reshaped some institutions and policies of the Visegrád

49. The following builds on Béla Greskovits, "Central Europe," in *Which Europe? The Politics of Differentiated Integration*, ed. Kenneth Dyson and Angelos Sepos (Houndsmills: Palgrave Macmillan, 2010), 142–55. We also drew inspiration from Peter Katzenstein, *A World of Regions: Asia and Europe in the American Imperium* (Ithaca: Cornell University Press, 2005).

countries, exposing them to competition for international recognition and investment. The seeds of intraregional rivalry were planted in the early days of transition, and can also be traced back to a long history of rivalry and outright hostility among some of the four countries. Rivalry was reinforced, however, by the EU's "hub-and-spoke" approach to integration and the increasing power of transnational firms, which enabled them to play different locations against each other in order to secure high returns on their investments.

Region of Rivals

The Visegrád area's history is no less replete with externally imposed but locally resented frameworks and processes of regional cooperation than with episodes of failed bottom-up initiatives to that end, which were routinely frustrated by the ruling empires and quasi-empires: the Austro-Hungarian Monarchy and the Soviet Union.

Péter Kende's study provides a perceptive overview of the *longue durée* of failed bottom-up attempts, from ideas of transforming the Habsburg Empire into a "Confederation of the Peoples of the Danube Valley" to various plans to integrate Czechoslovakia with Poland, or Romania with Hungary or Bulgaria, proposed after World War II by a few conservative and Communist leaders and blocked, in the latter cases, by Stalin. Kende asserts that despite their popularity in intellectual circles, the plans of confederation and integration were doomed to failure by their neglect of existing power relations and by the fact that they "never could rely on broad popular support, and were rather incompatible with economic 'interests' (or rather aspirations.)"[50]

Indeed, whatever economic cooperation among the industrialized and agrarian lands of the Habsburg Empire occurred, it took place in the context of fierce political competition among Hungarians, Czechs, Slovaks, Romanians, and other peoples. In light of their abundant legacies of rivalry and hostility, it is hardly surprising that after their forced incorporation into the military and economic bodies of the Soviet bloc, the Warsaw Treaty Organization and the Council for Mutual Economic Assistance (CMEA), the satellite states found it difficult to reinvent themselves as brothers-in-arms.

While outright hostility was kept at bay by Soviet interest in maintaining order in their sphere of influence, the satellite communist elites' mutual suspicion of each other's revisionism or anti-Soviet nationalism helped the Kremlin to resort to techniques of divide and rule. Soviet-type central planning and the CMEA further reinforced intraregional divisions, as their logics

---

50. Péter Kende, "Van-e még esélye és értelme egy közép európai államföderációnak? Kell-e nekünk Közép Európa?" [Does a Central European Federation still have a chance—and does it make sense? Do we need Central Europe?], special issue, *Századvég* [Century's end] (1990): 10.

backed autarky and import substitution rather than collaboration and export orientation, and gave priority to all-encompassing production profiles over specialization in selected production segments or niches. The evolving almost identical economic structures originated in socialist development strategists' undifferentiated preference for heavy industries.

Irony of ironies, the autarkic logic remained appealing during the 1970 and 1980s, when oil price hikes, détente, growing awareness of a West-East technological gap, and welfare considerations, all forced the CMEA to encourage a new division of labor based on specialization, transfer of technology and know-how, intra-industry trade—to advance toward complementary rather than structurally similar profiles.[51] The satellite economies did make some attempts to specialize: Hungary in production of buses and pharmaceuticals, Czechoslovakia and Poland in automobiles and heavy chemicals, and all three countries in varied branches of consumer electronics and computers. Yet these efforts were permanently hampered by the shortage syndrome characterizing the regional as much as the domestic economies. At the regional level, the syndrome manifested itself in insatiable demand for imported inputs, long delivery times, poor quality, lack of product differentiation and customer service, and other features analyzed by Kornai.[52]

As a consequence, individual countries remained interested in going it alone and keeping up parallel industrial structures and the longest possible supplier chains within their own economic spaces, in order to minimize dependence on unreliable, low-quality, and shortage-prone intra-industry trade with their neighbors. They were no less reluctant to share Western technology and know-how obtained through hard-currency purchase of licenses or accessed through smuggling and industrial espionage. Despite the efforts for specialization and cooperation through intra-industry trade, CMEA trade largely remained the same as it ever was: exchange of finished manufacturing products among the smaller member states, and manufacturing goods and foodstuffs for fuel and raw materials between these states and the Soviet Union.

Although national autarky was the quintessential legacy of the socialist system, its collapse heralded a heyday of regional cooperation—albeit more in political than economic matters. Three, respectively ideational, political, and economic manifestations, all dating to the first heroic period of systemic change, deserve to be mentioned: the revival of the Central European idea, the Visegrád Declaration, and the founding of the Central European Free Trade Area (CEFTA). The ideological and political initiatives reflected the new elites' own aspirations, whereas the new framework of regional economic cooperation was encouraged by the EU, and only reluctantly adopted by the postsocialist countries.

---

51. Márton Tardos, ed., *Vállalati magatartás—vállalati környezet* [Enterprise behavior—enterprise environment] (Budapest: Közgazdasági és Jogi Könyvkiadó, 1990).
52. Kornai, *The Socialist System*.

Breaking and Remaking Rivalry

The idea of Central Europe's cultural, political, and economic distinctiveness was revived by dissident artists and public intellectuals, such as the Czech novelist Milan Kundera, and Poland's Nobel Prize–winner poet Czesław Miłosz, to outline the region's exceptionalism and its natural affinity to the West. In his influential study of the issue, the Hungarian historian Jenő Szűcs, for instance, distinguishes among three historical European regions: the West, the East, and, in between, Central Europe. What distinguishes Central Europe from the East is that its history had long been shaped by Western influences.[53] Others have argued that Central Europe, while making little geographical sense, "conveys the political unity of those—Poles, Czechs and Magyars—who fought against communism, as distinct from their neighbours who did not."[54] The theme was subsequently picked up by U.S. political strategists, prominently Zbigniew Brzezinski, and persons who later became the region's political leaders, such as Václav Havel.

Most important in our context is the political career of the idea. As such, Central Europe has expressed the common ambitions of the countries of the region to return to the West, and has been adopted to justify demands for preferential treatment on the part of the West. In particular, the new elites used historicized regionalism as the ideological cornerstone of their strategies of fast and full EU integration.[55] Ironically, once the Eastern intellectuals and politicians reinvented Central Europe as a historical region, Western leaders who in the early 1990s were still ambivalent about EU enlargement bought into the idea and suggested to Czechoslovakia, Hungary and Poland to put their regionalism into practice and try to cooperate with each other before rushing to join the EU. So they did.

Led by shared interests in building democratic capitalism, security, stability, and a return to Europe, and concerned over the possibility of economic and political pressures from the Soviet Union in its death throes, in 1991 the three countries expressed their commitment to cooperation in the Visegrád Declaration.[56] However, while the fora and areas of cooperation were specified, the Visegrád group has never developed a robust institutional framework for regional collaboration.[57] Its actual achievements have been subject to constraints both before and after EU accession.

---

53. Jenő Szűcs, "Vázlat Európa három történeti régiójáról" [Europe's three historical regions], *Történelmi Szemle* [Historical review] 3 (1981): 313–59.

54. Perry Anderson, "The Europe to Come," in *The Question of Europe,* ed. Peter Gowan and Perry Anderson (London: Verso, 1997), 138.

55. Maria Todorova, *Imagining the Balkans* (New York: Oxford University Press, 1997).

56. Bunce, "The Visegrad Group," 251–52.

57. Rather "it is based solely on the principle of periodical meetings of its representatives at various levels (from Prime Ministers and Presidents to expert consultations). An official meeting of Prime Ministers takes place on an annual basis. Between these summits, one of the V4 countries holds presidency, part of which is the responsibility [*sic*] for drafting a one-year

Before 2004, haunted by historically ingrained fears of "Western be-trayal," Visegrád politicians suspected a hidden EU agenda for using their region as a buffer, and promoting (sub)regionalization as a poor substitute for full EU membership. (For the genealogy of the idea of Western betrayal see chapter 2, "Mobilizing Consent.") Their concern was reinforced by the EU's insistence on the importance of economic, rather than merely sluggish political cooperation for a true revival of the historical region.

The Visegrád leaders' fear was not unfounded, as in the early 1990s ideas such as a Europe of concentric circles, or a generic association between Eastern and Western Europe outside of the framework of the EU, still circu-lated widely. Moreover, in the Europe Agreements that were concluded in the early 1990s, the EU carefully avoided taking a position on the question of full membership. As a reaction, therefore, even if in 1992 the Visegrád states signed on to the CEFTA, they did so without much enthusiasm.

One rationale behind the CEFTA was that the bilateral Europe Agreements "gave more tariff advantages in trade with the EC than the 'Most Favored Nation' framework" under which the Visegrád group's members traded with each other, and the new agreement merely ensured equal treatment for them on the regional market. However, even if "CEFTA was a way to avoid the over-reaction in trade reorientation, the members did not seem to perceive it as such; rather, they had to be urged" by the EU.[58] Yet the further institutional development of regional economic cooperation has been minimal, not least because of the Visegrád states' fear that overdoing regionalization would give "the EU an excuse to put off the question of full membership of the central European countries."[59]

Regional economic cooperation faced yet other obstacles. Due to their inheritance of almost identical rather than complementary industrial struc-tures, the Visegrád economies did not have much to trade with each other to begin with. Arguably, this tendency was reinforced by the "hub-and-spoke" nature of the Europe Agreements, whereby each state in the region entered a legal relationship with the EU, and related to its neighbors principally via its relation with the Western hub.[60] Such a relationship did little to encourage multilateral trade, cooperation, and integration among the Visegrád coun-tries, and, as a result tended to marginalize the "spoke economies," which be-

---

plan of action." See the details at http://www.visegradgroup.eu/main.php?folder (accessed November 9, 2009).

58. Gergana Dimitrova, "The Limited Effectivenes of Transitory Regional Trade Arrangements in East-Central Europe: The Case of CEFTA," (M.A. thesis, Central European University, Budapest, Department of International Relations and European Studies, 1999), 4.

59. Bunce, "The Visegrad Group," 260.

60. Richard E. Baldwin, *Towards an Integrated Europe* (London: Center for Economic Policy Research, 1994); Peter Gowan, "Neoliberal Theory and Practice For Eastern Europe," *New Left Review*, no. 213 (1995): 3–60.

cause of their limited market size found it more difficult to attract FDI than would have been the case in a multilateral trade and investment architecture.

In order to "artificially" increase their attractiveness, the spoke economies therefore started to offer investors protection against imports from their neighbors, this way increasing the barriers of trade within the region. Evidence of trade deliberalization in the Visegrád countries in the wake of a first inflow of FDI into the automobile and electronics sectors bears out Richard Baldwin's analysis of the drawbacks of the hub-and-spoke model. Thus the EBRD finds that for the early transition period, "in Poland, FDI-intensive industries have average tariffs on imports that are 66 percent higher than in manufacturing as a whole. The corresponding figure for Hungary is 10 percent, but Hungary uses quantitative restrictions more heavily than Poland. When nontariff barriers are taken into account, the strong link between high protection and high FDI also appears in Hungary."[61] The *Financial Times* commented dryly: "Ironically, western multinationals have become Eastern Europe's most effective lobby for protection and their efforts to link investment commitments to guaranteed markets have become all the more intense as local demand has fallen below expectations."[62]

Interstate Competition

With the benefit of hindsight it can be argued that the exceptional—if limited—collaborative efforts of the heroic period—including, ironically, tacit cooperation in cutting back on the EU's overzealous efforts to craft a Visegrád region—left behind their own legacy, and that this legacy later proved to be important for the ways and mechanisms of regionalization, and for convergence on the institutions of embedded neoliberalism. Through their newly accumulated experience in effective collective action while leaving the East and returning to Europe, the Visegrád governments learned to consider one another as peer nations, whose moves in economic policy and political strategy deserved serious attention and scrutiny for their potential relevance for and impact on other states within the region. The short-lived experience of collaboration enhanced their mutual interest in one another, especially since, unlike in the Baltic area, there was no single Visegrád country that could be permanently followed as leader.

Overall, however, distinguishing themselves from their peers was the logic that prevailed. From the beginning on, governments made efforts to demonstrate leadership in particular policy fields—Poland with "shock therapy," Czechoslovakia with voucher privatization, and Hungary with incentives to attract FDI. Slovakia, which during the 1990s had spectacularly fallen behind its peers in terms of economic reforms, privatization, and political

61. *Transition Report 1994*, 137.
62. *Financial Times*, quoted ibid., 137.

democratization, made an equally spectacular comeback in the new millennium, with its flat tax and welfare reforms setting a new benchmark for economic strategy. Governments in all countries then tried at different times to capitalize on the international acclaim and material rewards that came with path-breaking accomplishments. In these endeavors, they could count on the backing of IFIs, which were eager to see success stories even if more often than not after short periods of popularity new challenges made "heroes go down."

The IFIs' interest in successful policy innovation can be explained by the fact that by the time socialism collapsed, these institutions had just completed a massive round of neoliberal policy advocacy which, however, brought about disappointing results in Africa and Latin America. Thus, they were in need of new proofs that their recipes could remedy economic malaise, and in this context the Visegrád states' "best practices" readily lent themselves to being advertised in other postsocialist countries and worldwide.

At the same time, the EU was less in need than the IFIs of picking success stories in the Visegrád region in order to motivate peers to catch up with leaders. With the exception of Slovakia, all Visegrád countries belonged to the first wave of East Central European countries that started entry negotiations with the EU in 1997. By this time, they fulfilled the political criteria for membership, and the commission considered the economic reforms to be going in the right direction.

The Visegrád countries' accession strategies focused on speeding their economic reform paths, strengthening their overall regulatory frameworks, and adopting the *acquis communautaire*. This also holds for Slovakia after the end of the Mečiar era. Arguably, therefore, the major impact of EU accession on the region's further development path was indirect: under the protective umbrella of EU candidate status, all countries started to attract massive FDI inflows, which contributed to reindustrialization, job creation, and enhanced competitiveness. As a consequence, policies of attracting FDI became a major hallmark of the Visegrád countries' embedded liberal regimes, bringing intraregional rivalry to a hitherto unknown level.

The socialist legacy of highly similar industrial structures, initially so disadvantageous for a fast reinvigoration of regional trade, later provided the essential foundations for the four economies' rapid foreign-led and export-oriented reindustrialization. As shown in chapter 2, the inherited complex industries helped attract complex-manufacturing TNCs whose first locational choices in the postsocialist East critically hinged upon the relative abundance of adequate human capital. The similarity of production profiles in the region, however, also spurred locational competition among the four countries, as in order to attract investment they needed to differentiate themselves from their neighbors.

Moreover, reflecting the production profile similarities, the evolving foreign-invested and controlled systems of production have adopted a transnational rather than a national character. By the early 2000s, the clustering of complex industries brought about tight cross-border integration of the Czech Republic, southwestern Poland, northwestern Slovakia, and northwestern Hungary that further enhanced the attraction of the fast-emerging regional economy. In this cluster, it is of minor significance for foreign investors on which side of a national border they ultimately locate production facilities. It is therefore easy for TNCs to engage the Visegrád countries in bidding wars over desperately needed investments.

And bidding wars there were. It was above all tax reforms and generous investment incentives that bore witness to the heightened locational competition within the Visegrád area. Corporate taxes in all four countries declined significantly already during the 1990s.[63] Poland revised its corporate income tax rate frequently during the 1990s, as a result of which it fell from 40 percent (1989) to 30 percent (2000). At the same time, personal income taxes, social security contributions, and indirect taxation went up. A similar pattern was visible in Hungary, where the government of Premier Gyula Horn halved the corporate tax rate on reinvested profits, with the consequence that Hungary was a regional leader in low corporate taxes. At the same time, personal income taxes, labor taxes, and consumption taxes were increased. In addition, this country was at the forefront in creating special tax exemptions for foreign investors. The Czech Republic followed a similar trend. Although it never dismantled its corporate taxes to the degree that the other Visegrád countries did, it nevertheless steadily decreased corporate taxation over the 1990s. Under the Social Democratic government, it also started to actively create special incentives for foreign investors.

From the end of the 1990s onward, tax competition took more dramatic forms, and has been closely linked to the agenda of attracting FDI. In 1999, Poland introduced another tax reform, and in 2000, the Czech Republic followed. A new round in the tax competition was initiated by Slovakia in 2004, when it introduced its flat tax rate regime of 19 percent for income, corporate, and value added taxes. With this step, the corporate income tax fell significantly below the EU average, and also below that of the new EU member states, prompting neighboring countries to lower their corporate taxes in return.

Low statutory tax rates are important tools for attracting FDI. Even if they do not tell much about the effective tax burden for investors, they signal a business-friendly environment, and set important parameters for the tax that de facto has to be paid.[64] Moreover, TNCs themselves have actively promoted

63. See, also for the following, Hillary Appel, "The political economy of tax reform in Central Europe: Do domestic politics still matter?" (2003), http://www.eurofaculty.lv/taxconference/files/Hilary_Appel.pdf (accessed May 7, 2008). See also Frank Bönker, "Steuerpolitische Aspekte der EU-Osterweiterung," *Vierteljahreshefte zur Wirtschaftsforschung* 72, no. 4 (2003): 522–34.

64. Steffen Ganghof, "The Politics of Tax Structure," MPIfG Working Paper 06/1 (Cologne: Max Planck Institut für Gesellschaftsforschung, 2006).

tax cuts. Thus, in 2003 the then executive director of the American Chamber of Commerce (AmCham) in Hungary, Péter Fáth, argued that given that EU accession puts limits on tax exemptions for TNCs, the next task for AmCham will be to lobby for a lower corporate tax rate, modeled after the Irish example.[65]

In addition to general reductions in corporate taxation, TNCs have been negotiating skillfully for investment incentives tailored to their particular needs. The type of demands foreign investors put on their host countries has changed over time. Whereas initially import protection and tax holidays were highest on the agenda, both were ruled out by the Visegrád countries' accession to the EU. Although foreign investors successfully pushed host country governments to defend their far-reaching tax concessions against the commission during the accession negotiations, demands have since shifted to other types of incentives.

One of the most striking results of Fergus Cass's empirical investigation of investment incentives in Eastern Europe is that incentive packages have become more generous since the late 1990s than in the early transition period. He argues that "this result is consistent with the extensive accounts of growing competition between countries for relatively mobile efficiency-seeking investments."[66] The trend is confirmed by Peter Kolesár's in-depth empirical study which finds that when locational features among competitors are similar, investment incentives play a major role in TNCs' choice of a specific location.[67]

Thus, in the case of the Hyundai/Kia investment in Žilina, the Slovak government outcompeted the Polish authorities in 2004 in the final round by adding a number of special-purpose incentives to the general support of 15 percent of the total investment as allowed by EU law. The government pledged additional subsidies for investment property, hospitals, housing, and English-language education for employees' children, as well as for the construction of a highway, a railroad link, and an airport. In addition, the government promised not to increase levels of corporate tax, employment protection, and employers' contribution to social protection. Kia did not have to give much in return—nor did it have to commit itself to a minimum of investment or employment.

Similarly, in the case of South Korean Hankook Tire's investment in Dunaújváros, it was investment incentives rather than locational advantages that made all the difference. This became clear when, following the Slovak government's decision in 2005 to cut back on some of its promised incentives,

---

65. Dorothee Bohle, and Dóra Husz, interview with Péter Fáth, executive director of the American Chamber of Commerce, Budapest, February 20, 2003.
66. Cass, "Attracting FDI," 41.
67. Peter Kolesár, "Race to the Bottom? The Role of Investment Incentives in Attracting Strategic Automotive Foreign Direct Investment in Central Europe" (M.A. thesis, Central European University, Budapest, Department of International Relations and European Studies, 2006). See also Drahokoupil, *Globalization and the State.*

Hankook Tire backed off from investing in Slovakia. This situation was hurriedly exploited by the Hungarian government that felt itself to be in desperate need of attracting at least one large investor, since the last major projects in the region had gone to its competitors Slovakia and the Czech Republic.

Locational competition became also deeply ingrained in the Visegrád countries' self-representation. Increasingly, they borrowed elements of the marketing strategies of competing private firms, and integrated them into their own policies to boost FDI. Acting as if they were firms, these states went far in differentiating their "products," namely their locations, from those offered by their regional competitors.[68] They also tried to mobilize broad popular support for their efforts to outcompete peer nations by conscious appeals to historically rooted national identity and pride. Politicians and the national media conferred symbolic meaning on massive green field investment projects, and interpreted the outcome of cross-regional competition for FDI as national victory of, say, "the tiger of the Tatra mountains," Slovakia, over the "Pannonian puma," Hungary (to mention only two of the many exotic terms adopted), or vice versa.

Manufacturing Miracles

Governments willing to capitalize on the legacy of socialist industrialization and TNCs eager to exploit locational advantages of the region eventually indeed produced a kind of manufacturing miracle. Whether measured by its share in output, employment or total exports, the complex industrial sector's performance appears as remarkable (table 1.7). Even when compared with some of the giant NICs, it is striking to recognize the extent of the region's success in attracting TNCs without whose involvement capturing large world market shares would not have been possible.

During the 1990s foreign penetration occurred primarily through acquisition of privatized property, but the inflows did not stop but rather accelerated during the 2000s when privatization was largely over. Although the bulk of foreign capital was invested in the service sector, manufacturing industry acquired close to 20 percent of the total stock. Within the manufacturing sector complex activities attracted one-third to two-thirds of foreign capital. No wonder, then, that in 2007, the ten large auto manufacturers and hundreds of suppliers located in the Visegrád countries produced the bulk of the three million units originating from the former socialist new EU member states, that is, about 15 percent of European production. Before the outbreak of the global crisis, the region's share was expected to climb above 20 percent in the coming years.[69]

68. Kolesár, "Race to the Bottom."
69. György Heimer, "Keletre Hajtás" [Driving east], *Heti Világgazdaság* [World economy weekly], July 12, 2008.

TABLE 4.1
FDI in the Visegrád countries and the NICs, late 2000s (billion USD)

	Inward capital stock (2010)	Value of green field investment projects (Apr. 2005–Jan. 2011)	Outward capital stock (2010)
Czech Republic	129.9	34.0	15.5
Hungary	91.9	45.7	20.7
Poland	193.1	109.8	36.8
Slovak Republic	50.7	41.3	2.8
Visegrád 4 total	*465.6*	*231.0*	*75.9*
Brazil	472.6	180.9	192.5
China	578.8	615.1	297.6
India	197.9	363.8	92.4
Mexico	327.2	119.8	66.1
Russia	423.1	255.5	433.6

Source: World Investment Report 2011 (New York: United Nations Conference on Trade and Development, 2011).

It is not only foreign physical capital and technology stock that have increased. Rather, large and sometimes even small or medium-sized domestic firms in the Visegrád economies have started to adopt transnational features and invest in service and manufacturing facilities mainly but not exclusively in the nearby countries. Hungarian enterprises' sizable acquisitions in the Visegrád area and its Southeastern European neighbors, and Czech and Slovak capitalists' cross-border operations within the former federal economic space, are cases in point.

Although lacking the heavy media coverage of China's successful or failed acquisitions of one or another piece of the advanced countries' "family silver," the rapidly increasing volume of the region's own transnational capital points to an additional aspect of its advancing developmental status (table 4.1).

What actual degree of development has been brought about by the leading role of export-oriented complex transnational industries? How successful have the Visegrád economies been in shifting factors of production to more efficient uses when assessed in microstructural rather than merely macro- or mesostructural terms? There is no easy and straightforward answer to these questions. On the one hand, the Visegrád states share membership with the most advanced states and a handful of successful newly industrializing countries in the elite club of exporters of cars, machinery, and equipment, electrical and electronics products, and chemicals including pharmaceuticals. From this viewpoint, their industrial transformation seems to be quite successful.

On the other hand, exporting cars or electronics equipment might involve different degrees of sophistication and skills in various economies. As Peter Evans pointed out, in the world of transnational production "it is not what you produce that counts so much as what role you play in producing it...what is important in the final analysis is not the sector per se but the set of productive roles that go with it."[70] It is precisely the gains from placing various production stages in locations characterized by distinct advantages (such as better infrastructure and larger local purchasing power versus lower wages, consistent with higher and lower levels of GDP) that motivate TNCs to organize their production systems and commodity chains globally and transnationally.[71]

With regard to efficiency, available data paint a mixed and changing picture that signals the need for more in-depth studies to arrive at solid judgments on the relationship between export roles and actual developmental status and prospects. A recent World Bank study, for instance, expresses optimism: "The positive effects of past FDI inflows into the region are visible in an increasing ratio of unit value of country exports relative to world exports and a shift towards higher export product quality. The shift towards higher technology exports is particularly evident in the Visegrád countries and Slovenia."[72] Evidence on labor productivity, however, indicates that the Visegrád economies still have a long way to go before catching up with the small Western European states.

Overall, in the Visegrád area, the self-propelling logics of regional competition encouraged by international and transnational actors and markets accelerated the convergence of national industrial policies on generous incentives to foreign capital, and provoked recurrent cycles of competition through lowered taxes. At the same time, however, the policies of embedding transnational capital added to the fiscal problems of the Visegrád states. Between 1995 and 2007, the tax to GDP ratio declined significantly in three of the four Visegrád countries, by more than 3 percent in Slovakia, 2 percent in Hungary, and 1.5 percent in Poland. In the Czech Republic the ratio also declined, but only by small amount. While there were many reasons for this trend, arguably corporate tax competition contributed to the weakening of the states' income base.[73] To some extent, then, embedding capital added to the fiscal stress that repeatedly brought welfare state retrenchment to the agenda.

Contesting the Euro

EU accession has not been particularly challenging for the Visegrád countries with the exception of Slovakia which, initially branded as a pariah state

70. Peter Evans, *Embedded Autonomy: States and Industrial Transformation* (Princeton: Princeton University Press, 1995), 251 n. 16.

71. Gereffi and Wyman, *Manufacturing Miracles.*

72. *World Bank EU8+2 Regular Economic Report* (Washington, D.C.: World Bank, January 2007), 24–25 and chart 38.

73. OECD, *Revenue Statistics 1965–2008* (Paris: Organization for Economic Cooperation and Development, 2009), 43.

and not considered for the first enlargement round, managed to catch up with its peers only at the price of a radical political and economic turnabout under the first and second governments of Premier Dzurinda. EU membership, however, also obliged the four countries to prepare for changeover to the euro. In the run-up to euro accession, the picture got reversed: despite the central banks' initial strong backing of a fast euro entry across the group, so far only Slovakia has qualified for membership in the eurozone.

Central banks, fiscal policymakers, and party politicians in Poland, Hungary, and the Czech Republic have engaged in protracted tugs-of-war, which have pushed eurozone membership to ever further future dates. For long, none of the governments were ready or able to break the existing welfarist social contracts by radical public sector reforms and welfare retrenchment. In addition, especially in Hungary, postponing euro accession was due to grave coordination problems with respect to macroeconomic policies. All this, in turn, raises the question of how to make sense of latecomer Slovakia's regional leadership in euro adoption.

Problems of Changeover: The Visegrád 3

Already before EU accession, central banks in the Czech Republic, Poland, and Hungary were advocating a fast adoption of the euro. National Bank of Hungary's (MNB) governor Zsigmond Járai declared that his country should join the eurozone by 2006, whereas National Bank of the Czech Republic's (NBČ) governor Josef Tošovský as well as National Bank of Poland's (NBP) governor Leszek Balcerowicz suggested 2007 as entry dates.

The rationale for joining soon was much the same in all the countries: staying out of the eurozone would expose their currencies to possible speculative attacks, but joining would reinforce fiscal and monetary discipline, decrease transaction costs, and be conducive to foreign trade and investment. Interestingly, central bankers also criticized some of the entry requirements. In particular, they requested a more flexible inflation rule, a shorter waiting time in the Exchange Rate Mechanism (ERM), and a widening of the exchange rate band within the ERM. Juliet Johnson argues that the major reason for central banks to push for fast EMU entry was that they were not strong enough to put an effective brake on public spending on their own, and assumed that tying the governments' hands by external rules would help.[74]

This points to a major difference in the institutional setups of the Baltic and Visegrád countries. Whereas in the Baltic states, independent central banks and the quest for stable national currencies were deeply embedded

---

74. Juliet Johnson, "Two Track Diffusion and Central Bank Embeddedness: The Politics of Euro Adoption in Hungary and the Czech Republic," *Review of International Political Economy* 13, no. 3 (2006): 361–86.

in the nation-building projects, and effectively constrained fiscal policies and welfare spending (see chapter 3), central banks in the Visegrád countries were much more embattled, and their stances on fiscal policies were more often than not ignored by governing parties for whom the use of social spending to appease vocal groups was essential in the electoral competition.

The NBČ arguably holds the record among the Visegrád countries for getting involved in controversy.[75] Modeled after the Bundesbank, the Czech Central Bank enjoyed a great degree of independence from the 1990s on. Its governor, Tošovský, was strongly committed to monetary orthodoxy. The fact that the Czech Republic managed to navigate the difficult years of early transformation with a fair record of macroeconomic stability was also a great source of self-confidence for the central bank. Nevertheless, from the mid 1990s on, NBČ's economic philosophy started to clash with the priorities of the Klaus government. Seeing its popularity waning, in 1996 the government engaged in fiscal spending to boost its electoral prospects. NBČ immediately reacted by tightening monetary policy, despite the fact that even after a substantial rise in public expenditure, the budget showed only a very tiny deficit.

This first conflict was a harbinger of the political fallout between the NBČ and a part of the political community, and especially Klaus, in the aftermath of the 1997 crisis. After his electoral defeat, Klaus staged a long and bitter attack against the bank, blaming its restrictive policies for the economic downturn. Klaus was not alone in this. Rather, the successor government led by Social Democratic Premier Miloš Zeman thought its policies were responsible for the sluggish recovery after the crisis.

The conflict escalated in 2000, when the conservative Civic Democratic Party (ODS) and the Social Democratic ČSSD joined forces to amend legislation in order to curtail the NBC's independence. Their proposition was that the central bank should set its inflation target and the exchange rate regime in agreement with the parliament, submit its budget to parliamentary approval, and give the government the right to recommend board members. The conflict further escalated when President Václav Havel, who strongly opposed the law, appointed a new governor just before its enactment. The conflict over the central bank's independence was finally settled by the Constitutional Court, which declared the law unconstitutional and confirmed the appointment made by President Havel.

With the central bank independence question settled, the conflicts moved to the terrain of EMU entry and fiscal consolidation. In the early 2000s, the Czech Republic registered the worst fiscal problems in its postsocialist history. Especially the bank bailout and the restructuring of the industry in the aftermath of the crisis, but also relatively high social spending and the refusal

---

75. For the following see Frank Bönker, "From Pacesetter to Laggard: The Political Economy of Negotiating Fit in the Czech Republic," in *Enlarging the Euro Area* ed. Dyson: 160–77; and Myant, *Czech Capitalism*, chaps. 5–6.

of successive governments to tackle the pension system contributed to the fiscal stress.

The ČSSD, which dominated several governments after 1998, lacked the capacity and the will to push through the type of fiscal consolidation program that would have made euro entry easier. Within the party, there was no consensus over the question of strong fiscal discipline and the desirability of a fast euro entry. The left-wing fraction of the party favored a real rather than merely nominal convergence with the eurozone, and was therefore concerned with the negative growth effects of fiscal adjustment programs. In addition to internal rifts, the ČSSD's position was also weakened by the fact that, although dominating the political scene, it never reached a comfortable majority in the parliament. Rather, it presided over unstable electoral coalitions, or over minority governments. Its vulnerability was reinforced by the fact that its electorate was volatile and euroskeptical. Politicians therefore shied away from unpopular reforms.

It was only after the elections of 2002 and the EU referendum in 2003, that the government of Vladimír Špidla eventually adopted a program for fiscal reform and with the NBČ worked out a strategy that foresaw the Czech Republic's euro entry around 2009–10. Although the fiscal consolidation plan was not overly ambitious, strong economic growth helped the country to meet the fiscal criteria of the Maastricht Treaty already in 2004. This overachievement, which opened up an opportunity to join the euro area much earlier than anticipated in the accession strategy, quickly brought President Klaus back into the equation.

Klaus had always been an ardent critic of EMU. Not only did he fear the prospect of a political union looming behind the monetary union, but he also thought it essential that less advanced countries pursue different monetary policies than the advanced ones, and therefore cherished the possibility of independent monetary policy. Quoting a Czech reform economist, Klaus argued that "When everything is frozen, you may go skating but you cannot run a rational economic policy."[76] In order to prevent a fast euro entry, Klaus used his presidential powers to appoint two well-known opponents of the EMU to the board of the central bank.

The Polish experience echoes that of the Czech Republic in that the NBP's orthodox monetary policy was highly controversial, and pitted it against spending-prone governments. The independence of the NBP and its focus on price stability were guaranteed in the constitution in 1997, "as part of the 'anticipatory' Europeanization of the Polish polity before the start of accession negotiations."[77] The bank took this mandate very seriously. It also

76. Václav Klaus, "The Future of the Euro: An Outsider's View," *Cato Journal* 24, nos. 1–2 (2004): 176.

77. See also for the following Radoslaw Zubek, "Poland: Unbalanced Domestic Leadership in Negotiating Fit," in Dyson, *Enlarging the Euro Area,* 201; Radoslaw Zubek, "Poland: From

favored a speedy entry to the EMU, and opted for monetary rather than real convergence.

The first open conflict around the bank's restrictive monetary policy occurred in 2001–2, when the incoming left-wing coalition government under Leszek Miller blamed the NBP for a sharp economic slowdown and threatened to limit its independence and change its mandate. As in the Czech case, this initiative failed. Henceforth, successive governments were pressured to match the NBP's quest for fast EMU convergence with corresponding fiscal adjustment.

In 2001–4, the Miller government repeatedly undertook ambitious attempts to cut public expenditure. In 2001, the cabinet negotiated a fiscal contract which would commit the government to fiscal prudence in the medium term. The consensus over fiscal consolidation, however, broke quickly down. The SLD was deeply divided over the necessity of such a step, especially since its commitment to budgetary prudence was seen as a major reason for its rapidly declining popularity. Ultimately, Premier Miller withdrew his support for the consolidation program, and appointed a new minister of finance, Grzegorz Kołodko, who was known for his pro-growth stance.

His reputation notwithstanding, Kołodko convinced Miller of the benefits of a fast-track entry to EMU envisaged for 2007, and prepared a comprehensive stabilization package. Like its predecessor, the package collapsed quickly in light of strong resistance within the party and a further decrease in the government's popular approval ratings. Trade unions and business groups were also opposed to the idea of sharp fiscal adjustment. Once again, Miller backed off from supporting a finance minister who was willing to tackle fiscal problems. Jerzy Hausner, newly appointed as Minister of Economy and Labor, saw no need for a speedy euro entry, and favored real rather than nominal convergence. Nevertheless, fast-growing public debt forced him to draft a new stabilization package. The Hausner Plan, although prepared in a more consultative way, shared the fate of its predecessors.

Meanwhile, due to the policy controversy and major corruption scandals, the SLD disintegrated and suffered a devastating defeat in the 2005 parliamentary elections. The national-populist successor governments under Premiers Kazimierz Marcinkiewicz and Jarosław Kaczyński were no longer concerned with fiscal consolidation and gave up any ambition for a fast-track EMU entry. In addition, they staged an attack on the NBP and its governor by setting up a committee to investigate the role of the bank in the privatization of financial institutions. As in the Czech case, it took the Constitutional Court's intervention to stop the attack. However, when Governor Balcerowicz's term expired, President Lech Kaczyński nominated one of his close associates, Sławomir

---

Pacesetter to Semi-Permanent Outsider?" in Dyson, *The Euro at Ten*, 292–306; and Rachel Epstein, *In Pursuit of Liberalism: International Institutions in Postcommunist Europe* (Baltimore: Johns Hopkins University Press, 2008).

Skrzypek, as new governor. Skrzypek backed the government's preference for delaying entry to the eurozone.

As with its neighbors, the Hungarian path to the eurozone was subordinated to partisan considerations reflecting domestic electoral risks and opportunities. Political struggles over the control of the Ministry of Finance and the central bank recurred over the whole transformation period, preventing these guardians of sound finances from establishing control over the spending ministries. The coordination of fiscal and monetary policies proved to be no less difficult.

Delegation of power for fiscal centralization, rationalization, and adjustment depended crucially on the extent to which prime ministers governed with cohesive legislative majorities and perceived finance ministers as brothers-in-arms rather than rivals in politics. Institutional reforms could advance in the former case but were watered down or stalled in the latter case.[78] Similarly, Hungary's muddling toward central bank independence reflected efforts at partisan control, which impaired the coordination of fiscal and monetary policies even after EU accession. Appointments of the new presidents of the MNB and measures to strengthen central bank independence occurred in a revealing sequence. "Unreliable" presidents were not allowed to enjoy the longer terms in office, legally protected positions, and enhanced policymaking authority guaranteed by the gradually Europeanized central bank laws. Instead, advances to stronger central bank independence typically favored and empowered their party-loyalist successors.

The tensions between welfare spending and fiscal consolidation in the run-up to EMU were even more pronounced in Hungary than in Poland and the Czech Republic. In 1998, public disappointment with the Left-led government and its Bokros package contributed to the conservative Alliance of Young Democrats–Hungarian Civic Alliance (FIDESZ-MPSZ) electoral victory, and lent some credibility to Prime Minister Viktor Orbán's later claim that his policies were superior to the left alternative, even in terms of social welfare.

To counter international recession, in 1998–2001 domestic output and consumption were boosted by fiscal measures. These included raising minimum wages by altogether 80 percent, large-scale development programs for transport infrastructure, tourism facilities, and public buildings, subsidized loans for residential construction and renovation, and incentives for domestic small and medium-sized businesses. Preparing for early euro entry in 2006, the MNB allowed the Hungarian forint to float within a 30 percent

---

78. Stephan Haggard, Robert R. Kaufman, and Matthew Shugart, "Politics, Institutions, and Macroeconomic Adjustment: Hungarian Fiscal Policy Making in Comparative Perspective"; and Béla Greskovits, "Brothers-in-Arms or Rivals in Politics? Top Politicians and Top Policy Makers in the Hungarian Transformation," both in *Reforming the State: Fiscal and Welfare Reform in Post-Socialist Countries*, ed. János Kornai, Stephan Haggard, and Robert R. Kaufman (Cambridge: Cambridge University Press, 2001), 75–110, 111–41.

band around its central parity against the euro. A policy of inflation targeting was introduced and the exchange rate was used as a tool of disinflation. Yet by 2006 the former pacesetter Hungary became a laggard. The reasons are mainly related to the specific features of party competition.

By 2002 the Hungarian political system consolidated as an essentially two-party democracy within which both FIDESZ-MPSZ and the Hungarian Socialist Party (MSZP) had to appear credible on the two issues that seemed important to the majority: social welfare and the issue of EU membership. This greatly impaired the country's ability to balance competing demands. In some sense, the Hungarian party system presents us with a paradox. For a long time, it has been among the most stable in the region, with two major parties and their junior partners capable of mobilizing large electoral blocs. At the same time, the two blocs have converged on many issues of economic reforms, integration with Western Europe and welfare policies. Yet convergence on policy issues has by no means dampened party competition. The struggle for votes has been excessive, but it has not been fought over divergent policy packages. Parties rather "dispute[d] each other's competence in achieving the desired result."[79] As a result, parties in opposition have steered all their efforts toward blocking the government's road to achieving a goal that both camps have in principle agreed upon.

The strategy for euro entry was one such battlefield of competences with lasting consequences. The Socialists, who returned to power in 2002, argued that lower interest rates, a weaker forint, somewhat higher inflation, and a high growth would allow for a gradual adjustment that would spare the population major shocks on the road to EMU. In their view, the necessary fiscal adjustment was easier to achieve under conditions of relaxed monetary policy. In contrast, FIDESZ in opposition backed the president of the MNB (an appointee of the first Orbán government) who prioritized disinflation and made relaxation of monetary policy conditional on convincing results in fiscal tightening. Eventually, the central bank's position prevailed. Over the 2000s, the MNB maintained high interest rates, which led to the appreciation of and repeated speculative attacks on the Hungarian forint, and an overall loss of export competitiveness.

These domestic struggles were the main cause of volatility, incoherence, and drift of policies. Faced with multiple political and economic pressures both Prime Minister Péter Medgyessy and Ferenc Gyurcsány, who succeeded him as premier in autumn 2004, let some of the most necessary reforms slide, and put their faith in muddling through. During the spring 2006 election campaign the opposition launched, and the government joined in a competition of promises of yet more generous welfare provisions. Uniquely in

---

79. Grzymala-Busse and Innes, "Great Expectations," 66–67.

Hungary's democratic history, voters granted the incumbent MSZP-SZDSZ coalition a second term.

The Hungarian welfarist contract started to expire, however. In response to the European Council's repeated demand for a credible new convergence path, shortly after his reelection Gyurcsány launched an austerity package that consisted of painful short-term measures to redress the budget deficit, as well as long-term structural reforms of the public administration, healthcare and pension systems. Alas, the premier's infamous leaked speech in which he admitted fooling the electorate about the actual state of the economy,[80] triggered a new round of cutthroat political rivalry, which virtually turned the government's whole term into a fierce election campaign, and prevented the country from getting any closer to eurozone entry.

Latecomer's Advantage: Slovakia

In contrast to the rest of the Visegrád group, Slovakia fulfilled all the conditions and introduced the euro in 2009. To demonstrate credible commitment to macroeconomic stability, it radically restructured its welfare state. We see two major factors that can explain this striking divergence from the Visegrád 3 and latecomer Slovakia's regional leadership on these issues. First, independence and new nation building brought Slovakia in some crucial aspects closer to the Baltic situation than was the case in other Visegrád countries. A political opportunity structure with a more accentuated nationalist element, and the related concern with the creation and maintenance of a stable currency, are among these aspects. Second, the international shaming and exclusion from the first round of EU accession brought about a major turning point in the country's political life.

Slovak politics has been characterized by stronger public support for macroeconomic stability and later, at least in the short run, somewhat greater tolerance of the related welfare losses. A number of factors are responsible for this. First, the communist regime left behind a fairly stable macroeconomy. Slovakia also inherited the Czechoslovak tradition of valuing price stability. After the "velvet divorce" this tradition was kept alive by the popularity of Mečiar's grand project, the sovereign Slovak nation-state, and its symbol, the stable new national currency. This strengthened the position of the National Bank of Slovakia (NBS) and can partly explain its relative independence even during the Mečiar regime. In striking contrast with the partisan skirmishes around all the other Visegrád central banks, not only could the first NBS governor Vladimír Masár serve his full term undisputed, but also his deputy Marián Jusko was appointed as his successor for the period 1999–2004 to prepare Slovakia for euro entry.

---

80. See for details http://www.timesonline.co.uk/article (accessed September 19, 2006).

The fiasco of being excluded from the first round of EU accession negotiations, undermined the capacity of Mečiar's regime to mobilize and harness Slovak nationalism for its own political survival. The external pressures opened a new window of opportunity for the opposition to effectively undermine Mečiar's credibility as a true representative of Slovak national interests. In 1998 a heterogenous coalition of the Christian democratic Slovak Democratic Coalition (SDK), former reform communist Party of the Democratic Left (SDL), and the Party of the Hungarian Coalition (SMK) defeated Mečiar's Peoples' Party–Movement for a Democratic Slovakia (HZDS) and formed a government under Premier Dzurinda. Their popularity lay in a new definition of Slovak nationhood that was compatible with Europeanization, ethnic inclusion, and competitive economic restructuring. As deputy prime minister for civic and minority rights in the first Dzurinda government, Pál Csáky of SMK asserted: "We are forming a government now; tomorrow we begin to change the regime."[81]

The new regime replaced the old one gradually and in a characteristic sequence. The heterogenous center-right/reform communist coalition of the first Dzurinda government reconquered the international arena for Slovakia. The country did not have to wait long for international recognition and admittance to OECD, NATO, and the group of EU accession countries. "International integration was the strongest driver for the Dzurinda cabinet and a unifying purpose for the ruling coalition....Slovakia would be joining the club that had previously welcomed its neighboring countries." [82] As far as economic policy is concerned, the government bailed out near-bankrupt commercial banks as well as large industrial firms such as the giant East Slovakian Steel Mills, and sold them to international strategic investors.[83]

After the 2002 election, relying on a more cohesive center-right coalition, Dzurinda formed his second government, which completed the break with the Mečiar legacy. First, the generous flow of subsidies to inherited old industries was redirected to TNCs, so that Slovakia could win bidding wars against regional rivals for major foreign investments in the automotive sector. Second, capitalizing on regained Slovak pride, Minister of Finance Ivan Mikloš launched an attack on the welfare state legacy. From 2002–3 onward, sweeping reforms of the pension and health care systems as well as of the tax system were enacted, the latter of which served as a model for the Czech and Hungarian reforms of 2007 and 2010, respectively. Adding to the stress, the government cut expenditures on family and child care, and restricted the availability of full unemployment benefits to those actively searching for a

---

81. Steven Fish, "The End of Meciarism," *East European Constitutional Review* 8, nos. 1–2 (Winter/Spring 1999): 51.
82. Katarina Mathernová and Juraj Renčko, "Reformology: The Case of Slovakia," *Orbis* 50, no. 4 (Fall 2006): 633.
83. Ibid., 634.

new job, which triggered a riot by the desperate Roma population of eastern Slovakia.

When asked about the societal acceptance of his reforms, Minister of Finance Mikloš pointed to "a schizophrenic state of mind. On the one hand, a majority of the people is critical about the reforms. On the other hand, a majority opposes a backlash against reforms. There have been attempts to depose us, but people want reforms. There is no alternative."[84]

However, the lack of alternatives bred disenchantment and apathy that contributed to the reformers' defeat in the 2006 elections. A mass exit of Slovak citizens from democratic politics paved the way for a radical victory at the June 2006 parliamentary elections. The turnout was at a record low level. Many of those who cast votes punished incumbents and thereby deprived reformers of a mandate to continue their thoroughgoing neoliberal course. A new administration under Premier Robert Fico, in which his Direction–Social Democracy (Smer) was allied with the radical nationalist Slovak National Party (SNS) and Mečiar's weakened HZDS, assumed power. EU-level actors, who were concerned about a revival of Mečiarism, resorted to the earlier routine of disciplining Slovak politicians through shaming and isolation. On account of its coalition with illiberal nationalists, Smer was initially denied membership in the European Parliament's socialist grouping.

Contrary to expectations, Slovakia's stability-oriented policy course was not significantly altered by the new government. Premier Fico's administration enjoyed the fruits of its predecessor's efforts. Up to 2009 rising wages, employment, and living standards, all due to rapid growth, boosted Smer's popularity. Indeed, Slovakia's compliance with the Maastricht criteria was in line with the plan inherited from the Dzurinda government to introduce the euro, which was accomplished on 1 January, 2009.

84. Interview, *Die Welt*, September 15, 2005.

Neocorporatism and Weak States

The Southeastern European Countries

A high degree of heterogeneity distinguishes the Southeastern European group from the Baltic and Visegrád regime clusters. Uniquely in the postsocialist world, Slovenia exhibits all the attributes of Western European small states: economic openness, protective and efficiency-enhancing compensatory policies, macroeconomic stability, and governance by established democratic and neocorporatist institutions. In contrast, economic opening, market institution building, and democratization proved to be slow and conflictual processes, while corporatism failed to acquire systemic significance, in Bulgaria, Romania, and Croatia.

Over time and across the Southeastern European cases, wide variation in state capacity and shifts in the balance of power among labor, capital, and the state are the key structural factors that underlie the diversity as well as the consolidation versus fluidity of new regimes. In concrete terms, a capable state enabled Slovenia's hegemonic center-left governments to coherently pursue a labor-inclusive transformation path and implement policies conducive to such a path. Conversely, overall state weakness constrained Bulgarian and Romanian political actors in "choosing" their countries' postsocialist history as their counterparts in other East Central European states did. In Croatia, nationalism and war significantly weakened the state. Unstable institutional configurations, poor growth performance, and recurrent macroeconomic instability over the 1990s all bear witness to state weakness in the majority of Southeastern European countries.

According to our Polanyian framework it is ultimately up to the political system in general and the state in particular to direct capitalist development to sustainable paths. If the required coordination and maneuvering capacities are in short supply, the framework predicts economic disorganization, social disintegration, and political crisis. Before the 1990s ended, all of these perils materialized in the weak Southeastern European states.

In circumstances of protracted and partial transformation, political change and limited stabilization have come in dramatic ways and at high costs. By the second half of the 1990s, deep crises of the economy and democratic legitimacy provoked political upheavals in Bulgaria, Romania, and Croatia alike. The turbulence helped reformist coalitions to occupy the headquarters of policymaking and accelerate the pace of economic and political transformation. Breaking with their predecessors' practices of vacillation between labor inclusion and exclusion, protectionism and liberalization, and promotion of national and foreign-led capitalism, the new governments significantly altered the earlier paths.

From the late 1990s, Bulgaria and Romania advanced toward the neoliberal pattern of radical stability-oriented institutions of macroeconomic coordination, minimal taxation, and a meager welfare state. In contrast, Croatia's concern with protecting selected social groups and some of its industries from the vagaries of marketization makes some of its features reminiscent of those of embedded neoliberalism. However, its reliance on a peculiar source of income, tourism, has allowed the country to stay on a more national and inward-oriented capitalist development path than has been the case with the Visegrád group.

The original weak state paths also left their mark on the emerging social order of the 2000s in the "successful laggards."[1] The crises of the 1990s erupted because captured as these states were by powerful domestic groups, they failed to act in the interests of national economic development. At the same time, the aftermath of the crises revealed and exacerbated yet another aspect of state weakness, namely the inability to filter and mediate the impact of external influences on the domestic political economy. In consequence, international actors and developments, such as the assistance and pressures of the IMF, and EU accession offered after the NATO bombing of Yugoslavia to Bulgaria, Romania, and ultimately also Croatia became disproportionately influential in shaping the new regimes.[2]

The EU made a deep impact on Southeastern Europe's regional dynamics as well, which reflected more its own stability and security considerations than these states' domestic agendas, and not infrequently contradicted the latter. Resolved to divide and pacify the Balkans, which it saw as a hotbed of instability, the EU imposed a logic that led to regional fragmentation via the European integration of different countries at different tempos. Below, we shall trace the impact of state strength and weakness and of international

1. Gergana Noutcheva and Dimitar Bechev, "The Successful Laggards: Bulgaria and Romania's Accession to the EU," *East European Politics and Societies* 22, no. 1 (2008): 114–44.
2. Vachudova, *Europe Undivided.*

and transnational influences on regime outcomes in the arenas of industrial relations, industrial restructuring, and monetary and fiscal coordination.

Labor's Won Battles and Lost Wars

Without doubt, the most spectacular regime outcome in Southeastern Europe is Slovenia's democratic neocorporatism which, despite the skepticism of some analysts and international institutions, earned the country acclaim among experts in postsocialist labor politics and inspired research into its origins.[3] Trade unions in Slovenia did have the power to build robust social partnership institutions, acquire material benefits for their members, and codetermine the direction of transformative policies. Especially given that the tiny country appears to have successfully followed the Western European small states' earlier paths of adaptation to world markets, the question arises: Was the Slovenian option open to other postsocialist countries as well?

Recently this question was answered in the negative by Stephen Crowley and Miroslav Stanojević. They argue that a number of factors had to collude to make the Slovene model work: export-oriented industry, a self-management legacy, and a major strike wave at the beginning of the transformation when Slovenia's institutions were being built. The combination of these factors was what made Slovenia exceptional, and it was hard to replicate them elsewhere.[4]

Is it the case that due to its roots in exceptional circumstances the Slovene path was indeed next to impossible to emulate? Given its pattern of similarities and differences, the Southeastern European group lends itself as a helpful comparative context for testing this proposition, and allows us to contribute to the broader debate on labor's fortunes after the fall of socialism. Briefly, we submit that there was more than a single path to postsocialist labor weakness, and that the Southeastern European unions walked their own, individual ways toward loss of strength, which were different from both the Visegrád and the Baltic trajectories.

Labor Movements: The Southeastern European Pattern and the Slovenian Exception

To begin with, there are reasons to believe that in the formative years of the early 1990s not only Slovenian but more generally Southeastern European

---

3. Miroslav Stanojević, "Successful Immaturity: Communist Legacies in the Market Context," *South-East Europe Review for Labor and Social Affairs* 2, no. 4 (1999): 41–55.

4. Stephen Crowley and Miroslav Stanojević, "Varieties of Capitalism, Power Resources, and Historical Legacies: Explaining the Slovenian Exception," *Politics and Society* 39, no. 2 (2011): 268–95.

labor still exhibited a measure of strength and influence, which goes against the generalization proposed in the so far most encompassing comparative volume on postsocialist labor politics. Its editors, Stephen Crowley and David Ost contend that the "point in Eastern Europe is not so much that labor has been *weakened* since 1989...but that it had been *created* as a weak actor. Thus, unions in Eastern Europe confront the new global economy not from an initial position of strength but of weakness."[5]

While this assessment might fit the Baltic or Visegrád cases, its validity in Croatia, Bulgaria, and Romania is doubtful. Since it is difficult to substantiate the claim that labor here had been weak *in statu nascendi,* it is important to understand the factors of its dramatic loss of political clout and policy influence by the late 1990s. In fact, the authors of the country studies in Crowley and Ost's volume are reluctant to depict the Southeastern European trade unions as uniformly weak at the onset of transformation, and rather tend to characterize them in the ambivalent terms of simultaneous power and powerlessness.[6]

For example, Marina Kokanović describes the Croatian labor movement as strong on account of its remarkable resilience in its frequent confrontations with President Franjo Tuđman's semiauthoritarian administration despite war and the collapse of economic and social welfare infrastructure. At the same time, labor weakness is indicated by unions' meager influence on "the creation of social reality, labor and welfare legislation, [and] tax policy."[7] David Kideckel suggests that Romanian unions, rooted in their organizational and mobilizing capacities, had the greatest power across Eastern Europe, which was also manifest in their leaders' large role in national politics. He adds, however, that despite the many battles won by Romanian labor, its "power has been ineffective in the overall war where it counts most: preserving or expanding jobs, improving working conditions, and preserving and extending labor's purchasing power."[8] Similarly, in Grigor Gradev's account, Bulgarian unions scored "a row of successes in particular policy areas and individual cases." Yet such accomplishments occurred in the context of

5. Crowley and Ost, *Workers after Workers' States,* 228. Emphasis in the original.

6. Recently, a detailed study has also challenged Crowley and Ost's generalization. On grounds of unique evidence on trade unions' plant-level conflicts and bargaining in postsocialist Romania and Ukraine, the study substantiates that there have been significant differences in labor's strength and accomplishments in the two countries. Concretely, the "representative" unionism of Romania has been overall much more successful at the level of industrial manufacturing plants than the "distributive" strategies of the Ukrainian labor movement. Mihai Varga, "Striking with Tied Hands: Strategies of Labour Interest Representation in Postcommunist Romania and Ukraine," (Ph.D. diss., University of Amsterdam, 2010).

7. Marina Kokanović, "The Cost of Nationalism: Croatian Labor, 1990–1999," in Crowley and Ost, *Workers after Workers' States,* 141; Marko Grdešić, "Mapping the Paths of the Yugoslav Model: Labour Strength and Weakness in Slovenia, Croatia, and Serbia," *European Journal of Industrial Relations* 14, no. 2 (2008): 133–51.

8. David A. Kideckel, "Winning the Battles, Losing the War: Contradictions of Romanian Labor in the Postcommunist Transformation," in Crowley and Ost, *Workers after Workers' States,* 97.

a "continuing loss of power" since "tripartism, and the social dialogue system, have been degraded by the government and persistently emptied of their main content as institutions of representative democracy."[9] Importantly, the statistical data on the slower (though still rather dramatic) deterioration of union density than in Poland, Hungary, and all three Baltic states, also lend support to the idea that in organizational terms labor in Southeastern Europe was not all that weak at the onset of transition.[10]

Since some explanations of postsocialist labor weakness stress the role of nonmaterial factors, the ideational resources of Southeastern European labor deserve our attention as much as its organizational strengths.[11] Could unions across Southeastern Europe draw on similar kinds of ideological and behavioral legacies as Slovenian organized workers? Without denying the importance of Yugoslavia's worker self-management and earlier corporatist experiences for the victory of neocorporatism in Slovenia, we question that the abundance of such resources per se would set this country apart from the rest of the region.

Evidently, Croatia had very similar legacies to those of Slovenia. So far as Romania is concerned, Mihail Manoilescu and other thinkers of the interwar years had been pioneers of theorizing and advocating corporatist regimes (albeit not their democratic but their authoritarian or outright fascist variants) as means to avoid class conflict and dependency.[12] Interestingly, without reference to the rich interwar tradition, a former Communist leading ideologue of Romania's early transformation phase, Silviu Brucan, contended that "if [Romania] wants to avoid becoming an exhausted half-colony of the West," it would need to "mix the South Korean and Austrian systems (*Sozialpartnerschaft*)."[13]

Even more important seems to be the fact that, as with other legacies, workers' self-management could be perceived as an asset (as in Slovenia) as well as a threat (as in Croatia and Serbia) from the viewpoint of the emerging new regimes.[14] Thus, the alleged contrast between the abundant ideational resources of the Slovenian labor movement and the meager endowment of the region's other unions is unlikely to provide a solution for the Slovenian puzzle. All this leads us from mapping the structural factors of labor strength to considering the role of workers' actual political agency. If in the formative years of systemic change Southeastern European unions had not lacked resources, could it be their varied ways of using their power that produced the later differences?

---

9. Grigor Gradev, "Bulgarian Trade Unions in Transition: The Taming of the Hedgehog," in Crowley and Ost, *Workers after Workers' States*, 122; Iankova, *Eastern European Capitalism.*
10. Visser, *ICTWSS*, accessed September 9, 2011 at http://www.uva-aias.net.
11. Ost, *The Defeat of Solidarity*, 193–96.
12. Schmitter, "Still the Century of Corporatism"; Love, *Crafting the Third World.*
13. Cited in Berend, "Alternatives of Transformation," 131.
14. Grdešić, "Mapping the Paths."

In this respect, Crowley and Stanojević propose that Slovenian neocorporatism originated most directly from workers' mobilization for the cause of a labor-inclusive capitalist regime at the right historical moment. Hard hit by the stabilization program of the last federal government led by Premier Ante Marković, Yugoslavia's economic collapse, and after independence, by a renewed attempt at macroeconomic stabilization on the part of the country's first democratic administration, workers responded to the sharp decline of their living standards with massive militancy. Workers' protest was well timed, as it peaked right at the historical moment when the new democratic and market institutions were being forged.[15] Among the factors of success Crowley and Stanojević also point to the importance of a unified union movement adhering to social democratic ideology, and to the fact that Slovenian businesses were as centrally organized as were workers, which allowed for a lasting compromise between their top representatives.[16]

The massive Slovenian protest wave was not without beneficial consequences for workers. It helped remove a right-wing coalition from power, build the foundations for more than a decade of center-left hegemony, shift the privatization debate toward acceptance of substantial employee ownership, and back the laws that established worker codetermination in 1993 and a Tripartite Council of trade unions, employer associations, and the state in 1994.[17] While this agency-centered line of thought does not lack plausibility, comparison with other Southeastern European cases indicates that it may not provide a full explanation of the Slovenian exception.

Although reliable statistical data are hard to come by, anecdotal evidence gives the impression that in the first half of the 1990s Bulgarian and Romanian labor was no less mobilized than Slovene workers (even if the frequency of strikes in all of these cases lagged behind their usual levels in Western or Mediterranean Europe.) Based on Bulgarian union federation data, Elena Iankova reports 1,300 industrial conflicts in 1990; 850 in 1991; 40 large and 1070 local strikes involving 1.1 million participants in 1992; and 750, 620, and 538 events in 1993, 1994, and 1995, respectively.[18] Similarly, Kideckel sees Romanian unions' power as "reinforced by constant militancy, from localized walkouts to nationwide general strikes to threatened invasions of cities and towns."[19]

Labor protest faced the greatest obstacles in Croatia, where the nationalist regime deplored strikes as unpatriotic, especially during but even after the war of independence. Nevertheless, strike activities never entirely subsided. Risking repression, unions managed to organize about three hundred

---

15. Crowley and Stanojević, "Varieties of Capitalism," 277–80.
16. Ibid., 281.
17. Ibid., 280–82.
18. Iankova, *Eastern European Capitalism*, chap. 3.
19. Kideckel, "Winning the Battles," 97.

protest events annually, including general strikes and other types of contentious collective action.[20]

Is it then the case that notwithstanding their comparable militancy Bulgarian, Romanian, and Croatian unions were sentenced to failure by the fact that—unlike in the Slovenian case—their cooperation was hampered by deep political divisions? Hardly so, as available evidence speaks against assuming an overly stark contrast. Stanojević himself confirmed that like other East Central European unions, in the early 1990s those of Slovenia exhibited strong political and ideological divisions, and competition was intense. As elsewhere in the region, the major split was between old—albeit often reformed—and new, independent trade unions. [21]

Other authors note that unions found ways of bridging political divisions and jointly mobilizing their rank and file at local and national levels in all the Southeastern European countries. Cooperation among unions was possible even in the hostile Croatian political atmosphere. While the old trade union federation reformed itself successfully and managed to keep the most numerous membership, the two major new union federations that were close to the government (one of them even founded by Tudman's nationalist ruling party, the Croatian Democratic Union—HDZ), soon increased their autonomy and repeatedly joined forces with other confederations to protest against government policies and to achieve collective agreements.[22]

It is also not the case that enterprises in Bulgaria, Romania, and Croatia were unorganized. Rather, state-owned firms either were members of inherited compulsory associations or founded new ones early on. Interestingly, where they lacked their own organizational resources, sometimes the successors of communist trade unions came to their help. Iankova notes that the Bulgarian National Union of Economic Managers was formed in 1990s with the assistance of the Confederation of Independent Trade Unions in Bulgaria (KNSB) "in its efforts to establish social partnership." Although the managers' association "was designed mainly to defend the interests of economic directors as state employees, it played an important role in laying the foundations for an organization of employers."[23]

Against this background it is unsurprising that Bulgarian, Romanian, and Croatian labor's struggles yielded results that were reminiscent of the

20. Kokanović, "The Cost of Nationalism," 143 and 152–59; Grdešić, "Mapping the Paths," 146.

21. Miroslav Stanojević, "From Self-Management to Co-Determination," in *Making a New Nation: The Formation of Slovenia,* ed. Danica Fink-Hafner and John R. Robbins (Aldershot: Dartmouth, 1997), 250; Miroslav Stanojević, "Social Pacts in Slovenia," in Pochet, Keune, and Natali, *After the Euro and Enlargement,* 321–22.

22. Kokanović, "The Cost of Nationalism," 151, 150–56; Marko Grdešić, "Transition, Labor and Political Elites in Slovenia and Croatia" (M.A. thesis, Central European University, Budapest, Department of Political Science, 2006), 18–19. For Bulgaria see Gradev, "Bulgarian Trade Unions"; and for Romania Kideckel, "Winning the Battles."

23. Iankova, *Eastern European Capitalism,* 56.

Slovenian unions' early successes. In particular, unions managed to press governments to set up national tripartite forums and reform labor codes. Under labor's pressure, a first Romanian attempt at tripartite cooperation was launched in 1990. A first agreement was signed in 1992, and in 1993 a secretariat for social dialogue was established. In Croatia the first meeting of the tripartite Economic and Social Council was held in 1993. In "transformative corporatist" Bulgaria in the first half of the 1990s hardly any coalition in office missed signing an agreement on social peace and setting up a plethora of tripartite bodies, before the National Council for Tripartite Cooperation was legally established in 1993 "for the resolution of problems of labor and labor relations, social insurance, and living standards at national level."[24]

Is it then the case that, contrary to Slovenia where tripartism granted labor genuine inclusion, in the rest of Southeastern Europe it was not a form of substantive but only of "illusory corporatism"? Ost coined this term to describe the purely symbolic concessions offered to labor unions by reform elites, who "sought to use tripartite bodies to rubber-stamp and legitimate neoliberal policies decided elsewhere."[25] This of course assumes that a neoliberal transformation strategy was actually being pursued and needed to be legitimized. Yet even if this might qualify as an appropriate interpretation of, say, the Polish and Hungarian situations, we consider its extension to the Southeastern European cases as problematic.

Although the erratically changing forms and participants and the overloaded agendas of Bulgarian, Romanian, and Croatian tripartism do seem to exhibit the symptoms of precariousness and inefficiency observed by Ost, reform elites' neoliberal zeal could hardly be blamed for corporatism's unfulfilled promises or paralysis. Bulgaria and Romania have been known above all for their limited reforms and stop-and-go policies. The marginal influence of "crusaders of monetarism" in Iliescu's Romania, in postcommunist Bulgaria, or on Tuđman's "Croato-specific transformation plan" that grew out of the rejection of Yugoslav Premier Marković's stabilization and liberalization program, all raise doubts about the validity of the idea that tripartism in Southeastern Europe could be a façade behind which lurked neoliberalism.[26]

---

24. Youcef Ghellab and Marketa Vylitova, "Tripartite Social Dialogue on Employment in the Countries of South Eastern Europe" (Budapest, International Labour Office, 2005); Kokanović, "The Cost of Nationalism," 152; Grdešić, "Transition, Labor," 30; Iankova, *Eastern European Capitalism*, 188–93.

25. Ost, "Illusory Corporatism," 507.

26. Venelin I. Ganev, "The Dorian Gray Effect: Winners as State Breakers in Postcommunism," *Communist and Postcommunist Studies* 34 (2001): 3. For a criticism of simplistic concepts of neoliberal hegemony in the East, see Venelin I. Ganev, "The 'Triumph of Neoliberalism' Reconsidered: Critical Remarks on Ideas-Centered Analyses of Political and Economic Change in Post-Communism," *East European Politics and Societies* 19, no. 3 (2005): 343–78. For the Croatian case see Bićanić and Franičević, "Understanding Reform," 10.

Rather than legitimizing market radicalism, early concessions to labor in Bulgaria and Romania can be better explained by a combination of initially strong and militant labor and the hegemony of unreformed postcommunist parties.[27] In addition to supporting tripartism, governments in both countries were ready to meet other demands of labor as well. Thus, the privatization plan of Bulgaria's first postcommunist administration in 1990–91 "supported broad privileges for managers and employees (including one proposal to sell them 49% of their enterprise at up to a 50% discount)" and was embraced even by Podkrepa, the anticommunist trade union.[28] In Romania, the first postcommunist government promised to accommodate the unions' quest for "the forty-hour week, indexed wages, and better working conditions."[29]

In this respect, Croatia was different. The right-wing government only willy-nilly engaged with unions. Besides the nationalist rulers' rejection of the Yugoslav legacy and particularly worker self-management, their reluctance is explained by the fact that HDZ was a populist party that sought to generate consent by directly paying off vocal groups, rather than by broader political economic settlements achieved through bargaining with unions in the tripartite arena. The fact that in this hostile political environment Croatian labor could acquire ad hoc concessions therefore reflects its perceived strength. It also helped that toward the end of the Tudman years unions started to behave as a democratizing movement, which instilled fear in the holders of power.[30]

Governments' fear of labor as a political force was a factor in Bulgaria and Romania too. More frequently than elsewhere in East Central Europe, incumbents in these two countries suffered devastating defeat from the "fist of the working class." Massive and sometimes violent labor protest routinely provoked or contributed to political turbulence that drastically shortened the life-spans of governments.[31] Indeed, in 1999 when the Jiu Valley miners attempted their fifth violent raid in a row on the country's capital, Romanian President Ion Iliescu, who had earlier used miners as a substitute riot police force against protesters for greater democracy, voiced his concern over the threat of "a labor inspired revolt."[32]

27. Romania's first five governments after 1989 were formed by postcommunist successor organizations. In Bulgaria, "the former Communist Party preserved its nearly absolute grip on power until the beginning of 1992, and generally retained its hegemonic position in national politics—on both the central and especially the local level—until 1997." Venelin Ganev, *Preying on the State: The Transformation of Bulgaria after 1989* (Ithaca: Cornell University Press, 2007), 43.

28. Andrew Barnes, "Extricating the State: The Move to Competitive Capture in Post-Communist Bulgaria," *Europe-Asia Studies* 59, no. 1 (2007): 80.

29. Kideckel, "Winning the Battles," 103.

30. Grdešić, "Mapping the Paths," 142.

31. On the (in)famous cases of coal miners' repeated armed raids on Bucharest, see Ion Bogdan Vasi, "The Fist of the Working Class: The Social Movements of Jiu Valley Miners in Post-Socialist Romania," *East European Politics and Societies* 18, no. 1 (2004): 132–57.

32. Cf. in Kideckel, "Winning the Battles," 99.

Thus, the question remains: If on grounds of labor's initial strength and in Bulgaria and Romania governments' willingness to accommodate union demands it is difficult to single out the factors of divergence of Slovenia's neocorporatist order from the paths of other Southeastern European states, then what building blocks of a labor-inclusive regime were missing in the latter cases?

We can solve the puzzle by "bringing the state back in."[33] The key issue to be considered is that the symptoms of precariousness, fluidity, and disfunction were not restricted to tripartism. Rather, in Southeastern Europe in the first half of the 1990s the same essential shortcomings characterized virtually all of the public policymaking institutions and apparatuses, whether their task was maintenance of law and order, privatization, promotion of FDI, fiscal or monetary policy, or social protection.

Accordingly, we contend that tripartism's ups and downs in Bulgaria, Romania and—albeit to a lesser degree—in Croatia originated from the syndrome of general state weakness rather than from any hard-headed pursuit of the neoliberal agenda. Lacking state capacity hampered the functioning of neocorporatist frameworks in more fundamental ways than the policy preferences of reformist elites ever could. Indeed, the vacillation of the latter between labor inclusion and exclusion was itself a symptom of state weakness. This is not to claim that the hostility of particular governments toward labor never played any role.[34] Our point rather is that state incapacity would impair the implementation of policy strategies across the board—even if their aim was inclusion rather than marginalization of workers.

No Capable State—No Democratic Corporatist Order

Further scrutiny of the juncture at which Slovenia's industrial relations took the turn toward neocorporatism, and of the factors that prevented similar developments elsewhere in Southeastern Europe, requires a shift in analytic perspective from the heroic early times to later years, and from the formal establishment of tripartism to its consolidation. According to Charles Maier, corporatism's "founding conditions are different from maintenance conditions."[35] Interestingly, his observation that in Western Europe

33. Peter Evans, Dietrich Rueschemeyer, and Theda Skocpol, eds., *Bringing the State Back In* (Cambridge: Cambridge University Press, 1985).

34. Ironically, even when market radicals had the upper hand, as in Premier Philip Dimitrov's short-lived neoliberal administration in Bulgaria, the IMF stepped in and asked the government to reconsider its social partnership policy. In response, "by early summer 1992, the government had reshuffled the Ministries of Finance and Industry and appointed a new Deputy Prime Minister, Nikola Vassilev, who was charged with maintaining contact with the trade unions." Iankova, *Eastern European Capitalism*, 67.

35. Charles Maier, "Preconditions for Corporatism," in *Order and Conflict in Contemporary Capitalism: Studies in the Political Economy of Western European Nations*, ed. John H. Goldthorpe (Oxford: Oxford University Press, 1984), 50.

"to maintain corporatist institutions took less energy and commitment than to erect them"[36] seems to apply in reverse to Southeastern Europe. Neocorporatist frameworks were fast established in all four countries, but it was only in Slovenia that they proved robust enough to adopt systemic traits. It is the presence or absence of a capable state, which can act in relative autonomy from societal interests, and has the capacity to implement and enforce its goals and policies, that provides the key to understanding the difference.[37]

For researchers of Western European labor politics, the salience of state capacity is evident to the extent that the assumption of a degree of stateness is part and parcel of the definition of corporatism and more broadly labor rights. In this vein, by corporatism Maier means "a broad concertation between employer and employee representatives across industries, which is usually established and sometimes continually supervised under state auspices....Corporatism suggests a coordination of national negotiations in which state agencies endow major private associations with quasi-public authority."[38]

Peter Katzenstein's influential notion of democratic corporatism also points to the centrality of small *states*—rather than particular governments or elites—recognizing their vulnerability in the world economy, and the need for domestic compensation.[39] Similarly, throughout history, a capable state had been crucial for the enforcement of a large variety of workers' rights. As Charles Tilly put it: "Over the whole range of workers' rights—not only unemployment insurance but also health and welfare benefits, vocational training, occupational safety, minimum wages, unionization, and the right to strike—the actual exercise of rights depended heavily on the state's capacity and propensity to discipline capital."[40]

What this amounts to is that neocorporatism relies on a state, which in Alfred Stepan's formulation is "more than the 'government.' It is the continuous administrative, legal, bureaucratic and coercive systems that attempt not only to structure relationships between civil society and public authority in a polity but also to structure many crucial relationships within civil society."[41]

36. Ibid., 56–57.
37. Libraries have been written about the relative autonomy of the state, and the origins and forms of state capacity. Our account builds loosely on Michael Shafer, *Winners and Losers: How Sectors Shape the Developmental Prospects of States* (Ithaca: Cornell University Press, 1994); Evans, Rueschemeyer, and Skocpol, *Bringing the State Back In;* and on the literature cited in notes 40–43 below.
38. Maier, "Preconditions," 40. See also Gerhard Lehmbruch, "Concertation and the Structure of Corporatist Networks," in Goldthorpe, *Order and Conflict*, 60–80.
39. Katzenstein, *Small States*, 38–47.
40. Charles Tilly, "Globalization Threatens Labor's Rights," *International Labor and Working-Class History* 47 (Spring 1995): 13.
41. Alfred Stepan, *The State and Society: Peru in Comparative Perspective* (Princeton: Princeton University Press, 1978), quoted in Theda Skocpol, "Bringing the State Back In: Strategies of Analysis in Current Research," in Evans, Rueschemeyer and Skocpol, *Bringing the State Back In,*

While the existence of states endowed with administrative, legal, bureaucratic, and coercive structures can be taken for granted in the advanced capitalist countries, this is much less the case in East Central Europe. As Max Weber pointed out, industrial "capitalism and bureaucracy have found each other and belong intimately together."[42] From this it can be inferred that in countries that industrialized late, and under the auspices of a communist rather than a capitalist system, states are likely to be significantly weaker.

This is the gist of Herbert Kitschelt's and his co-authors' account of regime diversity in East Central Europe. An important variable that shapes postcommunist institutional differences is the nature of precommunist and communist state legacies. Countries with little industrialization and political mobilization prior to the advent of communism also failed to build formal bureaucratic state apparatuses during communism. Instead, "patrimonial communist" rule relied on extensive networks of patronage and clientelism, and "vertical chains of personal dependence between leaders in the state and party apparatus and their entourage." In turn, legacies of this kind led to corruption and patronage-prone postcommunist regimes.[43] In this classification, Bulgaria and Romania share the legacies of patrimonial communism. In contrast, Croatia shares with Hungary and Slovenia the legacies of "national accommodative communism," a form of communist rule that allowed for a stronger bureaucratic apparatus.

While these scholars are mostly concerned with legacies and their consequences for different parties and party systems in the region, Venelin Ganev has recently argued that the early transformation, and specifically the mode of state and Communist Party separation, has made a profound impact on the organizational and institutional features of the state itself. Using the example of Bulgaria he demonstrates how the strategic behavior of elites has led to the weakening of available state structures. During their prolonged withdrawal from power, the Bulgarian Communist Party elites not only stripped the state of its most valuable assets, but their struggles for resource redistribution affected mechanisms and institutions of state control and governance, and weakened the administration's overall monitoring ability. As Ganev writes: "The concrete manifestation of this general trend toward fractured stateness may be depicted as inability to design and implement policy, acute organizational incoherence, and lack of infrastructure for salutary state interventions in largely spontaneous processes of social and economic change." His contribution is part of a burgeoning literature on the

---

7. See also Michael Mann's concept of infrastructural power of the state, namely "the state's capacity to actually penetrate civil society and to implement political decisions throughout the realm," which points to an important aspect of stateness. Michael Mann, "The Autonomous Power of the State," *Archives Européennes de Sociologie* 25, no. 2 (1984): 190.

42. Max Weber, *Economy and Society*, ed. Guenther Roth and Claus Wittich (Berkeley: University of California Press, 1968), 1395 n. 4.

43. Kitschelt et al., *Postcommunist Party Systems*, 21–28.

relationship between parties and party competition, the state, and reform capacities in East Central Europe.[44]

Taken together, this literature provides compelling reasons for why Bulgaria and Romania failed to build states capable of structuring the relationship between labor and the nascent capitalist class, and to reliably implement policies agreed upon in tripartite bargaining. The legacy of patrimonial communism gave the Communist Party and its successors the upper hand at the onset of transformation. Party elites then used the opportunities to "prey on the state," this way further undermining state capacity. In short, winners acted as "state breakers."[45]

The World Bank indicators of the quality of governance bear witness to that. According to this data, Bulgaria and Romania have significantly lagged behind Slovenia (as well as the Visegrád and Baltic states) as far as their governments' effectiveness, regulatory capacity, and ability to maintain the rule of law and control corruption are concerned (table 1.6).[46] It is puzzling, though, that Croatia is to be found among the weak states too. After all, this country shares with Slovenia similar communist and state legacies. Moreover, unlike in Bulgaria and Romania, the communist successor party lost the first multiparty election in both post-Yugoslav states.[47]

What explains Croatia's weak state capacity? In line with existing literature, we argue that unlike in Bulgaria and Romania where the postcommunist states were born weak (and weakened further in the early 1990s), in Croatia it was the combined effect of an unbalanced nationalism, war and its aftermath, and the semiauthoritarian nature of the Tuđman regime that undermined an originally capable state.[48] For a number of reasons, in Croatia nationalism played a much more dominant role than in Slovenia, to the extent that it soon outpaced all other forms of social integration.

The repositioning of opposition forces after Yugoslav Communist leader Josip Broz Tito's clampdown on the "Croatian Spring" in 1971, the ethnic

---

44. Ganev, *Preying on the State*, 9. For alternative concepts see above all Anna Grzymala-Busse, *Rebuilding Leviathan: Party Competition and State Exploitation in Post-Communist Democracies* (Cambridge: Cambridge University Press, 2007); Timothy Frye, *Building States and Markets after Communism: the Perils of Polarized Democracy* (Cambridge: Cambridge University Press, 2010); Conor O'Dwyer, *Runaway State-Building: Patronage Politics and Democratic Development* (Baltimore: Johns Hopkins University Press, 2006); Roger Schoenman, "Networks, Uncertainty and Institution Building in Europe's Emerging Market" (manuscript, 2011).

45. Ganev, *Preying on the State*, 95.

46. See also Patrick Hamm, David Stuckler, and Lawrence King, "The Governance Grenade: Mass Privatization, State Capacity and Economic Growth in Post-communist Countries," Working paper 222 (Amherst: University of Massachusetts Amherst, 2010), table W1, 53. On the basis of a different data set, this study confirms the large gap in state capacity between Slovenia and the other three Southeastern European countries.

47. Croatia also sits uneasy with Frye's argument that party polarization can explain the propensity of elites to weaken the state, because Croatia's polarization score is similar to that of the Czech Republic, Slovakia, and Latvia. Frye, *Building States and Markets*, 55.

48. see, e.g., Bićanić and Franičević, "Understanding Reform." We are very grateful to Višnja Vukov for forcing us to rethink the origins of Croatia's weak state.

heterogeneity of the republic, and a large and in part strongly nationalist émigré community, all contributed to robust nationalist sentiment. Arguably, however, the most important factor of Croatia's hardened nationalist course was the war of independence in 1991–95. On the one hand, "after the outbreak of the war, the nation accepted President Tudman's leadership almost unquestioningly, the war effectively providing him with far-ranging authority." Democratic institutions quickly degraded into a mere façade, with the parliament simply rubberstamping Tudman's decisions.[49] On the other hand, trade unions initially posed no challenge to the country's course. In 1991, the main trade union confederations and the government signed the so called "war agreement," whereby the unions exchanged social peace against social consultation.[50]

In addition to the negative impact of truncated democracy and of ad hoc rather than any regular neocorporatist coordination, Croatian state autonomy and capacity also suffered a heavy blow from the nationalizing policies of HDZ. As Bruno Schönfelder observes, ethnic Serbs (as well as Croats whose loyalty to HDZ was considered doubtful) left the public sector on their own, or were fired and replaced not least by nationalist re-migrants from the diaspora. The fact that many of the positions—whether in the public administration, judiciary, or the management of SOEs—were refilled with loyal but incompetent or inexperienced appointees, led to deterioration of an originally capable apparatus.[51] Combined with the impact of war, a similar selective approach led to swelling social expenditures. The bulk of benefits went to war veterans and invalids as well as their and the victims families, while spending on natalist policies was extensive too.[52] Fast-deteriorating democracy, loyalty-based and ethnic purging of the bureaucracy, narrowly targeted and unsustainable social spending, and the peculiar beneficiaries of privatization (discussed below) have all conspired against a capable Croatian state.

This background provides us with a better understanding of why neocorporatism could ultimately not gain ground in most of Southeastern Europe. Bulgaria and Romania simply lacked administrative and bureaucratic systems that were able to structure the relationship between capital and labor. The key problem therefore was the mismatch between an initially organized and vocal labor and a state that was too weak to refuse but also to consolidate social partnership and other concessions. Differently put: although labor's strength was certainly greatest early in the transformation, these were not yet the years when the basic institutions of Bulgarian and Romanian capitalism

49. Bruno Schönfelder "The Impact of the War 1991–1995 on the Croatian Economy: A Contribution to the Analysis of War Economies," *Economic Annals* 166 (2005): 13.

50. Grdešić, "Transition, Labor," 33.

51. Schönfelder, "The Impact of War," 21–22.

52. Paul Stubbs and Sinisa Zrinscak, "Croatian Social Policy: The Legacies of War, State-Building and Late Europeanization," *Social Policy and Administration* 43, no. 2 (2009): 121–35.

were forged. These states were simply unable to institutionalize *any* stable and permanent configuration—whether their ultimate aim was to include or exclude labor.

The consequences can be teased out when the mismatch is contrasted with Slovenia's balanced labor-state relationships. One factor of emerging Slovenian neocorporatism was that employers in export-oriented industries—both in labor- and in capital-intensive sectors—became alarmed at unsustainable wage increases, which were prompted by the choice of a managed float currency regime. Employers embraced centralized bargaining as a way to enforce wage restraint. It was against this background that tripartism was institutionalized.[53]

One key factor moderating labor's strategies across various sectors was the perception of short-term losers that the Slovenian state would fulfill its obligations following from the class compromise. Trust in the capacity and credibility of state and government made it easier for losers to view themselves as future winners, while their longer time horizons kept them in the camp of supporters of social partnership, which contributed to the institutionalization of neocorporatism.

This was precisely the phase, namely that of the consolidation rather than the purely formal establishment of tripartite institutions, at which the Southeastern European countries' paths sharply diverged. Their divergence was due to several reasons. First, moderate strategies could hardly acquire dominance in Bulgaria and Romania, after the social partners learned that the authorities were unable to reward them with future gains for their short-term sacrifices. Accordingly, growing awareness of the administrations' inability to translate class compromises into policy strategies led economic actors to pursue particularistic (sectoral or individual firm–based) tactics over those serving the public good including their own long-term and encompassing interests.[54]

To the extent that their unrestrained demands were met, this could only happen at the cost of further destabilization and fragmentation of state agencies, mirroring increasing fragmentation of the societal field. However, these dynamics undermined the very foundations of neocorporatism, since "the fragmentation of coherent public authority over economic and social policy should not be mistaken for the purposeful delegation of power to non-state actors."[55]

Second, the Southeastern European unions might at times have gone too far in using their political clout to challenge power-holders. For example, Kideckel notes that in Romania "due to those early successes and attempts by

53. Feldmann, "The Origins of Varieties," 346; Crowley and Stanojević, "Varieties of Capitalism," 276.

54. Aleksandra Sznajder Lee and Vera Trappmann, "Von der Avantgarde zu den Verlierern des Postkommunismus: Gewerkschaften im Prozess der Restrukturierung der Stahlindustrie in Mittel- und Osteuropa," *Industrielle Beziehungen* 17, no. 2 (2010): 192–231.

55. Maier, "Preconditions," 59.

political leaders to curry union favor, labor soon gained an unrealistic sense of power. Its leaders thus shifted their attention from labor issues per se to the character and organization of the national government."[56] In response, governments felt tempted to control unions by undemocratic methods.

To the extent that Bulgarian and Romanian organized workers managed to challenge power holders in the high politics of shaping the postsocialist political economy, their failure to win a decisive voice was in some ways reminiscent of the outcome of the conflictual processes that by the 1970s undermined Western Europe's postwar labor-inclusive settlement. All the obvious differences notwithstanding, in one respect at least the Bulgarian and Romanian unions seem to have walked in the footsteps of their Western predecessors, who during the massive strike wave of 1967–73 had demanded more than a capitalist order was ever willing to deliver.[57]

Croatia's failure to embrace neocorporatism was different, since here initially existing state capacities were directed toward the war effort and toward nurturing loyal allies, both of which significantly weakened labor's position in the polity. Even so, Croatian labor repeatedly challenged the semidemocratic government and ultimately contributed to its fall.

Consolidating tripartism is of course a game it takes three to play: strong labor capable of constraining employers' choices but also controlling workers and moderating their strategies, capital able to check but also willing to accommodate workers' demands, and a state able to assist the interaction and help enforce the mutual obligations of social partners. So far, the role of capital was largely missing from our analysis. We will now turn to the region's propertied classes, which emerged in the processes of privatization, foreign investment, and industrial restructuring.

Postsocialist Capitalism in Strong and Weak States

How far were the Southeastern European employers willing to tolerate trade unions and accommodate their demands? What impact did the new capitalists have on state capacity, and how did this change from the early to later years of transformation? We search for answers first by highlighting the peculiar character and policy preferences of the postsocialist "ersatz" classes that initially dominated the Southeastern European political economies. Second, we will elaborate on the specificities of transnational investors, whose role in industrial restructuring became crucial by the late 1990s.

---

56. Kideckel, "Winning the Battles," 103.

57. On the historical turning point in the West, see Jonas Pontusson, "Introduction: Organizational and Political-Economic Perspectives on Union Politics," in *Bargaining for Change: Union Politics in North America and Europe*, ed. Miriam Golden and Jonas Pontusson (Ithaca: Cornell University Press, 1992), 1–41.

Continuity of the Economic Elite

According to the literature, the features of postsocialist capitalists varied greatly depending on whether the transformation brought about a radical break with the socialist past. Valerie Bunce was one of the first scholars who pointed out the importance of political continuity versus discontinuity for the character of economic elites. She argued that "the pace of economic reform correlates highly with the pace of political reform."[58] Specifically, if the founding elections failed to dislodge former Communists from power, as in the Bulgarian and Romanian cases, this slowed down democratization as well as economic reforms, and led to sluggish growth of the private sector. What kind of "capital" could possibly emerge from such "slow, uneven and compromised" transitions?[59]

Empirically substantiating Bunce's original argument, Steven Fish suggested that "modest or no elite replacement" in the political realm led to continuity of the economic elite as well. The new party leaderships and central or local bureaucracies, which either represented or were captives of enterprise lobbies, strove to defend the inherited positions of "red" or "green barons." On the other side of the coin, "in Bulgaria, and Romania...the slowness of privatization checked the growth of a wealthy business class and a broad stratum of small entrepreneurs who could be counted on in some instances to support reformist (or at least non-communist or non-antiliberal) policies and candidates."[60]

How did the slow pace of privatization and limited elite turnover that (with the partial exception of Croatia) originally characterized all Southeastern European countries shape the economic elites' influence over organized labor and the state?[61] An important consequence, but one that has so far been neglected in the literature, was that by their reluctance to separate the public from the private economic sphere, the political and bureaucratic elites also delayed the process of differentiation between capitalism's defining classes.

In chapter 1, we recalled the proposition that initially East Central European capitalism had been one "without capitalists."[62] As far as Southeastern Europe is concerned, this argument can be stretched further, since for an extended period its new systems lacked not only capitalists but their main antagonists as well. The emergence of free wage labor lacking any control

---

58. Valerie J. Bunce, "Sequencing of Political and Economic Reforms," in *East-Central European Economies in Transition: Study Papers Submitted to the Joint Economic Committee Congress of the United States* (Washington, D.C.: U.S. Government Printing Office, 1994), 59. See for a similar argument on the relationship between the pace of political and economic reforms, World Bank, *From Plan to Market*.

59. Bunce, "Sequencing of Political and Economic Reforms," 59.

60. Fish, "The Determinants of Economic Reform," 67.

61. As demonstrated by the Slovenian case, the limited turnover of economic elites did not mechanically follow from sluggish democratization.

62. Eyal, Szelényi, and Townsley, *Making Capitalism*, 5.

over the means of production took longer in Southeastern Europe than in the Visegrád or the Baltic states because of both the overall slower pace and the preferred methods of privatization. As hinted above, all four countries lagged behind their northwestern neighbors in terms of the expansion of the private sector's contribution to GDP and employment. More important, the modest amount of privatization that did occur mainly benefited enterprise insiders: both managers and—though to a lesser extent—workers.

In concrete terms, Slovenia and Croatia adopted MEBOs as the primary and vouchers as the secondary method of privatization, while Romania and Bulgaria respectively combined MEBOs or vouchers with direct sales.[63] Unlike the method of competitive direct sales, which was first adopted in Hungary and later in all the Visegrád and Baltic states (see chapters 3 and 4), this insider-dominated privatization extended the period of highly fragmented ownership structures. It also delayed the second wave of takeovers by strategic (mainly foreign) investors,[64] and thus slowed down the process of differentiation between the "haves" and "have-nots" and, as a consequence, class formation. All this led to the persistence of peculiar forms of employer-employee relations, which helped organized labor to win some battles, but also paved its way to losing the war for a labor-inclusive capitalist regime.

If it is correct to assume that "the more private the economy, the less the union representation,"[65] then it follows that unions could rely longer on the opportunities offered by state ownership (as well as by fragmented insider ownership) to maintain their organizational strength. Against this background it is unsurprising that at the onset of the transformation SOE managers were not particularly hostile to their employees. They were willing to keep workers on the payroll (although wages were not always paid on time or at all), and join with them in demanding state subsidies to keep troubled firms afloat.

To be sure, this type of manager-worker alliance was less frequent in Croatian crony capitalism[66] than in other Southeastern European countries. Independent Croatia proceeded rapidly in etatizing its inherited "socially owned enterprises." The privatization program introduced in 1991 foresaw the immediate transformation of many of the largest firms into SOEs. Other enterprises that initially were scheduled for privatization also ended up in government hands. The rationale for these measures was to "prevent a political and economic coalition of ex-communist managers and workers,"

63. EBRD *Transition Report 2000*.
64. According to a recent analysis, this was the main factor of the wide divergence between the paths of the Czech Republic, Hungary, and Poland, and those of Slovenia, Russia, and Ukraine. Soós, *Rendszerváltás és privatizáció*.
65. Crowley and Ost, *Workers after Workers' States*, 226.
66. Bićanić and Franičević, "Understanding Reform."

and instead give the HDZ firm control over the choice of future owners and managers.[67]

It is hardly surprising, therefore, that many lucrative positions in Croatia's postsocialist economy made their way into the hands of the governing party's political friends. The government also aimed to target specific social groups, such as war veterans, refugees, displaced persons, and former political prisoners, all of whom were HDZ's core constituencies, with a voucher program.[68] Thus, in Croatia elite turnover in managerial positions was relatively high—albeit partly illusory as many former communist managers simply switched loyalties.[69] In the final account, however, the politically motivated exchange of managerial elites left labor bereft of allies in the workplace.

In contrast, in Bulgaria and Romania, rather than checking and moderating union strategies, initially employers had incentives to join their struggles even if these alliances sometimes led to noncreative industrial destruction. One striking example is that of Stara Zagora DZU, the flagship firm of the Bulgarian computer industry, where in 1990 workers of the Podkrepa trade union together with their managers struck for several weeks in support of a long list of demands, which included "an attack on the director, charges of financial mismanagement, demands for restructuring the plant, and the possibility for employees to privatize the units." In consequence, "the plant incurred heavy losses. It never fully recovered, and by 1999 there were less than one thousand employees (out of nearly six thousand originally)."[70]

Ultimately, however, labor's strength was undermined by the very coalition partner it had relied upon. Ganev has shown how in the mid-1990s Multigroup—a diversified "political capitalist" conglomerate that operated in a multitude of sectors from the gas trade to steel, tourism, and complex manufacturing—effectively looted DZU's few remaining assets by first degrading the firm to a producer of pirated compact discs for the Russian market and then leaving it to bankruptcy. He concludes, "the case of DZU suggests that the activities of winners might be directly related to what may be broadly defined as deindustrialization of SOEs in post-Communism."[71]

The above evidence points to a syndrome that was not specific to Bulgaria but plagued most of Southeastern Europe, where from the late 1980s to the late 1990s "winners of partial reforms" in the dominant state-owned sector and nascent crony capitalists picked up the pieces of property and power left

67. Vojmir Franičević and Evan Kraft, "Croatia's Economy after Stabilization," *Europe-Asia Studies* 49, no. 4 (1997): 675.

68. Ibid. See also Vojmir Franičević, "Privatization in Croatia: Legacies and Context," *Eastern European Economics* 37, no. 2 (1999): 5–54.

69. Bruno Dallago and Milica Uvalic, "The Distributive Consequences of Nationalism: The Case of former Yugoslavia," *Europe-Asia Studies* 50, no. 1 (1998): 85.

70. Gradev, "Bulgarian Trade Unions," 131.

71. Ganev, "The Dorian Gray Effect," 15. For the term political capitalism, see Staniszkis, *Political Capitalism.*

behind by the socialist system. Capitalizing on the weakness of the state and contributing to further losses of its capacity, powerful actors used former state assets to accumulate fragmented, special-interest or personal wealth, rather than wealth that accrued to the society and economy as a whole.[72]

Accordingly, during the 1990s Bulgaria, Romania, and, albeit to a lesser extent, Croatia suffered more than the front-runners of transformation "not only from the development of capitalist production, but also from the in-completeness of that development...not only from the living but from the dead"—as Karl Marx characterized late nineteenth-century Germany.[73]

However, if the continuity of political and economic elites proved to be an obstacle to the successful transformation of the majority of Southeastern European states, then the fact that Slovenia escaped the negative conse-quences poses a puzzle. After all, neither the dynamics of political elite turn-over nor those of economic elite change set the country clearly apart from its Southeastern neighbors. Rather, as noted by Nicole Lindstrom and Dóra Piroska: "No 'cleansing' of former Yugoslav socialists occurred in Slovenia. Former socialist party members went on to assume prominent positions in government and industry."[74]

On these grounds, some country specialists harbor skepticism concerning the merits of the Slovenian path and contend that the country could have done better by adopting a more radical approach to political and economic change.[75] Recently, Hungary's leading expert on former Yugoslavia Attila K. Soós has gone so far as to question whether Slovenia ought to be counted among the most Westernized postsocialist states at all. Unconventionally, he stressed Slovenia's similarities with Russia and Ukraine.[76]

Soós has argued that Slovenia did indeed suffer from its half-hearted break with the past, and paid a high price for its insider-dominated privatiza-tion process in terms of lost attraction for foreign investors. This was due to the fact that enterprise managers and organized workers successfully teamed up to fend off foreign competitors for ownership of their firms. At the same time, through the frequent redistribution of the gains of profitable compa-nies to loss-makers, Slovenian state intervention created uncertainty, harmed the transparency of business operations, and thus caused foreign investors to shy away.[77] Is this indeed the case?

---

72. Joel Hellman, "Winners Take All: The Politics of Partial Reform in Postcommunist Transitions," *World Politics* 50 (1998): 203–34; J. C. Sharman, "Who Pays for Entering Europe? Sectoral Politics and European Union Accession," *European Journal of Political Research* 43, no. 6 (2004): 797–822.

73. Karl Marx, *Capital,* vol. 1 (New York: Vintage, 1977), 91.

74. Lindstrom and Piroska, "The Politics of Privatization," 120.

75. Adam Frane, Kristan Primož, and Matevž Tomšič, "Varieties of Capitalism in Eastern Europe (with Special Emphasis on Estonia and Slovenia)," *Communist and Post-Communist Studies* 42, no. 1 (March 2009): 65–81.

76. Soós, *Rendszerváltás és privatizáció,* 109.

77. Ibid., 102–3.

Steering Foreign Capital Flows

At first glance the above criticism seems to be supported by evidence. Undoubtedly, during the 1990s foreign capital preferred the Visegrád and Baltic region to the Southeastern European group, not excepting Slovenia. It is also well established in the literature that the Slovenian state used a variety of protectionist measures to limit foreign takeover especially in strategic sectors.[78] Finally, when assessed by the status of investment promotion agencies and the comprehensiveness of the incentive packages granted, Slovenia's measures to attract FDI lagged far behind those of Hungary or Poland. Indeed, in the latter respect even Romania and Bulgaria seem to have surpassed Slovenia (table 1.2).

The puzzle, then, is: Given the continuity of Slovenia's economic elite, its protectionism, its meager incentives, and its overall limited inward FDI, how could it retain and deepen the same semicore profile of international integration as the Visegrád states, and enjoy overall no less economic dynamism than the latter? Conversely, how to make sense of the fact that Slovenia's most similar neighbors in Southeastern Europe lagged far behind it on all these dimensions, so that their international integration profiles exhibited semiperipheral traits and their performance in growth or macroeconomic stability was much inferior?

Critics of Slovenia's developmental model would explain the dual anomaly by suggesting that Slovenia's exceptionally favorable initial conditions counterbalanced the effects of its ill-conceived transformation strategy so that the negative consequences appeared in milder forms than in its southeastern neighbors. We do not deny the general importance of inherited assets, but we insist upon the necessity of identifying the exact factors to which the counterbalancing effects ought to be attributed. Just as in the case of consolidating tripartism, our master variable behind Slovenia's success in industrial restructuring is superior state capacity. In contrast, lack of state capacity goes a long way to explain the overall Southeastern European weak performance in restructuring industries and attracting FDI. This can be shown by examining some important similarities and differences between Slovenian restructuring through FDI and the experiences of the Visegrád group and the three other Southeastern European states.

A comparative analysis of the structure of inward FDI stock challenges Soós's vision about the Slovenian state's general hostility toward foreign investors. It also throws doubt on the idea that whenever the government did intervene against TNC takeovers, it used untransparent practices causing general uncertainty and confusion in economic transactions. Rather, we

---

78. Nina Bandelj, "Negotiating Global, Regional and National Forces: Foreign Investment in Slovenia," *East European Politics and Societies* 18, no. 3 (2004): 455–80; Lindstrom and Piroska, "The Politics of Privatization."

find that the priorities of Slovenian industrial policy were fairly rational and coherent, and hence we propose that state intervention as practiced in the country did not become part of its economic problems, but rather part of their solution.

The sectors that can partly explain Slovenia's inferior performance relative to the Visegrád states in attracting FDI include major public utilities, such as electricity, gas, water, transport, storage, and telecommunications. In terms of FDI penetration of these services Slovenia was a clear laggard. Yet the Slovenian state had more direct and effective policy tools at its disposal to manage its public sector than discouraging TNCs through redistributing profits, creating uncertainty, and undermining transparency. It could plainly reject or at least postpone marketization and privatization into foreign ownership—and this is how it actually proceeded. Nevertheless, such practices per se should not make Slovenia look "un-Western," especially given that many Western European states similarly limited foreign takeovers of their public utilities; in fact, it is the Latin American countries that have recently become the champions of this sector's foreign-led privatization.

Slovenia also lagged behind the Visegrád countries in attracting FDI into its traditional labor-intensive low-wage/low-skill manufacturing activities, such as the textiles and apparel, footwear, and timber and wood industries (table 5.1). Arguably, however, the country's overall wage level, which has been by far the highest in the postsocialist world, must have acted as a more powerful deterrent to transnational light industry investors than any threat of state intervention. All in all it seems that while in some sectors Slovenia was certainly less attractive for FDI than the Visegrád cluster, its disadvantages had little to do with the kind of state intervention that critics see as a consequence of insider-dominated privatization. Thus, such an explanation of Slovenia's limited FDI lacks convincing power.

Conversely, it seems reasonable to expect that untransparent ad hoc state intervention would make the largest negative impact on inward FDI flows into the physical and human capital–intensive complex-manufacturing industries, such as chemicals and pharmaceuticals, machinery, automobiles, and electronics. This is so because in order to minimize the risks associated with their usually sizable sector-specific investments, TNCs tend to prefer transparent and predictable industrial policies. Surprisingly, however, Slovenia was very successful in attracting foreign capital to its complex industries. In terms of the relevant per capita FDI stock in 2000, it was second only to Hungary but surpassed the Czech Republic and Poland, and even more Bulgaria, Romania, and Croatia (table 5.1).

Facts seem to challenge another criticism too. Soós asserted that "in the eyes of insider owners the limited separation of the public and private economy has questioned the very purpose of private capitalist accumulation, namely that profits are to be reinvested in the business in order to make it

TABLE 5.1
Slovenia's strategy of economic restructuring, mid-2000s

Country	FDI inward stock in public utilities (percent)[a]	FDI inward stock in traditional light industries (percent)[b]	FDI inward stock in the financial sector (percent)	FDI inward stock in complex-manufacturing industries (percent)[c]	Ratio of out-ward to inward FDI stock
Slovenia	9.1	1.8	20.7	22.4	51.0
Visegrád 4 average	11.7	6.9	16.2	16.7	11.1
Baltic 3 average	16.6	7.3	22.8	4.2	16.5
Bulgaria, Romania, Croatia average	12.5	7.8 (without Bulgaria)	26.2	9.3 (without Bulgaria)	3.7

Source: Authors' calculation based on wiiw Foreign Direct Investment Database Central and Eastern Europe (Vienna: The Vienna Institute for International Economic Studies, 2008).

Note: Data refer to 2006 except for Slovakia for which the latest available figures are for 2005.

[a] Electricity, gas and water supply, transport, storage, communications, education, health care, and social services.

[b] Food, beverages and tobacco, textiles and apparel, leather and leather products, and wood and wood products.

[c] Chemicals, machinery and equipment, optical and electronics equipment, and transport equipment.

even more profitable."[79] However, doubt is thrown on this proposition by the fact that Slovenia has been East Central Europe's leader in an important indicator of the drive for capitalist accumulation, namely in its own outward FDI.[80] In outward investments even Hungary has lagged far behind Slovenia. Especially given that the Western European small states have recently adopted similar strategies of selectively combining FDI inflows with strong outward investment activity, this feature also seems to support the view that Slovenia belongs to the most Westernized postsocialist political economies.

Finally, comparative analysis of FDI stock in the commercial banking sector also allows interesting observations. It is well known that Slovenia initially limited foreign takeovers in the financial sphere, raising dissatisfaction and continual criticism even on the part of the European Commission.[81] Until the early 2000s, Slovenia succeeded in imposing restrictions on FDI with the consequence that as late as in 2000 foreign banks' share in the country's total bank assets was just a fraction of their share in the Visegrád or Southeastern European countries. In light of this, the fact that in the same year Slovenia surpassed all the Visegrád as well as the other three Southeastern European countries in terms of the per capita FDI stock accumulating in its financial sector is surprising. A plausible explanation seems to be that Slovenia sold smaller pieces of its "family silver" at higher prices than all its neighbors.

Based on the above, our own interpretation of the Slovenian strategy of economic restructuring through transnationalization is as follows. State intervention has indeed constrained FDI penetration—but not in the particular sectors and ways suggested by critics of gradual transformation strategy. Without doubt, the government took the lead in delaying the foreign takeover of public utilities, commercial banking, and other key infrastructural areas. However, this resistance seems to have been based on a calculated rather than an ad hoc and misconceived restructuring strategy. Once Slovenia was ready to allow foreign involvement in these sectors—as eventually happened due to the EU's pressure in advance of accession—it could count on better conditions of foreign-led privatization than would have been the case in the buyer's markets of the 1990s, when all the Visegrád states tried to outcompete each other in marketizing their public and private services.

In attracting FDI to complex industries, Slovenia has not lagged behind the Visegrád states, let alone its Southeastern European neighbors. At the same time, Slovenian businesses appeared as East Central Europe's pioneers in relocating their labor-intensive activities to the less developed successor states of former Yugoslavia. They also started to establish their presence within the lagging economies' financial and other infrastructure sectors. As far as the impact of such industrial policy priorities on labor is concerned,

---

79. Soós, *Rendszerváltás és privatizáció*, 124.
80. Slovenian outward FDI mainly targeted the new countries of former Yugoslavia.
81. Lindstrom and Piroska, "The Politics of Privatization."

on the one hand, the threat of relocation may have disciplined organized labor in the traditional industries and oriented it toward accepting moderate strategies. On the other hand, the transnational restructuring of complex manufacturing through which employment was created, coupled with the relocation of low-wage/low-skill operations abroad, could help avoid the dra- ·
matic collapse of wages and spread of sweatshop work from which labor has suffered in other Southeastern European countries. In sum, we argue that this multifaceted strategy deserves attention even when compared with the restructuring experiences of Western European small states. Notwithstanding the obvious disparities in wealth and economic power, Slovenia seems to have embarked on a similar pathway to that of Austria, for instance, some time earlier.

The weak state paths of Bulgaria, Romania, and Croatia look markedly different. In some ways, their ultimately foreign-led restructuring seems to conform to two key observations on the impact of varied channels of international integration on domestic state capacity that have been proposed by students of less advanced countries in other parts of the world. First, different types of capital inflow affect on domestic state capacity in different ways, with some investments having an adverse effect. The best known example is of course oil, but portfolio investment or FDI in hypermobile industries also belong to those whose volatility can make it difficult for states to sustain economic strategies. In contrast, other investments—most notably in complex industries—might even reinforce state capacities to negotiate and administer projects, and provide for infrastructure and education.[82]

Second, according to Kiren Chaudry, initial institutional endowment matters too: "Countries still forging central institutions can potentially evolve almost solely in response to capital inflows, generating bureaucracies that are the direct products of the international economy.... In contrast, where strong institutions are in place, as in the East Asian cases...international capital is more likely to be used to promote economic goals."[83]

As far as the Southeastern European laggard countries are concerned, the main lesson we can draw from all this is that weak states are unlikely to attract anything but "impatient" foreign capital. The reason is that TNCs willing to settle more permanently in a national economy—in particular capital-intensive complex-manufacturing investors—tend to demand from their host a variety of resources and services that cannot be efficiently delivered by a weak state. On the other hand, the hypermobile foreign investors who commonly target less complex activities might just spend too short a period of time in any new location to significantly contribute to or even appreciate

    82. Kiren Aziz Chaudry, *The Price of Wealth: Economies and Institutions in the Middle East* (Ithaca: Cornell University Press, 1997), 25. See also Shafer, *Winners and Losers.*
    83. Chaudry, *The Price of Wealth,* 27–28; and Terry Karl, *The Paradox of Plenty: Oil Booms and Petro-States* (Los Angeles: University of California Press, 1997).

improvements in state capacity. As the authors of the VoC approach argue, "patient" capital is the key to coordinated market economies,[84] whereas its absence undermines strategic coordination by firms or states, since "nomadic" TNCs neither provide much strategic coordination on their own nor expect it from their hosts.

Especially from the late 1990s, impatient transnational capital has arrived in large amounts and varied forms in the Bulgarian, Romanian, and Croatian economies. Indeed, there is a clear asymmetry between the sectoral structure of FDI stock in Slovenia and in the other three economies. It is precisely in the traditional and labor-intensive, low-wage/low-skill "sweatshop" industries that the three laggard countries have outperformed Slovenia as attractive locations for inward FDI. Conversely, foreign investors have by and large avoided the laggard economies' complex-manufacturing sectors. Interestingly, this common pattern has developed in all three states despite their differing commitments to granting financial incentives and offering specific services to complex-manufacturing TNCs. Croatia essentially refused to adopt any measure to foster the transnational restructuring of its complex industries. Romania, for its part, designed one of East Central Europe's most comprehensive incentive packages. In this respect, Bulgaria has not lagged much behind.

The difference in approaches toward FDI among the three countries can by and large be explained by Croatia's reliance on tourism as a major source of hard currency earnings. Before the war of independence, international tourism contributed around 10 percent of GDP. At that time, Croatia was a net foreign currency earner not due to its manufacturing sector, which mostly exported to the Yugoslav and Soviet markets, but due to tourism. After 1997 tourism picked up again, surpassing the level of its contribution to the GDP under socialism already by 2000. Hence, the country did not have to rely so much on FDI in order to improve its external position. In addition, Croatia's major complex sector, shipbuilding, is perceived as a champion of national capitalism, and so far no government has been eager to sell this strategic asset to foreigners. The EU had to apply massive pressure to convince the Croatian government to even entertain the idea of the shipyards' privatization. [85]

Whereas Croatia did not feel pressure to offer FDI incentives, Romania's and Bulgaria's crucial problem lay in the coherent implementation of a strategic approach, as pointed out in several OECD studies. In Romania, tax laws have changed with "bewildering frequency.... Incentives have been

---

84. Hall and Soskice, *Varieties of Capitalism.*
85. Economist Intelligence Unit, September 2009; and Darjan Dragičević, "The Political Economy of Shipbuilding in Post-Socialist Transition: A Comparative Study of Croatia and Poland" (M.A. thesis, Central European University, Budapest, Department of International Relations and European Studies, 2007).

introduced, then removed when budgetary constraints demanded, only to be replaced within a short time with new incentives. The multitude of overlapping incentives and the frequency with which they have been changed make it difficult, even for Romanian tax authorities, to be sure which incentives apply at any given time for a given taxpayer situation."[86] Similarly, "since 1990, Bulgaria has introduced and repealed a 'bewildering' variety of tax incentives. Almost every year from 1990 onwards, changes have been made to the rules governing tax incentives."[87] Clearly, such industrial policy must have run in the face of its true objectives. By perpetuating uncertainty it deterred precisely those investors, namely the more demanding complex industry TNCs that it tried to attract by compensating for their risk.

Reminiscent of the ups and downs of tripartism discussed above, the flux of industrial policy measures reveals in yet another key area the inadequate capacity of Southeastern European states to devise and enforce clear and stable rules of the game. Consequently, foreign-led economic restructuring in much of the region has remained a matter of bargaining between unequals—between weak states and the least patient and most highly mobile types of TNCs. Despite lacking strategic capacities to attract patient and higher-quality FDI, the Southeastern European states could still meet nomadic TNCs' demands for uncontrolled mobility across borders and sectors, and cheap unskilled labor.

Against this background it should not be surprising that even in the few cases where complex industry TNCs attempted to make inroads into the Southeastern European economies, they tried to sell their hosts dubious projects carrying a high risk of fiasco. One example is Daewoo's acquisition of Romanian automobile factories shortly before the firm went bankrupt in its home country of South Korea. Even more striking are the adventures and misadventures of the British carmaker Rover, which in line with its strategy of relocating the assembly of its phased-out models to less advanced countries, tried to convince the Bulgarian authorities that its Maestro model that had earlier failed in its British home market would perform better if produced in Varna.[88]

Bulgarian automobile firms starved by dearth of capital for their restructuring projects welcomed the interest of a long-established Western European partner. The state-owned conglomerate Vammo, its automotive arm Terem, and their hurriedly established umbrella organization, the Daru Car group, competed in voicing their trust and confidence in the prospects of turning a

86. *Tax Policy Assessment and Design in Support of Direct Investment: A Study of Countries in Southeast Europe* (Paris: OECD, 2003), 141, 148, cited in Cass, "Attracting FDI," appendix 2b, 49.

87. *Tax Policy Assessment and Design*, 121, cited in Cass, "Attracting FDI."

88. Detelin Elenkov and Tonya Fileva, "Anatomy of a Business Failure: Accepting the 'Bad Luck' Explanation versus Proactively Learning in International Business," *Cross Cultural Management: An International Journal* 13, no. 2 (2006): 133.

British market failure into a Bulgarian success. "In fact, their goal turns out to be not so much to make profits from the deal, but to gain prestige of being a partner of Rover. Such collaboration might have been extremely beneficial for the image of a Bulgarian company like Daru Car."[89]

However, the British negotiators' optimism was grounded on an overestimate of the Bulgarian state's resolve and capacity to stick to the seemingly done deal. The Bulgarian privatization agency repeatedly changed unilaterally the terms of the deal without even notifying the British partner, and the government retreated from several of its promises. It delivered neither on the promised purchase of thousands of Maestros, nor on granting Rover exemption from a 10 percent excise duty on imported diesel engines and other import tariffs. Rover's Varna plant was quickly closed down.[90]

All this said, our purpose is not to question (or for that matter justify) the actions taken by any of these clearly desperate partners. We rather argue that their short-lived and unhappy marriage was sentenced to failure virtually from the beginning by the Bulgarian state's meager capacity to negotiate and assist transnational complex industry investments.

A last important indicator of the Bulgarian, Romanian, and Croatian states' weak capacity to pursue coherent industrial policies can be detected in the peculiar origin of a sizable part of their inward FDI stock. Relative to Slovenia or the Visegrád and Baltic states, a much larger share of foreign investment into these economies has originated from well-known tax havens such as the Virgin Islands, Liechtenstein, the Isle of Man, Cyprus, and Malta. From the early 1990s to the late 2000s, this kind of FDI has amounted to more than 12 percent of the total inward stock of each of the three countries, exceeding the volume of direct investment coming from individual large investor countries.

The mere existence of this feature is not, of course sufficient to prove that a large share of inward FDI is attributable to postcommunist early winners, who could maximize their gains by initially hiding their newly acquired riches in microstates, and later reinvesting their wealth in their native economies under even better conditions than in tax havens.[91] But perhaps a less ambitious but fairly self-evident proposition can be advanced: capital that investors move in and out of tax-heavens will hardly function as a reliable asset for the restructuring and development of a national economy. Instead, such investors are likely to exacerbate the danger posed by other less opaque but similarly mobile TNCs: they can easily "corner" (rather than as earlier was the case, capture) the public authority by threat of fast exit when facing

89. Ibid., 139.
90. Ibid., 135–38.
91. It is true, however, that the Bulgarian Multigroup started its operations in Malta, Liechtenstein, and Zug, Switzerland. Ganev, "The Dorian Gray Effect," 6–7.

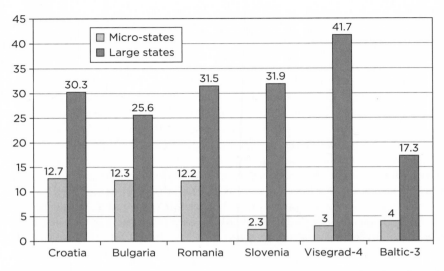

Figure 5.1 Origin of inward FDI stock in Southeastern Europe and other East Central European subregions. Average percent of total FDI stock in early 1990s through late 2000s. Authors' calculation based on wiiw Foreign Direct Investment Database on Central and Eastern Europe 2008. Investor microstates (also quasi-states and other tax havens) include Andorra, Bahamas, Belize, Bermuda, Cayman Islands, Cyprus, Gibraltar, Guernsey, Isle of Man, Jersey, Liechtenstein, Luxembourg, Malta, Marshall Islands, Netherlands Antilles, Panama, San Marino, San Vicent and Grenadines, Seychelles, Turks and Caicos Islands, Virgin Islands. Large investor states: France, Germany, Italy, United States.

unwanted policies—even if the latter would improve the host country's long-term development prospects.

Finally, let us make a related important point: the more impatient capital is, the less the likelihood that it will be labor-friendly. After all, high mobility empowers capitalists relative to workers in similar ways as it tends to shift the balance of power in favor of transnational companies vis-à-vis nation-states. It follows that, while the initially still modest FDI inflows to Southeastern Europe extended the grace period during which workers could count on some form of loyalty on part of their old employers, the hypermobile capital that by the late 1990s took the lead in industrial restructuring posed formidable challenges to organized labor.

To make things worse, the highly restrictive institutions of macroeconomic coordination adopted by some of the Southeastern European economies from the late 1990s strengthened state capacity at the expense of organized labor and the population at large. Instead of two unreliable earlier allies, namely "ersatz" capitalists and public administrations that lagged with reforms, in the new millennium Southeastern European labor had to face the coalition of two much strengthened adversaries: impatient (partly foreign)

capital and market-radical transformative states. All this heralded the end
of experimentation with neocorporatist and other labor-inclusive forms of
capitalism everywhere but in Slovenia.

Neocorporatist Balancing versus
Crisis-Driven Path Corrections

Along the lines of Katzenstein's earlier proposition that corporatist institutions can contribute to the efficacy of fiscal coordination, Torben Iversen
and Jonas Pontusson have argued that "the effects of monetary policies
cannot be understood without paying attention to the conditioning influences of wage bargaining structures and processes."[92] If wage bargaining
is centralized and coordinated, social partners concerned about economy-
wide levels of inflation and unemployment are likelier to respond to central banks' warning signals with wage restraint. Such a response in turn
preempts the need for overly restrictive monetary policies and this way the
desired macroeconomic goal can be achieved at lower social cost.

In contrast, highly decentralized, fragmented industrial relations systems—whether they result from conscious neoliberal design or the malfunctioning or atrophy of tripartism—make such accommodation unlikely.[93] In
these instances, central bank policy is not taken into consideration by the
parties to atomized wage bargaining and this increases the risk of monetary
stabilization measures overshooting.

Consistent with the above, when preparing for euro entry in the 1990s, the
Western European states tried to meet the new challenges of macroeconomic
coordination and adjustment by reliance on established neocorporatist practices and routines. In many of the countries that did not have neocorporatist
institutions before, employers, trade unions, and governments entered encompassing social pacts.[94]

Similarly, when faced with the even more challenging agenda of maintaining macroeconomic stability over the whole period of the 1990s to 2000s,
Slovenia embarked on the Western European small states' path. We will highlight the specificity of Slovenian coordination first by comparing it with the
experience of Croatia, which also succeeded in macroeconomic stabilization,
but by remarkably different means. Second, we will contrast the Slovenian

92. Torben Iversen and Jonas Pontusson, "Comparative Political Economy: A Northern
European Perspective," in *Unions, Employers, and Central Banks,* ed. Torben Iversen, Jonas
Pontusson, and David Soskice (Cambridge: Cambridge University Press, 2000), 12.
93. Robert J. Franzese and Peter Hall, "Institutional Dimensions of Coordinating Wage
Bargaining and Monetary Policy," in Iversen, Pontusson, and Soskice, *Unions, Employers,* 178–79.
94. See, e.g., Bob Hancké and Martin Rhodes, "EMU and Labor Market Institutions
in Europe: The Rise and Fall of National Social Pacts," *Work and Occupations* 32, no. 2
(2005): 196–228.

experience with the failure of Bulgaria's and Romania's early efforts to bring about macroeconomic stability.

Macroeconomic Stabilization and Social Partnership: Slovenia and Croatia Compared

Both Slovenia and Croatia faced a triple transformation to nation-state, democracy, and capitalism, a challenge that they also shared with the three Baltic states.[95] Some factors that empowered Baltic central bankers have therefore been at work in Slovenia and Croatia too. Their newly introduced currencies fostered identity through their national imagery, replaced the cacophony of a multiple-currency regime of Yugoslav dinars, German marks, and U.S. dollars with "unity in 'economic language,'" and consolidated the "trustworthiness of the institution that issued it or guaranteed its value."[96] However, neither the Slovene nor the Croatian central bank ever acquired the unchallenged hegemony of their Baltic counterparts. While in Slovenia monetary policy was meant to contribute to broader social and economic goals, and thus became embedded in a web of coordinated policymaking, in Croatia war and a charismatic and populist leader trumped central bankers in identity building and policymaking alike. These same factors also impaired coordinated policymaking.

One of the chief architects of the Slovenian transformation, then Deputy Prime Minister Jože Mencinger, wrote that macroeconomic independence had been sought through a "pragmatic economic policy and a floating exchange rate system for the new currency.... It was hoped that such a policy would result in smaller output losses and lower unemployment by allowing some inflation."[97] The same spirit also underlay macroeconomic policies toward the corporate sector. Banks and industrial firms were granted grace periods, subsidies, and loans to adjust and restructure so as to allow them a gradual transformation into genuine market actors.

Notwithstanding foreign advocacy of polar opposite strategies, the government stayed course. It is interesting to note that Slovenia was visited by the same team of advisers as Estonia, and was given very similar recommendations, namely fixed exchange rates, radical stabilization, liberalization, and privatization. But the suggestions of Jeffrey Sachs and his colleagues did not fall on fertile ground. As Mencinger recalled, "We listened to them, but did not follow their advice. Their agenda was based on ideology, not economics. And the U.S. advisors didn't see a difference between Slovenia and

95. Offe, "Capitalism by Democratic Design?"

96. Eric Helleiner, *The Making of National Money: Territorial Currencies in Historical Perspective* (Ithaca: Cornell University Press, 2003), 101, 112–13.

97. Jože Mencinger, "Transition to a National and a Market Economy: A Gradualist Approach," in *Slovenia: From Yugoslavia to the European Union*, ed. Mojmir Mrak, Matija Rojec, and Carlos Silva-Jáuregui (Washington, D.C.: World Bank, 2004), 78.

Mongolia."[98] One reason that Slovenian policymakers trusted their own opinions was that they had built up significant economic competence prior to the demise of socialism. Like their Hungarian and Polish colleagues, during the last two decades or so of the old regime many economists had studied abroad and gained thorough understanding of the state of the art in their field. They therefore saw little need for Western advice.[99]

National control over the commercial banking sector also mattered for the feasibility of a gradual and macroeconomically balanced transformation strategy. Even after recurrent EU pressures ultimately forced Slovenia to grant private and foreign capital freer access to its banks, caution in commercial bank transnationalization was still the rule, and reserve requirements remained effective tools of monetary stabilization at the Bank of Slovenia's (BS) disposal throughout the 1990s and beyond. Ironically, then, resistance to external pressures for the banking sector's hurried Europeanization in the course of EU accession helped the BS to succeed with the main task of Europeanization after accession, namely compliance with the Maastricht criteria for macroeconomic convergence.

An important asset for Slovenia's gradual and coordinated path toward macroeconomic stabilization was its specific socialist legacy. In Mencinger's words, Slovenian gradualists generally "considered the legacy of the past an exploitable advantage."[100] Independent Slovenia's embrace of the Yugoslav legacy of workers' self-management added a level of participatory decision-making unknown in other East Central European countries, and developed it into a system of negotiated industrial relations. After the initial recession, which removed from power the right-wing coalition that had won the first parliamentary elections, "political exchange between centre-left governments and organized economic interests became a permanent feature and the key mode of interest concertation, giving social legitimacy to market reforms."[101]

In line with the Slovenian gradualist strategy, which allowed the social partners to have a voice in the coordination of multiple and conflicting policy issues, central bank independence and an effective fiscal authority emerged in the context of a power-sharing arrangement with other important economic interests and institutions. Unlike in the Baltic and Visegrád states—where top macroeconomic policymakers were either celebrated as nation builders or continually distrusted and attacked for alleged partisanship—Slovenian central bankers and ministers of finance could build their legitimacy on a negotiated relationship with social partners.

---

98. Nicole Lindstrom and Dóra Piroska, interview with Jože Mencinger, conducted in Ljubljana, September 13, 2006, see Lindstrom and Piroska, "The Politics of Privatization, 121.
99. Mencinger, "Transition to a National," 76.
100. Ibid.
101. Miroslav Stanojević, "Workers' Power in Transition Economies: The Cases of Serbia and Slovenia," *European Journal of Industrial Relations* 9, no. 3 (2003): 290.

The Croatian path toward the new national currency and its stabilization was strikingly different. In the early 1990s, the war effort and a Keynesian demand stimulus to overcome the deep recession led to a heavily inflated economy. Incidentally, the governor of the Croatian National Bank (CNB) opposed printing money to keep the economy afloat. He saw his task as the stabilization of the newly introduced kuna, and was duly removed from office for this view.[102] It was only in 1993 that a serious effort at stabilization was made. By choosing an almost fixed exchange rate regime, Croatia followed the international mainstream. Massive demand for the new currency on the part of a population hitherto starved by a dearth of liquidity caused the kuna to appreciate. All of this contributed to successful stabilization, bringing inflation down to a level below that of Slovenia, at heavy cost.

The real appreciation of the kuna further undermined the external competitiveness of Croatia's manufacturing sector. Moreover, stabilization alone could not solve the problems of sluggish growth, dramatic decline of industrial production and wages, and persistent high unemployment. However, unlike their colleagues in Slovenia, Croatian policymakers did not embed the goal of stabilization in a broader economic strategy for the country, and were overall less willing to mitigate its costs.

True, Croatia's public expenditure increased significantly during the war and even the postwar years, in the latter period due not least to record levels of social protection spending. But as stated above, in contrast to the encompassing Slovenian strategy to embed markets, the bulk of compensation offered in Croatia was selectively geared toward the ruling party's cronies and core constituencies. Although the immense human toll taken by the war justified a measure of compensation for its heroes and victims, our point is that the structure of social spending was mediated by nationalist political considerations. After all, social suffering in transforming Croatia came in more than one single war-related form: real wages in 1993 were down to less than 50 percent of their level in 1990, and recovered only modestly in later years.[103]

A further difference can be traced to the Croatian elites' hostility toward the Yugoslav self-management inheritance.[104] As a combined consequence of power holders' strong will to transcend all the legacies of the past, and of their undermined capacity and skills to fulfill the obligations that would follow from regular tripartite bargaining, wage setting fast became decen-

---

102. Croatia introduced its national currency only at the end of 1991, after a first significant success in the war had been achieved. This should have made stabilization a relatively easy task, as the early war economy was financed by Yugoslav banknotes that the CNB had hoarded and gradually put into circulation. The second inflation wave from 1992 was the result of the government's economic policy choices. See Schönfelder, "The Impact of War," 27–28; Franicevic and Kraft, "Croatia's Economy," 670–71.

103. Franičević and Kraft, "Croatia's Economy," 672; Schönfelder, "The Impact of War."

104. Grdešić, "Transition, Labor."

tralized, which reinforced the divergence between the paths of these two Yugoslav successor regimes.

The contrasting strategies for institutionalizing new currencies and stabilizing economies allow us to highlight neocorporatism's contribution to strengthening state capacity. Not only was a degree of stateness a precondition for the consolidation of tripartite arrangements, but the opposite relationship applies too. Neocorporatism was Slovenia's unique asset for building East Central Europe's most capable state institutions, since this structure made it easier to coordinate fiscal, monetary, and labor market policies as well as claims on welfare spending, to distribute the burdens of stabilization and transformation equally among broad and diverse groups of actors, and to foster compliance. In contrast, Croatia's patronage networks prevented the country from finding mutually beneficial solutions to the problems of stabilization, the labor market, and an unbalanced welfare state. Unsurprisingly, many of the adopted policies proved unsustainable in the longer run.

Equally important, Slovenia's encompassing social partnership has become expression of a Europeanized and inclusive variant of nationalism. This contrasts sharply with Croatia's exclusive nationalism that is permanently on the look for enemies from within and without.

Last but not least, the tradition of social partnership helped Slovenia to enter the eurozone in 2007 as the first East Central European member state. Uniquely in the region, in April 2003 Slovenia's social partners signed an encompassing pact on future wages and income policy, thereby emulating the pacts that governments, labor unions, and employer organizations had signed in many old member states during their run up to EMU.[105] In Croatia, a similar plan was only considered after a deep economic and political crisis dislodged the HDZ from power. However, lack of trust among the partners, clashes over the necessary scope of reforms, the government's limited power to rein in crony capitalism, and the overly high expectations of trade unions led to the failure of social pacting in post-Tuđman Croatia.[106]

All in all, notwithstanding its specific features, Croatia has shared with Bulgaria and Romania an uncoordinated approach to economic, fiscal, and monetary policies, resulting economic and political traumas, and socially costly ways of stabilizing the economy.

The Failure of Uncoordinated Capitalism: Bulgaria and Romania

During the larger part of the 1990s, the Bulgarian and Romanian governments had to cope with conflicting pressures that begged for effective but

105. Stanojević, "Social Pacts in Slovenia."
106. Although the new center-left coalition government that succeeded HDZ in 2000 tried to pact with the unions, the attempt failed. See, e.g., Grdešić, "Transition, Labor."

unavailable mechanisms of macroeconomic coordination. Bulgaria's main challenge was to find a balance between the imperative of regaining control over its budget and inflation, the cost of appeasing losers by social welfare provisions (the initial generosity of which had not lagged far behind those of the Visegrád states),[107] and steering transformation's early winners away from "state-breaking" activities to productive investment. Similarly, Romania experienced an eruption of enterprises' and citizens' pent-up demands for protection in the aftermath of the immiserating regime of Nicolae Ceaușescu, the meeting of which came into permanent conflict with the requirements of macroeconomic stability.

To break the inflationary wage-price spiral, these states could either impose central wage regulation unilaterally (such as through prohibitive taxation of salary increases), or rely on tripartite and/or bipartite mechanisms of wage setting, the functioning of which required voluntary restraint on the workers' part. Governments tried to elicit cooperation by granting unions a voice in labor market and social policies, and labor-inclusive privatization schemes. However, since such concessions fell short of taming industrial conflict, policymakers were sentenced to permanent vacillation between negotiated and administratively imposed wage setting.

Unfortunately, the decentralized fiscal institutions and dependent monetary authorities inherited from socialism proved to be as ineffective a means for macroeconomic coordination as the nascent tripartite institutions. Most striking is the example of Bulgaria where, as noted by Veselin Dimitrov, "the position of the finance minister in the last years of communism was so weak that in 1987 Todor Zhivkov went so far as to abolish the ministry altogether." After the fall of socialism the Ministry of Finance was reestablished, but it still failed to gain significant administrative leverage. "Each minister was able to largely determine her or his own level of spending, with little regard to the consequences for the fiscal position. The finance ministry proved unable to control not only the preparation but also the implementation of the budget."[108] Moreover, the persistent instability of the party system, which until 1997 resulted in a series of short-lived and powerless governments, made a shift toward more centralized fiscal institutions virtually impossible. Subordinated to the government, the Bulgarian National Bank had no alternative to serving reckless spending agendas by printing money and lending to the state.

Romania, bled white by the immense cost of Ceaușescu's decision to force the country to fully repay its foreign debt during the 1980s, similarly lacked effective fiscal and monetary authorities. Although the varied coalition governments led by Iliescu's National Salvation Front initiated several

---

107. UNICEF, *Children at Risk in Central and Eastern Europe*, 135.
108. Veselin Dimitrov, "From Laggard to Pacesetter: Bulgaria's Road to EMU," in Dyson, *Enlarging the Euro Area*, 150.

stabilization programs in the 1990s, these efforts did not bring sustainable results. Typically stabilization measures were watered down once authorities faced social protest. Above all, these programs fell short of tackling one of the main problems behind high inflation and fiscal imbalances: "substantial quasi-fiscal deficits that were fuelled by bad debts between state-owned enterprises and tax arrears, as well as government subsidies on fuel for both industrial and domestic consumption."[109] To oil the wheels of fiscal overspending, governments continually intervened in the operation of the National Bank of Romania, thereby undermining trust in the national currency.[110]

The contrast between the quality of Slovenian state institutions and especially those of Romania and Bulgaria in the fields of labor relations, industrial policies and restructuring, and fiscal and monetary governance could hardly be more pronounced. In line with the expectations of the VoC approach the coordination of the Slovenian economy capitalized on the mutually reinforcing effect of complementary institutions, whereas during most of the 1990s the interactions among institutions in Bulgaria and Romania seem to have produced a rather perverse form of complementarity, tending to undermine each other's efficiency.

Distrust in tripartite frameworks hindered wage moderation, and made centrally imposed fiscal and monetary controls the only game in town. The harsh social consequences of these methods intensified demands for compensation, which perpetuated fiscal and monetary imbalances. In turn, savage cuts in welfare provisions to restore stability provoked new discontent and restarted the vicious cycle. Last but not least, the incapacity and low international credibility of these Southeastern European states impaired their prospects of securing the foreign resources—whether in form of loans or patient FDI—that could have helped to stabilize and reinvigorate their economies. Without simultaneous interventions across several political and economic arenas the problem of the vicious cycle could not be tackled. Under these conditions it took deep crises of economy and democratic legitimacy to open new windows of opportunity for large-scale institutional restructuring after the 1990s.

Rebuilding States and Redrawing the Symbolic Map

Political awareness of the urgent need for a radical path correction arrived first in Bulgaria at the turn of 1996–97, when Zhan Videnov's Bulgarian Socialist Party administration led the country into a nightmare of galloping inflation, skyrocketing budget deficits, massive commercial bank failures,

---

109. Dimitris Papadimitriou, "Persistent Laggard: Romania as Eastern Europe's Sisyphus," in Dyson, *Enlarging the Euro Area*, 220–21. According to Papadimitriou, the amount of quasi-fiscal deficits was estimated at over 50 percent of the GDP.
    110. Ibid., 221.

and labor militancy coupled with violent riots and protests against food shortages.[111] As both the economy and the democratic polity spiraled out of control, it took an "electoral revolution" to dislodge the postcommunist successor party from power and bring to power a new right-wing government. [112]

The moment of truth for Romanian political elites arrived first when the November 1996 election ended the rule of the postcommunist Romanian Social Democratic Party (PDSR), and brought to power a conservative coalition led by the Democratic Convention of Romania (CDR). Although the new government initiated a radical economic reform program, it failed to implement it, and soon faced a crisis when in "1999, a payment default was averted at the eleventh hour."[113]

Finally, the Croatian opposition used the political opportunity provided by Tudman's death to ignite a successful electoral revolution in 2000, and the new center-left government signaled its commitment to break with the semiauthoritarian and antimarket legacies of the past.[114] Despite the government's success in bringing down inflation, by the late 1990s the Croatian economy was in almost as dire straits as those of Bulgaria and Romania. The cost of keeping the flagship transport, shipbuilding, and tourism firms afloat put a huge burden on the budget, while their restructuring did not make much progress, opening a gaping hole in the balance of payments. The pension system was close to collapsing, also putting a huge strain on the budget. In addition, a credit boom that had followed the liberalization of the banking system in the early 1990s led to a major banking crisis at the end of the decade.[115]

In the aftermath of these crises, all three countries managed turnarounds, and started to close the gap with the rest of East Central Europe in terms of institution building, state capacities, and economic strategies. By the mid-2000s, the institutional configuration of Bulgaria, and to a lesser extent Romania, resembled that of the Baltic states. Croatian capitalism, on the other hand, shared many features with the Visegrád regime type. What accounts for this relative success in catching up, and how do these latecomer models differ from the capitalisms of East Central Europe's early movers?

The first important precondition for more consolidated stateness in the three Southeastern European countries was that their economic and political crises modified their earlier patterns of state capture to the benefit of only

111. Iankova, *Eastern European Capitalism*.

112. Veselin Dimitrov, "EMU and Fiscal Policy," Dyson, *Enlarging the Euro Area*, 261–78. On electoral revolutions, see Bunce and Wolchik, "Favorable Conditions and Electoral Revolutions."

113. Papadimitriou, "Persistent Laggard," 221.

114. For the role of unions in preparing the ground for the electoral revolution and further details on Croatia's turning point see Sharon Fisher, "Contentious Politics in Croatia: Civil Society and the 2000 Parliamentary Elections" (paper prepared for the 50th Annual Conference of the U.K. Political Studies Association, London, April 10–13, 2000.)

115. Bićanić and Franičević, "Understanding Reform."

a very few economic groups. Instead, a new kind of interest group politics emerged, which Andrew Barnes has termed "competitive capture." Its main attribute is an ongoing rivalry of particularistic interests and their representatives in bureaucratic and democratic politics over who controls (and thus gains from) various state policies and areas of influence.

According to Barnes, by the mid-2000s competitive capture reached a fragile equilibrium in Bulgaria, a finding that applies to Romania and Croatia as well. The new equilibrium has had important consequences for economic growth and state capacity. Although it has not ended interest group rivalry once and for all, it has led to a degree of accommodation and compromise allowing the winners to get their way without "taking it all." Therefore, from the early to late 2000s, competitive capture has been "compatible with economic growth and with enough state autonomy to monitor some parts of the system."[116]

Another important factor was the role of international organizations, which increasingly served as external reform anchors and institution builders. The earliest example is the IMF's role in crisis-ridden Bulgaria. After Bulgaria's inflation spiraled out of control in early 1997, the government had to turn to the fund for support. The IMF not only imposed a tough austerity package, but also made the country adopt the Baltic solution to its economic woes, namely a currency board. By the time of the eruption of the Bulgarian crisis, the IFIs no longer considered currency boards a mere "exotic" substitute for central bank independence. Rather, they became the IMF's standard remedy for countries that lacked a minimal ability to maintain the stability of the national currency, and keep current account and fiscal imbalances under control. As Dimitrov argues: "The board ... represented the ultimate recognition of the inability of Bulgarian governments to manage monetary policy. It substantially restricted their discretion in fiscal policy by making it impossible to finance the deficit by printing money, and by prohibiting the Bulgarian National Bank from lending to the government."[117]

Parallel to the intensified involvement of IFIs, once the accession process started the European Commission became the primary source of templates for new state institutions with reinforced coordination capacities. Because of Romania's and Bulgaria's meager performance, the EU Commission was initially reluctant to start entry negotiations with them, and its only reason for doing so was to reward their center-right governments for their support of the West during the Kosovo war. As a consequence, however, both countries were subject to the EU's unusually harsh conditionality and close monitor-

---

116. Barnes, "Extricating the State," 71, 92. For the changes in Croatian crony capitalism see Vojmir Franičević and Ivo Bićanić, "EU Accession and Croatia's Two Economic Goals: Modern Economic Growth and Modern Regulated Capitalism," *Southeast European and Black Sea Studies* 7, no. 4 (December 2007): 645.

117. Dimitrov, "EMU and Fiscal Policy," 273.

ing.[118] The same holds true for Croatia, which just barely had managed to escape its status as "a pariah and outcast requiring strict international conditionality" for meeting even modest performance standards.[119]

A major focus of the EU's conditionality and a source of much conflict was the reform of the administrative apparatus and the judiciary. The EU's insistence on the reform of key building blocks of the state, its credible and repeated threats to postpone membership if state reforms were not taken up in time, and its close postaccession monitoring of reform progress were without doubt a major factor that increased state capacity in all three countries. Pro-European domestic elites internalized the imposed conditions, and capitalized on the promise of full membership once their states acquired the capacity to break with the legacies of "balkanized" authority and politics. Both the attraction of leaving "the Balkans" and returning to Europe, and the strict sanctions in case of noncompliance, helped these Europeanizing coalitions prevail against their nationalist rivals in domestic arenas.[120]

As confirmed by improvements in the indicators of fiscal deficit, inflation, FDI inflows, and quality of governance, the macroeconomic coordination capacities of Bulgaria, Romania, and Croatia were indeed strengthened. On the other hand, the imposed logic of integration at different speeds exacerbated regional fragmentation, since the material and spiritual ties between the would-be EU insiders and the remaining outsiders were partly weakened and partly transformed by the fact that the weak or quasi-states still populating what Spyros Economides describes as the ever-shrinking "quarantine region" of the "Western Balkans" were left behind.[121]

As this suggests, the EU's effort to "divide and pacify" the Balkans by redrawing its economic and political boundaries in line with a new symbolic geography[122] has not been without costs. Although in the frameworks of the Stability Pact for Southeastern Europe and the Stabilization and Association Process the would-be insiders and the outsiders are seen as belonging to the same region, and on these grounds are asked to develop strong regional ties on their roads to Europe, their perspectives of EU membership remain starkly different. "While attempting to create a spirit of unity, and in more practical terms a regional market and trade interdependence, the overriding idea that EU accession can be achieved (and probably will be achieved) on a solitary basis is detrimental to regional cooperation."[123]

---

118. Noutcheva and Bechev, "The Successful Laggards."
119. Bićanić and Franičević, "Understanding Reform," 18.
120. Noutcheva and Bechev, "The Successful Laggards," 128–139; Papadimitriou, "Persistent Laggard." For an excellent analysis see Gergana Dimitrova, "From Bright Light to Blackout: The Influence of the Europeanization Paradigm on Bulgarian Foreign Policy and Transport and Energy Infrastructure Policy" (Ph.D. diss., Central European University, Budapest, Department of International Relations and European Studies, 2008).
121. Spyros Economides, "Balkan Europe," in Dyson and Sepos, *Which Europe*, 112–25.
122. Todorova, *Imagining the Balkans*, 160.
123. Economides, "Balkan Europe," 123.

Finally, both Romania and Bulgaria also adopted a number of policies and institutions that allowed them to enhance administrative efficiency while sparing them all the pain of building and maintaining sophisticated and costly administrations. Bulgaria's currency board and both countries' minimalist welfare states are cases in point. The flat tax system embraced by Bulgaria and Romania is another good example. It reduced public agencies' enforcement activities to a minimum at which they could appear as efficient. It is therefore not surprising that it is mostly states that lack an efficient tax administration, and where tax compliance is limited, that have chosen to adopt a flat tax system. At the same time, the flat tax is also a signaling device, indicating "to the rest of the world a fundamental regime change, shifting towards more market-oriented policies."[124] In this context, it is interesting to note that Croatia, being less dependent on FDI inflows, also did not share the enthusiasm for simple institutions with its Southeastern European peers.

As a result of competitive rather than monopolistic state capture, EU conditionality, and choices of institutions which do not require sophisticated administrative structures, by the mid 2000s, Romania and Bulgaria seem to have taken firm roots in the neoliberal camp. However, some essential differences remain. First, the institutional solutions adopted by the Baltic states reflected conscious elite choices. Thus in Estonia the currency board reflected the political elite's conscious decision of merging the agenda of economic transformation with that of building an independent nation state. In contrast, the laggards only adopted these institutions when a major meltdown severely restricted the alternatives open to them.

Second, the early choices of the Baltic states also revealed some skill and will for institutional innovation. When first adopted, the currency boards and flat taxes were still exotic solutions, rarely put into practice before. In contrast, at the time when Bulgaria and Romania adopted similar institutions, they had become mainstream solutions, propagated by IFIs, and tried and tested elsewhere. Third, domestic and external influences and agendas reinforced each other in the case of the early movers, thus producing relatively robust institutions. In contrast the same institutions were more externally imposed and have taken less deep roots in the laggards.

All of this implies that market radicalism was also the *backup option* adopted by some of the weakest postsocialist states in the aftermath of their dramatic failures to coordinate more complex and socially balanced transformation agendas. Since all three countries arrived to pure versus embedded neoliberal regimes after radically altering their initial weak state paths, their experience might be relevant for many other weak states populating

---

124. Keen et al., "The 'Flat Tax(es),'" 35. For a more detailed discussion of the flat tax revolution in East Central Europe, see chapter 3, "The Politics of Early Economic Reforms."

Southeastern Europe and the former Soviet Union, an issue we shall return to in the Conclusion.

Finally, as far as Croatia's muddling through its triple transformation is concerned, the differences with the more balanced paths of Slovenia and the Visegrád group are significant. Most important, the ideational foundations of this variant's embeddedness lay not in the appreciation but rejection of what Yugoslav socialism left behind. Nation building *on rather than with the ruins* of Yugoslavia goes far in explaining Croatia's rejection of neocorporatism notwithstanding all of its inherited prerequisites, as well as the drift toward embedded neoliberalism despite insufficient state capacity.

Nation building has also left its mark on Croatia's peculiar pattern of embeddedness. While the generosity of compensation exceeded the usual standards of the Visegrád states, welfare benefits were granted not on the ground of inherited status but rewarded individual sacrifices for the new nation, or served the cause of nationalizing as in the Baltic states. Furthermore, the selective but bloated welfare state did not rely for financing on the export economy, as Croatia so far has hardly developed one worth the name. The reason, again, is in the elites' lasting ambition to control the flagship firms of national capitalism.

Arguably, therefore, it is above all its lucky endowment of natural beauty that saved the country from travelling all the way down toward market radicalism. Without the receipts from tourism, hardly would it have been possible to maintain the combination of a selective but over-generous welfare, and an inward-oriented capitalist system in a state as weak as Croatia has become.

6

The Return of Hard Times

With the outbreak of the crisis of the late 2000s, the precariousness of the new postsocialist order has once again come to the fore. Global financial instability and recession have posed difficult challenges to all the variants of East Central European capitalism. By 2009, most of the new EU member states had accumulated major economic imbalances and had gone through deep recessions, which have in some countries lasted for several years. To defend their currencies and keep their economies afloat, three states—Hungary, Latvia, and Romania—had to turn for help to the IMF and the EU. In addition, governments have been confronted with the reform fatigue and disenchantment of their citizens, which in many cases set in well before the global crisis struck.

Like the earlier crises, the global financial crisis of the late 2000s and its repercussions have put the diverse development strategies and institutions of the region's market societies under stress. The drying up of international credits and the breakdown of export markets have forced many countries to make sharp adjustments. Amidst a new round of painful measures governments have also had to rethink their strategies for mobilizing support, since the key institutions that helped generate consent earlier have turned into liabilities for crisis management.

How far has the global crisis put into danger the few success stories that postsocialism has brought about? More precisely, how far have the East Central European countries succeeded in keeping the main challenges to their new orders—economic destabilization, social disintegration, loss of legitimacy, and impaired democracy—at bay under the adverse conditions of the Great Recession?[1] With the global crisis still unfolding, we cannot give a

---

1. Carmen Reinhart and Kenneth S. Rogoff, *This Time Is Different: Eight Centuries of Financial Folly* (Princeton: Princeton University Press, 2009).

definitive answer to any of these questions. Instead, we seek here to spell out the specific vulnerabilities of the different regimes and countries, and the resources on which they might be able to rely in their coping strategies.

The main proposition we put forward is that there is a nontrivial relationship between the economic challenges the East Central European countries and regimes have been exposed to, and their ability to deal with the fallout of the crisis. More specifically, our point is that whether and at what cost various states have been able to maneuver through hard times has ultimately depended on the capacities of the political sphere rather than merely on the specifics of crisis exposure. This is in line with our idea of the centrality of the political system to capitalist success.

To apply and substantiate this argument, we will show that there are differences in how regimes have been affected by the crisis. This variation can be traced to regime-specific patterns of international integration—whether through manufacturing FDI and exports or through the financial sector—as well as to the peculiar forms in which governments tried to maintain legitimacy once its original sources, namely identity politics or social and economic protectionism, were depleted or proved difficult to finance. This way, the East Central European regimes' varied institutions and performances have had a bearing on their strengths and weaknesses when facing hard times.[2]

First, statistical evidence shows that all countries belonging to the neoliberal regime type had accumulated multiple external imbalances, which made them highly vulnerable once the crisis broke out. In particular, their current account deficits, ratios of foreign debt to GDP, and high and fast-growing shares of mortgage-based and foreign currency–denominated loans to households, had by 2007 spiraled out of control.

In comparison, the countries of the embedded neoliberal regime cluster, as well as neocorporatist Slovenia, were less exposed along all of these dimensions. In this group, however, Hungary stood out for its high public and external debt, and its high share of loans in foreign currency within total credit to private households.

Second, we find that already before the economic crisis social and political tensions accumulated across the region that bore witness to a "new" political economy of protest and patience. Several developments illustrate this, such as the occurrence of violent demonstrations and riots, the rise of radical illiberal parties and the radicalization of formerly moderate centrist parties, a significant drop in voter turnout region-wide, and a strong dissatisfaction with democracy and lack of trust in its institutions revealed by opinion polls. In the literature these developments have been described as the

---

2. The importance of the links between the paths of international integration and features of the crisis is also a cornerstone of the argument of Joachim Becker and Johannes Jäger, "Development Trajectories in the Crisis in Europe," *Debatte: Journal of Contemporary Central and Eastern Europe* 18, no. 1 (2010): 5–27; and Myant and Drahokoupil, *Transition Economies*.

TABLE 6.1
Exposure to the global crisis, mid-2000s

	Financial and real estate FDI[a]	Manufacturing FDI[b]	Current account balance[c]	External debt[d]	Extension of credit to private sector[e]	Share of FX loans within the banks' household loans[f]	General government balance[g]
Estonia	60.6 (36.5)	14.4 (16.9)	−17.8 (−11.3)	119.3 (71.8)	285.0	82.4 (66.6)	2.6 (1.7)
Latvia	46.5 (38.8)	8.8 (15.6)	−22.3 (−8.2)	135.4 (84.0)	221.9	87.4 (58.4)	−0.4 (−1.6)
Lithuania	25.6 (23.1)	36.3 (31.1)	−14.5 (−6.9)	76.9 (44.8)	263.2	61.6 (29.2)	−1.0 (−1.3)
Bulgaria	38.1 (28.2)	17.8 (34.8)	−25.4 (−5.1)	107.6 (67.2)	250.2	29.8 (5.6)	3.5 (−0.9)
Romania	31.2 (16.1)	34.1 (50.9)	−14.4 (−5.8)	48.5 (37.6)	261.3	58.7 (29.3)	−3.1 (−1.5)
Czech Republic	31.1 (25.7)	36.1 (41.9)	−2.6 (−6.3)	44.4 (38.2)	233.6	0.1 (0.7)	−1.6 (−6.6)
Hungary	30.9 (27.0)	35.7 (45.7)	−6.9 (−9.4)	96.8 (61.6)	144.1	70.2 (5.0)	−4.9 (−7.2)
Poland	32.6 (28.2)	33.9 (35.9)	−2.8 (−2.5)	54.8 (49.5)	194.2	39.8 (29.7)	−1.9 (−6.3)
Slovak Republic	24.4 (26.5)	48.0 (35.8)	−4.8 (−4.3)	52.7 (39.5)	134.2	2.8 (0.5)	−1.9 (−2.8)
Croatia	55.1 (26.2)	23.0 (34.9)	−7.5 (−6.3)	77.6 (66.3)	136.4	n.a.	−2.5 (−4.8)
Slovenia	36.5 (27.9)	37.1 (48.5)	−4.8 (−0.8)	100.6 (52.5)	190.8	n.a.	0.5 (−2.7)

[a] Inward FDI stock in the financial and real estate sectors in percent of total inward stock in 2005–7 (depending on data availability). 2003 data in parentheses. wiiw Foreign Direct Investment Database Central and Eastern Europe (Vienna: The Vienna Institute for International Economic Studies, 2008).

[b] Inward FDI stock in the manufacturing sector in percent of total inward stock in 2005–7 (depending on data availability). 2003 data in parentheses. wiiw Foreign Direct Investment Database.

[c] In 2007, as percent of GDP. 2003 data in parentheses. EBRD, *Transition Report 2009*.

[d] In 2007, as percent of GDP. 2003 data in parentheses. EBRD, *Transition Report 2009*.

[e] Ratio of domestic credit to private sector as percent of GDP, March 2007. EBRD, *Transition Report 2009*.

[f] Foreign currency–denominated credit to households as percent of total bank loans to households, 2008. 2003 data in parentheses. National Bank of Hungary, *Report on Financial Stability* (Budapest, April 2009), chart 2/17.

[g] In 2007, as percent of GDP. 2003 data in parentheses. EBRD, *Transition Report 2009*.

region's "backsliding," and been associated with either the changing impact of the EU after accession, or domestic factors such as the weak roots of democratic political culture, and the negative effects of neoliberal transformation strategies.[3]

Backsliding, however, has not been a uniform trend in the region. We need to look for a closer connection between regime type, particular social tensions, and the forms of political radicalization that emerged prior to the financial crisis. We must also pay attention to the capacities of mainstream political actors to cope with destabilizing tendencies. These capacities differ within each régime, and different abilities to accumulate political resources during prosperity have also had an impact on abilities to cope with the financial crisis.

Briefly, neoliberal regimes, which drew heavily on the rapid credit expansion associated with EU accession, suffered most from the drying up of international finance. Governments in these countries also faced particularly challenging policy choices, as existing institutions required painful adjustments that put high burdens on their populations. Neoliberal regimes, however, stayed the course, as their party systems were unable to generate policy alternatives. Whether the citizenry accepted or contested the adjustment strategies depended to a large extent on whether they trusted that their governments would make sure the burden was fairly shared, or at least be able to control the critical situation. Moreover, trust in government was based on the experience of the previous years.

While the Visegrád countries were also badly affected by the sudden withdrawal of international liquidity, their dependence on credit was overall lower than that of the Baltic countries. Export-dependent as they are, however, these economies suffered from the breakdown of their major markets. In addition, prior to 2008 the Visegrád states' populations had shown disenchantment with the existing social and political opportunities. Whether the authorities were able to appease the citizenry, and which institutional devices they used for that purpose, had an important bearing on the gravity of the crisis.

Finally, the internal diversity of the Southeastern European group manifested itself in the varied severity and forms of exposure to the crisis. Slovenia's main vulnerability lay in dependence on exports. It comes as no surprise that Bulgaria and Romania, having joined the neoliberal camp, experienced troubles reminiscent of those of Latvia or Lithuania. This was also the case for Croatia. As to the governments' political resources, Slovene neocorporatism's unique capacity for negotiated burden sharing was undermined

---

3. See, e.g., "Is East-Central Europe Backsliding?" special issue of *Journal of Democracy* 18, no. 4 (October 2007): 5–63; Cas Mudde, "EU Accession and a New Populist Center-Periphery Cleavage in Central and Eastern Europe," Central and Eastern Europe Working Paper 62 (Boston: Harvard University Minda de Gunzburg Center for European Studies, 2004); Grzymala-Busse and Innes, "Great Expectations"; Ost, *The Defeat of Solidarity*.

both before and after the crisis erupted, while other Southeastern European countries' ability to cope with hardship was still overcast by the long shadow of past state weakness.

Recession, Austerity, and No Alternatives: The Baltic States

All three Baltic states shared a development pattern that made them particularly vulnerable to the global financial crisis. Their impressive annual growth rates of about 9 percent in 2003–7 were almost entirely based on domestic demand, fueled by massive FDI in the banking, construction, and real estate sectors. High growth went hand in hand with high inflation and an appreciation of the real exchange rate. While this hampered export competitiveness, imports grew at an accelerating pace. As a consequence, current account balances deteriorated to a degree unprecedented in recent economic history. Especially after the mid-2000s, deficits could only be financed by an increasing inflow of risky short-term capital.[4]

What made the Baltic growth pattern particularly vulnerable was that it provided fertile ground for an accelerating credit boom. Until the end of the 1990s, the Baltic financial sectors had left firms and populations starved of credits. The rapid foreign takeover of banks, together with the liberalization of capital movements and the adoption of institutional and regulative standards of a sound financial system that were part of EU entry requirements, changed this and led to rapid credit expansion (table 6.1). The Swedish banks, for which the Baltic economic space provided a welcome opportunity to expand internationally, were primarily motivated by high returns on equity. They were actively involved in developing new market segments, and could also easily tap into sources of credit expansion via borrowing from their parent banks.[5] Thus, these banks were also the originators of mortgage lending in euros (see chapter 3, "Internationalization, European Integration and the Baltic Economic Miracle").

For governments it was difficult to control the credit boom. This was above all due to the fact that the EU governance of transnational banking left a number of loopholes and ambiguities of which banks could take advantage.[6] The Baltic governments were also, however, not very interested in

---

4. For a discussion of the Baltic states' vulnerability in a comparative perspective, see Becker and Jäger, "Development Trajectories."

5. See for the general role of foreign banks in creating the credit boom, e.g., Arcalean et al., "The Causes and Nature," 23–24; Pistor, "Into the Void"; and the literature on housing booms cited in chapter 3, note 95.

6. Pistor, "Into the Void"; Mohácsi Nagy, "Financial Market Governance"; Claus Puhr, Markus S. Schwaiger, and Michael Sigmund, "Direct Cross-Border Lending by Austrian Banks to Eastern Europe," in *Finanzmarktstabilitätsbericht* 17, (Vienna: Österreichische Nationalbank,

controlling the credit boom. As for most governments around the world that shared the Baltic group's preferences for liberalized markets, low taxation, and limited income redistribution, easy credit was the way to keep their voters contented with their socio-economic situation, especially in light of persisting or increasing inequalities. As Raghuram Rajan put it: "Politicians love to have banks expand housing credit, for credit achieves many goals at the same time. It pushes up house prices, making households feel wealthier, and allows them to finance more consumption. It creates more profits and jobs in the financial sector as well as in real estate brokerage and housing construction. And everything is safe—as safe as houses—at least for a while."[7]

From Nationalist Social Contracts to Privatized Keynesianism

In the Baltic states, the availability of cheap credit was an unexpected and welcome device to solve a problem that had been troubling them from the mid- to late 1990s onward, namely the waning capacity of the nationalist social contract to generate popular support for and legitimacy of the new order. While initially politicians could rely on the mobilizing potential of national identity as well as the demobilizing impact of minorities' social and political exclusion, and even put their welfare states in the service of nation-building and nationalizing projects, identity politics lost much of its appeal over the 1990s. At the same time, the social dislocations created by radical reforms and meager welfare states—widespread poverty, high unemployment, high and increasing inequality—increased the potential for social tensions. Although exclusion had an ethnic dimension to it as well, it crisscrossed ethnic lines.[8] As a consequence, the social question partly overlapped with and partly replaced the ethnic divide as the major issue Baltic governments had to confront.

In Latvia, already by the mid-1990s teachers and doctors started to go on strike for higher wages. Early in the new millennium, pensioners, farmers, and health care workers took to the streets.[9] Overall, support for the new system stayed very low. In Estonia, a spreading sense of dissatisfaction came into the open when a number of leading social scientists published a memorandum titled "Two Estonias" in 2001, which deplored the political, ethical,

---

2009), 109–29; Claudio E. V. Borio and Ilhyock Shim, "What Can (Macro-)prudential Policy Do to Support Monetary Policy?" BIS Working Paper 242 (Basel: BIS Monetary and Economic Department, 2007).

7. Raghuram G. Rajan, *Fault Lines: How Hidden Structures Still Threaten the World Economy* (Princeton: Princeton University Press, 2010), 31.

8. see, e.g., Aasland, "Citizenship, States and Social Exclusion."

9. Diāna Kalačinska, "Social Protest in Latvia 2006–2010: Political Disenchantment and Identity Formation" (M.A. thesis, Central European University, Budapest, Department of Political Science, 2010), 15; Smith-Sivertsen, "Latvia.", 100.

and social crisis in which the country found itself. It blamed the political elite for being uniquely concerned with the external image of the country, in this way becoming alienated from the problems of ordinary people and neglecting the most urgent social problems. It called for a new domestic agenda, which, parting with the sole priority of Westernization, would also take the issues of social inequality and poverty into account. At the same time, trust in government had decreased to the lowest level since independence, and the presidential elections in 2001 brought a candidate with a Communist past to power, whose victory was interpreted as a success of the "second Estonia."[10]

In Lithuania, a poll in 2004 revealed that 34 percent of respondents characterized the period of 1990–2004 as the most unfortunate in the country's history, more than the 30 percent that thought the same of the Soviet period. As in Estonia, intellectuals and political commentators have begun to speak of "two Lithuanias," "a westward-looking and economically vibrant Lithuania, celebrating its dynamism, and rejoicing over accession to the European Union and NATO, and an elite-abandoned, long-suffering, divided and depressed Lithuania, longing for something like the 'equality in misery' it knew in the Soviet Union." [11]

The popular discontent with the course these countries had taken also manifested itself in an increasing appeal of populist parties, and, in the case of Lithuania, the breakdown of what had looked like a relatively stable party system formed by two electoral blocs, as well as the rapid rise and demise of a president whose aggressive campaign targeted those citizens who had been left behind by market reforms.

As Kevin Deegan-Krause argues, the Baltic brand of populism—Latvia's New Era, Lithuania's New Union and Labor parties, and Estonia's Res Publica—can be described as purely antielite populism "focusing entirely on the need for 'new faces in government' as part of a major fight against corruption" and the abuse of power in office, rather than combining a populist agenda with specific political ideologies.[12] With the exception of the

---

10. Marju Lauristin, "Social Contradictions Shadowing Estonia's "Success Story," *Demokratizatsiya* (2003), http://findarticles.com/p/articles/mi_qa3996/is_200310/ai_n9310188/ (accessed August 6, 2010); Marju Lauristin and Peeter Vihalemm, "The Political Agenda during Different Periods of Estonian Transformation: External and Internal Factors," *Journal of Baltic Studies* 40, no. 1 (2009): 14.

11. Leonidas Donskis, "The Promise of Certainty, Safety and Security in an Uncertain, Unsafe and Insecure World: The Emergence of Lithuanian Populism," in *The Baltic States and their Region: New Europe or Old?* ed. David J. Smith (Amsterdam: Rodopi, 2005), 146.

12. Kevin Deegan-Krause, "Populism and the Logic of Party Rotation in Postcommunist Europe," in *Democracy and Populism in Central Europe: The Visegrad Elections and Their Aftermath,* ed. Martin Bútora, Oľga Gyárfášová, Grigorij Mesežnikov, and Thomas W. Skladony (Bratislava: Institute for Public Affairs, 2007), 152. For the Baltic cases, Deegan-Krause builds on André Sikk, Highways to Power: New Party Success in Three Young Democracies (University of Tartu: Doctoral Dissertation, 2006). See also Peter Ucen, "Parties, Populism, and Anti-Establishment Politics in East Central Europe," *SAIS Review* 27, no. 1 (Winter–Spring 2007): 49–62. For the

Lithuanian New Union, all of these parties were founded in the early 2000s and immediately upon making their first appearance, became the largest parties in parliament. Inevitably, while they owed much of their appeal to new faces and the promise of new and clean politics, once in power, their leaders tended to become as corrupt and unpopular as those of any other party. The mere fact, however, that these parties could get so much support shows that antielite sentiment—be it economic or political by origin—ran deep through the Baltic societies.

Against this background, privatized Keynesianism—overwhelming reliance on private credit to secure income and employment—offered the Baltic governments an institutional device that allowed them to address social discontent while also being compatible with their market-radical orientation. In all three Baltic countries, aggressively expanding banks colluded with governments to set off housing booms that many times exceeded those of neighboring countries east and west.[13] These booms, combined with rapid wage growth and newly acquired exit opportunities, contributed greatly to easing existing social tensions, as they provided even lower strata with rising income, better employment opportunities, and new consumption possibilities. Inequality, however, stayed very high in the Baltic states, and in Latvia it even increased over the 2000s.

Arguably, therefore, Albert Hirschman's famous "tunnel effect" might have an explanatory power in the Baltic cases. As is well known, the tunnel effect explains the tolerance of societies for high and rising inequality by the fact that those left behind actually take comfort from others' good fortune, because this gives them hope that their turn will come in due course. At first glance, the Baltic social climate does not seem to be favorable to widespread "gratification over advances of others."[14] For acquiring dominance, such perceptions require the ability on part of temporary losers to identify with the winners. Yet, Hirschman argues, such empathy ought to be in short supply in ethnically, religiously, and regionally segmented societies. A number of factors, however, might have contributed to making the tunnel effect work.

First, by the time of EU accession a measure of social integration across ethnic lines was underway—witness the region-wide decline in public perceptions of Russian-speaking minorities as security threats (table 6.2). Due to high growth and increased opportunities for labor mobility, ethnic

---

absence of ideological populist parties see Daunis Auers and Andres Kasekamp, "Explaining the Electoral Failure of Extreme-Right Parties in Estonia and Latvia," *Contemporary European Studies*, 17, no. 2 (2009): 241–54.

13. For a more detailed discussion of the Baltic housing boom, see chapter 3, "Internationalization, European Integration, and the Baltic Economic Miracle."

14. Albert O. Hirschman, "The Changing Tolerance for Income Inequality in the Course of Economic Development," in his *Essays in Trespassing: Economics to Politics and Beyond* (Cambridge: Cambridge University Press, 1981), 40.

minorities also got increasingly better integrated into labor markets.[15] This created a new source of tolerance for temporary income disparities, since it weakened the perception that economic advance was merely due to ethnicity, language, or religion—rather than, for example, hard work, merit, or luck. The sluggish but ongoing extension of citizenship rights most likely had similar effects. Second, rapid growth may have made the tolerance for inequality easier because "economic change and the concomitant physical transformation of the country and its cities are more apparent, so that the expectation or possibility of improvement is persuasively communicated to various groups and individuals."[16]

As a combined result of these developments, the Baltic societies appear to have accommodated the growth-propelled "inequalities in an almost providential fashion,"[17] although the persistent disparities also contributed to the parallel spread of political apathy (attested by the drastic decline of participation in elections) and mass exit, for example through emigration. All in all, then, the combination of rapid consumer growth extending into the lower echelons of society, the tunnel effect, and enhanced exit opportunities underpinned a period of relative political stability in the Baltic states which, as we argue below, in the case of Estonia was also backed by trust in political institutions.

With the benefit of hindsight, the Baltic economic miracles of the 2000s appear as a market-based version of the kind of illusion fostered fifty years earlier by Juan Perón in his advice to Carlos Ibáñez, then president of Chile: "My dear friend: Give to the people…all that is possible. When it seems to you that already you are giving too much, give them more. You will see the results. Everyone will try to scare you with the specter of an economic collapse. But all of this is a lie. There is nothing more elastic than the economy which everyone fears so much because no one understands it."[18]

---

15. See, e.g., Mihails Hazans, "Ethnic Minorities in the Latvian Labour Market, 1997–2009: Outcomes, Integration Drivers and Barriers," in *How Integrated is Latvian Society? An Audit of Achievements,* ed. Nils Muiznieks (Riga: University of Latvia Press, 2010), 125–58. This is not to deny that in Estonia and Latvia ethnic tensions remained a major factor of social life, leading at times to violence. Both countries had their new "calendar demonstrations" organized on days of special significance for the ethnic communities, such as May 9 (the Soviet Victory Day) and March 16 (the Latvian Legionnaires Day). What is more, Estonia's first large-scale ethnic riots—triggered in 2007 by the relocation of the "Bronze Soldier" monument to Red Army soldiers killed in World War II—have revealed how precarious ethnic integration has been. Our point is merely that, overall, the credit and housing booms allowed a better life for all ethnic groups, thereby mitigating ethnic tensions. For an overview of the shifting significance of identity in Estonia, see, e.g., Martin Ehala, "The Bronze Soldier: Identity Threat and Maintenance in Estonia," *Journal of Baltic Studies* 40, no. 1 (2009): 139–58.

16. Albert O. Hirschman, "The Turn to Authoritarianism in Latin America and the Search for Its Economic Determinants," in *Essays in Trespassing,* 130.

17. Hirschman, "The Changing Tolerance," 40.

18. Quoted in Hirschman, "The Turn to Authoritarianism," 102.

TABLE 6.2
Sources of political stability and capacity for crisis management, mid- and late 2000s

Country	Fear of ethnic minorities[a]	Rate of unemployment[b]	Turnout at elections[c]	Trust in parliament[d]	Trust in government[e]
Estonia	6 (60)	4.7 (10.0)	50.8	30–	52 (66)
Latvia	8 (44)	6.1 (10.6)	50.2	10–	13 (34)
Lithuania	2 (40)	4.3 (12.4)	47.3	10	19 (29)
Bulgaria	25 (46)	6.9 (13.7)	55.8	10–	22 (21)
Romania	15 (60)	6.1 (6.7)	39.2	20	24 (34)
Czech Republic	32 (44)	5.3 (7.8)	64.5	10+	26 (29)
Hungary	13 (26)	7.4 (5.9)	64.4	20–	18 (35)
Poland	10 (35)	8.5 (19.3)	47.2	10	21 (17)
Slovak Republic	27 (53)	11.0 (17.4)	54.7	20+	41 (19)
Croatia	16 (57)	9.7 (14.4)	60.6	15	19 (20)
Slovenia	12 (14)	4.7 (6.7)	61.9	20+	34 (29)

[a] "Do you think national minorities pose a big threat, some threat, little threat, or no threat to peace and security in this society?" Percent answering "big threat" and "some threat," in 2004. 1992 data in parentheses. Rose, "Diverging Paths," 31.
[b] Percent in 2007. 2003 data in parentheses. EBRD, *Transition Report 2009*.
[c] Turnout at national parliamentary elections in 2003–8; for Romania, turnout in 2008; for Estonia and Lavia, percent of voting-age population. IDEA Database, http://www.idea.int/vt/country_cfm? (accessed February 5, 2011).
[d] "How much trust do you have in certain institutions?" Percent of answers "complete or some trust," in 2006. *Life in Transition: A Survey of People's Experiences and Attitudes* (London: EBRD, 2008).
[e] "I would like to ask you a question about how much trust you have in certain institutions. For each of the following institutions, please tell me if you tend to trust it or tend not to trust it." Average trust in national government in 2007–9. Average 2003–6 data in parentheses. Eurobarometer Surveys. http://ec.europa.eu/public_opinion/index_en.htm (several release dates).

The difference from Perón's advice is that in the Baltic cases it was not "old guard" populists but neoliberal political strategists and their external allies who embraced the idea that "there is nothing more elastic than the economy." Warnings about an imminent collapse were largely absent.[19] Importantly, European institutions also failed to take seriously the fact that macroeconomic imbalances may result in crash landings. This negligence was not due to lack of attention. As the Baltic states set their eyes on rapid eurozone entry, they stayed under close European scrutiny. Estonia and Lithuania were included in the ERM II right after EU accession, and Latvia followed in 2005.

Subsequently all three countries saw their hopes for early euro adoption shattered because they were unable to keep inflation in line with the euro entry target. Lithuania had a particularly painful experience, as its government believed that it had a realistic chance for introducing the euro. The country's inflation rate compared favorably with those of its Baltic neighbors and was only marginally higher than the euro reference value. The European Commission, however, had second thoughts about admitting a poor,

---

19. When such warnings were raised, they were ignored. The Latvian premier's defense of full-throttle growth despite warnings he received from economists is a case in point.

fast-growing, and inflation-prone country. When the EC rejected Lithuania's bid, it was also sending a strong signal to the whole region that it had no intention whatsoever of bending the rules even the tiniest bit.

The EC's decision triggered a controversy over the adequacy of the Maastricht criteria for fast-growing catching-up economies. It also did not go unnoticed that the EU was applying a double standard: whereas some old member states had been allowed to enter the eurozone despite the fact that their governments were cooking the books, new member states had to endure with much less tolerance. But none of these debates went to the core of what was going wrong in the Baltic states. While the benefits and drawbacks of inflation were being discussed, these economies could build up asset bubbles and unsustainable current account deficits right under the EU's scrutinizing eyes. It was the IMF that published one of the first critical analyses of the growing imbalances associated with the Baltic growth model.[20]

In the wake of the global financial crisis, the bubble eventually burst, leading to an extraordinary economic decline. In 2009, the peak year of the crisis, Estonia's GDP decreased by 16 percent, Lithuania's by 15 percent, and Latvia's by 19 percent. Industrial production contracted by 28, 16, and 15 percent, respectively. Unemployment soared, reaching between 14 and 18 percent.[21] The Baltic states thus experienced the sharpest reversal of fortune in the whole of Europe. What is more, they also faced particularly challenging policy choices. For countries that had all but lost their industrial base, exporting their way out of crisis was very difficult. Pegged currencies added to the problems. At the same time, the crisis made virtually impossible the pursuit of any strategy that was structurally dependent on capital and goods imports.

Trust and Mistrust in the Baltic Model

In light of this, perhaps the most striking feature of the Baltic states' coping strategies is that they did not generate any alternative to neoliberalism and its core institutions. While most of Western Europe initially responded to the crisis by fiscal expansion, from the beginning all three Baltic states embarked upon internal devaluation notwithstanding the extremely high costs, which, according to a *Financial Times* editorial, were not "belt-tightening but amputation."[22] Invariably, their adjustment packages involved huge public

20. "Republic of Latvia: Selected Issues," IMF Country Report 06/354, http://www.imf.org/external/pubs/cat/longres.cfm?sk = 19984.0 (accessed February 20, 2009).

21. Eurostat data referring to the third quarter 2009, on a year-on-year basis, http://epp.eurostat.ec.europa.eu/tgm/table.do?tab = table&init = 1&plugin = 1&language = en&pcode = tsieb020 (accessed October 23, 2010).

22. "Estonia Shows the Euro is Not Doomed Project," *Financial Times,* May 13, 2010. For an excellent discussion of the adjustment programs in the Baltic states and their consequences for labor markets and inequality see Jaan Masso and Kerly Krillo, "Mixed Adjustment

sector wage cuts and layoffs, further retrenchment of welfare programs, and only limited tax increases.

Within a single year, Estonia cut its public sector expenses by the equivalent of more than 9 percent of its GDP. This determination to belt-tighten to the point of amputation paid off: in May 2010, the EC ruled that the country now qualified to join the eurozone. Lithuania's and Latvia's austerity efforts are also motivated by their prevailing desire to introduce the euro as soon as possible, and are of a similar magnitude to that of Estonia. A comparison is useful to highlight just how unusually burdensome the Baltic austerity packages are: among the harshest Western European packages, that unveiled by David Cameron's Conservative–Liberal Democrat coalition in the U.K. in 2010 foresaw slashing public expenditures by an equivalent of 8 percent of GDP over five years. The Baltic states have done more in a single year.[23]

The draconian adjustment programs were closely linked to the Baltic states' determination not to let go of their currency peg. An episode in the negotiations between Latvia and the IMF sheds light on some interesting details. Among all Baltic countries Latvia was the hardest-hit by the crisis. In autumn 2008, both its banking system and its currency peg came under strong pressure. While the Swedish-owned banks could still rely on lending from their parent institutions, investors lost confidence in the domestically owned Parex Bank, which soon encountered serious liquidity problems. The government's injection of liquidity into the bank and its partial takeover failed to restore confidence. Simultaneously, the Bank of Latvia was forced to strongly intervene in order to defend its currency peg, which caused a heavy drain on the country's foreign reserves.

In December 2008, the Latvian government turned to the IMF to get support for its ailing economy. In the negotiations, initially the IMF delegation was open to a widening of the lats corridor. The government, however, would not budge on the question of the peg, but rather accepted an adjustment program that is tough even by IMF standards. IMF Managing Director Dominique Strauss-Kahn said as much: "It is centered on the authorities' objective of maintaining the current exchange rate peg, recognizing that this calls for extraordinarily strong domestic policies, with the support of a broad political and social consensus."[24]

Forms and Inequality Effects in Estonia, Latvia, and Lithuania," in *Inequalities in the World of Work: The Effects of the Crisis,* ed. Daniel Vaughan-Whitehead (Geneva: International Labour Office, 2011), 35–94.

23. Andrew Ward, "Baltic Trio Shows How Fiscal Medicine Tastes," *Financial Times,* June 24, 2010; Chris Bryant, "Daunted by Deficits," ibid., June 23, 2010.

24. Strauss-Kahn quoted in Edward Hugh, "Why the IMF's Decision to Agree a Latvian Bailout Programme without Devaluation Is a Mistake," posted December 22, 2008, http://www.rgemonitor.com/euro-monitor/254854/why_the_imfs_decision_to_agree_a_latvian_bailout_programme_without_devaluation_is_a_mistake (accessed January 23, 2009). On the initial IMF position see Nina Kolyako, "IMF Initially Demanded Widening Lat Peg Corridor," *Baltic Course,* January 13, 2009.

There is something puzzling here. Why is it that after the spectacular failure of a development model, governments in the Baltic states stuck to the very same ideas that underpinned this model? And why were they so adamant in defending their specific institutions, which made the pain of adjustment so much harder? For an explanation, we have to take a closer look at political and economic factors in the domestic and international arenas.

On the domestic side, the Baltic party systems are not well suited to bringing about alternative solutions to economic problems. On the one hand, talking about "systems" seems to be itself misleading, "in that to speak of a system of parties is to ascribe some degree of stability and predictability to the interactions between the parties concerned."[25] A party landscape characterized by politicians who refuse to show a minimum of loyalty to their organizations, where parties are constantly split, fused, rebuilt, and newly invented, and in the most extreme case elections are won by parties that were not even around at the time of the previous elections, cannot be conducive to the emergence of programmatic alternatives. On the other hand, because of the close connection of economic liberalism and nation and state building, parties with left-wing ideologies are in short supply or cannot make it to the government, as is the case in Latvia.

If political competition is not the way to generate alternatives to the dominant economic paradigm, it has also to be added that there has been little popular pressure to change course. In this respect, Estonia is the most striking example. Unparalleled in Europe, there has been no single protest event following the austerity packages. What is more, the Estonian public also continued to have a high level of trust in its government throughout the crisis (table 6.2). Thus, even if the Estonian population started to judge its economic situation much less favorably than before the crisis, it did not take issue with its government on how the situation was to be handled.

In this respect, Latvia and Lithuania differed. In both countries, partly violent antigovernment protests erupted. Though the protests were triggered by the austerity cuts, they were part of a broader frustration with unresponsive and corrupt governments that had accumulated for some time. This is particularly the case in Latvia, where the anticorruption efforts undertaken in the wake of the EU accession revealed the high-level collusion between political parties and oligarchs who grew rich on finance, oil, and transport. In many cases parties were simply a vehicle to promote the oligarchs' interests.[26]

---

25. Mair, *Party System Change,* 175. On the issue of unconsolidated party systems in the Baltic states, see Evald Mikkel, "Patterns of Party Formation in Estonia: Consolidation Unaccomplished"; Artis Pabriks and Aiga Stokenberga, "Political Parties and the Party System in Latvia"; and Aine Ramonaite, "The Development of the Lithuanian Party System: From Stability to Perturbation," chaps. 2 to 4 in *Post-Communist EU Member States: Parties and Party Systems,* ed. Susanne Jungerstam-Mulders (Aldershot: Ashgate, 2006). See, however, Kreuzer and Pettai, "Patterns of Political Instability," for an account of the systemic features of instability.

26. For this and the following, see Kalačinska, "Social Protest in Latvia"; Iveta Kažoka and Akule Dace, "Latvia: Extreme Political Turbulence," European Policy Institutes Network, Commentary No. 3 (February 2009); Rasma Kārkliņa , "Latvia: A Model of Political Integrity?"

These revelations, and legal procedures against some of the oligarchs, started to undermine public trust in government right after EU accession. They also triggered a backlash by the oligarchs and their political allies. The most controversial moves on the part of the latter included an initiative to change a number of laws regulating access to information on national security investigations, and the attempted and finally successful removal of the head of the anticorruption agency. Both events led to protests, demonstrations, and a number of legal appeals. The "umbrella revolution" of 2007 forced Premier Aigars Kalvītis's government to resign. Building on this success, Latvian protestors staged a second, so-called "Penguin Revolution" in January 2009, which brought about the downfall of Ivars Godmanis's government.[27]

What this sequence of events suggests is, that in Latvia (and arguably in Lithuania as well) at the base of societal discontent has been frustration with the fact that politicians abused their power in the narrow interests of a few, and could not be held accountable. In this respect, one of the major first moves of crisis management—the quasi-secretive takeover of the troubled Parex Bank—only confirmed established patterns, as it once more demonstrated the close interconnectedness of oligarchs and the political class. It also did not help matters that the government pushed its first austerity package through parliament virtually without debate.

Another sign of the "them versus us" divide was the call for a rebellion against the "fat cat" officials, which a hacker hoped to unleash by accessing millions of tax records to expose state salaries. Lavish remuneration of central bankers of more than thirty thousand euros per month did not sit well with a population that was asked to huddle together like penguins. There was also a growing frustration with successive governments' sheer incompetence in economic and social matters, as demonstrated for instance by Finance Minister Atis Slakteris, who in an interview with Bloomberg Television in 2007 described the situation of Latvia's economy as "nothing special."

Thus, while socio-economic grievances triggered the Penguin Revolution, what was really at its core was the unaccountability and incompetence of the whole ruling class. It was this class, rather than a specific economic model, that was held responsible for the economic crisis. Consequently, while the

---

in *Latvija 2020*, ed. Žaneta Ozoliņa and Inga Ulnicāne-Ozoliņa (Riga: LU Akademiskais Apgads, 2008). For an early account of the relation between oligarchs and parties see Marja Nissinen, *Latvia's Transition to a Market Economy: Political Determinants of Economic Reform Policy* (New York: St. Martin's Press, 1999). A particular feature made the Latvian party system especially prone to business penetration. There is no direct form of state funding for political parties, and substantial restrictions on party income and expenditures are largely absent.

27. While the term umbrella revolution simply refers to the rainy weather at the time of demonstrations, the Penguin Revolution got its cue from Prime Minister Godmanis who in his New Year's Eve address of 2008 suggested his people to learn from the penguins of Antarctica, which huddle up close to each other during the winter frost.

protestors were concerned with their economic situation, they mostly wanted to oust the government.

All in all, domestic politics goes some way in explaining why alternatives to drastic austerity and existing institutions were not being generated. But international actors played a major role too. Whereas the IMF suggested that Latvia widen its currency band, both the EC and the Swedish government took a different stance on the matter, and communicated this to all three Baltic countries. The Swedes came to the defense of their heavily exposed banks for which devaluation would have been very bad news. In turn, the EC allegedly opposed the IMF because the latter also urged it to prepare a fast-track EMU entry for Latvia.[28]

Largely due to the crisis of the eurozone, the EU's determination to play by the rules of the Maastricht criteria has, if at all possible, strengthened. One question left unanswered by the EU as well as by the Baltic determination to belt-tighten their way out of crisis is, how to restore growth and competitiveness and avoid social disintegration in countries that have lived for so long on housing bubbles.

Semicore Specialization, Polarized Democracy, and Austerity: The Visegrád Model in Peril

Given the Visegrád group's reliance for growth on complex-manufacturing export industries and the lesser role than in the Baltics of credit- and mortgage-based growth of domestic markets, financialization here typically did not reach critical dimensions. It was, therefore, mostly the breakdown of their export markets that drove Hungary, the Czech Republic, and Slovakia into recessions. Furthermore, a too hard landing of the Visegrád countries has to date been prevented by the relatively quick recovery of German industrial production.

Another vulnerability of the Visegrád countries, namely their relatively weak capacity to keep their public finances under control, has, however, attracted attention. As the crisis of the eurozone has brought about a new age of austerity, all members of the EU are constantly being scrutinized for the state of their public finances—and macroeconomic coordination, and in particular controlling the expenses of welfare states, has long been the Achilles

---

28. Becker and Jäger, "Development Trajectories"; Hugh, "Why the IMF's Decision"; IMF, "Republic of Latvia: Selected Issues," 10. Christoph Rosenberg, who led the IMF mission to Latvia, denied that there were differences between the stances of the IMF and the other donors on the issues of the peg and eurozone accession. Yet a number of newspaper articles around the time of negotiations pointed to such divisions. See, e.g., "Latvian PM Rules Out Currency Devaluation," http://www.eubusiness.com/news-eu/1238067121.77/ (accessed January 9, 2009); Kolyako, "IMF Initially Demanded."

heel of the Visegrád countries' development. How far and at what political cost the related problems could be resolved before 2008 has had a strong impact on the challenge each country is facing.

In this respect, Hungary stands out. Whereas Slovakia, Poland, and the Czech Republic could all rein in their budget deficits and public debt during the 2000s, in Hungary both spiraled out of control, turning the country into a hot spot of the global financial crisis and leading to political destabilization as well. What has made Hungary so exceptional among its peers?

Difficulties of Responsible Government

Governments in the Visegrád countries have faced a basic dilemma. On the one hand, they have relied on welfarist social contracts to appease vocal groups, and more generally to secure legitimacy for the new system. On the other hand, maintaining welfare state generosity resulted in recurring macroeconomic imbalances, provoked passive and increasingly also active resistance among those who financed the social security system, and put governments at loggerheads with European actors who kept pressuring the new EU member states to adhere to the Maastricht criteria.

More than in the other East Central European states, therefore, governments in the Visegrád countries have been exposed to what Peter Mair has termed a growing tension between responsive and responsible government.[29] According to Mair, recently there has been a widening of the traditional gap between responsive government, which is concerned with voters and public opinion, and responsible government, which follows legal procedures, rules, and conventions, and stands by its international obligations. There are a number of reasons for this.

First, it is increasingly difficult for governments to read public opinion and aggregate interests, as parties have decreased their engagement with civil society, and mass electoral opinion has become more fragmented. Second, governments find themselves increasingly constrained by a plethora of institutions and agencies. Globalization and Europeanization have played a major role in this, as governments are now accountable to a wide range of principals, many entirely outside of their control. Third, governments are trapped by policy legacies, namely the accumulating effects of previous policies and commitments that narrow their room for new decisions. Finally, with the rapid decline of party membership, parties have all but lost their control over the electorate.

---

29. Peter Mair, "Representative versus Responsible Government," MPIfG Working Paper 09/8 (Cologne: Max-Planck-Institut für Gesellschaftsforschung, 2009).

Previously, it was easier to bridge the (narrower) gap between responsible and responsive government by appeals to partisan loyalty, but this is no longer the case. A fragmented and disenchanted electorate is therefore up for grabs in every new election. Against this background, Mair also sees the bifurcation of many party systems between "mainstream" parties and a new form of opposition. On the one hand, the former stress their governing capacity and vocation, and get elected on this base. On the other hand, new parties emerge that do not want to govern but claim to represent, often using populist rhetoric. These "irresponsible or semi-responsible" opposition parties challenge government from outside.

Albeit devised for the West European context, Mair's dichotomy is helpful for our inquiry, especially as some of the developments he observes appear even more acute in the Visegrád democracies. Party systems all over East Central Europe were born with a "hollow core," that is, with a pervasive weakness of the popular component. The electorate is even more fragmented and volatile than in the West. Since it has never really been structured by durable cleavages, public opinion is more difficult to read, let alone aggregate. If responsible government increasingly involves an acceptance that institutions and actors beyond the nation-state are tying elected leaders' hands, then responsible governments in the East find their hands even more tightly bound than their counterparts in the West, because of EU conditionality and their own economic dependency.

Policy legacies—the accumulation of fiscal commitments that significantly narrow the space for policy autonomy and innovation—are important for the Visegrád countries as well, although they play out differently than in the West. While social programs in the region are more amenable to change, and debt service is less of a strain on budgets (with the exception of Hungary), lower capacities to raise taxes and the pressure on state revenues generated by competition over FDI put similar limits on the Visegrád countries' "fiscal democracy" to those encountered in the West.[30]

The bifurcation of "mainstream" and "irresponsible" parties, however, has not been characteristic for the Visegrád countries. Here, illiberal and populist parties move easily in and out of government, and mainstream parties are very likely to act irresponsibly when in opposition, partly to fend off their illiberal competitors, and partly to challenge parties in government. Under these conditions, responsible government does not pay off. Instead, governing parties are often tempted to maintain popularity at the expense of responsibility. While all four Visegrád countries have faced the challenges of reconciling the requirements of responsive and responsible government,

30. For the operationalization of policy legacies and fiscal democracy see Wolfgang Streeck and Daniel Mertens, "An Index of Fiscal Democracy" MPIfG Working Paper 10/3 (Cologne: Max-Planck-Institut für Gesellschaftsforschung, 2010).

and some degree of political destabilization has occurred everywhere, only in Hungary did it develop into an outright political crisis.

Political and Economic Instability

What set Hungary apart? Two developments there have combined to make the gap between responsive and responsible government particularly wide and difficult to bridge. On the one hand, Hungary showed multiple symptoms of economic malaise already long before the global crisis broke out. Alone in East Central Europe, the economy's annual average growth rate dropped after EU accession, not least because of the MNB's high interest rate policies, which were detrimental to domestic growth and export competitiveness alike.

Sluggish growth in turn put a heavier burden on the state, especially because in line with the welfarist contract, public social expenditures continued to increase over the first years of the new millennium, contributing significantly to massive fiscal overspending and ballooning debt. In addition, not only did several left-liberal governments maintain large welfare programs, but they also relied on privately issued loans and mortgages to allow the middle classes consumption well beyond their incomes.

On the other hand, the highly polarized party system and cutthroat party competition greatly impaired governments' capacities to react in a responsible way. Instead, there was a "politics of outbidding," where each political camp attempted to defeat its rival by promising better deals to the electorate. Once in government, parties could therefore hardly afford to turn away from earlier campaign promises. Polarization and fierce rivalry also implied that as a rule the opposition refused to overtly or even tacitly support reformist government initiatives. As a result, successive governments were unable and unwilling to cope with the deterioration of public finances. In particular, the government of Premier Péter Medgyessy and the first Gyurcsány cabinet backtracked from planned reforms of health care, pensions, and public administration, with dire consequences for the country's macroeconomic balances.

The moment of truth came when, reelected after yet another round of the politics of outbidding in the 2006 election campaign, Premier Gyurcsány admitted that the good times were over. He announced a draconian austerity package, combining existing with new taxes and fiscal expenditure cuts, with a new EMU convergence program that foresaw comprehensive structural reforms of the public administration, education, health care, and pensions. As a result, the government's popularity instantly plummeted. The loss of support did not stop there.

From September 2006, when the premier's (in)famous "lie speech" was leaked, the government had to face enduring massive protest from the opposition coupled with recurrent violent riots, organized by radical right-wing groups, never seen before in the new Hungarian democracy. Increasing radicalization gave also rise to a far-right newcomer to the Hungarian party landscape. The signs of a grave political crisis notwithstanding, this time the socialist-liberal coalition government was determined in its reform drive. Thus, the Socialist Party downsized its engagement with civil society by severing its remaining ties to the trade unions, turned a blind eye to an unprecedented drop in voters' support, and ignored popular protest. It tied its fate increasingly to a narrow circle of domestic and transnational actors eager to continue harsh economic reforms.

With the Socialists finally trying to correct for their earlier irresponsible economic policies, the main opposition party FIDESZ moved into the zone of responsiveness. It increasingly spearheaded popular dissatisfaction and protest. Continuously criticizing the left-liberals' austerity drive, thus joining forces with all those groups that bitterly contested the high social costs, FIDESZ at the same time refrained from spelling out any credible alternative.

It could also bank on a growing frustration among the Hungarian middle class whose members felt that their ascent was blocked by "a number of obstacles, rigidities, and discriminatory practices," and thus that "in spite of all their efforts and achievements, they are not really 'making it.' "[31] Long years of sluggish growth, high taxation and limited employment opportunities dampened the hopes of many to catch up with the living standards of the West. Even if the credit and mortgage boom tamed such frustrations, the opposition's nationalist and anticommunist rhetoric fell on fertile grounds. Blaming foreign capitalists and former communist "oligarchs" for blocking the upward mobility of many others acquired credibility in a situation where the state strategy was geared toward attracting foreign rather than supporting local capital, and ex–Communist Party members turned into billionaires could occupy leading state positions.

For some, however, FIDESZ opposition did not go far enough. Ever since the European Parliament elections in June 2009, the breakthrough of a far-right newcomer to the Hungarian party landscape, the Movement for a Better Hungary (Jobbik), has sent shock waves through the country's political establishment. Not only is Jobbik unapologetic about attacking those forces that allegedly have ruined the country from the top—Communists and Jews—but it also vehemently targets those who eat up the state's resources from the bottom: the Roma. Targeting these "welfare parasites," and rushing to protect the "true Hungarians" against "Gypsy" crime resonates particularly well in much of Hungary's countryside, where employment opportunities are scarce, salaries low, and poverty persistent.

When the global financial crisis struck, Hungary's economy and political life were thus in a state of disarray. Despite efforts at austerity, the country

31. Hirschman, "The Changing Tolerance," 46.

still fought against a twin fiscal and current account deficit, largely the result of past irresponsible government. Appeasing the middle classes by turning a blind eye to their rapidly rising foreign currency debts, the left-liberal coalitions magnified Hungary's exposure. Unsurprisingly, political polarization and grave instability did not enhance external actors' confidence in the country's capacity to stay course.

These accumulated problems turned Hungary into one of the prime East European victims of the global crisis in October 2008: its currency and stock markets plunged, and foreign finance dried up. In order to escape bankruptcy, stem savage speculative attacks against the currency, restore confidence in the forint, and ease the credit crunch, the country had to rely on a coordinated rescue package crafted by the IMF and the EU. The conditions attached to the bailout package prescribed yet another hefty dose of austerity.

The crisis has posed a formidable challenge to Hungarian democracy. The requirements for responsible government go well beyond what society is ready to accept. The devastating defeat of the Socialist and liberal parties in the spring 2010 elections bears witness to that. Premier Viktor Orbán's new government has decided to cut through the dilemmas of responsiveness and responsibility by giving up on both.

While the government's increasing determination to pursue a radical neoliberal agenda should in principle please markets and major EU actors, the fact that it combines this with policies of strengthening national against foreign capitalists, and implements these measures in ways oftentimes barely reconcilable with democratic principles, undermines the government's international reputation. As the government is resolved to terminate the welfarist social contract of the past, its efforts at dismantling all the checks and balances of the democratic system may prove even more important for cementing its power than its parallel attempts to appeal to the electorate with a strong dose of nationalism.[32]

Whereas a long prehistory of economic and political instability has made Hungary especially crisis-prone, the other Visegrád countries could escape such a dire fate. Poland and Slovakia had also had their moments of political turbulence and populist backlash against governments that tried to tackle macroeconomic imbalances and problems of the welfare state, but the dust had mostly settled by the time the global crisis hit.

---

32. Hungary's radical reforms encompass flat taxes, radical welfare state retrenchment, and peculiar workfare programs. Democratic principles have been curtailed by the modification of the electoral law in favor of incumbents; far-reaching changes in the constitution; legal restrictions on the Constitutional Court's authority; and curtailment of media freedom and purging from media, and other public bodies of critical or merely independent-minded members. The measures aimed to mobilize identity-based support include a new law offering citizenship to Hungarian minorities in neighboring countries; economic nationalist policies targeting foreign banks and foreign-owned monopolies; and welfare state retrenchment, which affects the Roma minority disproportionately.

On the one hand, economic rebalancing had occurred earlier in both countries than in Hungary, making their economies less vulnerable. On the other hand, less consolidated party systems and the formation of ideologically heterogeneous coalitions made it difficult even for illiberal parties in office to act irresponsibly for too long, as such coalitions tended to be less durable. Finally, the Czech Republic faced the mildest problems. After the bank bailouts of the late 1990s were digested, government finances were kept largely in order. This was greatly helped by a fairly consolidated and not excessively polarized party system, and by the remarkable absence of irresponsibility—be it in government or opposition.

The Polish "postaccession crisis,"[33] manifest in the dramatic electoral defeat of the postcommunist successor party SLD and the formation of a nationalist-populist government coalition in 2005, anticipated in some ways the political turbulence that was to occur in Hungary a few years later. Similar to the first and second Gyurcsány administrations in Hungary, successive SLD-PSL coalition governments had tried uneasily and ultimately unsuccessfully to maneuver between the need for fiscal retrenchment and welfare reforms, as required by the preparation for EMU entry, and the need to take account of popular hostility toward such measures (see chapter 4, "Contesting the Euro"). The resulting conflicts were aggravated by a series of severe corruption scandals. As a result, SLD disintegrated rapidly, lost its majority in parliament, and could prolong its life in office only by forming a caretaker government. For the Polish Socialists, the 2005 elections "became more a struggle for parliamentary survival than a serious contest to win."[34] Their electoral defeat was even more devastating than that of Hungarian Socialists in 2010.

As in Hungary, a right-wing nationalist party skillfully moved into the Polish political space vacated by the Socialists and liberals. Framing the electoral choice as one between "liberalism," which allegedly had put Poland on the pathway toward corruption and misery from the early transformation onwards, and "solidarity," the Law and Justice Party (PiS) scored a surprise victory not only against the Left, but also against its moderate right-liberal competitor Civic Platform (PO).[35]

It is here that the parallels with Hungarian developments end. Instead of a comfortable two-thirds majority, PiS had only 27 percent of votes cast (and, due to very low turnout, the support of less than 11 percent of eligible

33. It was Attila Ágh who coined the term postaccession crisis. See his "Instability and Extremism in the New Member States: A General View and the Hungarian Case," paper presented at the workshop "Political Turbulences in Central Europe: Symptoms of a Post-Accession Crisis?" Friedrich-Ebert-Stiftung. Budapest, January 25–27, 2007.

34. Radosław Markowski, "The Polish Elections of 2005: Pure Chaos or a Restructuring of the Party System?" *West European Politics* 29, no. 4 (September 2006): 824.

35. PiS's candidate the late Lech Kaczynski also won the presidential elections held on the same day.

voters). It was not strong enough to form a government on its own, and instead had to rely on two, respectively left- and right-wing populist and xenophobic parties, Self Defense (SRP) and the League of Polish Families (LPR). Not only had PiS scored its victory due to irresponsible opposition, but by aligning with SPR and LPR, it took irresponsibility right into the government.[36] Henceforth, governing was dominated by the efforts of PiS to suffocate its junior partners by hijacking and implementing their programs. In consequence, the government combined aggressive foreign policies geared toward remedying historical grievances with an antidemocratic and antipluralistic domestic platform combined with a prolabor and pro–social policy stance.[37]

The aspiration of PiS for dominance on the entire right of the party spectrum culminated in its call for early elections in 2007. As is well known, this step backfired: although the elections brought PiS more votes, it lost its coalition partners in the process. At the same time, PO increased its support massively, and formed a coalition government with the Peasant Party (PSL). It is interesting to note that PO did not challenge the prolabor and pro–social policy agenda of its predecessor, and also made clear promises to public sector workers and the poorer strata.

As Radosław Markowski observed, "all electorates of relevant Polish parties show leftist, socially sensitive socio-economic attitudes and policy preferences."[38] Like in Hungary during the first half of the 2000s, parties competed over socio-cultural issues and policy style rather than over economic questions. As the Hungarian example shows, however, the fate of governments depended strongly on whether they could deliver on their socio-economic promises. In this respect, the PO-PSL government acted under much more favorable conditions than the second Gyurcsány government or the contemporary FIDESZ one did. Poland's EU accession was accompanied by fast-accelerating economic growth and declining unemployment. Unemployment also decreased because of massive emigration. In addition, EU funds greatly helped improve the situation of the Polish peasantry.

For these reasons Poland was in a much better situation than Hungary when the global crisis hit. Due to faster growth and a larger domestic market, its economy was in a relatively solid shape.[39] Despite the almost uninterrupted

36. According to Markowski, in the run-up to the 2005 elections, "PiS underwent a spectacular change from a fairly typical conservative party with noticeable though weak nationalist and populist leanings, into a radical nationalist, and visibly populist-socialist one." Markowski, "The Polish Elections of 2005," 820.

37. Guglielmo Meardi, "More Voice after More Exit? Unstable Industrial Relations in Central Eastern Europe," *Industrial Relations Journal* 38, no. 6 (2008): 510.

38. Radosław Markowski, "The 2007 Polish Parliamentary Election: Some Structuring, Still a Lot of Chaos," *West European Politics* 31, no. 5 (September 2008): 1065.

39. Becker and Jäger, "Development Trajectories"; Joachim Becker, "Osteuropa—das neue Argentinien? Der halbierte Kontinent in der Wirtschaftskrise," *Blätter für Deutsche und internationale Politik* 6 (2009): 97–105.

dominance of the welfarist social contract, its public finances were largely in order. Poland also experienced slower credit growth than many of its peers. The government had attempted to impose tight lending standards on mortgages prior to the crisis, which, albeit not entirely successful, had slowed the growth of mortgage lending. Finally, interest rate and currency developments put Poland in an advantageous position too.

During the crisis the Polish government used its room for maneuver to implement some countercyclical measures.[40] In addition, the Monetary Council consistently pursued a policy of monetary easing. By resorting to an IMF-granted flexible credit line, the Polish government also sent reassuring signals to the markets that a larger deficit resulting from fiscal stimulus would not derail the economy. Poland's recovery was moreover helped by a sharp devaluation of the zloty at the onset of the crisis. While all of this has allowed Poland to weather the storms of the global financial crisis more easily than most of its peers, the government has since faced challenges stemming from increased budget deficits and public debt. It may be that the gap between responsible and responsive government, which Premier Donald Tusk's government was for some time able to bridge successfully, will open wide again.

In Slovakia, popular dissatisfaction with neoliberal policies swept the left-populist Smer to power in 2006, which formed a coalition government with the radical anti-Hungarian and anti-Roma SNS and the remnants of Vladimír Mečiar's HZDS. Although Premier Robert Fico had promised to reverse most of the reforms previously enacted by Mikuláš Dzurinda's government, he finally left most of them untouched, or corrected them only at the margins. The major difference with its predecessor was that the Fico government actively sought the collaboration of trade unions. This paved the way for coordinated policymaking, which helped dismantle the last barriers not only to Slovakia's entry to the eurozone, but also to crisis management.[41]

The Fico government's unexpectedly responsible policy course was greatly helped by the fact that the country's distributional struggles had been largely resolved by the time it assumed power—even if, as the food riot of 2004 indicated, the outcome was very costly for the Roma. Indeed, after 2006, the Slovak economy started to expand at a rate that came close to the stellar Baltic figures without, however, significantly increasing foreign debt or social disparities. The fiscal and social policy legacies of the Dzurinda

40. See, also for the following, e.g. Becker and Jäger, "Development Trajectories"; "Republic of Poland: Staff Report for the 2010 Article IV Consultation," IMF Country Report No 10/118 (2010), http://www.imf.org/external/pubs/ft/scr/2010/cr10118.pdf (accessed September 1, 2010).

41. Dorothee Bohle and Béla Greskovits, "Slovakia and Hungary: Successful and Failed EMU Entry without Social Pacts," in Pochet, Keune, and Natali, *After the Euro*, 345–69; Lajos Héthy, "Tripartite Answers to the Economic Downturn in Central and Eastern Europe: Social Dialogue and the Crisis—the Situation in Central and Eastern Europe," paper prepared for the conference "Negotiating out of the Crisis," Turin, November 25–27, 2009 (Turin: International Training Center of the ILO, 2009).

government as well as the period of high growth based on a successful export drive made the country initially less vulnerable to the global financial crisis. The challenge for the government came when the country's major export markets broke down, forcing its economy into a recession. The Fico government maneuvered its way out of crisis with a moderate fiscal stimulus, automatic stabilizers, a coordinated policy approach, and the support of the recovering export markets. On the downside, unemployment rose rapidly and stayed high.[42]

Throughout the crisis, Premier Fico remained popular. His popularity was also boosted by the fact that he entered a cultural bidding war with his radical populist coalition partners on the issue of whose party was more representative of Slovak national identity and interests in domestic and international arenas. Frequent conflicts with the split ethnic Hungarian parties of Slovakia, and recurrent skirmishes with the Hungarian government, offered ideal terrains for Fico to win all the battles—and thereby sow the seeds of losing the war. Similar to the Polish PiS in 2007, Smer performed very well in the summer 2010 parliamentary elections. However, as the support for SNS plummeted and HZDS was practically swept from the political arena, it was the incoherent and fragmented opposition that formed the new government. Fico, leader of the Visegrád group's hitherto most trusted government, was forced into opposition.

The return to power of economic neoliberalism under the new Slovak Premier Iveta Radičová indicates that, as in Poland, there is a possibility for a renewed cycle of fiscal retrenchment and liberal reform that is likely to clash with popular demands for social safety and security, thus opening the terrain for new political turmoil.

The Czech Republic was unique among its Visegrád peers in that it escaped their political troubles during the first decade of the 2000s. More generally, if politics in Hungary, Poland, and Slovakia often tended to be high voltage, this was less the case in the Czech Republic.

The contrast is sharpest with Hungary. True, the Czech Republic has the second most consolidated party system after Hungary, characterized by decreasing fragmentation and bipolar party competition.[43] However, there are two important differences. First, Czech parties compete on socio-economic issues, and are thus better prepared for representing societal groups than is the case in Hungary, where party rivalry has few such underpinnings.[44]

---

42. "Slovak Republic: 2010 Article IV Consultation—Staff Report; and Public Information Notice on the Executive Board Discussion, International Monetary Fund Country Report No. 10/290 (2010), http://www.imf.org/external/pubs/ft/scr/2010/cr10290.pdf (accessed October11, 2010); Héthy, "Tripartite Answers."

43. See, e.g., Petr Kopecký, "The Rise of the Power Monopoly: Political Parties in the Czech Republic," in Jungerstam-Mulders, *Post-Communist EU Member States,* 125–45.

44. Ibid., 128–29. See also Kitschelt et al., *Post-Communist Party Systems;* 309–17; Geoffrey Evans and Stephen Whitefield, "The Structuring of Political Cleavages in Post-Communist

Second, whereas the Hungarian electoral system has contributed to sharp party polarization by producing strong governments, the Czech proportional system tends to produce weak and often minority governments. This has encouraged cooperation among elites of opposing camps, something unthinkable in Hungary where not only is party competition exceptionally bitter but, as noted by Zsolt Enyedi, polarization is taken to the extreme by "politicians of the government parties [who] regard the members of the opposition (and vice versa) not as colleagues, but as enemies, whose complete eradication from the public sphere is an unlikely, but worth-trying project."[45]

The weakness of governments, and the checks and balances institutionalized by the Czech party system also prevented radical liberal reforms of the type introduced by the second Dzurinda government in Slovakia.[46] Even Czech center-right governments tended to take a gradual rather than radical approach to reforms, and could afford gradualism thanks to the country's balanced economic situation. Relatively high growth rates made it easier for governments to continue running a generous welfare state while reducing taxes and keeping public finances in order. This also allowed the Czech National Bank to keep interest rates below those of the euro area. Largely as a consequence, the trap of private borrowing in foreign currency could be avoided. Conservative bank lending policies also contributed to limited credit growth. When the economy started to suffer from the breakdown of export markets, a decrease in FDI, and the credit crunch, the government reacted with modest fiscal stimulus, which was reinforced by the central bank's policy of monetary easing.

Crisis and its management, however, led to an increase of the public deficit and debt, which became a major issue during the May 2010 elections. Against the background of the Greek and eurozone crises and the excessive deficit procedure launched against the Czech Republic by the EU, the Czech Social Democrats' campaign promise of increasing welfare expenditure proved to be controversial. Although the party emerged strongest from the election, its overall electoral support (22 percent of the vote) was unimpressive. Since the Social Democrats also lacked suitable coalition partners, a three-party formation of the Center-Right could assume power.

All these parties had campaigned on the necessity of spending cuts and cracking down on "welfare state abuse." What is more, two of the governing

---

Societies: the Case of the Czech Republic and Slovakia," *Political Studies* 46, no. 1 (1998): 115–39. If our argument is correct, then recent developments question to some extent Frye's argument about the perils of polarized democracies (see his *Building States and Markets*). He argues that party polarization around socio-economic issues hinders economic reforms. In contrast, we find the Czech party competition over socio-economic issues served the country well, whereas Hungary's competition over everything other than socio-economic issues was a major obstacle to reforms.

45. Zsolt Enyedi, "Party System Concentration in Hungary," in Jungerstam-Mulders, *Post-Communist EU Member States*, 191.

46. O'Dwyer and Kovalcik, "And the Last Shall Be First."

parties are newcomers to the Czech political landscape. Campaigning on an antiestablishment, anticorruption and pro-austerity ticket, Public Affairs (VV) and Tradition Responsibility Prosperity 09 (TOP 09) could unexpectedly gain 10 and 17 percent of the vote, respectively. The rise of antiestablishment parties with a bent for radical neoliberalism may signal turbulent times ahead in Czech politics.

All in all, then, the major challenge for governments in the Visegrád countries does not stem from the global crisis directly, but rather from the need to adjust to the emerging postcrisis context of "permanent austerity." While all governments have taken up the cause, past experience casts some doubt on whether a significant downsizing of the welfarist contract can be achieved without alienating an important part of the population and the risk of dire political consequences.

The Crisis, Neocorporatism, and Weak States: Southeastern Europe

The vulnerabilities of Southeastern European economies were to a large extent akin to those of the Visegrád and Baltic economies. After 2008, Slovenia suffered from receding demand for its complex-manufacturing export products, which raised new concerns about industrial competitiveness. Slovenia is, however, harder hit than most of its Visegrád's peers, as the crisis also spilled over to its banking sector. Meanwhile, Bulgaria, Romania, and to some degree also Croatia exhibited many symptoms of the "Baltic disease": their current account balances were in peril, and their financialized development paths proved unsustainable under conditions of evaporating international liquidity. At the same time, the latter countries' overall weak industrial bases have limited their ability to combat recession by enhanced export performance.

As far as political capacities for crisis management are concerned, it must be borne in mind that as with the Visegrád group, Southeastern Europe did not escape political turbulence prior to the crisis. However, the center of gravity of conflicts in Southeastern Europe lay in their peculiar governance patterns that distinguish them from the Visegrád and Baltic states alike. Concretely, the Slovenian political struggles centered directly on the neocorporatist (rather than partisan) structures of regime coordination, while the political instability of Bulgaria, Romania, and Croatia is a manifestation of their weak states.

Eroding Slovenia's Neocorporatism

Like the Visegrád countries, and especially the Czech and Slovak Republics, Slovenia entered a recession in 2009 that was directly related to the breakdown of its export markets. In addition, its banking sector became highly exposed. A new wave of privatization through MEBOs had led to a rapid growth of bank loans to the private sector, that were concentrated in sectors strongly affected by the crisis. Due to these sectors' reliance on foreign, mostly short-term finance, Slovenian banks were confronted with a significant deterioration in credit quality.[47] The center-left coalition government under Borut Pahor, which took office just as the crisis started to hit the country, faced difficult challenges. What is more, the government could rely much less on democratic corporatism than its predecessors. On the one hand, the center-left hegemony of the 1990s had given way during the 2000s to more polarized political competition. On the other hand, neocorporatism has started to show signs of exhaustion.

In Slovenian politics, a new era of heightened political contestation and civil strife was heralded by the 2004 parliamentary elections, which led to the formation of a center-right coalition government dominated by the Slovenian Democratic Party (SDS). As Danica Fink-Hafner points out, this was a turning point in Slovenian politics. In the 1990s the "competition between the two ideological clusters was not perceived as a zero sum game," but rather targeted not yet mobilized or unrepresented voters; by 2004, however, the "newly established centre-right parties consolidated sufficiently and fully learned the rules of the political game in achieving governmental majority," and thus were able to overcome the center-left hegemony.[48] Even so, ideological competition stayed within the center, and was not affected by the political radicalization observed in the Visegrád countries. For example, euroskeptical and radical populist parties had only limited influence in Slovenia.

However, the swing of the ideological pendulum brought a neoliberal breakthrough in transformation strategy. Janez Janša's administration initiated sweeping reforms of the tax system, labor market, and welfare state and pushed for completing privatization. All these measures were fiercely contested by trade unions, as they threatened to alter the balance of power between capital and labor, and the government had to partly backtrack on them. Yet the abolition of mandatory membership in the Chamber of Commerce and Industry in 2006 meant a formidable challenge to neocorporatism.[49]

According to Miroslav Stanojević, the right-wing government's assault on major ingredients of the Slovene model coincided with broader tendencies

47. EBRD, *Transition Report 2009*, 224.

48. Danica Fink-Hafner, "Slovenia: Between Bipolarity and Broad Coalition Building," in Jungerstam-Mulders, *Post-Communist EU Member States*, 223.

49. On the neoliberal reforms and their impact on corporatism, see Stanojević, "Social Pacts," and Miroslav Stanojević, "The Europeanisation of Slovenian Corporatism," paper presented at the Industrial Relations in Europe Conference, Oslo, September 8, 2010; Igor Guardiancich, "The Uncertain Future of Slovenian Exceptionalism," *East European Politics and Societies*, online publication, July 29, 2011, doi: 10.1177/0888325411415518.

of the erosion of neocorporatism, which are reminiscent of similar processes of gradual but transformative change toward a more liberal system of industrial relations observed in West European coordinated market economies.[50] Specifically, accelerating privatization, transnationalization, and the change from mandatory to voluntary membership in peak associations have shifted the priorities of Slovenian business. The massive loss of members had a radicalizing impact on the Chamber of Commerce, which started to take much tougher positions in negotiations with labor.[51] Increasing pressures for competitiveness have also brought about a differentiation of policy preferences among employers in sheltered and exposed sectors. Especially the employers in "high road" export-oriented sectors, which relied on flexible quality production, saw neocorporatism as a straightjacket, and turned instead to individual firm-based industrial relations.

In addition, organized labor also underwent processes of collapsing membership and preference fragmentation. This was partly due to structural causes. For instance, the adoption of flexible production methods created an army of workers in precarious employment and undermined the traditional networks and solidarities of valley communities of the Alpine foothills on which, in Stanojević's view, Slovenian corporatism originally thrived. Partly, the significant decline of union density might have been the result of the social pacts that multiplied in the run-up to Slovenia's EMU entry. The series of pacts on incomes, employment, and public sector reform inevitably led to tensions between union leadership and their rank and file's demands for higher wages and safer employment. Labor's exit from responsible unions, the eruption of wildcat strikes, and the rise of militant labor organizations have been some of the consequences.[52]

All in all, then, upon the advent of the global crisis political competition in Slovenia showed stronger polarization than before, while neocorporatism's capacity to coordinate responses to the crisis weakened. As a consequence, responses to the crisis were overshadowed by contentious politics, such as massive strikes and harsh employer reactions, which threatened to further undermine the capacity of the Slovenian polity for coordination.

The period of stress for Slovenian corporatism is not over. As almost everywhere in East Central Europe, the public sector deficit has significantly increased due to the crisis and its management, and the government is now hard-pressed to find an exit strategy from its various fiscal stimulus

50. Stanojević, "Europeanisation." For the concept of gradual transformative change, see Wolfgang Streeck and Kathleen Thelen, eds., *Beyond Continuity: Institutional Change in Advanced Capitalist Economies* (Oxford: Oxford University Press, 2005); and for the erosion of the German corporatism Streeck, *Reforming Capitalism*.

51. Stanojević, "Europeanisation," 11–14.

52. Ibid, 4, 13–15.

measures.[53] In addition, it plans to tackle structural reforms above all in the pension and health care systems. In Stanojević's' assessment, future policy responses will remain coordinated in some form. But instead of fully fledged neocorporatism, Slovenia is likely to see social pacts among much weakened and/or less committed partners: trade unions with decimated membership, less disciplined employers, and an embattled government.

The Long Shadow of State Weakness: Bulgaria, Romania, and Croatia

After the shocks of the mid- to late 1990s and in the course of European integration, Bulgaria and Romania joined East Central Europe's neoliberal regime family populated originally by the Baltic states. Before the crisis, most comparative studies tended to overemphasize the differences and disregard the similarities between the modified Southeastern European and the seemingly very successful Baltic paths, but the global crisis showed that there existed a "Baltic-Balkan group" with important shared attributes.[54] Features of precrisis trajectories, specific vulnerabilities, policy and political responses to financial instability and recession, and obstacles to sustained recovery can all be counted among the aspects in which in recent years the development of Bulgaria and Romania has mirrored the Baltic experiences.

In a similar vein, Croatia's growth path over the 2000s was reminiscent of the Baltic one, notwithstanding the fact that its industrial structure, welfare state, size of public sector, and labor relations made it similar to the Visegrád group's embedded neoliberalism. Its precrisis growth relied almost entirely on domestic consumption, with the construction sector taking the lead. The bulk of FDI went into finance and trade. Foreign-owned banks with privileged access to cross-border borrowing fueled rapid credit growth, most of which financed service activities. Croatia's monetary policy was traditionally geared toward maintaining a stable kuna exchange rate, which was conducive to euro financialization. Thus, Croatia's foreign exchange liabilities were comparable to those of the Baltic states and Bulgaria (table 6.1).[55]

---

53. Slovenian stimulus measures were the most generous in the whole region. As a consequence, the government deficit widened from 1.7 percent of GDP in 2008 to 5.5 percent in 2009. IMF, "Slovenia—2010 Staff Visit Mission Concluding Statement," http://www.imf.org/external/np/ms/2010/061110.htm (accessed October 10, 2010); Republic of Slovenia, "Slovenian exit strategy 2010–2013," http://www.vlada.si/fileadmin/dokumenti/si/projekti/Protikrizni_ukrepi/izhod_iz_krize/SI_exit_strategy.pdf (accessed October 11, 2010); Hermine Vidovic, "Slovenia: Catching Up Slowly," *wiiw Monthly Report*, no. 10 (2010): 21–23.

54. Torbjörn Becker, Daniel Daianu, Zsolt Darvas, Vladimir Gligorov, Michael Landesmann, Pavle Petrovic, Jean Pisani-Ferry, Dariusz Rosati, André Sapir, and Beatrice Weder di Mauro, "Whither Growth in Central and Eastern Europe? Policy Lessons for an Integrated Europe," Bruegel Blueprint 11 (Brussels: Bruegel Institute, 2010), 1.

55. "Republic of Croatia: 2010 Article IV Consultation," IMF Country Report No. 10/179, June 2010, http://www.imf.org/external/pubs/ft/scr/2010/cr10179.pdf (accessed October 10, 2010).

In spite of these similarities with the Baltic states, one important difference is apparent. While the former were much harder-hit by the crisis than any of their peers including the Southeastern European countries, they have also tackled the challenges of the crisis head on, no matter the costs for their societies. Indeed, their determination has earned them international acclaim, and pundits have advertised the Baltic way of handling the crisis as the model for Europe's southern periphery to follow. In contrast, governments in all three Southeastern European countries have been drifting and inconsequential in their policy responses, and have been frequently challenged by massive protest waves. In this way, governments themselves have contributed to prolonging the crisis.

Thus the Bulgarian Borisov administration first responded to the recession with an austerity package that according to critics amounted to a gross mishandling of the crisis. Not only was the austerity program unnecessary painful, but it also missed its target. The package trapped the economy "in a largely self-inflicted vicious circle of an economic downswing and a swelling fiscal imbalance."[56] Further, the administration shied away from proposing any coherent and realistic long-term exit strategy, but simply put all its hopes on a fast euro entry. Such hopes were much less realistic than in the case of the Baltic states given that the country had not even joined ERM II.[57]

In the end, even austerity failed. Faced with evaporating popular support, the government abandoned fiscal stringency, put on hold all further structural reforms, and did little to curb the growth of wages, which by far outpaced productivity. Nevertheless, while wages and salaries kept rising, domestic demand continued to be on the decline, indicating a sharp drop in consumers' and investors' confidence.[58]

Romania was even harder-pressed than Bulgaria to respond in a determined fashion to the crisis. While in the latter country the currency board and prudent fiscal policies had kept the budget balanced, the Romanian authorities had significantly raised public sector employment and pensions prior to the crisis, both of which measures weighed heavily on public expenditures. Romania's multiple macroeconomic imbalances left the country more vulnerable than Bulgaria. In spring 2009, pressed by the rapid deterioration of the country's external financing position and the fragility of the national currency, the newly elected prime minister of the Liberal Democratic Party government, Emil Boc, had to turn to the IMF for assistance. The resulting standby loan agreement was conditional on harsh adjustment measures. Despite the IMF's preference for a mixture of tax increases and expenditure cuts, the Boc government was reluctant to raise the income tax, and opted

---

56. Anton Mihailov, "Bulgaria: In the Trap of Macroeconomic Mismanagement," *wiiw Country Analyses and Forecasts*, no 6 (July 2010): 63, 65.

57. Ibid.

58. Ibid., 64.

instead for doing it the hard way. The premier proposed drastic cuts in public sector wages and pensions.[59]

Romanian political actors responded with resistance. The Constitutional Court judged the pension cuts unconstitutional, and the opposition parties staged petitions and frequently repeated (albeit failed) no-confidence votes against the minority government. There was massive labor and general popular protest as well. At the same time, Romania's dismal macroeconomic indicators and dependence on IMF emergency loans soon put an end to hopes for a fast adoption of the euro. All in all, successive Romanian governments have had to act in an atmosphere of political disaffection, mistrust, and social protest, and have shown little skill in maneuvering through the crisis.

The Romanian and Bulgarian policy responses to the crisis were similar in yet another respect. In their attempts at fiscal consolidation, both countries shied away from or failed to implement measures that would have required sophisticated administrative and political skills. Thus, Romanian policymakers have been reluctant to raise low personal income taxes or carefully target fiscal expenditure cuts. Similarly in Bulgaria, while "a skillful restructuring of revenue and, especially, spending in times of crisis can in principle produce a robust countercyclical effect…it is in this territory that the government produced a series of blunders."[60] That both governments failed to invest sufficient time and administrative effort in adequate policy design seems to confirm that a lack of state capacity to propose and implement sustainable policy strategies continues to plague these countries.

Of all the Southeast European countries, it is Croatia that has faced the most peculiar mix of challenges.[61] The country's growth path by the second half of the 2000s was reminiscent of that of the Baltic states, the existence of major complex industries notwithstanding. The overvalued exchange rate and Croatia's wage setting, which prioritized the sheltered over the exposed sector, can account for this. During the 2000s, public sector salaries grew rapidly, pulling private sector wages along. A laggard in privatization, Croatia also did not attract large amounts of FDI to its manufacturing sector.

At the same time, however, the fate of Croatia's complex industries is illustrative of the country's significant divergence from the neoliberal model. Like most of the Visegrád countries, but for a longer period than, for instance, the Czech and Slovak Republics, Croatia cherished the idea of national capitalism, and rejected fast privatization in order to keep many of its economy's commanding heights in the hands of the domestic elite. In particular, the shipbuilding industry, which—accounting for 15 percent

59. Joan Hoey, "Romania's Austerity Package and Public Finances after the Crisis," Economist Intelligence Unit, http://rbd.doingbusiness.ro/en/2/general-economic-trends/1/361/romanias-austerity-package-and-public-finances-after-the-crisis (accessed March 11, 2010).

60. Mihailov, "Bulgaria," 64.

61. Our assessment of the Croatian crisis builds on Vojmir Franičević, "Croatia: Prolonged Crisis with an Uncertain Ending," in Vaughan-Whitehead, *Inequalities,* 139–208.

of total exports and employing around 11,500 people—in the late 2000s still constitutes the core of the country's complex manufacturing, has been kept afloat by state assistance, protectionism, and lavish subsidies.[62] Moreover, Croatia's generous but pathological welfare state sets the country apart from the neoliberal model as well. Overall, the state continues to assume a much more important role in the economy than in the neoliberal cluster. Consequently, when it comes to public debt, Croatia falls closer to the Visegrád group.

In addition to its peculiar socio-economic mix, Croatia is unique for its belated approach to the EU. It was only in 2005 that the EU opened accession negotiations with the country, and the most difficult areas—competition policy and judiciary reform—were still ahead when the global financial crisis broke out. Therefore, it is not the gravity of the recession alone that has made crisis management a difficult task for successive Croatian governments, but rather the multiplicity of challenges and the problem overload resulting from its late development and delayed Europeanization.

Consequently, euro financialization is forcing the country down the path of internal devaluation in order to restore competitiveness. The related pressures on public sector employment and wages are being reinforced by the need to control the public debt and deficit. The EU has added fuel to the fire by insisting that subsidies to the shipbuilding industry be downsized. EU conditionality has been extended to at least three more areas considered as very sensitive: cooperation with the International Criminal Tribunal for the Former Yugoslavia, settlement of a territorial dispute with Slovenia, and the fight against corruption.

As with the political situation in its Southeastern European peers, Croatia's ruling HDZ has contributed to the crisis rather than coming up with a solution. Intensifying anticorruption investigations have led to a number of high-profile arrests that revealed how deeply leading HDZ officials were involved in illegal practices. The fallout from corruption kept the ruling party busier than that from the economic crisis. For long HDZ simply ignored that there was a crisis at all. It took Prime Minister Ivo Sanader's resignation from office in July 2009 for his successor Jadranka Kosor to tackle the country's economic problems in a more determined fashion. It was not before the spring of 2010 that under the pressures of declining output, surging unemployment, and public finances spiraling out of control, an economic recovery program was at last presented.[63] The Kosor government's advance on this agenda has been far from convincing.

---

62. *EIU Country Report Croatia September 2009* http://www.eiu.com/report_dl.asp?issue_id=1484828933&mode=pdf (accessed December 12, 2010); Dragicevic, "The Political Economy of Shipbuilding."

63. Zoran Daskalović, "Die Bilanz der Regierung Kosor," *Blickpunkt Kroatien* (Friedrich-Ebert-Stiftung), no. 10 (August 2010), 1; *EIU Country Report Croatia*, nos. 6–10, (2010),

In December 2009, voters' disaffection with corruption scandals, their deteriorating social conditions, and what is seen as the government's belated and inadequate response to the crisis swept a Socialist president to power. Ever since, tensions between President Ivo Josipović and the government over economic matters have been on the rise.[64] The country has also seen severe tensions between the administration and trade unions. There have been conflicts over public sector salaries, privatization of shipyards, and a new labor code.[65] Widespread popular dissatisfaction, intraparty fights, and upcoming parliamentary elections have all led the government to backtrack from some of its crisis management plans.

In sum, Croatia's capacity to combat the economic crisis is not particularly convincing. After its predecessor's denial of the very fact of crisis, it took the Kosor government another ten months to come up with an encompassing recovery program, and even this belated plan is being derailed by fierce opposition from several quarters. When it comes to socioeconomic issues, the Croatian government seems to be no less trapped between responsiveness and responsibility than its counterparts in the Visegrád group. In contrast to Poland, Slovakia, and Czech Republic, and as with Hungary, the severity of this trap impairs the country's capacity to respond to the crisis.

Responsible Government or the Specter of Ungovernability

As we have shown throughout, crises have been an integral part of the postsocialist regimes' foundation and further development. The transformational recession of the early 1990s was crucial for the coming about of the initial reform strategies. It was instrumental in forging an elite consensus on the need for radical solutions in the Baltic states, and justified the Visegrád reformers' efforts to compensate selected socio-economic groups for the costs of transformation. In Bulgaria, Romania, and Croatia, social dislocation gave impetus to labor's initial militancy and political influence, and in Slovenia it paved the way for the lasting hegemony of political forces ready for cooperation with social partners.

The crises of the second half of the 1990s partly reinforced and partly corrected these initial choices. In the Baltic countries the hard times caused by the Russian crisis strengthened elite preferences for market radicalism,

---

http://www.eiu.com/index.asp?layout=displayIssue&publication_id=1210000921   (accessed December 12, 2010).

64. *EIU Country Report Croatia*, March 2010, http://www.eiu.com/report_dl.asp?issue_id=425289027&mode=pdf (accessed December 12, 2010).

65. Tihomir Ponoš, "Der Aufstand der Gewerkschaften," *Blickpunkt Kroatien*, (Friedrich-Ebert-Stiftung) no. 10 (August 2010); *EIU Country Report Croatia*, nos. 6–10 (2010).

notwithstanding the social costs. In Bulgaria and Romania macroeconomic destabilization after the originally half-hearted reforms eventually led to a neoliberal breakthrough. Several Visegrád countries experienced the limits of the national capitalist paths they initially embarked upon, and shifted to foreign-led development strategies.

Twenty years after embarking on rough but so far passable paths toward capitalism and democracy, East Central Europe has again been put to a dire test. The global financial crisis was delayed in spreading to the region, but once it struck, its impact was severe. During 2008–10, with the exception of Poland all economies went through steep recessions. In more than half of the countries, the very models on which the economic miracles of the 2000s relied turned into developmental traps. It is small wonder then, that some observers came to the conclusion that seen from the vantage point of the Great Recession, "the whole process of transformation appeared to be a failure."[66]

More recently, however, East Central Europe has also been admired for its remarkable capacity to cope with the repercussions of the Great Recession. While the crisis has had a deep impact, in many countries recovery has come fast. This stands in contrast to the countries in the northwestern and Mediterranean peripheries of the EU, where the specter of sovereign default has loomed large. Already in early 2010 the *Economist* contended that "the continent's biggest financial upheaval is in Iceland...and the biggest forecast budget deficits in the European Union next year will not be in some basket-cases from the ex-communist 'east' but in Britain and in Greece,...None of the ten 'eastern' countries that joined the EU is in so bad a mess."[67]

In a similar vein, in a recent book Anders Aslund praises the region for its responsible politics in the face of the crisis. In his interpretation, East Central European governments have engaged in virtuous policies of heroic fiscal reform and limited state interference, and have been by and large supported by voters who placed concern for the long-term perspectives of their countries above their narrow short-term interests. Parliamentary fragmentation was an alleged asset too, as it allowed for flexible policy responses.[68]

In light of the still unfolding crisis it is too early to tell whether it is the depth of recession, the remarkable capacity for adaptation, or unexpected new developments in global financial markets or the EU that will eventually determine the region's future trajectory. The theoretical perspective developed in this book generally suggests that present economic performance indicators are both too narrow and too volatile to support reliable judgments

---

66. Jens Hölscher, "Twenty Years of Economic Transition: Successes and Failures," *Journal of Comparative Economic Studies* 5 (December 2009): 10.
67. "Eastern Europe: Wrongly Labelled," *Economist*, January 9, 2010, 27.
68. Anders Aslund, *The Last Shall Be the First: The East European Financial Crisis, 2008–2010* (Washington, D.C.: Petersen Institute for International Economics, 2010).

on the success versus vulnerability of capitalism and its varieties. Our yardstick of success as defined at the outset measures the capacity of the political system to combine over time market efficiency and social protection in viable ways, and to exploit the varied potentials of neocorporatist, pure, and embedded neoliberal capitalisms to provide economic freedom, social cohesion, and political liberty.

Any postcrisis settlement, therefore, will have to be assessed by focusing on the reconfigured overall balance among social integration, marketization, and democracy—especially given that, in Polanyi's words, "Improvements,...are, as a rule, bought at the price of social dislocation. If the rate of dislocation is too great, the community must succumb in the process."[69]

This chapter has shown that the global crisis—while far from fully undermining the viability of East Central Europe's capitalist regimes—has already contributed to unsettling previously established balances and social contracts, and sometimes dangerously so. Four developments stand out. First, in all regimes the balance is shifting toward a stronger dose of markets and a lesser degree of social protection. The attempted new settlement shows particularly worrisome features in pure neoliberal regimes, where the impact of the global recession has reached the population almost unmitigated, threatening these societies with even less cohesion than they had before.

Second, whatever meager means for economic and social protection remain, governments tend to redistribute them in a highly unequal manner. Their motives reflect regime-specific and country-specific mixtures of electoral considerations and generational, ethnic, and antipoor biases—all intensified by the hard times. Not infrequently, resources crucial to mitigating poverty and inequality go instead to better-off social and economic groups in ways that, as James Kurth long ago observed in the different context of Third World development, may even lead to reverse forms of income redistribution from poorer to wealthier households and from labor and small businesses to corporate giants.[70]

It is also true that where governments try to put at least a part of adjustment burden on the large financial, commercial, and manufacturing firms that gained the most from the mismanaged consumption boom, as is the case in Hungary, they face the danger of retaliation in the form of these firms' raising prices, withholding planned investments, and shedding labor force.

Third, it is noteworthy that all regimes have suffered loss of capacity to prevent social disintegration. The rise of popular protest, lack of trust in public authority, and frequent government turnovers have weakened the political sphere so crucial for holding capitalist societies together. As a consequence,

---

69. Polanyi, *The Great Transformation*, 76.
70. James Kurth, "The Political Consequences of the Product Cycle: Industrial History and Political Outcomes," *International Organization* 33 (Winter 1979): 1–34.

the specter of ungovernability is haunting a number of countries in all the regimes. The political troubles do not end here. Across East Central Europe, radicalizing political forces and desperate constituencies alike seem ready to scapegoat their rivals and neighbors on ethnic, class, or other grounds, or at least to stand by without much protest while others do the dirty work, even if punishing those allegedly responsible for the new avalanche of social suffering comes at the cost of impaired democracy.

In at least one case democratic breakdown has become a real option. Ironically it is in Hungary, formerly the region's front-runner in democratic and party system consolidation as well as in welfarism and foreign-led re-industrialization, that embedded neoliberal capitalism and democracy now face the greatest danger of being dismantled. That this process could advance so far and fast in that country is a warning signal for other states within the region and outside of it. It should also give pause to those observers who seem to be enamored of the region's "responsible" politics of handling the crisis. What is being praised today as responsibility for the market economy can easily turn out to be colossal irresponsibility in terms of the future prospects of capitalist democracy.

All this implies that the region is likely to be confronting the postcrisis environment against the background of significantly weakened institutional foundations and capabilities. A fourth development adds to this: the exhaustion of the institutional solutions each regime had earlier found to mitigate the tensions inherent in capitalist democracies. Identity politics in the Baltic states, welfarism in the Visegrád countries, and neocorporatism in Slovenia have all shown signs of erosion. During the 2000s, the abundance of transnational capital flows and the capacity-building efforts of the EU sufficed partly to prolong the life of these institutions, and partly to provide market-based substitutes. The novel context of global austerity has put an end to this, and innovative new solutions to the problem of reconciling markets and democracy seem to be in short supply.

Conclusion

Postsocialist Capitalism Twenty Years On

Two decades ago Valerie Bunce suggested that East Europeanists take seriously the fact that "while post-communism can be defined by where it is heading (or, more to the point, might be heading), it must also be defined by its point of departure: that is, by state socialism and its collapse."[1] She also stressed that the systemic change was "under-determined" and might lead to varied and surprising outcomes. This book responds, as it were, to these important early suggestions with new insights into the intricate relationships between socialism and the emerging capitalism. Concretely, we see our contribution in theorizing the patterned diversity of the new order; in analyzing domestic legacies, choices, and external risks and opportunities that have kept in motion the process of regime formation; and in highlighting the systemic factors of fragility of even the few postsocialist success stories.

Here we will develop some of our key themes a step further, reflect on alternative explanations, and specify our position in old and new debates of broader theoretical interest. We revisit the issues of legacies, initial choices, and repressed alternatives; compatibilities and trade-offs among market, welfare, democracy, and identity; the virtues and vices of international integration; and the processes of convergence and divergence in the capitalist world. Finally, we point to the relevance of our framework for other cases, summarize its conceptual implications, and tie all of this together by evaluating the merits and limits of Polanyi-inspired accounts of the ongoing transformation of the global political economy.

1. Bunce, "Leaving Socialism," 36.

Legacies, Initial Choices, and Repressed Alternatives

The main focus of the book is the phenomenon of capitalist diversity after socialism. This diversity can be seen as surprising, given the widely shared view that the socialist system was remarkably successful in forcing uniform structures and institutions on its integral parts. How could so variegated a socioeconomic architecture have been built on and with socialism's allegedly uniform "ruins?"[2]

Our answer is based on the idea that in setting their countries on the road toward capitalist democracy, politicians were confronted with a host of ambiguous legacies. Incomplete nation and state building, encompassing but paternalistic welfare states, and socialist industrialization that created an army of skilled and experienced but inefficiently employed workers: all of this left transformative actors with a number of liabilities to cope with and a fair amount of assets to build upon. Which legacies were to be interpreted as assets or threats was, however, by no means predetermined. Rather, the impact of socialist and presocialist pasts on postsocialist futures also depended on how reformers perceived the assets and threats from the viewpoint of attractive or at least feasible political agendas.

Thus, reform elites in the Baltic states urged the citizenry to rally around the flag of idealized visions of their interwar nations, states, and economic institutions. Conversely, the Soviet legacies were presented as dangerous obstacles to the most important task the reformers set themselves. Soviet industry and the ethnic composition of its workforce, and the inherited welfare state including the in-kind contributions of enterprises, were perceived as threats to national independence and its economic ramifications. Baltic politicians, therefore, made the most radical break with the past, and paid little attention to the costs involved. With varied and changing enthusiasm, though, Baltic populations (save for the excluded minorities) have bought into the elite project of trading social welfare and industrial upgrading for national independence and security.

In contrast, reformers in the Visegrád area embraced the socialist industrial legacies and qualified workforces as foundations for successful reindustrialization, and the paternalistic welfare institutions as a means to divide and pacify the feared opposition to market reforms, and thereby protect society. Hence, these countries embarked on less radical paths of change, which allowed sheltering workers and businesses from the extreme hardships of transformation. Although not without reluctance and occasional resistance, societies followed their elected leaders on paths of socially sensitive forms of neoliberal capitalism.

2. Stark and Bruszt, *Postsocialist Pathways,* 6.

Whereas in the Baltic and Visegrád subregions the perceptions that mattered most for the chosen trajectories were those of political elites, Slovenian politicians were early on challenged by and had to learn to cooperate with a powerful labor movement, which had its own view on what elements of the inheritance ought to survive. Trade unions, center-left politicians, and the reformist bureaucracy backed by businesses that maintained strong links to the state have embraced the legacies of Yugoslav self-management and market socialism, and eventually transformed these into durable institutions of neocorporatist interest mediation.

Finally, while in the above cases perceptions mattered and initial choices led to coordinated yet open-ended policy experimentation, in Romania, Bulgaria, and Croatia key actors, with or without visions of how to cross the bridge between the past and the future, initially lacked the capacity and/or willingness to follow clear road maps. In these laggards of transformation, weak state legacies and further state weakening in the first half of the 1990s conspired to reduce the chances for coordinated moves from the old to any new order. For an extended period of time the defunct socialist system was replaced by anarchic priorities and measures bringing the destructive aspects of macrosocial change to the fore.

But how much had the reform elites' perceptions really mattered for the crucial early choices? After all, our findings seem to imply a degree of co-variance among aspects of diversity under socialism and capitalism. Once we abandon the assumption that socialist legacies were uniform and acknowledge the existence of varieties within the socialist system, it can also be argued that reform radicalism versus gradualism or welfarist versus identity politics and their social and political consequences have had little to do with perceptions and choices, but have largely resulted from "objectively" given differences in inheritances.

In this view, rather than allowing freedom of choice, different legacies would impose strict priorities upon politicians. Is it not the case that Baltic reformers were "forced" into nation building and reform radicalism by the imperative of having to confront the least favorable legacies among our cases, namely Soviet occupation, wasteful dependent industrialization, and colonizing immigration? And is not the abundance of inherited assets a sufficient explanation for Slovenia's gradual, inclusive, and balanced transformation path?

We submit that even if co-variation between legacies and outcomes exists, it is unsatisfactory to explain the latter by inherited structures alone. Most important, Mark Blyth argues, "structures do not come with an instruction sheet."[3] In order to link outcomes with inherited structures in a convincing way, actors' interpretations of legacies and the way these perceptions inform

---

3. Blyth, *Great Transformations*, 7.

choices, and thus political opportunities and risks, must be factored in. This is especially true in the context of radical uncertainty, of which there has been plenty in East Central Europe. Actors were uncertain about the defunct system, the collapse of which came as a surprise to most and "like the collapse of all orders, was partial" only,[4] and they could not foresee the specifics of the emerging new order. In this context ideas provided the "instruction sheets" that reduced uncertainty and offered guidelines for collective action.

We have found many examples of this. Take, for instance, the Baltic states' institutional choices. While their past indeed left behind daunting tasks, it could hardly have been predicted that their paths toward "Baltic miracles" would be paved with ideas and measures far more radical than the neoliberal consensus of the time, such as currency boards and low flat tax regimes. For a contrast, consider the Czech reformers' initial confidence in the value of their country's industrial legacy and the way this helped them combine visionary neoliberalism with economic and social protectionism.

We have also paid much attention to potentially viable paths of transformation that were initially considered but later abandoned, or not entered at all: the "suppressed historical alternatives" of winning choices.[5] The critical early years of transformation were replete with political and policy experimentation. In the Baltic states, for example, initial reform ideas still included citizenship rights based on territoriality, the expansion of the welfare state, and a gradual changeover to new national currencies. All four Visegrád states had their neocorporatist moments, when reformers still hesitated between forms of substantive and merely formal inclusion of labor in the polity. Three countries of this group originally opted for national capitalism and efforts to strengthen local businesses against foreign competitors. Conversely, Slovenia's first, short-lived conservative government rejected gradualism and initiated radical reforms.

Our contention that in the transformation process nothing was preordained and the course of regime formation could have taken different turns could still be challenged by advocates of geographical determinism. Although we are unaware of systematic accounts of postsocialist varieties in this vein, the argument that geography made (almost) all the difference could be developed on grounds of purely physical location as well as of its cultural effects.

Physical distance evidently plays a role among the locational factors of TNC operations. Why not, then, explain the divergent development of complex-manufacturing sectors in the Visegrád and Baltic areas simply by the fact that it is cheaper to transport, say, equipment or spare parts from Germany to the Czech Republic than to Latvia? We doubt, however, that distance from

4. Bunce, "Leaving Socialism," 37.
5. Barrington Moore, Jr., *Injustice: The Social Bases of Obedience and Revolt* (London: Macmillan, 1978), 376.

Western markets and capital-rich countries could alone provide a compelling explanation. After all, the Baltic states are far from Germany, but they are neighbors to Finland and Sweden. Yet both the Finnish cell phone manufacturer Nokia and the Swedish household appliances producer Electrolux have established their largest production plants (and Nokia a sizable R&D facility) in distant Hungary rather than in their Baltic backyard.

We are faced with similar anomalies in regard to shared cultural orientations of neighboring countries and regions. For instance, if cultural proximity has indeed been an important factor in regime choices, then how to make sense of the fact that in their neoliberal economic and limited democratic institutions the Baltic states appear to be the least "Nordic," and social democratic corporatist Slovenia the most "Nordic," in all of East Central Europe?

In sum, even if particular patterns of inherited assets and liabilities or features of physical and cultural geography may have made certain choices likelier than others, the observed large-scale experimentation and innovation in combining inherited with imported and newly invented institutions point to the prominent role of perception and agency as causes of the key regime features. In turn, the complexity of encompassing change and radical uncertainty about its true risks and opportunities can account for the fact that the new regimes emerged, to quote Stephan Haggard, "by default, trial-and-error, and compromise; [took many] years to crystallize; and [were] often plagued by internal inconsistency."[6]

Market, Welfare, Democracy, and Identity: Compatibilities and Trade-offs

Our second conceptual proposition refers to the relationships among the market, welfare, democracy, and identity. Conspicuously, in the formative period of the 1990s, almost no country could establish a regime that was economically neoliberal and fully democratic, yet socially unprotective. Hence, we contend that the interplay of economic and political freedom during the transformation was more complex than predicted by the neoliberal vision, and that its outcome was conditional upon factors external to the market-radical agenda. What can this tell us about systemic transformation and consolidation?

Challenging the optimism of the neoliberal vision, a central concern of the early literature was the incompatibility among the key aspects and processes of transformation. Claus Offe famously contended that while the agendas of creating a market economy, democracy, and a nation-state were inextricably linked, they were also mutually contradictory.[7] Thus, Offe and

6. Haggard, *Pathways*, 23.
7. Offe, "Capitalism by Democratic Design?"

other skeptics saw a danger that the triple transformation would either result in weak economies left without effective coordination, or in a weakening or breakdown of democracy, or a combination of perils.

The book explains the fact that East Central Europe's market societies proved more resilient to the perilous tendencies than was expected, by their politicians' reliance on specific resources to mediate tensions and generate support for the new order. Put simply, there have been two main kinds of resources that enabled these states to pursue marketization and economic restructuring in relatively stable albeit sometimes imperfect democratic contexts. Political elites either drew on the legacies of socialist welfare states or revitalized ideological traditions oppressed under the past system, most importantly nationalism. While welfare states and economic protectionism directly mitigated social dislocation by compensatory material arrangements, nationalism gave the citizenry a sense of identity, belonging, and pride, which could to some extent compensate for material losses and insecurity. Occasionally, welfarism and identity politics occurred in combination rather than as alternatives.

As we have shown, the reliance on nationalism was most prominent in the Baltic states and Croatia, where an acute sense of threatened national survival formed strong bonds between political elites and populations, and crystallized in nation-building or nationalizing projects. That is not to say that nationalism was absent in the rest of the region. However, even if nationalism has played a role in the Visegrád group and Slovenia, it has not been invoked as a single major legitimizing force of the new order. This group of democracies would have had a harder time surviving, had political elites not also pledged a welfarist social contract.

Our interpretation of nationalism thus differs from that in the early literature on postsocialist transformation, which under the impression of the Yugoslav and post-Soviet secession wars stressed its pathological traits: irredentism and xenophobia. Surely, the unfinished tasks of nation building have haunted all countries, and nationalists did question civil liberties and minority rights. However, especially given that unlike in the interwar years the pathologies rarely condensed into fully articulated antidemocratic and anticapitalist projects, we see reasons for stressing nationalism's ambiguous rather than uniformly negative impact on the transformation.[8] On the one hand, "imagined communities" could create new or reinforce existing bonds of solidarity that could help combat atomization produced by the expansion of markets. On the other hand, the appeal to national pride became a common element of broader strategies for catching up with the West in the new competitive environment, which pitted countries against each other in their quest for FDI and EU integration.

8. For this argument see Tom Nairn, *Faces of Nationalism: Janus Revisited* (London: Verso, 1997).

These considerations allow a few generalizable claims. First, consistently pursued agendas of some kind of solidarity, whether based on social protection, national identity, or a combination of the two, appear as necessary conditions for the viability of capitalist democracies, since without them no postsocialist country has managed to adopt the new order. Second, in a dynamic view of political impact we sense a trade-off between welfarist and identity politics. Once embedding neoliberalism in socially protective arrangements becomes untenable, democratic politics is likely to lose balance, and stabilization may occur via larger doses of identity politics leading, in the worst case, to sacrifices of democratic quality.

In fact, the trade-off has worked both ways, as neither welfare nor identity politics could be counted on as stabilizers forever. By the mid-2000s, welfarist social contracts have been repeatedly challenged by fiscal crises of the state, while creeping institutional reforms have led to unpopular retrenchment. Conversely, identity politics has also exhausted much of its mass appeal, bringing the social rather than the national question to the fore. How could legitimacy be kept once its original sources became depleted? Part of the answer lies in the role of the international system.

Virtues and Vices of Deep International Integration

From the late 1990s, there has been growing interest in the effects of deep international integration on postsocialist capitalism. For advocates of convergence under neoliberal hegemony, the emerging capitalist diversity must have been surprising. In this perspective, once the Soviet empire fell apart, its pieces moved from the frying pan to the fire, entering the global economy viewed by convergence theorists as no less powerful a homogenizing agent than Soviet-type socialism had been. But if strict external constraints have narrowed the room for local agency across the globe, why have they allowed a significant degree of institutional experimentation in Europe's most exposed latecomer societies?

We account for latecomer capitalism's diverse paths by questioning and problematizing the assumption that East Central Europe has been affected by a uniform set of global pressures. First, the related opportunities and risks tend to vary across cases. Since the region's political economies have captured dissimilar world market segments and niches, attracted TNCs in different sectors, and in some cases have faced specific demands from international and supranational institutions, they have been exposed to a host of new factors of differentiation which, in interplay with their legacies and political choices, have contributed to divergent development.

Second, the impact of external factors has varied over time. When witnessing the failure of pessimistic predictions, many analysts tended to explain the success of East Central European transformations by the role of IFIs, the

EU, and TNCs. Especially the perspective of EU membership was considered to be crucial. Stability was attributed to a combination of accession negotiations and conditionality, transnational linkages between socio-economic and political actors, and the deep penetration of the region's economies by FDI.

Many examples confirm the thrust of Europeanization literature. EU accession has endowed the postsocialist transformation with greater legitimacy, as it has offered a concrete perspective for the region's return to the West. It has also lengthened the time horizons of politicians who, especially when faced with waning popular support, might otherwise have backslid on transformative measures. In Slovakia, Bulgaria, Romania, and Croatia, accession tipped the balance in favor of democratic promarket forces. In addition, the pressure for conformity with the EU's laws, regulations, and norms and the assistance provided by the EU have strengthened government effectiveness.

Nevertheless, the eruption of the global financial crisis shed light on different and more controversial factors that helped Europeanization to foster economic and political stability in the short run, but also challenged this stability in the medium run. The crisis raised awareness of the crucial role played by abundance of foreign capital in easing regime-specific social tensions. Accession to the EU encouraged massive investment by TNCs in general and tempted transnational banks in particular to inject a significant amount of liquidity into many (but not all) of the new member states' domestic markets.

Easy access to foreign finance fueled rapid growth and foreign currency–denominated lending granted households a larger share in the new system's wealth, but all of this came at a heavy cost. The crisis hit the Baltic states, Hungary, and Romania very hard. The pure neoliberal regimes experienced some of the steepest recessions in the world due in a large part to the extreme harshness of their adjustment programs. Making things worse, the period of financialized growth had all but destroyed their anyway modest industrial competitiveness.

The dire fate of neoliberal regimes is also a manifestation of a deep fault line running through Europe, a "hidden fracture" that threatens the EU's economy and polity.[9] During the last decade before the global crisis, a deep divide between what Martin Wolf has so aptly dubbed the economies of "ants" and "grasshoppers" has emerged.[10] While some European economies industriously pursued strategies of wage restraint and export competitiveness, others relied on easy access to cheap credit, built up asset bubbles, and lost their competitive edge in the process. The financial sectors, most notably German and French banks, bridged the gap between the "underconsuming" European core and its "overconsuming and overstimulated" periphery.[11]

---

9. We borrow the term hidden fracture from Rajan, *Fault Lines.*
10. Martin Wolf, "The Grasshoppers and the Ants—a Contemporary Fable," *Financial Times,* May 26, 2010.
11. Ibid.

The crisis of the eurozone has brought the fault line into the open. Ever since, the EU's elites have been struggling with reforming the principles and institutions of the union's socio-economic governance in order to reduce economic imbalances and the risk of sovereign debt crises. At the core of reformed governance are a renewed commitment to austerity and financial discipline, and strict limits on solidarity. In consequence, the costs of adjustment are likely to put the largest burden on the heavily indebted societies.

We sense a danger, therefore, that the EU's earlier positive influence is turning into a straightjacket that adds to the already difficult challenges East Central Europe has to face. An externally imposed procyclical debt management strategy that (according to some economists at least) has a good chance of being self-defeating is unlikely to gain popular support, and governments may increasingly be tempted to break away from the resurgent orthodoxy. After all, why take the sticks if there are no carrots left? A wholesale repoliticization of socio-economic issues, putting at risk the earlier hard-won gains in state capacity, is far from excluded.

Challenged by waning democratic legitimacy and increasing politicization at home, European governments may also be less inclined to enforce democratic values abroad. Under these new external constraints, the short-term perspectives of democracy and capitalism in East Central Europe are bound to depend on the ability of national governments to impose austerity without losing legitimacy. Such ability, our analysis indicates, varies more across countries than across regimes.

Global Convergence versus Capitalist Diversity

Our findings also help to clarify our position within the larger debate on convergence and divergence in the global economy. For East Europeanists inspired by the VoC approach, the diversity of postsocialist capitalism is not puzzling at all. They claim to have discovered cases that already display the features of LME or CME. Since superior efficiency should help these fittest of postsocialist capitalisms withstand global pressures and survive as clear alternatives, a new variation on the once popular theme of *The End of History* could be applied to the region: when it all ends, there should be not a single "Last Man" but a pair of viable twins, a Liberal and a Democratic Corporatist.[12]

However, we do not view the diverse outcomes of transformations as a milestone marking the end of East Central Europe's peculiar history. Rather, our inquiry has revealed both the persistence of diversity, and a clear shift of all new regimes—and thus of the whole region's political economy—in the neoliberal direction.

---

12. Francis Fukuyama, *The End of History and the Last Man* (New York: Free Press, 1992).

Initially it was only the Baltic regimes that could be rightly termed pure neoliberal. In the first half of the 1990s all the other countries were still involved in experiments with various aspects of the Western European small state model—from open markets to welfare states and, indeed, to some kind of democratic corporatism. From the end of the 1990s important shifts in institutional configurations have altered the region's macrosocial landscape. Both the pure and the embedded neoliberal regime families adopted new members from Southeastern Europe. The early neocorporatist experiments of the Visegrád states were discontinued, leaving Slovenia as the sole representative of Katzenstein's small state model.

The 2000s have witnessed further gradual changes and occasional radical ones. Slovakia reformed and retrenched its welfare state and flattened and lowered its taxes, approximating in these (but not other) aspects the pure neoliberal type. At the same time, gradual welfare retrenchment became the norm in other Visegrád countries too, while Hungary became stuck with overgenerous welfarism and its pathologies. Lastly, with the arrival of the global crisis even Slovenian neocorporatism has weakened.

All in all, in a dynamic perspective our typology appears to be "closed" at its neocorporatist end, which was all but vacated by the late 2000s, but wide "open" and increasingly populated at the opposite end, that of pure neoliberalism. This asymmetry helps us identify other cases to which our typology might apply. Two groups of countries come to mind: some of the many weak states of Southeastern Europe and the CIS, and the crisis-ridden states on the EU's Mediterranean and northwestern periphery.[13]

We have argued that almost all the East Central European countries that shifted to neoliberalism belatedly in the 2000s came from originally weak state paths. Hence the possibility that other small states currently still plagued by weak capacity might emulate them in future. For example, Albania, Montenegro, Macedonia, Serbia, Georgia, and Armenia seem to have chances of adopting orderly forms of neoliberalism.

For this to happen, these would-be members of the neoliberal regime family ought to forge durable settlements with their neighbors and ethnic minorities on their territories: issues they have not fixed so far. They also ought to (re)build and/or import some administrative capacity to pursue at least a minimalist agenda of marketization, stabilization, and control of corruption with more coherence than earlier. Just as in Bulgaria, Romania, and Croatia, external actors ought to play a key role in this limited kind of state

---

13. We are skeptical about the relevance of our varieties for Azerbaijan or the central Asian states, because the Soviet system left these countries at a largely preindustrial stage, without a sizable manufacturing sector, skilled labor forces, and welfare arrangements, or sufficient state capacity in general. While this goes far in explaining their failure to achieve capitalist breakthrough, with no capitalism in place our typology loses its validity. These states are also trapped by natural resource dependency, just like Russia, which we excluded on the grounds that our book is about resource-poor small states, not resource-cursed giant ones.

building. Yet, as the EU's resolve to enlarge is waning, these countries might also fail to adopt any new order and instead join the camp of all but stateless Bosnia-Herzegovina, Kosovo, and Moldova.

The wider universe covered by our typology might expand in other ways than through countries rising from the bottom of the developmental hierarchy by means of enhanced state capacity thanks to the benevolent influence of external actors. Another group of newcomers might arrive after backsliding from positions closer to the top of the ladder of economic advance. Decline in these cases would be the result of weakened state capacity, traceable partly to less benevolent international pressures.

Such backsliding became a realistic possibility once the specter of a sovereign debt crisis triggered a radical transformation of a number of Western and Southern European states. Iceland, Greece, Portugal, Spain, Ireland (and most recently Cyprus and, indeed, Italy), hard-pressed by global markets, IFIs, and the EU, are in the process of drastically retrenching their welfare states, terminating social contracts recently achieved through limited social partnership, and downsizing public agencies and utilities. Austerity has fueled political disaffection and instability in all of these countries.

It is not excluded that once the EU's "old" peripheral capitalisms escape their current state of disorder, they will end up with features reminiscent of the fragile varieties on Europe's "new" periphery. Such an outcome would make the region's two-decade-long Sisyphean efforts to sustain markets and democracy in adverse conditions appear as precursors of a situation to which the West itself is heading: a new round of open-ended struggles against capitalism's propensity to weaken its own social and political foundations.

New Global Transformations

We began by outlining a Polanyian framework for understanding the diversity of postsocialist capitalism. In contrast to other approaches in comparative political economy, this framework makes it possible to detect the contradictory and conflicting nature of capitalism stemming from the simultaneous pushes for market deepening and social protection, the hard to reconcile demands on the polity from the forces of capital and the society at large, and the multilevel governance of the capitalist system. Based on this framework, we have shown how over the last twenty years each regime has developed specific configurations and abilities to deal with these tensions, and has avoided succumbing to any of the perils of capitalism: social disintegration, economic disorganization, and/or political breakdown. But we have also demonstrated that the drift toward less and less embedded forms of neoliberalism, a drift reinforced by the Great Recession, has put existing compromises at risk. Under the pressure of an international environment in which the survival of markets has once again taken precedence over the

security of societies or states, the space for social compensation and democratic decision making has shrunk dramatically.

Can pure neoliberalism survive? Can it entrench itself in global, European,
and national institutions? Are societies—Western and non-Western—able
and willing to bear the costs of saving a global financial system from the
destruction it has brought on itself? Are they ready to take the remedy that
has been proposed to solve the crisis, namely to discount the fact that "the
financial crisis concerned banks and their behavior," and to redefine its resolution "as a need to cut back, once and for all, the welfare state and public
spending"?[14] Or are we likely to see a renewed cycle of movement and countermovement, out of which a more embedded economy can emerge? In the
remainder of this chapter we will show that the Polanyian perspective developed here makes it possible to detect some of the tensions running through
contemporary capitalism, while also pointing to the difficulties of striking a
new balance between capitalism, social protection, and democracy.

Recently three challenges to pure neoliberalism have been identified.
Pointing to mass protest, spreading xenophobia, nationalism, and the spectacular rise of radical right-wing populist parties, all of which are developments that are by no means confined to the East, some recall Polanyi's analysis
of the "fascist situation" of the 1930s. That time, governments' defense of the
market system and commitment to the gold standard triggered an ultimately
deadly confrontation with a labor movement increasingly frustrated by rising
unemployment and falling wages. All this led to an insurmountable tension
between business and labor, which entrenched themselves in industry and
the parliament, respectively. The deadlock was "resolved" by fascist dictatorship, which rescued the national economy at the price of abandoning democracy and the global system alike.[15]

There are indeed a number of parallels between Polanyi's account of the
interwar period and the contemporary nationalist tendencies and malaise
of democracy. There are, however, important differences too. We have tried
to capture some of these differences by building on Peter Mair's thoughts
on the gap between responsive and responsible government and the related
polarization of unresponsive parties that govern and responsive ones that do
not aspire to form governments.[16]

For Mair, the problems for responsive government do not only stem from
international constraints, as in Polanyi's account. He also stresses the difficulties that governments face in reading public opinion and aggregating interests, as the links between parties and civil societies have weakened, and mass
electoral opinion has become more fragmented. In addition, because of low
party membership, parties have all but lost their control over the electorate.

14. Colin Crouch, *The Strange Non-Death of Neoliberalism* (Cambridge: Polity Press, 2011), viii.
15. Polanyi, *The Great Transformation*, 235–36.
16. Mair, "Representative versus Responsible."

Translated into Polanyi's language, Mair's concept implies that currently the forces of countermovement are amorphous, fragmented, and unclear about their preferences, and therefore unlike in the 1920 and 1930s, typically lack the organizational and ideological resources to firmly entrench themselves in parliaments.

It follows that the main challenge to capitalist democracy may not originate from a Polanyi-type deadlock and the assault by fascist or newer breeds of illiberal forces that deadlock provokes. Not questioning that such threats are also part of the region's and Europe's reality, we rather see the imminent danger in the erosion of the foundations of democracy due to widespread and permanent frustration with its poor performance. To the extent that this frustration cannot find its outlet and remedy within the confines of formal politics and existing party systems, it is likely to transform into political apathy. At worst, then, democracy would pass away—to paraphrase T. S. Eliot— not with a Polanyian bang but a whimper—just as in many cases communist autocracy did. If that is the case, it is difficult to see how existing popular frustration and anger can be elevated to an effective countermovement capable of reembedding capitalism.

Acknowledging the limited role national democracies can play in reining in market forces and actors that have increasingly become organized on a global scale, a number of authors point to trans- and supranational sources of countermovement. For example, in a recent article James Caporaso and Sidney Tarrow propose that due to interventions on the EU level "a structure of *supranational embedded liberal compromises*" is evolving, and support their claim by evidence that the European Court of Justice is gradually shifting its emphasis from decisions to enhance labor mobility within the EU to upholding decommodifying regulations aimed at strengthening the pension, family, and citizenship rights of migrant workers at the transnational level.[17]

Not trusting European institutions so much, Colin Crouch rather sees the need to bank on global corporations to build up "a more negotiated, voluntary regulatory system" in which "regulations will be exchanged for lightly monitored guarantees of good behavior by the large firms."[18] The expected improvement in corporate social responsibility is compatible with Polanyi's idea that firms threatened by deregulated markets and elements of capitalist elites seeking not merely profits but also "social recognition" can be recruited to the forces of countermovement.[19] As to why global corporations should become interested in more responsible behavior, Crouch points to the pressure that consumers can exert on them. "Even giant TNCs...need

17. James A. Caporaso and Sidney G. Tarrow, "Polanyi in Brussels: Supranational Institutions and the Transnational Embedding of Markets," *International Organization* 63 (2009): 593–620. Emphasis in the original.
18. Crouch, "What Will Follow," 485.
19. Polanyi, *The Great Transformation*, 153.

to sell their products if they are to maximize shareholder value, and this can make them vulnerable and sensitive to certain pressures."[20] This opens a window of opportunity for citizens as consumers to force corporations to respect a number of essential human rights and values, which results in the constraint of pure profit-seeking behavior.

John Ruggie's recent work exhibits a similar trust in the combined resources of global corporations and consumers to reembed liberalism on a global, rather than national scale.[21] Appointed as the UN special representative on human rights and transnational corporations, Ruggie has acquired first-hand experience on the political opportunities and risks of making the TNC–civil society relationship more fruitful through implementation of the UN Global Compact. However, Ruggie also specifies the political constraints faced by such a new international architecture. The first of these constraints stems from individual states' limited capacity to enforce the new business and human rights agenda in domestic arenas, or to align with each other for the same purpose on the international level. Second, "an individual liability model cannot fix larger imbalances in the system of global governance." Most importantly, a renewed effort at embedding neoliberalism will not emerge unless social movements and encompassing political coalitions that support this agenda are forged.[22]

To some extent, these visions of a new age of globally tamed liberalism bear greater resemblance to the nineteenth-century order secured by the balance of power and *haute finance,* than to the postwar compromise of embedded liberalism, predicated on a delicate balance between the domestic and international realms. It is not difficult to see some parallels with the role of *haute finance*—that cohesive elite of transnational bankers whose main motivation was gain and who, in order to attain that aim, had to act in responsible ways. As Polanyi asserts, a hundred years of peace were due to *haute finance*'s determination to avert wars, which would have undermined its possibilities for maximizing profits. To this end, it exerted power on governments and, if needed, provided "de facto administration for those troubled regions where peace was most vulnerable."[23]

A reenactment of a global liberal order held together by a socially responsible transnational elite is however unlikely to occur. This is for two reasons. First, as Wolfgang Streeck contends, elite interests today are more than ever

20. Crouch, *The Strange Non-Death,* 138–39.
21. John G. Ruggie, "Taking Embedded Liberalism Global: The Corporate Connection," in *Taming Globalization: Frontiers of Governance,* ed. David Held and Mathias Koenig-Archibugi (Cambridge: Polity Press, 2003); John G. Ruggie, "Business and Human Rights: The Evolving International Agenda," *American Journal of International Law* 101, no. 4 (October 2007): 819–40; and John G. Ruggie, ed., *Embedding Global Markets: An Enduring Challenge* (Aldershot: Ashgate, 2008).
22. Ruggie, "Business and Human Rights," 838–40.
23. Polanyi, *The Great Transformation,* 14.

"divorced from interest in system survival," as the striking inequality characterizing the neoliberal global system effectively does "away with traditional ideas of elite 'stewardship.' " Instead, we are facing a "situation in which the very rich have become so rich that their consumption can sustain economic growth, and the profits that depend on it, even in the face of advancing impoverishment of mass consumers."[24] As a corollary, the degree to which firms and consumers might contribute to reembedding market society must be further scrutinized.

Secondly, however, even if global elites could be lured into a greater sense of responsibility, in order for the system to become sustainable, they would also need to find a way of effectively reducing popular democracy to its nineteenth-century level. Even if popular democracy is increasingly being hollowed out, the fate of national governments still depends on electorates. Important sections of societies are not likely to be content with an agenda that relies on extension of human rights and consumerism, while having little to offer in terms of substantive social protection. This issue is bound to remain prominent on the national political level, and the fate of governments is closely tied to their stances on matters connected with it. Frictions between the multiple levels of capitalist governance are therefore likely to stay severe and the danger of disintegration real for some time to come.

In line with these thoughts, some observers do not put much trust in transnational governance and elites, but rather point to a new era in the international balance of power that in the long run can lead to reembedding capitalism. In particular, the rise of China and the other BRIC countries poses a challenge to American-style liberalism. The apparently successful contemporary wave of state-directed industrialization that also relies on manufacturing exports and foreign capital imports has catapulted Chinese capitalism into a position to engage in a worldwide shopping spree. China's rise seems to be unfolding in the same historical moment that the U.S. hegemony is threatened by a financial meltdown and domestic political stalemate. These developments may well indicate that "the global financial expansion of the last twenty years...is the clearest sign that we are in the midst of a hegemonic crisis. A more or less imminent fall of the West from the commanding heights of the world capitalist system is possible, even likely.... If the system eventually breaks down, it will be primarily because of U.S. resistance to adjustment and accommodation. And conversely, U.S. adjustment and accommodation to the rising economic power of the East Asian region is an essential condition for a non-catastrophic transition to a new world order."[25]

---

24. Streeck, "Taking Capitalism Seriously," 15.

25. Giovanni Arrighi and Beverly J. Silver, *Chaos and Governance in the Modern World System* (Minneapolis: University of Minnesota Press, 1999), 273–74, 287–88. It is remarkable that these propositions were advanced already in 1999. In a more recent work, the late Arrighi

All of this reminds us of one of Polanyi's powerful messages. In our reading of Polanyi, market expansion and market regulation did not develop in a tightly coupled pattern, but occasionally followed each other with considerable time lags. Since not all challenges from either side could be responded to by its counterpart in due time or with comparable force, the pendulum logic of the double movement could lead to extreme swings in either direction, the one propelled by the forces of market expansion and the other by their adversaries. Written from the vantage point of the Great Depression, Fascism and World War II, Polanyi's book is also a striking account of the difficulty and occasional impossibility of balancing regulation by a politically agitated mass society against the basic needs of a functioning market economy.

In light of all of this, it remains to be seen whether any combination of the developments presented here will ever add up to an overarching settlement that can rightly be termed global or European embeddedness. If this fails to happen, the loose patchwork of partial compromises among new transnational movements and countermovements, as well as among declining and new hegemons, will mirror the fragmentation observed in national arenas. Such an outcome may resemble a "new medieval" pattern, which in Katzenstein's interpretation denotes "a move, more or less halting in different regional settings, toward multiple, nested centers of collective authority and identity" interacting with a challenged American hegemon and whichever counterhegemon arises as the challenger.[26]

With the global crisis still unfolding, there is great uncertainty regarding the course capitalist development is about to take. This should give pause to overconfident predictions. However, we hope we have demonstrated that an adapted Polanyian framework remains pertinent for the analysis of market society's paths—even if these might lead to a prewelfarist and predemocratic new medieval future. In important respects, then, ours is still a century of the Great Transformation.

---

further elaborated on the question of China. See his *Adam Smith in Beijing: Lineages of the Twenty-first Century* (London: Verso, 2007).

26. Katzenstein, *A World of Regions*, 245, citing Hedley Bull, *The Anarchical Society: A Study of Order in World Politics* (New York: Columbia University Press, 1977), 254–55.

Index

Figures and tables are indicated by an *f* or *t* appended to the page number.

Albania, 268
American liberal hegemony, challenges to, 273–74
Antall, József, 149, 155
Armenia, 268
Asia, newly industrializing countries (NICs) in, 34, 37, 140n1, 170, 171*t*
Aslund, Anders, 48, 60, 78n68, 80n72, 256
Atlas Economic Research Foundation, 124
Austria, 44, 67, 70, 72, 74, 78, 92, 186, 206
automotive industry
  in Bulgaria, 208–9
  in Visegrád countries, 89, 163, 166, 169–70, 171
Azerbaijan, 268n13

backsliding, 226, 269
Bączkowski, Andrzej, 151
Balcerowicz, Leszek, 60n14, 61, 150, 173, 176
Balkan states. *See* Southeastern European countries
Baltic states, neoliberal capitalism in, 3, 5, 96–137. *See also* global economic crisis of 2008 in Baltic states; Russian-speaking residents of Baltic States; taxation in Baltic states
  central banks, 104, 106–10, 113, 173–74, 236
  credit, access to, 92, 95, 131, 133–35, 227–30
  crises of 1990s and, 5–6, 255–56
  currency boards, 104–10, 111, 113–14, 119, 128
  deindustrialization, 119, 125, 131
  differences between, 96–97
  economic miracle of Baltic Tigers in 2000s, 131–37
  emigration, 135–36
  "Estonian miracle," narrative of, 124–31
  ethnic aspects of social policy, 119–24, 120*t*
  EU accession, 131–33, 136
  EU and, 97, 110–11, 111*t*, 129, 131–34, 223, 232–34
  euro, move to, 110–11, 111*t*, 232–34
  exclusionary and inclusionary citizenship policies, 99–103
  FDI inflows, 88–91, 96, 133, 227
  financial and banking sector in Latvia, 130–31
  foreign commercial banks in, 133–35
  historical legacies and political opportunity structures, 75, 76, 77, 79
  home ownership and real estate boom, 134–35
  IFIs and, 126, 131
  IMF and, 106, 109, 110, 111, 128, 223, 233, 234, 237
  labor conditions, 120*t*, 123, 133, 135–36, 228–31

Baltic states *(continued)*
  LME, Estonia identified as, 10
  machinery and electrical equipment
    industries in Estonia, 125, 127
  macroeconomic stability, 51–53, 52*t*
  market opening, regulating, and stabiliz-
    ing, 25–29, 26*t*
  nation-building and state-building in, 96,
    97, 98–99, 104
  national currencies, 104–11, 113–14, 233,
    234
  nationalist social contract, 113–24, 228–30
  paths to, 60, 84, 85, 252, 260–61
  pensions, 114–19, 117*f*, 133, 156
  political parties, 101–3, 229–30
  popular consent, obtaining, 62, 65, 136–
    37, 228–30
  privatization, 122–23
  Russian oil and oil products, transit man-
    agement of, 127
  semicore versus semiperipheral interna-
    tional economic integration, 44–48, 45*t*
  social cohesion/stress, 48–51, 49*t*, 123,
    133
  Southeastern European countries com-
    pared, 182, 184, 185, 186, 194, 199, 202,
    204*t*, 209, 212, 213, 218, 219, 221, 222
  state governance capacities, 36–44, 39*t*,
    41*t*, 43*t*
  transformation costs, compensating for,
    29–36, 32*t*, 35*t*
  transformative corporatism versus neolib-
    eralism debate, 18–19
  typological definition of, 19, 22, 23*t*
  Visegrád countries compared, 138, 139,
    173–74, 179
banking and financial institutions. *See also*
    central banks; credit, access to; foreign
    commercial banks; international finan-
    cial institutions
  EBRD, 25, 59–60, 166
  financial and banking sector in Latvia,
    130–31
  free banking, 106–7
  Parex Bank, Latvia, 130, 133, 234, 236
  Swedish financial institutions, eastward
    enlargement of, 92, 133, 227
Barnes, Andrew, 219
Becker, Uwe, 15n23
Belarus, 78n68
Berend, Iván T., 59, 70, 71
Bibó, István, 73–74n53

Birkavs, Valdis, 116
Bismarck, Otto von, social reforms of, 72
Blyth, Mark, 261
Boc, Emil, 252
Bokros, Lajos, and Bokros package, 149,
    177
Borisov administration, Bulgaria, 252
Bosnia-Herzegovina, 269
Brazauskas, Algirdas, 110
Bretton Woods Conference (1944), 17–18
Britain
  Baltic austerity package compared to, 234
  Rover (car manufacturer) in Bulgaria,
    208–9
  Speenhamland welfare regime of 1795, 79
Brubaker, Rogers, 68n37, 97
Brucan, Silviu, 186
Bruszt, László, 9
Brzezinski, Zbigniew, 164
Bulgaria. *See* Southeastern European coun-
    tries
Bunce, Valerie J., 69, 198, 259

capitalism postsocialist. *See also* postsocialist
    capitalism in East Central Europe
Caporaso, James, 271
Cardoso, Fernando H., 12
Cass, Fergus, 169
Ceauşescu, Nicolae, 216
CEFTA (Central European Free Trade
    Area), 163, 165
Center for Research into Post-Communist
    Economies, 124
central banks, 28–29, 104
  in Baltic states, 104, 106–10, 113, 173–74,
    236
  in Southeastern European countries,
    211–14, 219
  in Visegrád countries, 173–78, 179
Central Europe, as distinctive region, 164.
    See also postsocialist capitalism in East
    Central Europe
Central European Free Trade Area
    (CEFTA), 163, 165
Chaudry, Kiren Aziz, 206
China, 106, 171, 273
CIS (Commonwealth of Independent
    States), 10, 268
CMEA (Council for Mutual Economic Assis-
    tance), 162–63
CMEs (coordinated market economies),
    10–11, 267

common goods, common bads, and tensions in postsocialist East Central Europe, 20–21, 21*t*

Commonwealth of Independent States (CIS), 10, 268

compensation for transformation costs, 29–36, 32*t*, 35*t*, 64–65

competitive capture, 219

complex industries and goods
    deindustrialization, 90, 92, 119, 125, 131, 200
    FDI inflows supporting, 88–91
    as measure of international economic integration, 44–48, 45*t*

conditionality, 85–88.219–220, 221, 239, 254, 266

Confederation of Industrialists, 118

The Constitution of Liberty (Hayek), 112

coordinated market economies (CMEs), 10–11, 267

corporate income tax rates, reduction of
    in Baltic states, 112–13
    in Visegrád countries, 168–69

corporations, transnational. *See* transnational corporations

Council for Mutual Economic Assistance (CMEA), 162–63

Councils of Economic and Social Agreement (RHSD), 146–48

credit, access to, 92–93
    in Baltic states, 92, 95, 131, 133–35, 227–30
    in Southeastern European countries, 92, 95, 251
    in Visegrád countries, 92

Croatia. *See* Southeastern European countries

crony capitalism, 199, 200, 215–16

Crouch, Colin, 134–35, 271–72

Crowley, Stephen, 184, 185, 187

Csáky, Pál, 180

currencies. *See* euro; national currencies

currency boards
    in Baltic states, 104–10, 111, 113–14, 119, 128
    global economic crisis and, 252
    as paths to postsocialist capitalism, 28, 33, 84–85
    in Southeastern European countries, 219, 221
    welfare, markets, democracy, and identity, interplay between, 262

Czechoslovakia/Czech Republic. *See* Visegrád countries, embedded neoliberal capitalism in

Daru Car group, 208–9

debt
    Ceaușescu's decision to fully repay Romanian foreign debt, 216
    Latin American debt crisis, 128
    Visegrád countries, external debt in, 142–44
    Yugoslavia, debt burden of, 51

Deegan-Krause, Kevin, 229

deindustrialization, 90, 92, 119, 125, 131, 200

democracy, identity, market, and welfare, interplay between, 263–65

democratic governance capacities of post-socialist states. *See* state governance capacities

dependent market economies (DMEs), 11–12

Dimitrov, Philip, 191n34

Dimitrov, Veselin, 216, 219

Dlouhý, Vladimír, 78

DMEs (dependent market economies), 11–12

double movement theory, 13–14, 16, 56, 274

Drahokoupil, Jan, 10

Dreifelds, Juris, 79

Dubček, Alexander, 153

Dzurinda, Mikuláš, 148, 157–58, 173, 180, 181, 245–46, 247

East Central Europe. *See* postsocialist capitalism in East Central Europe
    as distinctive region, 164

EBRD (European Bank for Reconstruction and Development), 25, 59–60, 166

Economic and Monetary Union (EMU), 87, 134–35, 139, 173–78, 215, 237, 240, 243, 250

economic crisis of 2008. *See entries at* global economic crisis of 2008

Economic Ethics of the World Religions (Weber), 76

education
    in Baltic states, 121, 123
    socialist regime, under, 71, 79

Eglitis, Daina, 115, 119–20n62

elderly, pensions for. *See* pensions

electrical equipment and electronics
  industry
  in Estonia, 125, 127
  in Visegrád countries, 89, 163, 166, 171
Electrolux, 263
Eliot, T. S., 271
embedded neoliberal capitalism
  in Croatia, 3, 22, 182, 218, 251, 253–54
  global economic crisis and, 224, 225*t*, 226,
    242, 245, 246, 248, 251
  in Visegrád countries. *See* Visegrád coun-
    tries, embedded neoliberal capitalism in
emigration from Baltic states, 135–36
employer relations. *See* labor relations
employment/unemployment. *See* labor conditions
EMU (Economic and Monetary Union),
  87, 134–35, 139, 173–78, 215, 237, 240,
  243, 250
The End of History (Fukuyama, 1992), 267
England. *See* Britain
Enyedi, Zsolt, 247
ERM (Exchange Rate Mechanism), 173,
  232, 252
Esping-Andersen, Gösta, 17
Estonia. *See* Baltic states, neoliberal capitalism in
ÉT (Interest Reconciliation Council), Hungary, 149–50
ethnic minorities. *See also* Russian-speaking
  residents of Baltic States
  German interwar interference on behalf
    of, 68
  Roma peoples, marginalization of, 159–
    60, 241, 242n32, 245
  threat perceptions across East Central
    Europe, 230–31, 232*t*
EU accession
  Baltic states and, 131–33, 136
  deep international integration and, 266
  global economic crisis and, 226, 229, 230,
    232, 235–36, 240, 243, 244, 254
  paths to postsocialist capitalism and, 5, 28,
    44, 85–88, 92–93, 95
  in Southeastern European countries, 183,
    205, 213, 219–20
  Visegrád countries and, 151, 161, 164,
    167, 169, 172–73, 175, 177, 179, 180
EU conditionality, 85–88.219–220, 221, 239,
  254, 266
EU enlargement, 5, 44, 87, 92, 129, 164,
  173

euro
  Baltic national currencies pegged to, 109,
    134, 233, 234
  Baltic states' move to, 110–11, 111*t*,
    232–34
  Bulgaria and, 252
  global economic crisis and, 247, 267
  macroeconomic coordination and, 211
  private euro-denominated loans in Baltic
    states, 134–35
  Slovenia's entry into eurozone, 215, 250
  Visegrád countries' move to, 172–81
European Bank for Reconstruction and
  Development (EBRD), 25, 59–60, 166
European Court of Justice, 271
European Union (EU)
  Baltic states and, 97, 110–11, 111*t*, 129,
    131–34, 223, 232–34
  deep international integration and,
    265–67
  democratic governance in, 43
  global crisis of 2008 and, 50, 223, 232–33,
    232–34, 238, 239, 242, 243, 247, 252, 254
  hub-and-spoke approach to integration,
    162, 165–66
  legislation and regulation compliant with,
    28, 33
  path to postsocialist capitalism and, 1, 5,
    28, 44, 55–57, 74, 85–88, 92, 93–95
  postaccession crises, 95, 220, 243
  Southeastern European Countries and,
    183–84, 215, 219–21, 223, 250, 252, 254
  Visegrád countries and, 138, 162, 163,
    165–69, 172–81, 223, 238, 239, 242, 243,
    247
  waning of urge to enlarge, 269
Evans, Peter, 171–72
Exchange Rate Mechanism (ERM), 173,
  232, 252
Eyal, Gil, 9

Faletto, Enzo, 12
fascism, 14, 186, 270–71, 274
Fáth, Péter, 169
FDI. *See* foreign direct investment
Fico, Robert, 181, 245–46
financial crisis of 2008. *See entries at* global
  economic crisis of 2008
financial institutions. *See* banking and financial institutions
Fink-Hafner, Danica, 249
First World War, 68, 74

Fish, Steven, 198
The Flat Tax (Rabushka and Hall, 1983), 112
flat tax regimes
    in Baltic states, 111–13
    in Bulgaria and Romania, 221
foreign commercial banks
    in Baltic states, 133
    market penetration by, 31–33
    in Southeastern European countries, 213,
        251
foreign direct investment (FDI)
    in Baltic states, 88–91, 96, 133, 227
    deep international integration and, 266
    diversity of types of, 12
    EU entry negotiations encouraging, 88
    during global economic crisis, 224, 225*t*
    industrialization in East Central Europe
        often dependent on, 69
    international economic integration, mea-
        suring, 44–48, 45*t*
    in Southeastern European countries,
        88–90, 202–11, 204*t*, 210*f*, 217, 251, 253
    typological theories based on, 10
    variations in inflows across East Central
        Europe, 88–91, 95
    in Visegrád countries, 88–90, 95, 142, 144,
        161, 166–68, 170, 171*t*, 172, 239, 247
free banking, 106–7
Free Market Institute, 109, 118
Free to Choose (Friedman and Friedman),
    112, 125
Friedman, Milton, 59, 61, 112, 125
Friedman, Rose, 112
Frye, Timothy, 194n47, 247n44
Fukuyama, Francis, *The End of History*
    (1992), 267

Ganev, Venelin, 190n27, 193, 200
Gdańsk agreements of 1980, 150
Georgia (country), 60, 268
Germany
    Bismarckian welfare reforms in, 72
    ethnic Germans, interwar interference on
        behalf of, 68
    expansionist policies of, 74
    financial institutions, eastward enlarge-
        ment of, 92
    industrialization process in East Central
        Europe and, 70
    social market economy of, 60n14
Gerschenkron, Alexander, 54, 55n1
Gilbert, Emily, 113

Glasman, Maurice, 79n70
global economic convergence and diver-
    gence, 267–69
global economic crisis of 2008, 5–6, 223–58
    "backsliding" and, 226
    consequences of, 255–58, 269–74
    currency boards, 252
    deep international integration and,
        266–67
    embedded neoliberal capitalism during,
        224, 225*t*, 226, 242, 245, 246, 248, 251,
        253–54
    EU accession and, 226, 229, 230, 232,
        235–36, 240, 243, 244, 254
    in Greece, 247
    neocorporatism during, 225*t*, 226–27,
        248–51
    neoliberal capitalism during, 224, 225*t*,
        226, 251, 257
    political responses to, 224, 235–37,
        240–48, 254–55
    sources of political stability and capacity
        for crisis management, 232*t*
global economic crisis of 2008 in Baltic
    states, 227–37
    alternatives to draconian austerity mea-
        sures, failure to generate, 233–37
    credit boom as means of accommodat-
        ing inequalities and social discontent,
        228–32
    credit boom, reliance on, 227–30
    economic decline triggered by crisis, 233
    IMF and EU, Latvia's need to obtain assis-
        tance from, 223, 234, 237
    inflation rates and euro entry target,
        232–33
    neoliberal capitalism, performance of,
        224, 225*t*, 226
    political unrest, 235–37
    trust in government during crisis, 232*t*,
        235–37
    vulnerabilities and strengths, 227–28
global economic crisis of 2008 in Southeast-
    ern European countries, 248–55
    Bulgaria, Croatia, and Romania, 251–55
    embedded neoliberal capitalism in Croa-
        tia, performance of, 224, 225*t*, 226, 251,
        253–54
    IMF and EU, Romania's need to obtain
        assistance from, 223, 252–53
    neocorporatist Slovenia and, 225*t*, 226–27,
        248–51

global economic crisis of 2008 in Southeastern European countries *(continued)*
  neoliberal capitalism in Bulgaria and Romania, performance of, 224, 225*t*, 226, 251
  political instability, 248, 254–55
  vulnerabilities and strengths, 248
global economic crisis of 2008 in Visegrád countries, 237–48
  embedded neoliberal capitalism, performance of, 224, 225*t*, 226, 242, 245, 246, 248
  IMF and EU, Hungary's need to obtain assistance from, 223
  political instability, 240–48
  responsible and responsive government, tension between, 238–40, 270–71
  vulnerabilities and strengths, 237–38
global transformation of liberalism, 269–74
Godmanis, Ivars, 237
gold standard, 13, 17, 106–7, 108n34, 270
Gorbachev, Mikhail, 126
Gourevitch, Peter, 62
governance capacities of postsocialist states. *See* state governance capacities
Gradev, Grigor, 185–86
Great Britain. *See* Britain
Great Depression of 1929–33, 5, 14, 108n34, 274
Great Recession of 2008. *See entries at* global economic crisis of 2008
The Great Transformation (Polanyi, 1944), 8, 29n50, 60n12
Greece, 247, 256, 269
Gyurcsány, Ferenc, 178–79, 240, 243, 244

Habsburg Empire, 66, 67, 72, 162
Haggard, Stephan, 34, 263
Hall, Peter A., 10
Hall, Robert, 112
Hanke, Steve H., 106, 109
Hansson, Ardo, 106, 118
Hausner, Jerzy, 151, 176
Havel, Václav, 164, 174
Havelka, Jan Amos, 79
Hay, Colin, 134
Hayek, Friedrich August von, 59, 61, 106–7, 112, 144
Helleiner, Eric, 113
Hirschman, Albert O., 2, 88, 230, 231
historical legacies and political opportunity structures, 75–81, 82*f*. *See also* socialist legacy
Holocaust, 70

Horn, Gyula, 168
housing boom in Baltic states, 134–35
hub-and-spoke approach of EU to integration, 162, 165–66
Hungary. *See* Visegrád countries, embedded neoliberal capitalism in
Husák, Gustáv, 145
Hyundai/Kia investment in Žilina, Slovakia, 169

Iankova, Elena, 18, 42, 187, 188, 191n34
Ibáñez, Carlos, 231
Iceland, 256, 269
identity politics, 64–65, 263–65
IFIs. *See* international financial institutions
Iliescu, Ion, 189, 190, 216
IME program, Estonia, 104
IMF. *See* International Monetary Fund
income inequality, unemployment, and poverty, 48, 50, 92, 123, 133, 154, 228–31, 257
industrial relations. *See* labor relations
Industrial Revolution, 48–50
industrialization process in East Central Europe, 69–72
Inglot, Tomasz, 72, 152
Institute of Economic Affairs, 124
Interest Reconciliation Council (ÉT), Hungary, 149–50
international corporations. *See* transnational corporations
International Criminal Tribunal for the Former Yugoslavia, 254
international economic integration
  deep international integration, benefits and drawbacks of, 265–67
  semicore versus semiperipheral, 44–48, 45*t*
international financial institutions (IFIs)
  Baltic states and, 126, 131
  deep international integration and, 266–67
  EBRD, 25, 59–60, 166
  marketization encouraged by, 27
  paths to emergence of postsocialist capitalism and, 55, 57, 59–60, 91–93
  in Southeastern European countries, 219, 221
  in Visegrád countries, 142, 167
International Monetary Fund (IMF)
  Baltic states and, 106, 109, 110, 111, 128, 223, 233, 234, 237
  global crisis of 2008 and, 223, 233, 234, 237, 245, 252–53

paths to postsocialist capitalism and, 84, 85
Southeastern European countries and, 191n34, 219, 223, 252–53
Visegrád countries and, 142, 223, 245
investment incentives, 31, 32t, 95, 168–69
Ireland, housing boom in, 134–35
Iversen, Torben, 211

Jacoby, Wade, 83, 84, 87, 93
Janša, Janez, 249
Járai, Zsigmond, 173
Jewish Holocaust, 70
Johnson, Juliet, 105, 173
Johnson, Paul M., 71n46
Josipović, Ivo, 255
Jusko, Marián, 179

Kaczyński, Jarosław, 151, 176
Kaczyński, Lech, 176, 243n35
Kádár, János, 141
Kallas, Siim, 107, 108
Kalvītis, Aigars, 136, 236
Katzenstein, Peter J., 17, 19, 24, 37, 53, 54n85, 55n1, 66n34, 67, 192, 211, 268, 274
Kaufman, Robert R., 34
Kazakhstan, 60
Kende, Péter, 162
Keune, Maarten, 160
Keynesianism, 18, 84, 134–35, 214, 230
Kideckel, David, 185, 187, 196–97
King, Lawrence, 9
Kitschelt, Herbert, 65n32, 80, 193
Klaus, Václav, 60–61, 79, 140, 144–45, 147, 159, 174–75
Kokanović, Marina, 185
Kolesár, Peter, 169
Kołodkom Grzegorz, 176
Kornai, János, 8n2, 34, 142, 163
Kosor, Jadranka, 254–55
Kosovo, 219, 269
Kundera, Milan, 164
Kuroń, Jacek, 153, 154–55
Kurth, James, 257
Kyrgyz Republic, 60

Laar, Mart, 78, 79, 99, 106–8, 112–14, 119, 124–26, 128, 134
labor conditions
in Baltic states, 120t, 123, 133, 135–36, 228–31
centralized wage setting in Southeastern European countries, 216
emigration from Baltic states, 135–36

unemployment, income inequality, and poverty, 48, 50, 92, 123, 133, 154, 228–31, 257
labor relations
in Southeastern European countries, 184–91, 196–97, 210–11, 213–17
state governance capacities and, 191–97
in Visegrád countries, 146–52
Lace, Tana, 115, 119–20n62
Ladányi, János, 160
Landes, David, 63–64
Landsbergis, Vytautas, 103
Latin America
debt crisis, 128
NICs (newly industrializing countries) in, 34, 37, 140n1, 170, 171t
Latvia. See Baltic states, neoliberal capitalism in
League of Nations, 108
legacies and political opportunity structures, 75–81, 82f. See also socialist legacy
legal restorationism, 99–101
Leontjeva, Elena, 109
liberal market economies (LMEs), 10–11, 267
liberalism, global transformation of, 269–74
Lieven, Anatol, 100
Lithuania. See Baltic states, neoliberal capitalism in
LMEs (liberal market economies), 10–11, 267
Love, Joseph, 58, 73

Macedonia, 268
machinery and electrical equipment industries in Estonia, 125, 127
MacIver, Robert M., 29n50
macroeconomic stability in postsocialist countries, 51–53, 52t, 211–17
Mair, Peter, xii, 102, 238–39, 270–71
Majone, Giandomenico, 86
management employee buyouts (MEBOs), 122, 143, 144, 145, 199, 249
Mann, Michael, 193n41
Manoilescu, Mihail, 186
Marcinkiewicz, Kazimierz, 176
markets
opening, regulating, and stabilizing, 25–29, 26t
welfare, markets, democracy, and identity, interplay between, 263–65
Marković, Ante, 187, 189
Markowski, Radosław, 244

Marx, Karl, 201
Masár, Vladimír, 179
Mazowiecki, Tadeusz, 150
MEBOs (management employee buyouts),
    122, 143, 144, 145, 199, 249
Mečiar, Vladimír, 76, 85n80, 145–48, 157–58,
    167, 179–81, 245
Medgyessy, Péter, 150, 178, 240
Mencinger, Jože, 212–13
Mexican currency crisis of 1994, 128
Mikloš, Ivan, 180–81
Milanovic, Branko, 115
Miller, Leszek, 176
Miłosz, Czesław, 164
minorities. *See* ethnic minorities
Moldova, 60, 269
money. *See* euro; national currencies
Mont Pelerin Society (MPS), 106
Montenegro, 268
mortgage boom in Baltic states, 134–35
MPS (Mont Pelerin Society), 106
multinational corporations. *See* transnational
    corporations
Munich Agreement of 1938, 74
Murrell, Peter, 18–19
Myant, Martin, 10

nation-building and state-building process
    in Baltic states, 96, 97, 98–99, 104
    market, welfare, democracy, and identity,
        interplay between, 263–65
    as path to emergence of postsocialist capi-
        talism, 67–69
    popular consent, identity politics as means
        of mobilizing, 64–65
    in Southeastern European countries in
        ruins of Yugoslavia, 222
national capitalism efforts in Visegrád coun-
    tries, 141–46
national currencies. *See also* currency boards
    in Baltic states, 104–11, 113–14, 233, 234
    gold standard, 13, 17, 106–7, 108n34, 270
    in Southeastern European countries, 212,
        214, 215, 217, 221
NATO (North American Treaty Organiza-
    tion), 180, 183, 229
Nelson, Joan M., 27
neocorporatism, 3, 5
    global economic crisis and, 225*t*, 226–27,
        248–51
    macroeconomic stability and, 211
    in Slovenia, 3, 5, 23*t*, 24, 182, 184, 187,
        196, 215, 248–51

state governance capacity and, 195–97
    typological definition, 23*t*, 24
    Visegrád countries, failure in, 146–52, 262
neoliberal capitalism. *See also* Baltic states,
    neoliberal capitalism in; embedded
    neoliberal capitalism; Western neolib-
    eral states
    in Bulgaria and Romania, 3, 22, 182, 218,
        251
    challenges to pure neoliberalism, 269–74
    deep international integration and, 266
    global economic crisis and, 224, 225*t*, 226,
        251, 257
    global shift toward, 267–69
    market, welfare, democracy, and identity,
        interplay between, 263–65
newly industrializing countries (NICs) in
    Latin America and Asia, 34, 37, 140n1,
        170, 171*t*
Nokia, 263
Nölke, Andreas, 11, 12
North American Treaty Organization
    (NATO), 180, 183, 229

OECD (Organisation for Economic Co-
    operation and Development), 136, 180,
        207
Offe, Claus, 72–73, 104, 263
oil and oil products, Russian, Baltic transit
    management of, 127
Orbán, Viktor, 150, 177, 178, 242
Orenstein, Mitchell A., 83
Organisation for Economic Co-operation and
    Development (OECD), 136, 180, 207
Ost, David, 18, 42, 120n62, 185, 189

Parek, Lagle, 127–28
Parex Bank, Latvia, 130, 133, 234, 236
paths to emergence of postsocialist capital-
    ism, 3–5, 55–95, 260–63
    compensation for transformation costs,
        64–65
    dual influence of transnational and inter-
        nal factors, 4–5
    East, desire to leave, 58–62
    EU, influence of, 5, 18, 55–56, 57, 74,
        85–87, 92, 93–95
    FDI inflows, 88–91, 95
    first phase of regime formation, 81–82, 82*f*
    identity politics, appeals to, 64–65
    IFI investment, 55, 57, 59–60, 91–93
    industrialization process, 69–72
    initial choice of transformation strategies, 4

nation-building and state-building process, 67–69
political agency, importance of, 3–4, 55–57
political opportunity structures, historical legacies of, 75–81, 82*f*
popular consent, mobilizing, 62–67
second phase of regime formation, 93–95, 94*f*
socialist legacy as part of, 56, 58–59, 65–67, 70–71, 75–82
TNCs, role of, 55, 57, 87–91, 92, 93
transnational actors, institutions, and markets, role of, 4–5, 82–87
uncertainly and crisis, influence of, 4
welfare arrangements, 72–73
West, contradictory and strained relationship with, 73–74
pay-as-you-go (PAYG) pension arrangements, 117, 157, 168
Penguin Revolution of 2009, 236
pensions
in Baltic states, 114–19, 117*f*, 133, 156
NDC (notional defined contribution) scheme, 117–18
PAYG (pay-as-you-go) arrangements, 117, 157, 168
"under-age" pensioners, 36, 154, 157
in Visegrád countries, 116, 152–59
Perón, Juan, 231–32
Poland. *See* Visegrád countries, embedded neoliberal capitalism in
Polanyi, Karl
paths to emergence of postsocialist capitalism and, 56, 57, 60n12, 63, 64
social dislocation and improvement, connection between, 257
tensions in contemporary capitalism and, 270–74
typography of postsocialist capitalism derived from, 2, 8, 13–17, 29n50, 48–50, 269
political agency, importance of, 3–4, 55–57
political opportunity structures, historical legacies and, 75–81, 82*f*
political parties
in Baltic states, 101–3, 229–30
in Southeastern European countries, 188, 190, 195, 200, 215, 218, 249, 254
in Visegrád countries, 141, 144, 161, 174–79, 180, 181, 240–48
political unrest
global economic crisis of 2008 and, 224, 235–37, 240–48, 254–55

neoliberalism, current challenges to, 270–71
Pontusson, Jonas, 88, 211
popular consent, mobilizing
in Baltic states, 62, 65, 136–37, 228–30
identity politics as means of mobilizing, 64–65
as path to emergence of postsocialist capitalism, 62–67
in Southeastern European countries, 62, 65
in Visegrád countries, 62, 65
postaccession crises, 95, 220, 243
postsocialist capitalism in East Central Europe, 1–54, 259–74
in Baltic states, 3, 5, 96–137. *See also* Baltic states, neoliberal capitalism in
common goods, common bads, and tensions, 20–21, 21*t*
countries covered by, 1
deep international integration, benefits and drawbacks of, 265–67
embedded neoliberalism, 3, 5. *See also* embedded neoliberal capitalism
global economic crisis, response to, 5–6, 223–58. *See also entries at* global economic crisis of 2008
global transformation of liberalism and, 269–74
historical trajectory of, 25
literature, review of alternative conceptualizations in, 9–13, 18–19
macroeconomic stability and, 51–53, 52*t*, 211–17
market opening, regulating, and stabilizing, 25–29, 26*t*
market, welfare, democracy, and identity, interplay between, 263–65
neocorporatism, 3, 5. *See also* neocorporatism
neoliberalism, 3, 5. *See also* neoliberal capitalism
paths to emergence of, 3–5, 55–95, 260–63. *see also* paths to emergence of postsocialist capitalism
Polanyian framework used in analyzing, 2, 8, 13–17
postwar Western European small states compared, 17–18, 53–54
semicore versus semiperipheral international economic integration, 44–48, 45*t*
social cohesion/stress, 48–51, 49*t*, 123, 133

postsocialist capitalism in East Central
    Europe *(continued)*
    socialist legacy and, 260–61. *See also* social-
        ist legacy
    in Southeastern European countries, 3,
        182–222. *See also* Southeastern Euro-
        pean countries
    state governance capacities, 36–34. *See also*
        state governance capacities
    success, fragility, and diversity of, 1–9, 260,
        267–69
    transformation costs, compensating for,
        29–36, 32*t*, 35*t*
    typology of, 2–3, 19–25, 21*t*, 23*f*
    in Visegrád countries, 3, 5, 138–81. *See also*
        Visegrád countries, embedded neolib-
        eral capitalism in
poverty, unemployment, and income inequal-
    ity, 48, 50, 92, 123, 133, 154, 228–31, 257
privatization
    in Baltic states, 122–23
    Russian oligarchs' exploitation of, 142
    in Southeastern European countries, 122,
        190, 199, 249
    in Visegrád countries, 122, 142, 144, 145
product cycle theory, 89

Rabushka, Alvin, 112
Radičová, Iveta, 246
Rajan, Raghuram G., 228
real estate boom in Baltic states, 134–35
Repse, Einars, 108
responsible and responsive government, ten-
    sion between, 238–40, 270–71
retirement. *See* pensions
Rhodes, Martin, 160
RHSD (Councils of Economic and Social
    Agreement), 146–48
Ritenis, Jānis, 116
Roma peoples, marginalization of, 159–60,
    241, 242n32, 245
Romania. *See* Southeastern European coun-
    tries
Rose, Richard, 121
Rosenthal, Christoph, 237n28
Round Table agreements of 1989, 141, 150
Rover (British car manufacturer) in Bul-
    garia, 208–9
Ruggie, John G., 17, 272
Russian Federation
    oil and oil products, Baltic transit manage-
        ment of, 127
    privatization, oligarchs' exploitation of, 142

Russian-speaking residents of Baltic States
    decline in perception of threat from,
        230–31, 232*t*
    exclusionary and inclusionary citizenship
        policies regarding, 99–103
    narratives of "Estonian miracle," 126
    nation-building and state-building pro-
        cess, 96, 97, 98–99
    social policy, ethnic aspects of, 119–24,
        120*t*
    Soviet migration of, 98–99

Sachs, Jeffrey, 7, 19, 48, 63, 84, 106, 212
Sanader, Ivo, 254
Savisaar, Edgar, 104
Scharpf, Fritz, 86
Schneider, Ben Ross, 11
Schönfelder, Bruno, 195
Schuler, Kurt, 106, 109
Second World War, 14, 68–70, 72, 162,
    231n15, 274
Selgin, George, 106, 109
semicore versus semiperipheral interna-
    tional economic integration, 44–48, 45*t*
Serbia, 186, 268
Siimann, Mart, 118
Sinkey, Joseph, 109
Šķēle, Andris, 130
Skrzypek, Sławomir, 176–77
Slakteris, Atis, 236
Šleževičius, Adolfas, 109, 110
Slovak Republic/Slovakia. *See* Visegrád coun-
    tries, embedded neoliberal capitalism in
Slovenia. *See* Southeastern European coun-
    tries
social cohesion/stress, 48–51, 49*t*, 123, 133
Social Insurance Institution (ZUS), Poland,
    153
social movement theory, 75
social partnerships
    in Southeastern European countries,
        186–91, 197, 211, 213–17
    in Visegrád countries, 146–52
social protections. *See* welfare
socialist legacy, 260–61
    paths to emergence of postsocialist capi-
        talism and, 56, 58–59, 65–67, 70–71,
        75–82
    in Southeastern European countries, 186,
        213, 214–15
    welfare state and, 72–73
SOEs (state-owned enterprises), 60, 142,
    159, 195, 199–200

Solidarity, 141, 143, 150, 153
Soós, Attila K., 201, 202–4
Soskice, David, 10
South Korea, 169–70, 186, 208
South Korean Hankook Tire, 169–70
Southeastern European countries, 3,
    182–222. *See also* global economic cri-
    sis of 2008 in Southeastern European
    countries
  automotive industry in Bulgaria, 208–9
  Baltic states compared, 182, 184, 185, 186,
    194, 199, 202, 204*t*, 209, 212, 213, 218,
    219, 221, 222
  central banks in, 211–14, 219
  centralized wage setting, 216
  CME, Slovenia identified as, 10
  credit, access to, 92, 95, 251
  crises of 1990s and, 5–6, 255–56
  currency boards in, 219, 221
  economic elites in, 198–201
  embedded neoliberal model in Croatia, 3,
    22, 182, 218, 251, 253–54
  EU accession, 183, 205, 213, 219–20
  EU and, 183–84, 215, 219–21, 223, 250,
    252, 254
  FDI inflows, 88–90, 202–11, 204*t*, 210*f*,
    217, 251, 253
  flat tax regimes in Bulgaria and Romania,
    221
  foreign commercial banks in, 213, 251
  heterogeneity across, 182–84
  historical legacies of political opportunity
    structures, 75–77, 80–81
  IFIs, involvement of, 219, 221
  IMF and, 191n34, 219, 223, 252–53
  industrialization process in, 70
  labor relations, trade unions, and tri-
    partism in, 184–91, 196–97, 210–11,
    213–17
  macroeconomic stability, 51–53, 52*t*,
    211–17
  market opening, regulating, and stabiliz-
    ing, 25–29, 26*t*
  national currencies in, 212, 214, 215, 217,
    221
  neocorporatist capitalism in Slovenia, 3, 5,
    23*t*, 24, 182, 184, 187, 196, 215, 248–51
  neoliberal model in Bulgaria and Roma-
    nia, 3, 22, 182, 218, 251
  paths to postsocialist capitalism in, 261,
    262
  political parties in, 188, 190, 195, 200, 215,
    218, 249, 254

  popular consent, obtaining, 62, 65
  privatization, 122, 190, 199, 249
  rebuilding of weak states in, 217–22
  semicore versus semiperipheral interna-
    tional economic integration, 44–48,
    45*t*
  social cohesion/stress, 48–51, 49*t*
  socialist legacy in, 186, 213, 214–15
  state governance capacities, 36–44, 39*t*,
    41*t*, 43*t*, 191–97, 202
  TNCs and, 203, 207, 208, 209
  transformation costs, compensating for,
    29–36, 32*t*, 35*t*
  transformative corporatism versus neolib-
    eralism debate, 18–19
  transnational influences, 84, 85, 92, 95
  tripartism in, 186–91
  Visegrád countries compared, 182–85,
    194, 199, 202–5, 204*t*, 209, 213, 216,
    218, 222, 255
  welfare systems in, 221
Soviet Union
  Baltic states flooded with Russian-speaking
    workforce under, 98–99
  "Estonian miracle," narratives of, 126
  industrialization process and, 70–71
  intraregional rivalries between Visegrád
    countries under, 162–63
  nation-building and state-building process
    in East Central Europe and, 68–69
  socialist legacy of. *See* socialist legacy
Speenhamland welfare regime of 1795,
    Britain, 79
Špidla, Vladimír, 175
Stalin, Josef, 71, 98n2, 162
Stanojević, Miroslav, 184, 187, 188, 249–51
Stara Zagora DZU, Bulgaria, 200
Stark, David, 9
state-building. *See* nation-building and state-
    building process
state governance capacities, 36–44
  in Baltic states, 36–44, 39*t*, 41*t*, 43*t*
  EU, democratic governance in, 43
  global economic crisis of 2008 affecting,
    257–58
  labor relations and, 191–97
  neocorporatism and, 195–97
  responsible and responsive government,
    tension between, 238–40, 270–71
  in Southeastern European countries,
    36–44, 39*t*, 41*t*, 43*t*, 191–97, 202
  in Visegrád countries, 36–44, 39*t*, 41*t*, 43*t*,
    238–40

state-owned enterprises (SOEs), 60, 142, 159, 195, 199–200
Steen, Anton, 122
Stepan, Alfred, 192
Strauss-Kahn, Dominique, 234
Streeck, Wolfgang, 18, 272–73
Suchocka, Hanna, 150
Sweden
    financial institutions, eastward enlargement of, 92, 133, 227
    pension advice in Baltic states and Visegrád countries provided by, 116–17, 156
    social democracy in, 7, 60
Szalai, Júlia, 157, 159–60
Szelényi, Iván, 9, 160
Szűcs, Jenő, 164

Tarrow, Sidney G., 75, 271
Tatur, Melanie, 18
tax regimes, flat, in Bulgaria and Romania, 221
taxation in Baltic states
    corporate income tax rates, reduction of, 112–13
    flat tax regimes, 111–13
    home ownership, provisions favorable to, 134
taxation in Visegrád countries
    corporate income tax rates, reduction of, 168–69
    welfare funding and collection issues, 160
Terem, 208
Tilly, Charles, 192
Tito, Josip Broz, 194
TNCs. *See* transnational corporations
Tomeš, Igor, 153
Tošovský, Josef, 173, 174
Townsley, Eleanor, 9
trade unions. *See* labor relations
transformation costs, compensation for, 29–36, 32*t*, 35*t*, 64–65
transformative corporatism versus neoliberalism debate, 18–19
transnational corporations (TNCs)
    deep international integration and, 265–66
    locational factors, 262–63
    paths to emergence of postsocialist capitalism and, 55, 57, 87–91, 92, 93
    social responsibility of, 271–72
    Southeastern European countries and, 203, 207, 208, 209
    transformation costs, compensating for, 31

in Visegrád countries, 11–12, 138, 140, 145, 167–70
tripartism
    in Southeastern European countries, 186–91, 197, 211, 213–17
    in Visegrád countries, 146–52
Tuđman, Franjo, 185, 188, 189, 190, 194, 195, 215, 218
"tunnel effect," 230–31
Tusk, Donald, 245

Ukraine, 74, 98, 142, 185n6, 199n64, 201
umbrella revolution of 2007, 236
UN Global Compact, 272
"under-age" pensioners, 36, 154, 157
unemployment, income inequality, and poverty, 48, 50, 92, 123, 133, 154, 228–31, 257
unions. *See* labor relations
United Kingdom. *See* Britain
U.S. liberal hegemony, challenges to, 273–74

Vagnorius, Gediminas, 109, 110, 118
Vammo, 208
Vanhuysse, Pieter, 155
Varieties of Capitalism (VoC) approach, 10–13, 207, 217, 267
Vassilev, Nikola, 191n34
Vernon, Raymond, 89
Videnov, Zhan, 217
Visegrád countries, embedded neoliberal capitalism in, 3, 5, 138–81. *See also* global economic crisis of 2008 in Visegrád countries; taxation in Visegrád countries
    automobile industry, 89, 163, 166, 169–70, 171
    Baltic states compared, 138, 139, 173–74, 179
    central banks, 173–78, 179
    credit, access to, 92
    crises of 1990s and, 5–6, 255–56
    DME model, Visegrád countries associated with, 11
    electronics industry, 89, 163, 166, 171
    EU accession, 151, 161, 164, 167, 169, 172–73, 175, 177, 179, 180
    EU and, 138, 162, 163, 165–69, 172–81, 223, 238, 239, 242, 243, 247
    euro, move to, 172–81
    external debt in, 142–44
    FDI inflows, 88–90, 95, 142, 144, 161, 166–68, 170, 171*t*, 172, 239, 247

historical legacies of political opportunity structures, 75–78, 79, 81
IFIs, 142, 167
IMF and, 142, 223, 245
intraregional rivalries and cooperation, 161–70
macroeconomic stability, 51–53, 52*t*
manufacturing miracle in, 170–72, 171*t*
market opening, regulating, and stabilizing, 25–29, 26*t*
national capitalism, attempts at, 141–46
neocorporatism, failure of, 146–52, 262
paths to, 60, 61, 138, 260–61, 262
pensions, 116, 152–59
political parties in, 141, 144, 161, 174–79, 180, 181, 240–48
popular consent, obtaining, 62, 65
privatization, 122, 142, 144, 145
Roma peoples, marginalization of, 159–60, 241, 242n32, 245
semicore versus semiperipheral international economic integration, 44–48, 45*t*
similarities and differences, 139–41
social cohesion/stress, 48–51, 49*t*
social partnership institutions, rise and demise of, 146–52
Southeastern European countries compared, 182–85, 194, 199, 202–5, 204*t*, 209, 213, 216, 218, 222, 255
split of Czechoslovakia into Czech and Slovak Republics, 141, 145, 147
state governance capacities, 36–44, 39*t*, 41*t*, 43*t*, 238–40
TNCs and, 11–12, 138, 140, 145, 167–70
transformation costs, compensating for, 29–36, 32*t*, 35*t*
transnational influences, 85n80, 92, 95
typological definition, 22–24, 23*t*
welfarist social contracts in, 138, 152–61, 180–81
Western neoliberal regimes, strained relationship with, 74
Visegrád Declaration, 163, 164
Vliegenthart, Arjan, 11, 12
VoC (Varieties of Capitalism) approach, 10–13, 207, 217, 267
Vuolo, Lo, 116n54

wage inequality, unemployment, and poverty, 48, 50, 92, 123, 133, 154, 228–31, 257
Warsaw Treaty Organization, 162
Washington consensus, 57, 59, 128

weak states in Southeastern Europe (Croatia, Bulgaria, Romania). *See* Southeastern European countries
Weber, Max, 14, 15, 24, 76, 193
welfare systems. *See also* pensions
Baltic states, nationalist social contract in, 113–24, 228–30
ethnic aspects of social policy in Baltic states, 119, 120*t*, 124
global economic crisis of 2008 affecting, 257
legacy of welfare state in East Central Europe, 72–73
market, welfare, democracy, and identity, interplay between, 263–65
social cohesion/stress, measuring, 48–51, 49*t*
in Southeastern European countries, 221
Visegrád countries, welfarist social contracts in, 138, 152–61, 180–81, 238
Western neoliberal states
influence of, 57, 58–59, 212–13
post-crisis backsliding, risk of, 269
strained and contradictory relationship with, 73–74, 165
White, Lawrence, 106
World Bank, 40, 116–18, 142, 156, 172, 194
World War I, 68, 74
World War II, 14, 68–70, 72, 162, 231n15, 274

Yugoslavia
debt burden of, 51
International Criminal Tribunal for the Former Yugoslavia, 254
labor relations and, 186, 187, 189, 190, 194
liberalized economies of successor states, 26
macroeconomic stability in Southeastern European countries and, 205, 207, 212–15
monetary stability plan for, 106
nation-building in Southeastern European countries on ruins of, 222
NATO bombing of, 183
paths to emergence of postsocialist capitalism and, 66, 69, 71n46, 74, 75, 80

Zeman, Miloš, 174
Zhivkov, Todor, 216
ZUS (Social Insurance Institution), Poland, 153